Accession no.
36208660

D1765702

Stone Worlds

WITHDRAWN

PUBLICATIONS OF THE INSTITUTE OF ARCHAEOLOGY, UNIVERSITY COLLEGE LONDON

Director of the Institute: Stephen Shennan

Publications Series Editor: Peter J. Ucko

The Institute of Archaeology of University College London is one of the oldest, largest, and most prestigious archaeology research facilities in the world. Its extensive publications programme includes the best theory, research, pedagogy, and reference materials in archaeology and cognate disciplines, by publishing exemplary work of scholars worldwide. Through its publications, the Institute brings together key areas of theoretical and substantive knowledge, improves archaeological practice, and brings archaeological findings to the general public, researchers, and practitioners. It also publishes staff research projects, site and survey reports, and conference proceedings. The publications programme, formerly developed in-house or in conjunction with UCL Press, is now produced in partnership with Left Coast Press, Inc. The Institute can be accessed online at http://www.ucl.ac.uk/archaeology.

ENCOUNTERS WITH ANCIENT EGYPT Subseries, Peter J. Ucko, (ed.)
Jean-Marcel Humbert and Clifford Price (eds.), Imhotep Today (2003)
David Jeffreys (ed.), Views of Ancient Egypt since Napoleon Bonaparte: Imperialism, Colonialism, and Modern Appropriations (2003)
Sally MacDonald and Michael Rice (eds.), Consuming Ancient Egypt (2003)
Roger Matthews and Cornelia Roemer (eds.), Ancient Perspectives on Egypt (2003)
David O'Connor and Andrew Reid (eds.), Ancient Egypt in Africa (2003)
John Tait (ed.), 'Never had the like occurred': Egypt's View of its Past (2003)
David O'Connor and Stephen Quirke (eds.), Mysterious Lands (2003)
Peter Ucko and Timothy Champion (eds.), The Wisdom of Egypt: Changing Visions Through the Ages (2003)

CRITICAL PERSPECTIVES ON CULTURAL HERITAGE Subseries, Beverley Butler (ed.)
Beverley Butler, Return to Alexandria: An Ethnography of Cultural Heritage Revivalism and Museum Memory (2007)
Ferdinand de Jong and Michael Rowlands (eds.), Reclaiming Heritage: Alternative Imaginations in West Africa (2007)
Dean Sully (ed.), Decolonizing Conservation: Caring for Maori Meeting Houses outside New Zealand (2007)

OTHER TITLES
Andrew Gardner (ed.), Agency Uncovered: Archaeological Perspectives (2004)
Okasha El-Daly, Egyptology, The Missing Millennium: Ancient Egypt in Medieval Arabic Writing (2005)
Ruth Mace, Clare J. Holden, and Stephen Shennan (eds.), Evolution of Cultural Diversity: A Phylogenetic Approach (2005)
Arkadiusz Marciniak, Placing Animals in the Neolithic: Social Zooarchaeology of Prehistoric Farming (2005)
Robert Layton, Stephen Shennan, and Peter Stone (eds.), A Future for Archaeology (2006)
Joost Fontein, The Silence of Great Zimbabwe: Contested Landscapes and the Power of Heritage (2006)
Gabriele Puschnigg, Ceramics of the Merv Oasis: Recycling the City (2006)
James Graham-Campbell and Gareth Williams (eds.), Silver Economy in the Viking Age (2007)
Barbara Bender, Sue Hamilton, and Chris Tilley, Stone Worlds: Narrative and Reflexivity in Landscape Archaeology (2007)
Andrew Gardner, An Archaeology of Identity: Soldiers and Society in Late Roman Britain (2007)
Sue Hamilton, Ruth Whitehouse, and Katherine I. Wright (eds.) Archaeology and Women: Ancient & Modern Issues (2007)
Gustavo Politis, Nukak: Ethnoarchaeology of an Amazonian People (2007)
Sue Colledge and James Conolly (eds), The Origins and Spread of Domestic Plants in Southwest Asia and Europe (2007)
Timothy Clack and Marcus Brittain (eds), Archaeology and the Media (2007)
Janet Picton, Stephen Quirke, and Paul C. Roberts (eds.), Living Images: Egyptian Funerary Portraits in the Petrie Museum (2007)
Tony Waldron, Paleoepidemiology: The Measure of Disease in the Human Past (2007)
Eleni Asouti and Dorian Q. Fuller, Trees and Woodlands of South India: An Archaeological Perspective (2007)
Russell McDougall and Iain Davidson (eds.), The Roth Family, Anthropology, and Colonial Administration (2007)
Elizabeth Pye (ed.), The Power of Touch: Handling Objects in the Museum Context (2007)
John Tait, Why the Egyptians Wrote Books (2007)

Stone Worlds

Narrative and Reflexivity in Landscape Archaeology

LIS LIBRARY

Date	Fund
02/05/14	i-Che

Order No

2478687

University of Chester

BARBARA BENDER
SUE HAMILTON
CHRIS TILLEY

WITH

ED ANDERSON, STEPHAN HARRISON,
PETER HERRING, MARTYN WALLER,
TONY WILLIAMS, AND MIKE WILMORE

Left Coast
Press Inc.

Walnut Creek, California

LEFT COAST PRESS, INC.
1630 North Main Street, #400
Walnut Creek, CA 94596
http://www.LCoastPress.com

Left Coast Press Inc.

Copyright © 2007 by Left Coast Press, Inc.

All rights reserved. No part of this publication may be reproduced, stored in a retrieval system, or transmitted in any form or by any means, electronic, mechanical, photocopying, recording, or otherwise, without the prior permission of the publisher.

Library of Congress Cataloging-in-Publication Data

Bender, Barbara.
  Stone worlds : narrative and reflexivity in landscape archaeology / Barbara Bender, Sue Hamilton, Chris Tilley ; with Ed Anderson, Stephan Harrison, Peter Herring, Martyn Waller, Tony Williams, and Mike Wilmore.
      p. cm. — (Publications of the Institute of Archaeology, University College London)
  Includes bibliographical references and index.
  ISBN-13: 978-1-59874-218-3 (hardcover : alk. paper)
  ISBN-13: 978-1-59874-219-0 (pbk. : alk. paper)
  1. Leskernick Site (England) 2. Landscape archaeology—England—Cornwall (County) 3. Cornwall (England: County)—Antiquities. 4. Bronze Age—England—Cornwall (County) 5. Excavations (Archaeology)—England—Cornwall (County) I. Hamilton, Sue. II. Tilley, Christopher Y. III. Anderson, Ed. IV. Title.
  DA670.C8B33 2007
  936.2′37—dc22

2006035672

Printed in the United States of America

∞™ The paper used in this publication meets the minimum requirements of American National Standard for Information Sciences—Permanence of Paper for Printed Library Materials, ANSI/NISO Z39.48–1992.

07 08 09 10 11   5 4 3 2 1

Contents

List of Illustrations

FIGURES

TABLES

COLOUR PLATES
Plates appear after page 288.

Participants in the Stone Worlds Project

Supervisor and Site Manager

MIKE SEAGER THOMAS

Survey Team Artist and Illustrator

WAYNE BENNETT

Illustrator

JANE RUSSELL

Website Designer

PAUL BASU

Installation and Media Artists

MARTIN HUBBARD, HEATHER KEIR CROSS, SIMON PERSIGETTI, AND MIKE VENNING

Site Planners

SHARON ADNITT AND JUSTIN RUSSELL

Site Photographers

LESLEY SMITH, JEREMY STAFFORD-DEITSCH, AND FAY STEVENS

Site Poet

JAN FARQUHARSON

Trench Supervisors

NICHOLAS BEAUDRAY, CHRIS DERHAM, CHRIS GREATOREX, RICHARD HOYLE, ERIC JONES, GARY ROBINSON, DIANE SPROAT, FAY STEVENS, AND HELEN WICKSTEAD

Excavators and Survey Team

1995 PHIL ABLESON, GILL ANDERSON, CATH BAYNTON, ALAN BENN, HENRY BROUGHTON, MARY HINTON, JASON HUTTER, PIPPA PEMBERTON, AND HELEN WICKSTEAD

1996 WAYNE BENNETT, HENRY BROUGHTON, CHRIS GREATOREX, PENNI HARVEY-PIPER, PATRICK LAVIOLETTE, PIPPA PEMBERTON, JANE RUSSELL, ASH RENNIE, MIKE SEAGER THOMAS, CHRISTEL SJÖSTRÖM, SOPHIE SEEL, MARYLYN WHAYMAND, HELEN WICKSTEAD

1997 CERI ASHLEY, WAYNE BENNETT, HENRY BROUGHTON, CHRIS DERHAM, PENNI HARVEY-PIPER, ANGUS GRAHAM, CHRIS GREATOREX, ERIC JONES, DAN KING, MATT LAKE, LESLEY O'ROURKE, STUART RANDALL, GARY ROBINSON, JANE RUSSELL, JUSTIN RUSSELL, MIKE SEAGER THOMAS, FAY STEVENS, STEVE TOWNEND, HELEN WICKSTEAD

1998 SHARON ADNITT, NICK BEAUDRY, WAYNE BENNETT, HENRY BROUGHTON, CHRIS DERHAM, ANGUS GRAHAM, RONALD GRIFFITHS, SUE HARRINGTON, JENNIFER HOLT, PENNI HARVEY-PIPER, RICHARD HOYLE, DAN KING, MARK LANDYMORE, PATRICK LAVIOLETTE, IAN MARTIN, ANDREW MAYFIELD, ASH RENNIE, GARY ROBINSON, JANE RUSSELL, JUSTIN RUSSELL, CLIFF SAMPSON, LESLEY SMITH, SIMON SMITH, DIANA SPROAT, JEREMY STAFFORD-DEITSCH, FAY STEVENS, HANNA STEYNE, ELIZABETH STONE, AND KEN YANDALL

1999 SHARON ADNITT, WAYNE BENNETT, HENRY BROUGHTON, DON COOPER, MARION CUTTING, CHRIS DERHAM, NIGEL FIRTH, TANIA FRASER, JANE GARWOOD, SUE HARRINGTON, RICHARD HOYLE, PATRICK LAVIOLETTE, MICHAEL LEASURE, ANDREW LOADER, ANDREW MAYFIELD, REBECCA MILLAR, CONNOR MCCAULY, RICHARD MACPHAIL, TESSA MORAY, RANJANA PIERIS, TOM PINFOLD, ANDREW POOLE, GARY ROBINSON, KATIE ROSE, JANE RUSSELL, ROSALIND OSWALD, CLIFF SAMPSON, KATIA SCHAER, SIMON SMITH, GARETH SPICER, FAY STEVENS, AND LOUISE WOOD

Acknowledgments

So many people to thank –

We start with local people. First, the Commoners. Bodmin Moor, though 'owned' by a mysterious figure (it is, in fact, part of the Duchy of Cornwall), is occupied by Commoners who have rights to the moor attached to the houses that they live in. We thank them warmly for giving us permission to work on the moor.

Second, the 'local' archaeologists. The Cornish Archaeological Unit had recently brought out, with the Royal Commission, a wonderful prehistoric overview of the moor, complete with detailed survey maps which, from the beginning to the end of our project, provided an essential 'grounding' for us (Johnson and Rose 1994). Of the unit, Pete Herring was most particularly and passionately associated with Bodmin Moor. He could have made us feel like intruders, but never did. He visited us often, worked with us, shared his intimate knowledge of the moor and the past with us. At the Summer Solstice, he would arrive with his faithful archaeological cohort and move around, quietly watching, waiting, and, if the sun was visible, hurrying to various viewing places. It was he who had originally 'found' the stone row and northern stone circle, and the Propped Stone behind which the sun sets on the longest day. When the manuscript was nearing completion, Pete read it with scrupulous, and quite critical, attention. His arguments seemed so well reasoned that we have often incorporated them into the text. For us, this dialogue seems to add an extra, and important, dimension to our work at Leskernick.

Dave Hooley of English Heritage also made life much easier for us. He cut the red tape, talked into the night, and walked us off our feet ('It's just a few hundred yards further on,' he'd say after a long day, striding effortlessly forward, and knowing full well that it was at least another mile or two …)

And finally, Tony Blackman, Cornish Nationalist and doyen of the young archaeologists. He was less enthused by our presence – academic aliens with no experience of the 'patch' – but he came with his youngsters, showed them what we were doing, and generously showed us the many discoveries he had made on the hill and beyond.

In the first year, 1995, we were a small group and we camped to the south of the moor, near Jamaica Inn. There were midges and a disapproval of late night carousing. So from the second year onwards we moved to the north of the moor, to the caravan site at Julliet's Well, Camelford. We came to know, and love, the intricate hierarchy of furniture and fittings in the different grades of caravan; we appreciated the facilities and though we didn't necessarily always approve the music, spent much time at the bar. John Watkins, the caravan-park owner, was very tolerant, and generous.

Of a morning, some of us used to take the northern way onto the moor, others the western one. Sheila and Brian Charman lived at Westmoorgate. They not only put up with the untidy litter of cars outside their gate, but offered encouragement after grisly days of rain, stored our equipment, and recharged our batteries (literally and figuratively).

Of an evening, wending home, there was the Rising Sun at Altarnun. The food was good and cheap; the owners welcoming of boots and wet gear; and, most importantly, it was the place where we began to meet and talk with local people who were often part of the farming community that had run their livestock on the moor for generations. An important place …

There were two teams working on the moor – the anthropology/surveying team, and the archaeology team. The survey team was small (around six people) and two people (Henry Broughton, Wayne Bennett) came back year after year and, in the Summer of 1999, helped Chris Tilley complete the wider settlement and landscape survey of the moor. Wayne Bennett also drew all the house plans for this part of the project. The archaeology team was larger (around 20 people) and involved quite a number of students who were doing their fieldwork requirement and only stayed a season. But again there were several who came back year after year, in particular Gary Robinson, Fay Stevens, and Helen Wickstead. There were also professional archaeologists who worked with us throughout the project: Mike Seager Thomas, and Justin Russell and Sharon Adnitt who did the field planning. We would like to thank all of these people, and also Jane Russell for drawing up for publication plans and sections; Mike Wilmore and Tony Williams – 'the sociologists'; Patrick Laviolette who undertook some in-depth interviewing; Paul Basu, the web-site designer; Stephan Harrison and Ed Anderson, the geologists; and Martyn Waller and Jane Entwhistle, the 'environmentalists'.

During the last season we put on an exhibition about Leskernick in the Church Hall at Altarnun. The vicar facilitated our presence; the WI ladies kindly tolerated us; and local people encouraged us, brought things, talked, and came to the opening and closing ceremonies. It felt very good indeed to move off the moor and into the community.

Later, when the exhibition began to tour around, a group of installation artists and media people – Martin Hubbard, Simon Persigetti, Heather Keir Cross, and Mike Venning – added their own interactive interpretations. We'd like to thank all of them for turning the exhibition into a happening.

Finally, we wish to express our gratitude to the various grant-giving bodies that made the work possible: the British Academy and AHRB generously funded us over five years, and the Department of Anthropology at UCL and the Institute of Archaeology weighed in with additional funding. The Prehistoric Society gave us some 'starter' funds.

Working on the moor was very special – a sort of privilege. We hope that in the course of this book we will be able to express something of our gratitude and our feeling of engagement with this very particular place and people.

Part One

Introduction

Chapter One

Stone Worlds,
Alternative Narratives,
Nested Landscapes

This is a book about landscape. About embodied landscapes, about the way in which people engage with the world around them, how they make sense of it, how they understand and work with it. And how it works on them. It is primarily about prehistoric landscapes, but also about contemporary ones.

It is about a project that involves both archaeologists and anthropologists. It also involves sociological projects, art projects, an exhibition, and a website. It attempts to question and work across disciplinary boundaries.

It is the culmination of five summers' work at Leskernick, a small hill in the northern part of Bodmin Moor in Cornwall, in which the archaeologists excavated 21 trenches, and the anthropologists surveyed both at Leskernick and across the moor (Figure 1.1).

In hindsight, the project began when Chris Tilley, who works in both the Department of Anthropology at University College London (UCL) and at the neighbouring Institute of

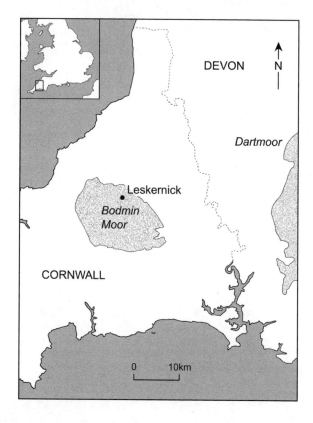

fig. 1:1 Location map: Leskernick, Bodmin Moor, Cornwall.

Archaeology (also part of UCL), undertook a survey of Bodmin Moor in 1994. His work focussed on ritual sites: the stone rows and circles, the cairns, and hilltop enclosures. His intention was to discover how they related to each other and to features in the landscape, most particularly the high tors. He wanted to show the link, both cause and effect, between people's symbolic evocation of their world and their experience of living in and moving around the landscape (Tilley 1995). In his work on the moor, Chris avoided the dense clusters of house circles, partly because it was almost impossible to survey them on his own and partly because his attention was drawn to the overtly ritual monuments.

CT (1994): I could see the settlement area from the cairn – a massive tangle of stones – and decided to avoid it. It seemed impenetrable, aloof, impossible to investigate compared with the stone circles and stone rows where I had a methodology and knew what I was to do. I took pity on a solitary wind-blown hawthorn tree eking out a solitary existence on the lower slopes of the hill among the clitter spreads. Why should anyone want to live in this desert of stone?

The houses seemed, at first glance, to be more mundane, more everyday. But this division between the sacred and profane, or the secular and the spiritual, is a contemporary one.[1] It is a distinction that is neither valid in our own world, where the most mundane activities and places are infused with ritual, nor is it appropriate for other times and places. If our work on the Leskernick hillside has done nothing else, it has shown, beyond a shadow of doubt, that the domestic is as ritualised, as symbolic as any lonely cairn or stone row.

Early in 1995, recognizing that there was something missing in his story, Chris talked with Sue Hamilton (Institute of Archaeology, UCL) and Barbara Bender (Department of Anthropology, UCL) about the possibility of working together on the moor (Figure 1.2). Chris mentioned the site of Leskernick, and he and Sue discussed what sorts of excavations would be practicable and in what order they might be undertaken. They ascertained, with some relief, that Leskernick had not been scheduled and that Dave Hooley, the monuments protection officer for English Heritage, might look favourably upon an application to excavate. They also got in touch with the Cornish Archaeological Unit, some of whom had been involved in the creation of the prodigiously detailed map of the settlement (Johnson and Rose 1994). They too seemed happy that we would work on the moor.[2]

And so, on a fine spring morning, the three of them walked across the moor to Leskernick (Figure 1.3).

fig. 1:2 Clockwise starting top left:
Chris Tilley; Unknown Sleeper;
Sue Hamilton; Barbara Bender.

fig.1:3 View of the southern hillside of Leskernick taken from Codda. Looking carefully the enclosures and house circles begin to emerge. Photo J. Stafford-Deitsch.

BB (1995): A warm milky day, the path worn into the granite. Chris inducting us into the names of places. Leskernick: a gentle hill, with a great rock tumble, just possible, from a distance – knowing what to look for – to see the occasional enclosure wall. On the lower slopes and the plain, no stones, just tussocky grass. Occasionally, as we walked, we'd stumble over slightly elevated grassy square shapes. 'Medieval,' Chris said. Most times I didn't notice them. Equally, I guess I wouldn't have noticed the stone row. Such very small stones, and half covered with matted grass. Chris showed us the mound and then the stone row which led off and away across a gully. … A strong sense of not 'seeing' much …

SH (1995): As we came over Codda Hill Tor the southerly slopes of Leskernick Hill came into view. The prehistoric settlement appeared as a patterned mass of stones merging into scree-strewn hillside where loose clitter and earth-fast boulders were anarchically juxtaposed. … The hillside looked fractured and grey against the smooth yellow-green moor below.

On the sides of the hill were two extensive houses clusters and numerous sinuous walled enclosures (Figure 1.4). To the south, on the plateau below the hill, was a small stone row and two stone circles. At the top of the hill was a large propped stone and a large ruined cairn. Here, then, were all the elements for an integrated project involving both daily life and more ceremonial occasions.

It was a place to capture the imagination. It was also, as Chris had discovered earlier, rather daunting.

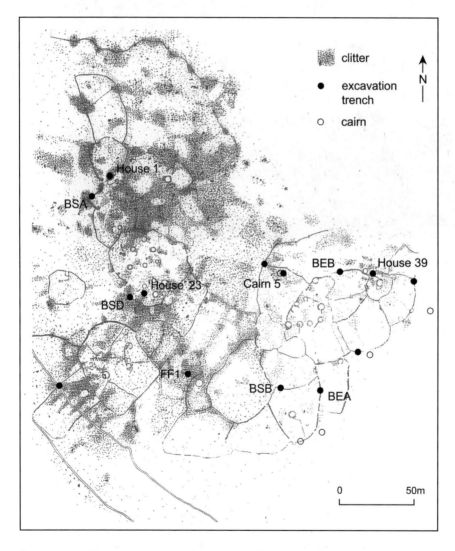

fig. 1:4 Map of Leskernick showing the clitter, settlements, enclosures, cairns, and locations of the excavation trenches. Only the excavation trenches discussed in the text are labelled (BS=boundary section; FF=field feature; BE=boundary entrance). All of the excavation trenches are discussed in Hamilton and Seager Thomas (in prep). The map is adapted from that produced by the Royal Commission of Historic Monuments (England).

SH (1995): It was easy to feel 'lost' in the stone row area. … I felt at home in the settlement area. We searched for some cairns on the perimeter of the settlement. Without a large-scale plan it was difficult. The 'natural' clitter played tricks, mimicking mounds and enclosure boundaries, or was it vice-versa?

Already, in that first encounter, people's different perceptions of place and landscape began to surface.

BB (1995): Sue worries about how to tie an excavation trench to the three stones that make up the terminal of the row. Chris shows us the way in which, at a certain juncture as you walk the stone line, Rough Tor comes into sight. The Elder inducting the juniors.

Up to the settlement: slowly bits of wall become clearer … and a small cairn with a cist … then three round small hut floors. We talk about entrances and what they would have seen. Of wooden structures, water availability. Sense that Chris becomes uneasy if the conversation becomes too 'functional'.

Having got a hesitant feel of the place, we agreed that during the first – modest – season the excavation would focus on the western terminus of the stone row that lay below and to the south of Leskernick Hill. The fallen stones at this end were much larger than along the rest of the row and, quite apart from discovering their original placement, there was the possibility that there might be ritual offerings. Meanwhile, the survey team would begin to work on the hillside, familiarising itself with the settlements and enclosures and checking the orientation of the house doors. The surveyors wanted to find out whether the sort of linkages that Chris had found between ritual constructions – long mounds, stone rows, and so on – and particular places in the landscape such as the high tors also held good in more everyday settings.

In the summer of 1995 the group consisted of the three directors and nine students.

BB (1995): We were camping quite close to Jamaica Inn and so we used to walk in from the southern part of the moor. It was a fantastic walk, down a very old, deeply entrenched track, over

*a ford. ... Then, after half a mile or so, the path gave out and
we walked for about a hundred metres until, cresting a shallow
incline, we saw, across the moor, the low stone grey hill of
Leskernick.[3]*

Slowly, we began to work our way into the site, physically, intellectually, and emotionally. In that first year we all tried our hand at everything.
A year later, the numbers had increased, we began to bring specialists on
board, and, as people became more knowledgeable and more passionate
about either the excavations or the surveying, fairly inevitable divisions of
labour emerged (chapter 11). There were nine on site in 1996, 17 in '97, 25 in
'98, and 31 in 1999.

During the second season (1996), the archaeologists finished work on the
terminal to the stone row and began work on the settlement. Over the course
of four summers (1996–99), they excavated three houses and adjacent outside
areas, a 'cairn', numerous sections of enclosure wall including entrance areas
and wall junctions, the area in front of the 'Shrine Stone', and parts of the
North Stone Circle. Meanwhile, the surveyors, having spent their first year
looking outwards from the house doors towards the surrounding hills, went
on to survey each and every house and field enclosure on the hill.

*BB (16 June 1996): In the first year we focussed on a structured
universe. This year we found out much more about the way it was
played out – worked out – through complex changing ... activities
and actions. ...*

*Working on the southern settlement, [we] felt more and more
strongly that the houses were not all lived in at the same time.
Some were ruined whilst others were being built. There were
also spaces and places that had already accumulated meaning,
... [places where] the walls took appropriate respectful avoiding
action. ... More obviously, the enclosures were a process of
accretion, abandonment and change. In one field it seems that
an old wall had gone out of use, and had been robbed to make a
new stout wall enclosing a larger area. In the western settlement,
Chris and Wayne found more dramatic evidence of this process,
with houses being decommissioned and then sometimes re-used
as cairns. Life on the hillside, over hundreds of years, was
complicated and nuanced.*

And then, in the last two seasons, they moved out into the larger
landscape.

In the first half of the book, chapter 2 discusses the nature of the moor, chapters 4–9 chart the progress of the archaeological excavations and anthropological survey work on and below the hill, and chapter 3 looks at the methodologies involved. Towards the end of the book, chapters 16–18 open to the wider prehistoric landscape.

It was always intended that the project would be about contemporary as well as prehistoric landscapes. Because we can only come to the past through the present, it seemed important to spend time trying to understand our attitudes, preconceptions, and engagement with the world around us. The anthropologists – often with help from the archaeologists – worked on, and with, the contemporary landscape, creating art installations and a travelling exhibition. Two anthropologists spent parts of two seasons at Leskernick looking at the ways in which we, in the present, engaged with the landscape, at our material culture, and at the social practices involved in the work we undertook. Another anthropologist created the Leskernick website. These contemporary preoccupations form the centre part of the book, chapters 10–15.

Prehistoric Landscapes

By the end of the summer of 1999 when the last trench was back-filled and hill and caravan park had reluctantly been left behind, we had an enormous amount of data. How were we to present these? We wanted this to be a book that opened in many directions, that crossed disciplinary boundaries, and that questioned long-established conventions on how scientific work should be presented. We did not want to write a monograph or a book with endless appendices. We wanted to write something that was readable, but it has to be admitted that, with 50 house circles and many kilometres of enclosure wall, not to mention the innumerable contexts uncovered in excavation, and the details of other settlements across the moor, we have not always succeeded.[4]

In the chapters on prehistoric sites and landscapes, excavation and survey are woven together and spliced with diary entries, dialogues, and other narrative interjections. One of the purposes of these interjections is to undermine the closure that usually occurs when findings are reported and interpreted.

Dialogue between CT and geologists Stephan Harrison [StH] and Ed Anderson [EA] (see chapter 9)

CT: (standing behind the mini-tor) … What we were wondering about was these slabs here that appear to be kind of wedged in round the back of this very large outcrop – as if they've been placed there to … demarcate or enclose the back of this small tor.

StH: I would say that certainly … one or two of the clasts that …

have very high dip angles appear to be natural, but I think there are others that are sort of perched on top of them, supported by them, [that] I would suggest may well be cultural. Yeah, I think you could argue for a cultural origin of the clasts standing up now to the south of the block.

CT: What they may be doing here then is, basically, enhancement, possibly of a rather minimal nature, of a feature that was already formed here. Something was recognised so they were just altering a few stones to make ... the pattern they recognise in it clearer.

EA: You haven't said much about the big block on top of the massive stone outcrop. I mean, one of the things that occurs to me when looking at it from down below is that it's actually been rotated through maybe about fifteen degrees, so that, in fact, it looks more cultural than natural. Any thoughts on that?

StH: I think this has been moved ... I don't think it's *in situ*. I don't know what criteria I use to make that decision, but it doesn't fit right ...

EA: The fact that it's a very large block, it probably weighs something in the region of five or six tons, and it's in a very unnatural position, sat on top of a large granite block – I can't think of any physical process that put it there. Nothing behind it – so where does the momentum come to actually push it there? ... Yeah ... I'd say that it's been culturally modified.

We wanted to emphasise the processes involved – the hesitations, the acceptance, and the rejection of ideas. The way in which, for example, the daily process of excavation generated alternative site histories that were then abandoned, forgotten, perpetuated, or transformed. We wanted to acknowledge the way in which even the most intensely mundane procedures – the identification of a feature, the decision on how to record it, how to assign meaning to it – involve some degree or level of interpretation.

SH (Thursday, 15 June 1995): With further trowelling [we found] a semi-circular area of mid-brown friable silt (Context 7) which continued across the end of one of the recumbent stones. ... [Within this was the top of] a circle of granite pieces (Context 4) ... deliberately placed. Perhaps we had a stone-lined hearth? Or a cremation pit? But the stones were not affected by heat. Alternatively, it might be a specially lined pit for the deposition of offerings: pieces of quartz, charcoal from non-local oak timbers. ... The uppermost fill (Context 5) within (and possibly encircling:

> *we were not sure yet) the circle of granite pieces was all that was revealed. This fill was dark and of soft consistency. A new possibility emerged: we might have the post-pipe of a substantial rotted post, c. 0.30 m wide, which could be part of a post alignment preceding the stone row. Perhaps the terminal area had incorporated timbers as well as standing stones? (see chapter 4).*

By highlighting the processes involved, we have tried to create a counterpoint to the spurious fixedness of excavation reports or of archival material including context sheets that provide minimal space for the recording of interpretative processes and strategies.

The diary entries also serve as a reminder that although the main text is written by the three directors, it is based on the work of all the people involved in the project. The diary entries allow some of the different voices to come through (see chapter 3 on Methodologies).

> *Steve (9 June 1997): Sue has said before the project that each trench has its own character and it's certainly true. The trowelling technique that Helen required of me was very different from what had been required by Chris G. the day before. This was also true of Mike's 'hut' 23 in the afternoon. There's an awful lot in the way of soil changes in that structure and it takes quite a bit of concentration to get to understand what you're seeing. Mike's great though, he makes a point of telling you what's going on in the soil and what you're looking for.*

> *Ash (6 June 1996): It quickly became apparent that a certain amount of friction had occurred between those excavating and those working on the field survey. From what I can gather a gulf was starting to emerge between the two camps. Which camp will I be placed in? Neither I hope!*

> *Fay (24 June 1997): With a little trepidation, fed by comments and ribbing last night and this morning about my 'defection' and a little uncertainty as to what I might be doing, I found myself very much at home and excited trying to find structures among the clitter. It made such a difference to raise my eyes from an excavation trench and explore the site, this freedom of vision inspiring new thoughts and ideas enabling a more holistic approach to the site, its surrounds, and what the aspirations of our work here are.*

Contributions to the e-mail discussion list attached to the project's website (www.ucl.ac.uk/leskernick) also allow some local, or more distant, voices to be heard.

Robin Paris, Local artist (Leskernick website, 10 June 1999): ... What sort of after-effect will [the books] leave on the communities that live around Leskernick today? And how will they affect the future of Leskernick itself? It's your last year here (officially) – you can walk away from any changes you may bring to the area, we will have to live with them.

There will be times when some readers will pause, perhaps critically, and say 'But you're just telling a story. You don't have any proof'. In response, we would stress that all interpretations are subjective. All accounts, no matter how seemingly factual, how dryly presented, are, in reality, a sort of narrative, a sort of story. We would stress that although there is a 'real' world 'out there', we can only access it through our concepts, words, and metaphors: our stories. At the same time, we would also insist that even though our interpretative biases affect how we assemble and understand the material evidence, this evidence has an integrity, an ability to resist certain interpretations, narratives, or stories. It is our job to be as rigorous as possible in defining and assembling the evidence, as honest as possible in admitting when it goes against the grain of a prior interpretation, and as open as possible to rethinking and reconceptualising interpretation, narrative and evidence. Recently, in a BBC 3 history series (November 2002), Simon Schama recounted the story of a 19th-century Boston murder. Schama felt that he had become so intimate with the evidence that he could put words into the mouths of the different protagonists. Some historians appearing on the programme were resistant to this, feeling that this overstepped their brief; others felt that these invented words had the potential to open up new avenues of investigation and thought. This latter is how we feel about the more speculative narrative elements within this text.

In the chapters on prehistoric Leskernick, we have worked with a new series of calibrated radiocarbon dates that our work has generated (Table 4.1). They are very interesting indeed and, used with considerable caution, they do suggest that the stone row and circles predate the settlements (see chapter 4); that some of the earliest settlement was on the southern side of the hill (see chapter 5); and that at least some of the houses were in use for considerable lengths of time. In one instance, the case of the shrine stone in the corridor between the two settlements, the radiocarbon date makes our interpretation look very questionable (see chapter 8). Even so, since most of the radiocarbon dates for the houses bunch within the Middle Bronze Age, the story of how the hill was settled is still open to a number of different interpretations. There are also, of course, many structures on the hill that were not excavated and that therefore do not have radiocarbon dates. Thus, for example, quite where the Propped Stone and the Great Cairn on the top of the hill fit into the story remains open to question.

As you will have noted, we continue to use the well-worn Neolithic/ Bronze Age terminology. We could, perhaps, have tried to be more aggressive about these terms but we find that they still offer adequate pegs on which to hang some of the changes that occur on the moor. First, it is the case that, following the Neolithic and Early Bronze Age construction of ritual monuments on the moor, there was, in the Middle Bronze Age, at around 1600 cal BC, a seemingly rapid population expansion onto the moor. There was more permanent settlement, more intensive husbandry, and also more construction and activity around the high places. And second, during the Early and Middle Bronze Age, bronze and gold objects began to appear at places beyond the moor, and some of the tin that went into the making of the bronze almost certainly came from the streams that flowed through the moor. Although we found no indisputable evidence of tin working at Leskernick, we have to allow for the possibility that alongside herding, fishing, collecting, and hunting, and perhaps a little cultivation, there were times when people were down by the river and streams panning for tin or excavating chunks of alluvial tin-rich cassiterite from the stream beds.[5] Or they might even have been crushing or smashing the cassiterite out of quartz veins in the moor's granite (see chapter 7).

Contemporary and Reflexive Landscapes

We wanted our work to contribute to a more reflexive approach to field archaeology, one in which trying to understand how we worked, and the *process* of interpretation, was as important as the end result – the narratives that we constructed. This was reflected in the publications that have arisen from this project (Bender, Hamilton, and Tilley 1997; Tilley, Hamilton, and Bender 2000; Tilley, Hamilton, Harrison, and Anderson 2000). This concern with the manner in which the past is *written* and *presented* develops directly out of the 'postprocessual' or 'interpretative' archaeology that emerged in the late 1980s and the realisation that 'writing' and 'illustrating' the past were not simply transparent, neutral, and value-free vehicles for transmitting information or 'facts' for others to passively consume (Bapty and Yates 1990; Hodder 1989; Hodder et al. 1995; Tilley 1989a, 1989b, 1990, 1993). Rather, they are creative and empowering acts that actively produce, rather than simply transmit, what we call the past between writers and readers.

Standard archaeological texts with their plans, diagrams, and figures usually represent a rhetoric of authority in which closure is created and debate shut-down: 'It *was* like this, here are the results'. These completely fail to recognise (or don't wish to recognise) that archaeology is always an ongoing and very open interpretative discourse in which there are always *other* possibilities, and *multiple* interpretations. Standard texts protect themselves and their own (always shaky) internal coherence from criticism by systematically filtering out the manner in which some interpretative possibilities come to be preferred to others, by excluding from discussion or debate the very processes by which we arrive at certain understandings rather than others. A 'reflexive' methodology, by contrast, makes such issues a central concern. Fieldwork has its own social, political, and emotional context that needs to be considered: a network of powers both facilitating and inhibiting the manner in which the past is understood (Berggren and Burström 2002; Chadwick 2003; Hodder 1997, 1999; Lucas 2001).

We knew that we wanted to look at our contemporary engagement with the landscape and with the past, but we also knew that it would be very difficult for any of the three directors to be both completely absorbed in the project and able to stand back and analyse the interactions and perceptions in which they were immersed. So we asked Tony Williams (chapter 12) and Mike Wilmore (chapter 11), both from the Department of Anthropology at UCL, to work alongside us. Tony Williams had just finished his first degree and we asked him to attempt a phenomenological approach to the landscapes that we moved across and interacted with both at Leskernick and back at the Camelford campsite. He also looked at the way in which material culture formed part of the expression of our identities, our sense of place, and our social relationships. We asked Mike Wilmore, a PhD student, to consider the social, political, and economic practices involved in the creation and interpretation of the Leskernick record.[6] Among other things, he addressed some of the causes for the fault-lines that appeared between the archaeologists and anthropologists.

Other chapters in the book also worked with our contemporary, reflexive engagement with the past. Thus, in chapter 13 we moved towards a present-day *physical* highlighting of prehistoric stone settings. We tried various 'art' interventions. The most important, because it seemed to create a potent dialogue between past and present, involved cling-filming and then painting many of the tiny prehistoric interventions – the almost invisible short runs of stone or encircled boulders in the stony clitter of the hillside – and also some of the more dramatic intercessions such as the Shrine Stone, the Propped Stone, and other large rocks piled one upon another. By using flags, we also brought more animation to the hill. And, through the pouring of coloured liquid offerings, we reactivated the solution hollows hidden in the high places (chapter 19).

We were 'outsiders' coming into an unfamiliar place. There were many people, including all the archaeologists working in Cornwall, who knew the place far more intimately than we did. We were blessed with Cornish colleagues – in particular Pete Herring of the Cornish Archaeological Unit and Dave Hooley of English Heritage – who spent hours and days on site with us, discussing, arguing, and sharing their profound knowledge. We had a debt to them and to all the local people from round and about, including the Commoners who gave us permission to move around the moor. It seemed important to share our ideas with them, to provide a forum for them to share theirs with us. In chapter 14, we discuss the travelling exhibition that we created. We used the opportunity of the exhibition being on show at Altarnun on the edge of the moor to talk with people about their attitudes to the moor, to Leskernick, to our work, and to the exhibition. In the process, we got a better sense of the different ways in which people engage with a sense of place and time.

These discussions also continued via the 'virtual' landscapes accessed via the website (www.ucl.ac.uk/leskernick) created by Paul Basu.[7]

Nested Landscapes, the Power of the Stones, and the View from Beyond

In the following chapters we plunge into detail, but before we begin we offer a first glimpse of the place, the landscape, and the power of the stones.

The hill and the monuments below it

Leskernick Hill is 329 m high – or low in comparison to the surrounding hills. Grey with stone where the other hills are green. An oval hill that feels circular as one moves around it.

At the top of the hill, on the western side, are large tabular granite outcrops. They have not weathered into stack-like tors but, instead, form platform-like surfaces. From these outcrops, moorstone or clitter tumbles down the western slope. Sometimes the clitter takes the form of large boulders, sometimes much smaller ones. Sometimes, where there is a hollow in the hillside, the stones heap up; other times they spread out. The southern slope of the hill also has clitter streams but they are not as dense, and the northern and eastern slopes are relatively stone free.

There are about 50 round Bronze Age house circles on the Leskernick hillslopes. They form two discrete settlements (Figure 1.5). Between the western edge of the southern settlement and the eastern edge of the western settlement there is a wide 'pathway' or corridor that leads towards the top of the hill. The houses are sited on the lower stony slopes of the hill. The ones on the southern side of the hill are set among a fair amount of clitter; the ones on the western side lie within a dense mass of stones. The house circles vary in size from 6 to over 10 m in diameter, and some of the wall-stones are up to 0.7 m high. Sometimes the house walls ride over and encapsulate large earth-fast boulders (also called grounders).

Both settlements have associated enclosures and compounds marked by

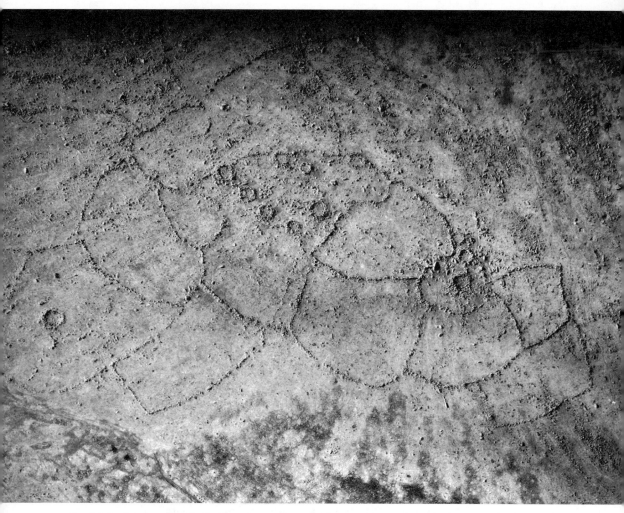

fig. 1:5 Aerial photograph showing the southern settlement (the enclave, the house circle, the outlying House 46 to the west) and its enclosures. The stone row and circles are not visible but lie just to the south of the most south-easterly enclosure. Kind permission of the RCHME.

low stone walls. The enclosures, which extend among the clitter on the slopes of the hill, vary in size from 0.25 to 1 ha. Some of the enclosures are so small and so rocky that they can have been of little practical use.

Near the foot of the hill, in the liminal space on the edge of the southern enclosures are a number of small cairns (c. 2 to 3 m diameter and 0.5 m high). Another cairn is found further up the hill, beyond the houses but still within the enclosures.[8] Because one of these cairns contains a cist, we can assume that some at least were used for burial.

There are also 'cairn'-like piles of stones within and between some of the houses in the western settlement. It seems as though a number of houses moved from being houses of the living to being houses of the dead.[9]

At the top of the hill, out of sight of nearly, but not quite all the houses is a large flat-topped stone, propped up on the top of a piece of tabular bedrock. At the summer solstice, the dying rays of the sun shine through the hole between the bedrock and Propped Stone just before the sun slips below the skyline (Color Plate 1a). We are uncertain of the Propped Stone's antiquity but believe it to be as old, if not older, than the Bronze Age settlements (Herring 1997). Also on top of the hill, but deliberately located out of sight of both settlements, is a very large cairn. On the basis of analogies with other excavated examples elsewhere on Bodmin Moor and beyond, it probably covered timber and/or stone-post settings, and would have acted as a focal point for ceremonies and offerings.

Below the hill, to the south, lies an undulating plateau area and, in among the springy turf and the remains of the old turf steads and disturbances created by medieval and later tin-streaming, are the remains of a modest Late Neolithic or Early Bronze Age stone row. The stones are less than 0.5 m high except at the western end where there are three large recumbent stones. Associated with the western end of the stone row is a stone circle and a much disturbed large cairn.[10] Another circle lies about 300 m to the south.[11]

Based on our work on the hill and in the surrounding landscape, we believe that the enclosures and house walls did much more than simply contain people or animals; they touched and contained the ancestral forces that were essential to people's ability to 'go on' in the world. For the people who lived both on and off the moors (Bodmin and Dartmoor), the stones were the ancestors or the ancestral beings or the work of the ancestral beings. The people of Leskernick lived within this ancestral stone world – an empowering place but one that required attentiveness and nurturing. The austere tabular stones at the top of the hill, like the tors on other hill tops, were particularly powerful – they were, perhaps, the source stones – the *ur* stones. The enclosure walls stopped short of these tabular stones. The Propped Stone was positioned on a piece of tabular bedrock. One of the largest houses, House 3, was located upslope from the rest and within view of outcrop and Propped Stone. It was also almost the only house from which Rough Tor, the most powerful of all places on the north moor was visible. Some of the angular backstones in the houses lower down the slopes had been sought out and brought down the hill, and the square-edged stones used in the stone row terminal below the hill were brought down from the high places.

The high places were important, but so, too, were the clitter streams and boulders. People incorporated earth-fast stones into their houses; joined up dense areas of clitter, large boulder and rock outcrop with enclosure walls; cleared away stones from around important rocks; encased boulders with uprights; and moved the stones within the clitter formations in subtle ways.

Life on these hillsides was one in which every movement in and around and about, and beyond, was imbued with a sense of ritual. In these people's engagement with the stones there was a cosmological reiteration that worked to and fro between the most intimate house interior, the compounds, and enclosures, out to the ceremonial monuments, and out across the landscape to the punctuated skyline of the tors and cairns. The practices of everyday life, feast day, and ceremony bled into each other. Although there may have been leaders or shamans in the community, what struck us, working at Leskernick, was that much of the ritual and knowledge was dispersed throughout the houses and fields, visible and available to all: a communal empowering.

Cliff Sampson (18 June 1998): It's hard to engage with the landscape when one's looking on the ground all of the time so as not to trip over stones.

[But perhaps it was different for people who were completely at home on the hill? Pete Herring (pers. comm., 12 April 1999) considers how it might have been:]

Will they have learnt the position and angle of each stone through life-long familiarity, and so skip through country we cross very gingerly? This seems important to think about as it forces us to consider whether their views were static, as ours tend to be when in clitter, ... or whether their views were what I call transitory. ... Transitory views are obviously more complex and mesmerising, especially in undulating landscapes like Cornwall. Hills and rocks move across each other (while shadows of clouds may move across them). Dream-like trances can develop when you concentrate on both foreground and background.

A nested landscape

Leskernick is surrounded by a circle of ridges and hills, all at a distance of just over 2 km. Standing on the top of Leskernick Hill, next to the large cairn on its summit and looking out, one has the feeling of being in an enclosed world, with only hints of a wider landscape beyond. Leskernick is the *omphalos* of the saucer; the Beacon, Tolborough Tor, Catshole Tor, Brown Willy, High Moor, Buttern Hill, Bray Down, and Carne Down form the rim. Rough Tor (4 km to the north-west) and Brown Gelly (7 km away to the south, down the line of the Fowey Valley), and the blue haze over the horizon to the north-east, are glimpses of a more distant world (Figure 1.6).

The hills to the north-east, east, and south-east are smooth contoured. Occasionally, they are broken by a large outcrop such as Black Rock and Elephant Rock. The hills on the western side are more dramatic. Codda, Tolborough, and Catshole are punctuated by rocky tors, while Brown Willy forms a long, gaunt spinal ridge.

32

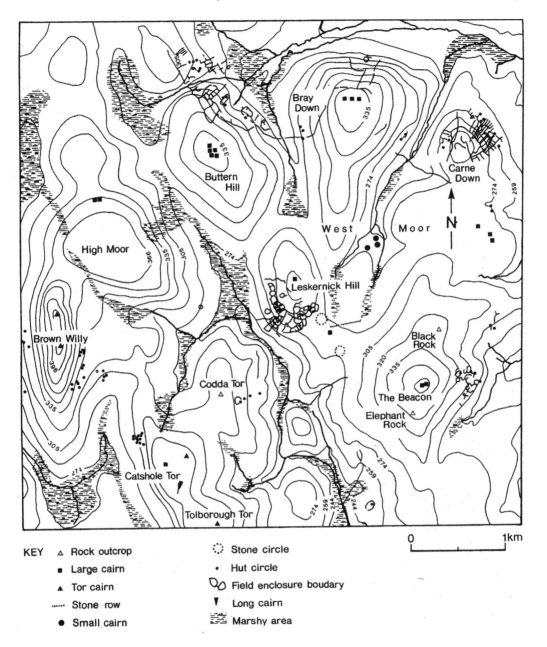

fig. 1:6 A nested landscape – Leskernick encircled by hills surmounted by Great Cairns. After Johnson and Rose 1994, map 1.

Nearly every one of the encircling hills has a large cairn or cairns on their summit. In some cases, the cairns encircle, build upon, or incorporate rock stacks and tors (Tolborough, Catshole, Brown Willy). In other cases, the piles of stones forming the cairns break the smooth contours of the hills to create, in effect, artificial tors. There are, in total, 21 such large cairns and *all* are visible from Leskernick. They seem to mark out and delimit a universe that centres on the hill, its settlement, and nearby ceremonial complex. On the eastern side of the circle, the hills, with their cairns, also delimit the edge of this part of Bodmin Moor. Beyond them, to the east, the land falls away.

Within this encircled territory there is only one large cairn, the one on the top of Leskernick Hill (but see Note 4:4 for alternative view). Within the territory there is also a scatter of small cairns. Apart from those intimately associated with the Leskernick settlement, there are another ten or more possible cairns on the lower slopes of Codda Tor, and another [three cairns a km] north-west of Leskernick on a flat, low-lying area near a stream confluence. From these small cairns many of the large hilltop ones are visible, but they themselves are only apparent from a short distance. This distinction between large prominent cairns on the hilltops and small cairns in low-lying and more hidden locations fits the general pattern known elsewhere on Bodmin Moor (Tilley 1995). It seems likely that the large prominent cairns acted both as boundary markers and as ceremonial foci, whereas at least some of the small constructions probably covered simple cremation burials.

Within the circle formed by the hilltop cairns not only is there an absence of large cairns, but also of traces of prehistoric settlements and field enclosures. The only traces of prehistoric settlement within this circle are some small concentrations of house circles lacking fields and enclosure walls at Codda, Catshole, and on the eastern slopes of Brown Willy. It seems quite possible that these houses were seasonally used by the inhabitants of Leskernick (see chapter 16). More extensive settlement and enclosure areas are usually found just beyond the large cairns on other hillslopes out of sight of Leskernick. It would seem that these neighbouring settlements hold their distance from Leskernick and at the same time their inhabitants built their ceremonial cairns in places that link them one with another, and with the central focus of Leskernick.

The Leskernick people lived within a nested landscape. Closest and most immediate was the lived space of their own settlement. On the margins of the settlement was the ambiguous liminal space of their own dead in the small marker cairns. At the top of the hill was the Propped Stone or Quoit. And out across the undulating plain was the stone row and circles.

On the hilltop, out of sight of the Propped Stone, was a ceremonial ground that was eventually covered and marked by the construction of the Great Cairn. On the other hilltops that encircled Leskernick were the other Great Cairns. They were the effective visual and spatial markers of the limits of people's day-to-day life-world, sites of different myths and stories.

This nested landscape, criss-crossed by paths of herds and people, was not the totality of the Leskernick world. There were other communities, other nested landscapes across the moor, and these local landscapes interdigited. The moor was a kind of kinscape, and there would have been high days and feast days when the Leskernick community and the others moved off to one or other of the great tors – most particularly to Rough Tor – to take part in major ceremonies.

The landscapes of the Leskernick people rippled out beyond the moor. There would have been expeditions and contacts in which moorland people were caught up in other webs of exchange and signification. There would have been some people who journeyed much further. They would have brought back fantastic tales and strange objects. There would also be travellers who arrived, and things that came from distant places that had passed down the line from hand to hand, trailing stories of far-off worlds.

From the outside in

For most of the book, we stand with the Leskernick people at the centre of their world. Just briefly, towards the end, we pause to wonder how Leskernick, how the moor, would have appeared to those who lived beyond it (chapter 18). And we surmise that in the wider geography of Bronze Age Britain, Cornwall, Bodmin Moor, and the communities that lived out their lives there were not perceived as marginal. They were central to the scheme of things; they inhabited a significant, and rather awesome place and landscape.

fig.2:1 Rough Tor

After descending to the De Lank river ... , the mists lifted like a curtain, unveiling the mountainside of Brown Willy and the ridge, on which a man was moving towards the cairn at the end: the grey light and the distance made the man resemble a thin black rod, or a microscopic bacillus. (Malim 1936: 34)

It is a land in which human creatures appear very small, yet, because of their rarity, of special significance. ... It is a quiet landscape in which the chief movement is in the clear washed sky across which move long wagon-trains of dazzling white clouds. ... Silently matching the clouds' aerial progress, violet blue shadows fly over the hills and valleys beneath. (French 1979: 1)

There is an air of immemorial antiquity within the noble granite of Bodmin Moor, which touches the spirit and heightens one's awareness of our primeval roots.
(Chalmers and Bird 1998: 7)

(The Moor has) a certain starkness, an almost brutally present structure suggesting petrified waves, crested at the tors, otherwise in deep wide undulations. The deep recessions of ochre and golden grass in the winter and of greens in spring only lightly cover a sculpture you know to be black as iron or bronze. ... Even the cattle on the Moor tend to be black. (Miskin cited in Val Baker 1973: 11–12)

It is not only the general profile of the tors which is striking; the individual rocks exert their fascination too. Some of them seem to have the significance of modern sculpture and to be imbued with a life of their own. They seem to be alive, waiting motionless as a wild animal might wait until you have gone away. ... The rocks are piled in such a way that they convey an atmosphere that is grim, almost terrifying. (Axford 1975: 44)

And now we made for the top [of Kilmar Tor]. It was more like scaling the ruined walls of a gigantic castle than a hill. Boulders are piled on boulders, as if dropped from some Cyclopean hand. ... Wander yourself over these great moors ... and see if you do not find yourself, after a while searching for meanings, seeing resemblances, and hearing voices such as you never saw or heard before. (Folliot-Stokes 1928: 341–44)

Chapter Two

Bodmin Moor
The Living Bedrock

LONELY, WILD, TIMELESS, FORBIDDING,

DREARY, TREACHEROUS, DANGEROUS, SINISTER, UNCANNY,

SILENT, A WASTELAND, BLEAK, STARK,

EERIE, ENIGMATIC, MYSTERIOUS,

RUGGED, MOUNTAINOUS,

FANTASTIC, MAGICAL, WINDSWEPT,

MENACING, SULLEN, MOROSE,

IMMENSE, PURE, UNADULTERATED, EMPTY,

PRIMEVAL, GRIM, UNTAMED, MAJESTIC, PERILOUS

These are the words used over and over again in 20th-century guide-books, novels, brochures, literary descriptions, and topographic accounts of Bodmin Moor. This small granite upland, no more than 20 km across from north to south and the same from west to east, has exerted a fascination and hyperbole out of all proportion to its size.[1]

The descriptions on the opposite page derive from people's sense of place. The reactions are personal and variable, but nonetheless they answer to understandings and sensibilities that are historically and socially particular. Again and again, the moor is constructed as a lonely wilderness. Something almost sublime. The solitary walker catches the moodiness of the place: on a balmy summer's day, it seems like a tranquil paradise. When the winds roar and the rain beats down, it seems like one of the most inhospitable places on earth. But always it remains the moor experienced at a distance. The forms of the stones are awe inspiring but our modernity has disengaged us from them. The visitor 'sees' the grazing animals but – often – fails to see the working landscape, the human labour that supports them. For the present-day moorland farmer or the Commoner with grazing rights, the moor is something quite different – it is an intimate place experienced in memory and encounter. It answers to a rather different set of social and economic relationships.

We, as archaeologists and anthropologists, are betwixt and between: we behold from a distance and yet, through returning to the same place again and again, and through working the hill, we begin to feel an intimacy.

In this chapter, we mainly 'see' the moor from a distance. We start with an explanation and description of the hard bedrock – the spinal structure of the place; then move to the vegetational 'skin' of the moor. We look at the scribbled palimpsest of human engagement with the moor and the changes it has wrought on bedrock and surface; and, in a little more detail, we pause to consider the pollen and other forms of evidence that document the changing prehistoric and later environment.

Later in the book, in chapter 16, we return to the land forms, the hills and the tors. This time we treat them in more attentive detail as we try to show how the formations were caught up in a prehistoric world view, invoking quite different responses.

Peter Herring: Notes on 'Bodmin Moor as Wilderness' in the Stone World Exhibition, Altarnun, 1999

Bodmin Moor as wilderness?

Terrain is uneven, hills are steep, and valleys are filled with spreading marshes. Streams are fast and strong, surprisingly strong – they could carry you away. Rocks are hard and naked: they seem to rear up at you in the mists; they draw blood when you slip or trip on them. Soils are dark and obviously poor, a lot of them are peaty and oozy. They support poor, but beautifully healthy vegetation: simple and tough.

Buzzards kill, and crows eat the dead. Bones are dragged around and scattered by scavengers. Those bones are large, long and very white. Lapwings and plovers swarm above you, regardless of you, enjoying the wind and the sun. But nearer to you, hopping from rock to rock are the little wheatears and stonechats. They seem to know and call you, leading you away from your track, like spirits. You become mesmerised by their company and only break from your trance when a ragged fox breaks from its cover; its redness startles.

Cattle, sheep and ponies, shaggy and hardy, nibble at the wiry grass and stubbly heather like wild animals on great untamed plains.

But is this place a wilderness?

When we look closely the wilderness retreats and becomes more of a modern state of mind. Bodmin Moor is a wilderness only in a romantically figurative way, and in a relative way, relative to a cultivated field or a busy road, relative to Altarnun village or Truro town, relative to the safety of home ...

The shaggy animals did not find their own way on to the hills. They, like the land itself, are owned. Owners ride or drive out to check, feed and herd them, to earn their living from them. The tough grass, heather and furze these animals graze is subdued and altered by them, and has been by the millions of farm animals that have been turned out onto the moors for at least two thousand years, and probably for four thousand. ...

People have developed paths and trackways; places have been named; maps drawn, bought and used; stories have been heard and learnt. Archaeologists and historians have described, studied and pondered and either drawn lost meanings from the Moor or imposed preferred meanings on it. ...

The wilderness becomes more familiar each time we return to the moors. ... We coin our own place-names, draw our own mental maps, and the wilderness is broken into parts and its power is weakened. The wilderness recedes and Bodmin Moor comes closer to home.

The Living Bedrock

The moor is a complex mosaic of marsh and granite, streams, ridges, and undulating plateaux. The highest points are near to its edges in the north-west and the south-east. It is criss-crossed by sluggish streams, associated with extensive marshy areas. The rivers have almost no fall, only gathering pace and losing height rapidly as they come off the granite and onto the surrounding softer rocks. Between the watercourses, the rounded and oval-shaped grass- and heath-covered hills and ridges are often dominated by granite rock tors. The highest, on the summit of Brown Willy, rises to 420 m. Cornwall's only natural inland lake, Dozmary Pool, lies in a saucer-shaped depression in the centre of the moor under the shadow of the Brown Gelly ridge. It is late glacial in origin (Brown 1977).

The granite boss of Bodmin Moor is intruded through sedimentary rocks of Devonian and Carboniferous age. The granites vary significantly in texture and composition depending upon the manner of intrusion and speed of cooling of the molten lava. They are generally finer in texture near to the edge of the moor because of the more rapid crystallisation of magna as it came into contact with the surrounding sedimentary rocks. These, in turn, were converted to form a variety of bedded slates ('killas') rich in mineral deposits such as tin, copper, lead, zinc, and wolfram, all of which have been exploited at some time in the past. The moor is broadly divisible into three parts: first, those areas of the hardest and most solid granite forming ridges, hills and outcropping rock stacks or tors; second, areas of more easily eroded kaolinised granite; and third, the main mass of granite, more or less decomposed at the surface, forming the more smoothly rounded profiles of the land visible today over much of the area, giving rise to rotted brown subsoil (rab or growan) (Reid, Barrow, and Dewey 1910; Reid et al. 1911).

Although the rocky tors occupy only a small part of the surface area of the moor, they dominate the landscape. They are the main lure for the visitors, and their most vivid memory. Despite the modern rational geological explanation, they still elicit a sense of awe and wonder (Figures 2.1, 2.2, and 2.3). The tors are created out of hard lenticular blocks of granite. The gently rounded surfaces rest horizontally on each other, and the individual sheets are often of great size. Sometimes they rest precariously on each other hence the name logan (logging or rocking) stone. The fantastic shapes of the high tors are caused by the horizontal and vertical cracks that formed as the granite cooled and crystallised from its molten state. These joints, running at right angles to each other, caused the rock to split naturally into cubes and rectangular blocks, dividing the mass into columns separated by openings up to 6 cm or more wide. Weathering and the freeze-thaw action occurring during prolonged periglacial episodes during the Pleistocene Ice Age, have both rounded these joints and enlarged them.[2]

Although the tors are quite small and not very high, the hyperbole used to describe them is justified, for they have a striking visual power and dramatic quality.

fig. 2:2 Tor and Texture: (top) Cheesewring, Stowe's Pound; (middle) top of Leskernick Hill; (bottom) rock close up.

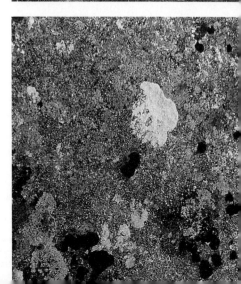

40

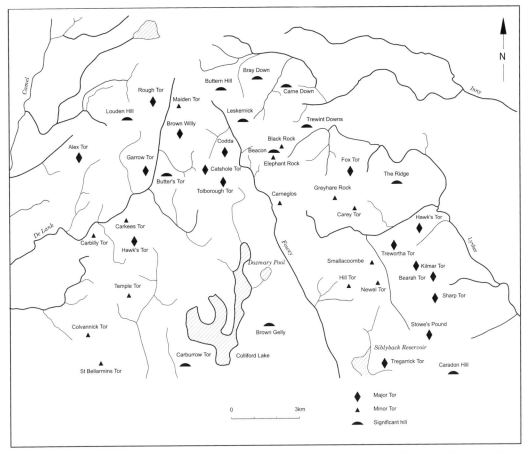

fig.2:3 The tors of Bodmin Moor.

The top stones of the highest tors are frequently riddled with solution hollows or basins, some of which are permanently filled with water. They are often interconnected by channels and the water erodes over the lips of the rock to create incredible arc-like shapes when seen from below (see chapter 19).

Below the rock outcrops on the tops of the hills there are characteristically extensive areas of tumbled blocks of stone and fallen slabs known locally as 'clitter' or 'moorstone'. This clitter, like the tors themselves, was the result of prolonged periglacial action, more particularly the permafrost creep of numerous bedrock outcrops (Harrison et al. 1996). Such areas make walking slow and arduous, and sometimes impossible. There are voids and chamber-like spaces amongst the tumbled blocks on the upper slopes, and often the clitter forms distinctive streams running down the hill slope or lobes that follow the contours of the hill. Individual rocks within the clitter and huge earthfast boulders, known as grounders, often catch the attention because of their strange shapes, textures, weathering lines, quartz and mica inclusions, and the lichens growing on their surface. Mostly grey and dull, the rocks are transformed and glow rose pink at sunset. Sometimes the sunlight glints brilliantly on mica inclusions that are only visible from particular angles and directions at particular times of day and seasons of the year.

The tors, the individual rock formations, the tangled clitter spreads, the massive grounders, and the slabs forming chambers all create the sculptural landscape that is Bodmin Moor. These formations, though they may seem 'rock solid', are, like everything in nature, always in process, caught up in long cycles of uplift, erosion, and deposition. And even in the whisper of time that is human time, the complex and changing ways in which people have understood and engaged with these land forms have had their effect.

A Working Surface

Working on the moor, we have marvelled at the richness of the prehistoric palimpsest and tried to understand how prehistoric people might have worked and walked in this landscape. In the Middle Bronze Age – the time that interests us most – the moor had a high concentration of settlement, and today it remains one of the best preserved prehistoric landscapes in Britain. Why? Partly because, despite much 19th- and 20th-century clearance in the centre and south-west of the moor, large areas remain rough pasture land, unenclosed and unimproved. And partly because settlement over the last 2,000 years, with the exception of a short period of medieval encroachment, kept to the edges of the moor. There is, therefore, an unparalleled record of stone row and circle, barrow, cairn, settlement, and enclosure.

Our attention has focussed on a particular moment in history. But as we walk the moor, we have recognised the sunken drove-ways and negotiated the field walls that are part of an ongoing story. Many of the field walls and abandoned houses go back to medieval times, to the period from about AD 1000 when people established longhouses and farmed extensive strip-based field systems. Many of the later medieval farms are still worked, but others were abandoned in the 14th, 15th, and 16th centuries, leaving houses, fields and cultivation ridges as part of today's palimpsest. Other farmhouses, both medieval and later, have been abandoned much more recently.

Peter Herring: Notes on 'Bodmin Moor as   an abandoned landscape' in the Stone World Exhibition, Altarnun, 1999

Many families, unable to find work or make a living from small Victorian farms, have left the moor in the last fifty years. Their ruined cottages, roof timbers and floors collapsing onto rusting stoves and rotting dressers, are among the most poignant elements of the moorland palimpsest. They remind us that all the archaeological remains were produced by people. And, as we picture plates on the dresser and smell the pasties being taken from the stove we know that it is possible, with care and imagination, to repeople the abandoned moor.

Sometimes, as we surveyed the prehistoric houses at different settlements across the moor, we recognise that there were later additions. Pete Herring has painted a vivid picture of an early medieval usage that involved members of the farming communities from around the edge of the moor driving their farm animals up to the high ground for the summer pastures (Herring 1996). They would often build small rough oval shelters up against or even inside the earlier prehistoric houses. Such huts have been found at Rough Tor, Brockabarrow Common, and probably at Leskernick.[3]

We acknowledge, but only out of the corner of our eye, the evidence of all this activity, of the continual working and reworking of the landscape. We witness the scars of the leats or channels – some that follow the contours of the base of the hills and collect the run-off water from them, others that cut cross-contour, collecting this run-off water and directing it into a downslope torrent. These channels, and the untidy dumps of grassed-over stone and soil, are the remains of medieval and later tin stream working.

There is also, on the very hill that we have worked on over five summers, much evidence of medieval and later quarrying of the surface moorstone. Scattered on the high slopes of Leskernick are fragments of broken or rejected millstones, of stone gateposts, and straddle stones[4] that would have been placed on stone posts. Sometimes, looking down on an almost complete millstone, seeing how it broke just before it was completed or perhaps even as it was being moved, it is not hard to hear the groans that must have gone up from the assembled stone workers (Figure 2.4). It is noticeable that the stone workers seem to have avoided the prehistoric houses on the hill. Perhaps, as Pete Herring (Notes on 'Bodmin Moor as an abandoned landscape' in the Stone World Exhibition, Altarnun, 1999, above) suggests, the houses were protected by stories of giants or spriggans.

We stumble over the remains of sub-rectangular peat drying platforms –

fig.2:4 (left) medieval stone walling; (right) a mill-stone that cracked before completion.

known as steads. There are over 1,000 steads on the moor.

Tony Blackman: Notes on 'Turf as fuel on Bodmin Moor' in the Stone World Exhibition, Altarnun, 1999

The number of turfs required for a household per year varied but was usually around 10,000. A day's 'journey' was about 1,000 turfs ... and these were all laid out around the cutting area to dry. They were regularly titched (turned) and after that 'crossed up' to ensure proper drying. As soon as they were dry enough they were built into a rick. ... The oblong rick with its pitched top would be thatched with rushes, scythed, and bundled in the marsh, to protect it from the weather. A ditch would then be dug around the rick, creating a platform under it called a stead, which helped keep the platform dry and stopped cattle using the rick as a 'scratching post'.

As well as all these small-scale industries, there were much larger ones. It is difficult to imagine that in the 1850s the south-east of the moor produced more tin than anywhere else in the world. Hard to imagine that this was an industrial landscape. On other parts of the moor there are the remains of extensive granite quarries and the tips and dressing floors of the china clay works.[5]

All these workings are part of the landscape of the moor. They are part of what we see today. In the main, because of our focus on the prehistoric landscape, we chose to ignore them. When we put on the exhibition at Altarnun we discovered how strange our myopia seemed to most of the local people (see chapter 14).

Changing Vegetation

(with Martyn Waller)

Although most people recognise the palimpsest of moorland activities, they (both archaeologists and visitors) often find it hard to imagine that the vegetation has ever changed. The tough grasses and the bracken and gorse on the higher slopes seem to be synonymous with what a moor should look like. But having worked on the vegetational evidence – creating an off-site pollen record and analysing 130 pollen samples from a variety of contexts within the settlement – we found that there had been changes, both during the time when Leskernick was settled and between then and now. Our find-

LIBRARY, UNIVERSITY OF CHESTER

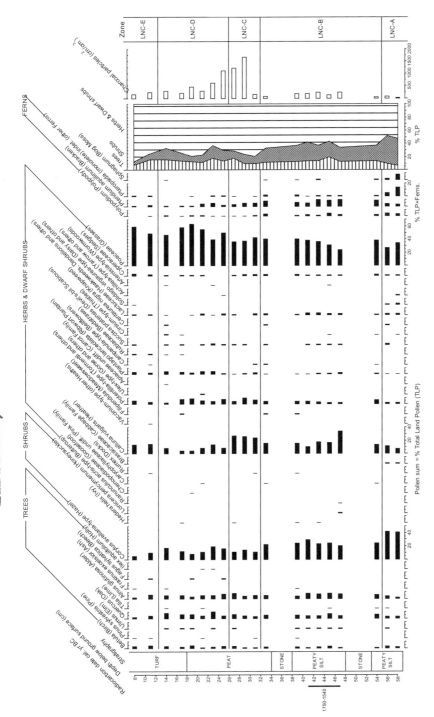

fig. 2:5 North Stone Circle percentage pollen diagram for the stone quarry hole (M. Waller).

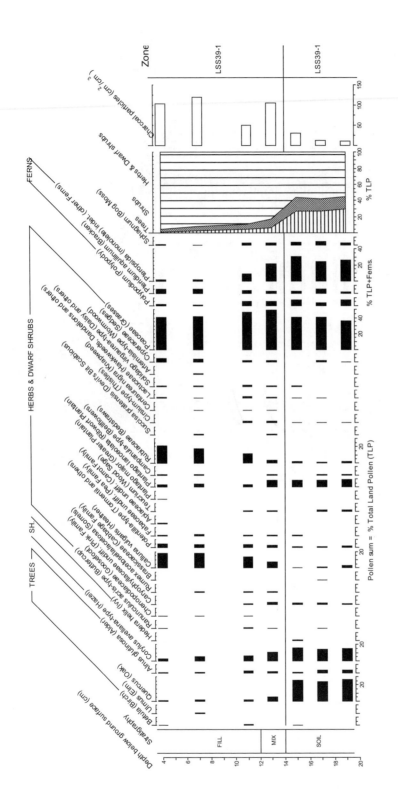

fig.2.6 House 39, southern settlement, percentage pollen diagram for the land surface sealed by the stone wall of the house (M. Waller).

ings complement those from other parts of the moor, particularly Rough Tor (Gearey et al. 2000). The pollen evidence from the North Stone Circle at Leskernick suggests that already in the Early Bronze Age the ritual area below the hill was covered in grass and heather moorland (Figure 2.5). The limited tree pollen from the circle is dominated by high hazel pollen counts and it seems likely that there were hazel stands quite close by on the hill slopes of Leskernick. There was also some oak pollen, and oak dominates the charcoal from the Bronze Age features and deposits associated with the

fig. 2:7a) How the Fowey Valley might have looked in prehistoric times (picture taken on the edge of the moor).

fig. 2:7 b) Herding animals on a treeless moor.

47

Leskernick houses. These oak trees are likely to have been sessile oaks, a type associated with western Britain. On the rather exposed high ground they would have been low growing and rather scraggy.

The on-site pollen evidence from soils and deposits contemporary with the Leskernick settlement confirms the presence of oak trees (and lesser amounts of hazel trees and scrub) in the wider environment of Leskernick, and there would have been concentrations of these trees, and of alder, along the river courses. It also indicates that the immediate environs were more or less open grassland and the presence of *Plantago lanceolata* (ribwort plantain) and *Pontentilla*-type (probably Tormentil) pollen suggests that it was used for animal grazing (Figure 2.6)[6]. It also seems that although there were pockets of peat at lower elevations, the peat did not really extend onto the higher ground.

It seems, therefore, that at the time when people were living on Leskernick Hill the landscape was relatively open and thus visibility between places would have been good, the soils and the grassland were of better quality than today, and there were trees dotted over the hillsides and more densely congregated within the river valley (Figure 2.7a).

The pollen and charcoal evidence is particularly interesting because it seems to undermine a long-accepted scenario in which people left the moor in the later Bronze Age – around 1000 BC – because of deteriorating soil conditions associated with wetter climatic conditions. It now seems that most of the soil deterioration at Leskernick and the other settlements developed after the prehistoric communities had left.[7] At Rough Tor South, Gearey et al. (2000: 505) suggest that the increase in *Calluna vulgaris* (heather) pollen is probably due to a decrease in grazing pressure following the abandonment of the Bronze Age settlement, rather than the effect of soil deterioration. At Leskernick, increases in heather pollen and fern spores from the time of abandonment again suggest a lessening of grazing pressure. It seems therefore that the animals have been taken off the moor before the effects of the wetter climate set in, or at least before it was manifest in terms of soil deterioration.

This situation seems to have been somewhat reversed during the later Iron Age. The pollen diagrams from the early medieval period at Rough Tor and East Moor (Gearey et al. 2000: 506) and the offsite record at Leskernick all suggest a reintensification of moorland grazing and even patches of cultivation.[8] In the last 1,000 years, with the permanent medieval settlement and enclosure of parts of the moor, grazing has been maintained though the intensity seems to have varied. Descriptions in the 16th century of abundant heather on the moor, for example, may indicate a lessening in the grazing pressure. By the middle of the 19th century, overgrazing and repeated burning had reduced the area of heather (Figure 2.7b).

Far from the landscape being 'timeless', it seems clear that the vegetation that we see today – the rough grasses, the bracken, and gorse of the high stony places – is a product of the last couple of hundred years (Johnson and Rose 1994: 3) (Figure 2.8).

fig. 2:8 Sheep and rare windblown trees at the foot of Leskernick hill.

Chapter Three

Methodologies

Introduction

For the most part, we have chosen to write this book as a collective 'we', one that represents the collaborative understanding of the three directors as well as – although as always in such enterprises insufficiently acknowledged – inputs from all the people that worked on and off site over the years. But in this chapter, it seemed sensible to allow each director to write about the methodologies they used for the different parts of the project that they were (more or less) in charge of. So Chris Tilley – with the help of Wayne Bennett who did all the sketching – talks about the house surveys. Barbara Bender talks about working with the enclosures. And Sue Hamilton talks about excavation methods.

It could be said that the anthropologists were dealing with some fairly novel problems, in part because they were asking questions about the meaning of 'things' that went beyond the sort of questions more usually posed, in part because – both literally and metaphorically – they had to cover a great deal of ground. They had, therefore, to think through their strategies in quite basic ways. No doubt there was some reinvention of the wheel but the process of finding adequate ways to represent their findings was, as Chris discusses later, part of the process of uncovering meaning. For Sue, the problems were somewhat different. The basic excavation methods were more or less in place, the novelty – and anxiety – lay, on the one hand, in the very particular problems of the terrain, and, on the other, the desire to humanise the craft of excavation and to find ways to acknowledge that that craft is as much about relationships – to people and to places – as it is about techniques. It is these aspects that Sue has focused on in this chapter. There is also another dimension to Sue's contribution: it enters into, as the observant reader will appreciate, a kind of dialogue with the sociologist's interpretation of what was happening on the hill (see chapter 11).

Chris Tilley and Wayne Bennett Talking About House Surveying

In 1995, we set ourselves the task of locating all the houses and establishing their house-door orientation. We had the great good fortune that the Royal Commission on the Historical Monuments of England (RCHME) had already undertaken a quite detailed survey (Johnson and Rose 1994). The associated report numbered off the houses and gave brief descriptions. Unfortunately, the numbers were not on the map. So, the first thing we had to do was to collate description and coordinate numbers with what was on the map and on the ground. We moved from the description to numbering the map, then locating and pegging the house floors. The numbered pegs gave us a sense of security – we now knew where the houses were!

CT (1995): After tea Sue and Helen came up to join us in locating more huts. Having seen us stumbling around they decided the compass might well be employed to help us find the right direction in which to walk. With this method we did find some huts. But in other cases the compass proved a dismal failure with Barbara's tried and proven semi-random stumbling method being far more effective. It was with a great sense of satisfaction that I found a hut before the compass did. The compass seemed to spoil the spontaneity of the process and represented an intrusion of what was going on in the excavation trench into the world of the settlement survey.

We wanted to see whether there was any pattern to the house entrances. More specifically, were they orientated to particular places within the land-scape? Where to start? One problem was the general lack of visibility of the overgrown stone row and the stone circles and distant cairns from the settle-ment areas. We solved this problem by the use of white marker flags. Then we built a portable doorway (height: 1.40 m, width: 0.5 m). The width was a rough average of the house doorways. The height was Sue's height – chosen because she was the shortest person on the project and the closest we could come to an imagined Bronze Age person!

With this doorway we framed the landscape (Figure 3.1). We stood it up in the entrance to each house. We checked the orientation, took photographs,

fig. 3:1 a) Recording orientations through the wooden house door – Barbara looking, Mary Hinton holding; b) Gill Anderson standing in for House 39; c) the view to the Fowey valley through a doorway on the southern settlement.

and noted down on record cards what could be seen as you looked straight ahead.

We were, in the first instance, somewhat confused. Were we plotting what we could see from the doorway in literal terms? In other words, if the view from a house doorway was blocked by another house was that significant? Or was there a 'right' way of orientating a house quite regardless of what might block the immediate view – was there a ground plan that conformed to the symbolic world view of the people of Leskernick? With hindsight, we think the second notion is right. But, without hindsight, we tied ourselves into a fair number of knots and made life harder for ourselves than we needed to.[1] Thus, we recorded (1) the house-door orientation, (2) all the names of the distant hills and tors that could be seen through the frame, (3) the numbers of all the other houses that would have been visible, and (4) whether the stone row, stone circles, and cairns could be seen.

Here is an example of the unnecessary lengths we sometimes went to:

CT (June 1995): *The greatest practical problem in recording was the proximity of other huts blocking the view. … This problem was resolved by people walking over to the other huts, standing on the walls and becoming the huts themselves. 'You go over and be hut 23 and I'll be hut 24'; 'Which hut are you?'; 'O.K. Can you now go over and be hut 27?' and so on. Looking out of the door in all these different directions, with people metamorphosing into hut walls, took an incredibly long time. It might take an hour or more to record the views from one hut doorway and everyone was rolling around with laughter at the madness of it all. Weather would create difficulties. If the mist came down the exercise would be impossible. Wind was another problem. You simply couldn't hear what hut someone was supposed to be in if it was any distance away. This had to be resolved by relay signalling.*

CT (June 1995): *There was this strange thing about temporality. In the excavation people seemed to be doing the same thing all the time, yet they were recording and doing different things every day. In the settlement work there seemed to be continuous variety, yet we doing pretty much the same thing all the time.*

During the second season, we finished checking the house door orientations and, turning our backs to the landscape, started to look at the house structures. We used a house recording form developed on the basis of observations we had made in 1995 and those incorporated in the Johnson and Rose

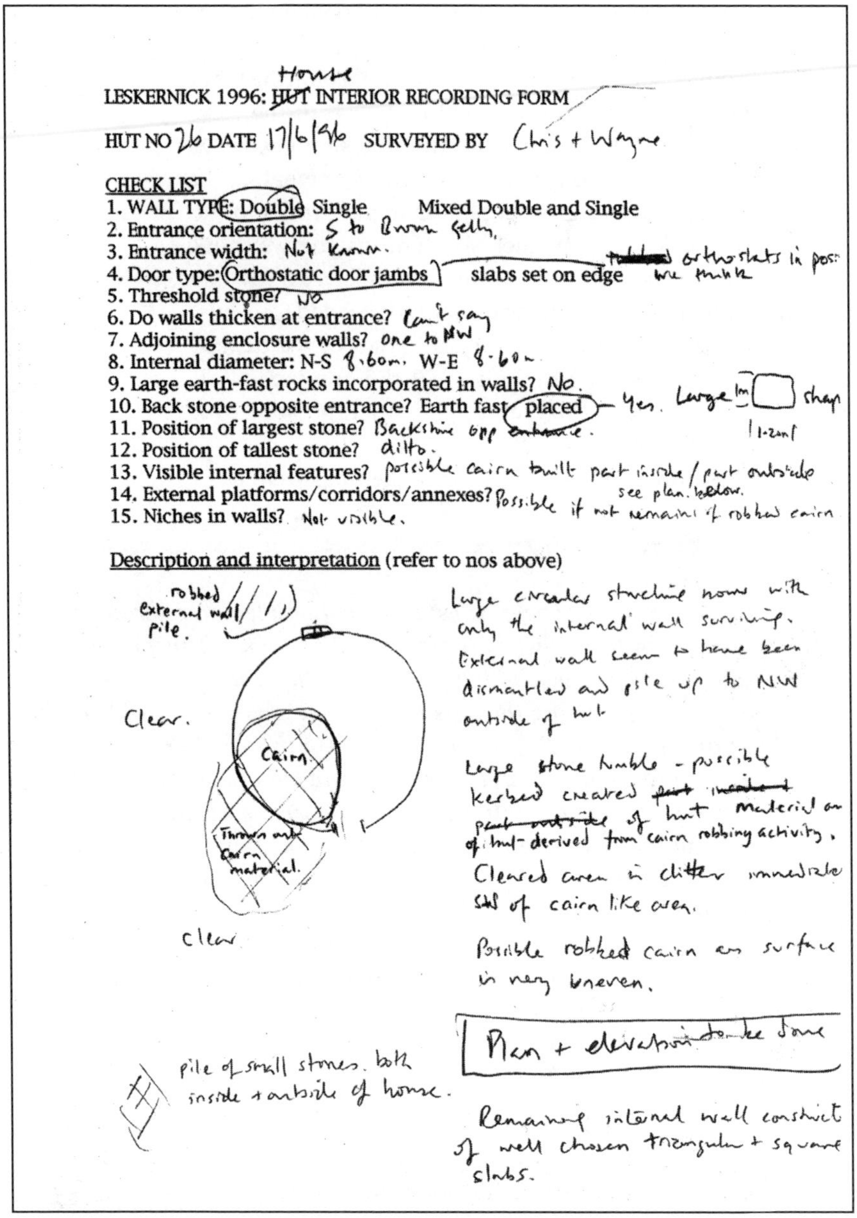

LESKERNICK 1996: ~~HUT~~ House INTERIOR RECORDING FORM

HUT NO 26 DATE 17/6/96 SURVEYED BY Chris + Wayne

CHECK LIST
1. WALL TYPE: Double Single Mixed Double and Single
2. Entrance orientation: S to Brown Gelly.
3. Entrance width: Not known.
4. Door type: Orthostatic door jambs slabs set on edge — orthostats in pos? we think
5. Threshold stone? No
6. Do walls thicken at entrance? Can't say
7. Adjoining enclosure walls? one to NW
8. Internal diameter: N-S 8.60m. W-E 8.60m
9. Large earth-fast rocks incorporated in walls? No.
10. Back stone opposite entrance? Earth fast placed — Yes. Large 1m shape 1.2m
11. Position of largest stone? Backstone opp entrance.
12. Position of tallest stone? ditto.
13. Visible internal features? possible cairn built part inside / part outside see plan below.
14. External platforms/corridors/annexes? Possible if not remains of robbed cairn
15. Niches in walls? Not visible.

Description and interpretation (refer to nos above)

Large circular structure now with only the internal wall surviving. External wall seem to have been dismantled and pile up to NW outside of hut

Large stone rubble - possible kerbed created ~~part inside part outside~~ of hut material on of hut - derived from cairn robbing activity.
Cleared area in clitter immediately SW of cairn like area.

Possible robbed cairn as surface is very uneven.

Plan + elevation to be done

Remaining internal wall consist of well chosen triangular + square slabs.

fig.3:2 A house recording form.

Bodmin Moor survey (Johnson and Rose 1994) (Figure 3.2). We retained the numbering code used in this survey with houses numbered from H1 to H50. We wanted to develop a methodology that detailed both house plan and elevation. This work proceeded on the basis of our conviction that, for the prehistoric house builders, the stones possessed symbolic qualities, and that, amongst other things, shape and size would have been significant in determining their precise location within the house interiors.

CT (June 1995): The excavation was dominated by technological procedures, a rhetoric of recording. In the settlement work there was no obvious starting point or procedure to follow, no standard context sheets. But we rapidly tried to create standardization in recording and got very concerned if things were not being done in the 'right' way. At one stage, we even had someone shouting out where we were to stand next and what we were to look at.

SH (June 1995): The process of finding the hut doorways, finding that other huts are blocking the views, what can be seen and what cannot, in many ways is identical to recording colour changes in the soil profiles of a feature ... but there is more of an illusion of freedom.

Given the large number of houses (c. 50) on the hillside, we had to develop a relatively quick but accurate method of drawing. We decided that annotated sketch plans of the surface stones and elevations of the interior wall-face should be made for all reasonably well-preserved houses (Figure 3.3). Where structures were too fragmentary, we simply described them on the house recording forms.

In 1996, two teams of three persons were used. We found, however, that despite an agreed practical methodology, differences in drawing style and interpretative approach made the comparison of the work increasingly problematic. So, in 1997, we decided that only one team should undertake the work.

In both seasons, the drawings and interpretative accounts detailed on the house recording forms were double checked by other members of the project team. Later on, as we became more skilled and knowledgeable in our work, the drawings and the interpretations on the recording forms were rerechecked and revisions were added, dated, and the authors credited, allowing us to acknowledge the changes in our thinking through time and differences between members of the survey team.

Each house was drawn on metric graph paper to a scale of 1:50. Usually, a central position within the house represented the centre of the drawing. Occasionally, this was adjusted to allow external components to be included on the drawing. The upslope back of the house was always placed at the top of the drawing.

Once a centre had been established and pegged, a compass was used to peg out the cardinal points within the inner circuit of the house wall. Two measuring tapes were laid out crossing through the centre point and the opposing cardinal positions to the outer limit of what was to be drawn.

Using two 1 m² drawing frames with 50 cm subdivisions, it was easy to move across the interior of the house using the measuring tapes as reference points. Traversing the walls using the frames was more difficult. It was often

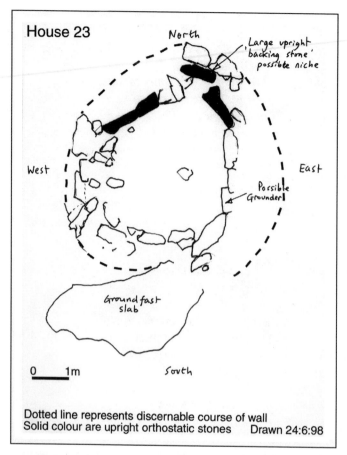

House 23

North

Large upright
'backing stone'
possible niche

West

East

Possible
Grounder

Ground fast
slab

0   1m

South

Dotted line represents discernable course of wall
Solid colour are upright orthostatic stones   Drawn 24:6:98

fig. 3:3 Annotated plan
and elevation of House 23.

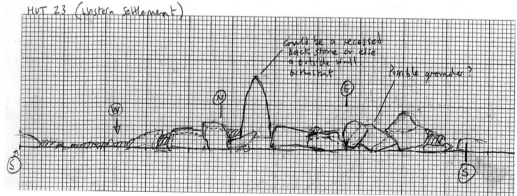

HUT 23 (Western settlement)

could be a recessed
back stone or else
a outside wall
orthostat

Possible grounder?

necessary for the person drawing to view through the frame from different angles to assess the shape and position of the stones. Sloping stones were especially difficult to represent. This process of moving over the stones engendered a dynamic approach to the drawing – less grounded in the principles of Euclidean geometry and more akin to a cubist appreciation of form.

The drawing of a sketch plan took between two and eight hours, depending on the size and complexity of the house remains. This compares with a figure of about eight hours for one house and 24 hours for a more complicated one for an archaeologist's pre-excavation plan. The elevation sketch of the interior wall face usually took between 10 and 20 minutes.

We used a 2b or softer pencil that enabled the drawings to convey something of the material qualities of the stones not normally shown in traditional archaeological drawing. We were conscious that the rough crystalline and weathered qualities of the granite should not be ignored and also that, although the use of the drawing frames allowed for a quite accurate sketch plan to be made, the two-dimensional drawn image could never really convey the three-dimensional experience of standing over the stones and the suggestive but inconclusive possibilities of their form beneath the coverings of turf and moss.

Elevation drawings were only done for those houses with well-preserved internal wall components (Figure 3.3). The person drawing sat in the centre of the house while another person moved a vertically held drawing frame around the internal circumference of the wall at 1 m intervals starting with a cardinal point. Essentially only those wall stones that appeared *in situ* were drawn but sometimes, when it was obvious that a stone had tumbled into the house interior, it was re-erected on the elevation drawing and the stone was marked with a dashed line.

All drawings were dated, initialled, and annotated. The annotation included the identification of the largest and/or tallest stone, earth fast grounders, any unusually shaped stones, the course and width of the apparent wall footing, areas of turf covered rubble, adjoining features such as porches, bench-like grounders and field walls, the entrance, compass orientation, etc. The first part of the house recording form permitted the further registration of important details such as whether a threshold stone could be seen or if the door jambs were still in place. The second part of the form asked for a descriptive and interpretative account by the survey team. There was also space on the form for a thumbnail sketch showing any important relationships between the house and any nearby structure or landscape feature.

The time taken in looking, drawing, and discussing the houses was central to the investigative and interpretative process. We began to get a feel for the houses and to see in ways that were quite different from our initial encounters. Because our work was not locked into the rigid technical procedures associated with standard excavation practice, it was easier for us to think imaginatively about the subject that was being drawn and studied. Thus, for example, we slowly came to recognise that some of the houses appeared to have been converted into cairns (see chapter 7).

CT (June 1999): Wayne and I then walk to the top of the tor and survey the area around the north of the cairn where we have found a house platform and an 'orator's' stone. We then go and sit on the massive cairn top and write a general description of the hill. It starts to rain. Wayne puts on his poncho and uses it as a tent, writing beneath it while I describe the hill and the landscape. The technique works wonderfully except that Wayne can't see anything that I am referring to. Likewise, I can't see what he's writing so he could be putting anything down we joke! We have another discussion about representing reality in words, something we started some days earlier while sitting on the top of Brown Willy in the swirling mist. We can never describe reality. It is a mess. In order to explain and interpret we have to simplify, make things clearer than they really are, sort out the essential from the inessential. What is there on the hill is a tangled mess and our descriptions tidy it up, make it neat. ... It is all a process of creating order, searching for a pattern and establishing links between things.

Barbara Bender Talking About Surveying the Enclosures

In the first instance, in our first year, we moved between peering at the survey map created by the RCHME and stumbling across the hillside. The survey map is wonderful and incredibly detailed. It was produced from aerial photographs and shows all the clitter – dense concentrations, thin spreads, large boulders, relatively clear areas, and so on – as well as the house and enclosure wall locations. The map both orientates and disorientates. What it does not show are the contours of the land. And without them the terrain is curiously flattened: there is no way of orientating oneself in terms of slopes or hollows, uphill or downhill. The countourless map nullifies the topography and – perhaps advantageously – we had to experience it for ourselves and learn to relate the house floors and enclosures to an intimate topography.

BB (June 1995): I find the process of map reading and walking very interesting – Gell's 'practical mastery',[2] though not much of that! From slight elevations, certain angles, the walls become very clear, but then they swim out of focus again.

In the second and third season, as we focused on the enclosure walls, we had to find a way to record them. On an unpublished overlay to the main RCHME map, some of the walls had been annotated, but this survey had been done very rapidly and the annotations were rather minimal.[3]

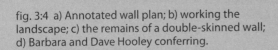

fig. 3:4 a) Annotated wall plan; b) working the landscape; c) the remains of a double-skinned wall; d) Barbara and Dave Hooley conferring.

We, too, used an overlay. We enlarged the RCHME plan to a scale of 1:500, laminated it and fixed it to a portable board. We covered the plan with tracing paper and, as we tracked along the walls, one person numbered the walls and features and annotated the plan, whilst another person marked up a recording sheet for each wall (Figure 3.4a).

In the first instance, we created a recording sheet that separately detailed wall entrances, wall junctures, and so on. The advantage of this format was that we got used to thinking about the different categories of information. The disadvantage was that the information on a given wall was dispersed between different sections on the recording sheet. Checking the sheets against the annotated overlay was unnecessarily time consuming. Eventually, we created a much simpler recording sheet that flowed with the wall. The sheet was divided longitudinally and on the right-hand side, the line of the wall was sketched and the stones, entrances, etc., were marked and numbered as on the plan. On the left-hand side, more detailed comments were made about the shape of the stones, type of wall, form of entrance, and so on.

BB (12 June 1996): Such a lovely cool sunny afternoon. The shadows slowly lengthening. Moving quietly around with Christel taking notes in her rather mysterious Germanic handwriting, and Pippa annotating the plan – her thoughts occasionally slipping away …

These procedures seemed adequate to our needs. One thing that we did not do was to measure in precisely the position along the wall of 'singular' stones or cairns, etc. They were located by eye.

CT (19 June 1996): In surveying the enclosure walls we are not creating a new minutely surveyed master plan of Leskernick but are more interested in generalities: qualities and characteristics, the 'narrative' sequence of the stones in the different walls: whaleback to grounder to triangular to entrance to cairn to adjoining enclosure wall etc.

We had hoped to be able to locate entrances within the enclosure boundaries. But, with rare exceptions, the gaps in the walls remained ambiguous. Very often, we suspected that they were made later, after the site was abandoned, and that often they had served to facilitate access by cart or sledge to the stones that were to be taken off-site for use elsewhere or were to be moved to some more convenient place on the hill to be worked upon before transport. Where there were piles of stone close to the entrance, we could be fairly sure that the entrance was a later breach and these we labelled 'B'; where we were happy that they were original, we labelled them 'E'; and where we were uncertain 'E?' or 'B?' To us, entrances had seemed an important element in our story because we wanted to understand more about people moving around the hill – people walking between places, going around places, creating secret places, and so on. But perhaps it was a little naive to think that everyone would have always stuck to the 'official' entrances:

Peter Herring (pers. comm., 12 April 1999): Entrances and movement: I share your sadness. [But] I also wonder whether openings in walls are so significant for identifying lines of movement within the settlements. Although there would have been 'highways', there must also have been by-ways. Even in early modern Cornish field systems I wouldn't just use the gateways. Loads of built stiles (not just on footpaths), and many more casual ones take farmers, trespassers etc. around the countryside. Would it be easier to work from nodes (e.g., houses and activity areas like the spring, the ceremonial sites) and key areas (the hilltop, the fields and pastures beyond) to suggest route-ways?

The interior of the enclosures was annotated using the same procedures. During the 1997 season, Dave Hooley[4] began the process of marking negative and positive lynchets[5] onto a smaller-scale copy of the survey plan (Figures 3.4, 3.5). These were then transferred to the annotated large-scale plans.

Dave Hooley (pers. comm., 18 June 1997): I felt it impossible to distinguish negative from positive lynchetting along any of the walls on the basis of surface evidence, or [to distinguish] whether the effect is due to human activity within the fields or to natural processes post-abandonment, without making unwarranted assumptions. I have adopted a convention of drawing my green 'lynchet' line on the upslope side of the walls affected, but do not wish to imply they are all 'positive lynchets'. In each case identified, the 'lynchet' appears as a distinct (but usually slight – 0.1 m to 0.25 m) step in the slope level from turf-covered ground on one side of the wall to that on the other side.

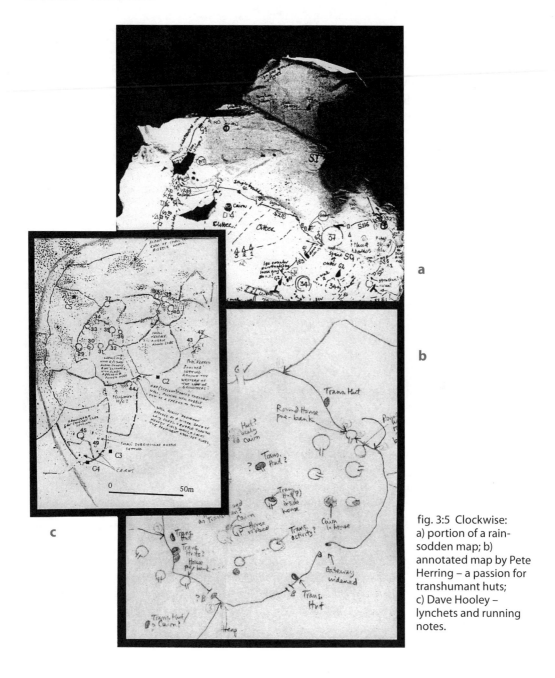

fig. 3:5 Clockwise: a) portion of a rain-sodden map; b) annotated map by Pete Herring – a passion for transhumant huts; c) Dave Hooley – lynchets and running notes.

As we shall see, the archaeologists resolved some of the questions posed by Dave Hooley: the 'lynchets' that they excavated turned out not to be lynchets after all! (chapter 5).

'Cairns' or 'stone-piles' presented a particular problem. Apart from the Great Cairn on the top of the hill, they were small (rarely more than 3 m in diameter). Leaving aside the precise *use* of such stone piles, we simply attempted to distinguish those that demonstrated some degree of structure from those that did not. There were certainly some 'stone piles' that appeared to have kerbs, some – a very few – even had the remains of a central cist. All these were labelled as 'cairns'. Many such cairns were located actually on, or within, enclosure walls and many appeared to have been constructed after the wall – and presumably the enclosure – had gone out of use. Often the length of wall close to the cairn appeared to have been robbed.

But there were many 'stone piles' that appeared completely amorphous. Many of these were located within the walls and enclosures along the southern perimeter of the southern settlement. Many, we can assume, were caused by later people – medieval or later still – piling up stones that were redundant to requirements as they searched for and extracted boulders and slabs to be taken off site, or stacking stones in order to breach a wall. At one point, our map was liberally splattered with such piles, but eventually some of those that 'looked' as though they were not part of the history of Bronze Age use and reuse and abandonment were eliminated. Others were left with query marks – some as '?cairn' some as '?stone pile'. It has to be admitted that this was a somewhat arbitrary procedure and a cause of considerable debate, and – as so often – the creation of cut-off points that eliminated later usage of the hill from our record felt uncomfortable.

Most of the time two or three people undertook the surveying. Almost all the results were rechecked in the field by another group – a process both tiring and sometimes tense!

HB (Wednesday, 1996): Once we started showing Barbara and Chris around the wall, disagreements inevitably arose. … Barbara continues to check everything in minutiae: 'Have you recorded this? I think this should definitely be recorded'.

Chris: 'Why? That's just a natural feature'.

Barb: 'I think it has been placed there'.

And so it carries on, with Chris and Barbara winding each other up.

'You can't always go around making everything cultural', says Chris to Barbara with both his hands in the top pockets of his shirt.

Just as we used Dave Hooley's expertise to help us plot the (assumed) lynchets, so we used Pete Herring's[6] knowledge to re-examine the wall abutments.[7] He worked independently from us and we then cross-checked our findings.

BB (23 June 1997): At lunch in House 28 Pete [Herring] produced his survey maps of the enclosure walls. Quite small, very neat – not at all like my big scruffy map. He said mine looked 'antiquarian' – I was mildly mortified! But then he was only marking wall butts, not 'singular' stones, potential cairns, possible entrances, and different wall structures!

With Helen and Gary participating we compared wall butts. As I expected we had about 90% agreement.

We located a few choice problems and set off around the hill looking at difficult butts. Gary and Helen prodded, pried and discussed. It was great to see how the expertise they had gained in the excavation carried over into the survey. They were very confident and we came to a lot of decisions – mostly agreeing with Pete's earlier assessments, but not always.

Pete knows the feel of the land, he walks confidently from place to place, ponders how they used the land.

Pete Herring (pers. comm., 12 April 1999) … The tension between archaeologists when recording: Is this partly due to investing effort and thus values into our observations and records which we don't want to see wasted or devalued by being persuaded by others to alter or delete them? You were very patient when I went round the southern settlement with you, Helen and Gary. But I worry about how you will feel about my differences of interpretation now that your work has been worked up into a draft, more effort expended and a rather more definite set of interpretations. Will you be so patient now? Will I in turn be making my comments less absolutist to reduce any tension?

In much the same way that the archaeologists needed to lift their heads above the excavation trench and move around to retain a sense of relationship between the grainy detail of the trench and the landscape from which it takes its being, so we found that the head-down procedures of planning needed to counteracted by moving more freely so that we could keep in sight the relationships between walls and houses and clitter and hillside, and think about the overall scheme of things.

CT (8 June 1996): Standing in the southern settlement, Leskernick Hill appears circular, though it is really oval in shape. Objective measurements and maps run contrary to bodily feeling and perception. To the prehistoric inhabitants of Leskernick their hill probably was circular, mirroring the circularity of their houses and their cairns and stone circles – a circle embracing all the other circles.

Pete Herring (pers. comm., 12 April 1999): Are you being seduced by the archaeologists' plan more than you want to be? When I have no map to guide me I see or feel the hill as island, dome, or slope. The circle comes only on geometrical analysis – dome having a presumed circular plan. Are houses, cairns, even stone circles perceived/experienced as circles? Not as ellipses (circles viewed from the oblique angles given by the adult eye), or domes (the cairns), or cones (houses with their roofs on)?

The process of recording is tiring. By the end of each season, we began to suffer from a surfeit of stones.

HB (Friday, summer solstice, 1996): Walls are beginning to grind and words like 'significant', 'cairn', 'interesting,' and 'stone' have become very stale. The words no longer express the enthusiasm of a week ago. Instead they are said flatly, something to be noted down on a form. Once said the words are carried off by the wind and we move to the next piece of wall.

And So to Sue Hamilton and Excavation Methodologies

One of the pragmatic aims of the Leskernick excavations was to establish the absolute and relative chronologies of the western and southern settlements and enclosures and their chronological relationship with the adjacent ritual landscape of the stone row and stone circles. We also wanted to know why and how people lived at the site and the nature of the local environment at the times of site use. We hoped to ascertain the architectural construction, spatial organization, and function(s) and uses and life-cycles of the various domestic and ritual structures. The specific relationship of the architecture to the boulders and stone spreads on the hill fascinated us right from the start, and we particularly wanted to elucidate why the 'Leskernick people' had chosen to live their lives amongst the stones. These questions seemed simple, but their resolution was hard won in an environment that has suffered the distorting and destructive effects of soil acidification, intense animal burrowing, and stone robbing, and has in places been smothered by peat.

Additionally, I chose to excavate in a particular way. Excavation is characterised by intense labour at a fixed location. Particularly in rural environments, this can engender a strong sense of, and reaction to, place, yet little of this is evoked or utilised in the interpretation and publication of excavations. Because Leskernick's landscape is strongly contained by a screen of enclosing hills, there was a good potential to focus on our awareness of place. I chose to maximise this. We walked onto and across the moor each day to and from our work. This was a 45-minute hike each way over hilly terrain. Much of our working equipment was backpacked on to site on a daily basis. Once on site, we did without even the basic facilities that form the paraphernalia of most excavations. We lacked shelter, lavatory facilities, and a 'site caravan'. The excavation trenches were widely dispersed across the site, forcing us to continuously walk through and around the surface ruins of Leskernick's prehistoric architecture. Over five years (1995–99), for a total of 19 weeks (each May and June), we deturfed, excavated, back-filled, and reconstituted c. 400 square m of Leskernick Hill wholly by hand.

The craft of excavation

> Date: Sunday, 2 June 1996
> Place: Dinner in Barbara's caravan
> Question: 'Why did you agree to join the team?' SH
> Answer: 'Because I wanted to visit Cornwall.' MST

The character of any excavation is site specific. Climate, geology, topography, plants and animals, and humanly constructed environments all affect the work patterns and ethos of the excavation team. With time, these aspects add to the participant's sense of identity of belonging to a particular project. Many people join, or are selected for projects and return year after year to the same excavations, not because of their knowledge or skill with respect to the project's archaeology, but because they are contributors to, and willing participants in, the conditions and collective character of the project. On the Leskernick excavations you most likely had to be interested in the Bronze Age, and be positive about or at least tolerant of constant debate and scrutiny of your attitudes and daily habits by the sociologists. Liking stones and hill walking was essential, as was thriving, or at least being able to cope with, working in exposed conditions. It probably helped to get on with at least one of the project directors.

The weather

June 1995 was sunny in North Cornwall and provided a gentle initiation into the moor's climate. Mostly, however, we toiled in the wind, rain, and mist in the best weatherproof clothing each of us could afford or invent (Figure 3.6).

But nothing keeps today's weather out on Bodmin Moor for eight plus hours. We know it to have been better in the Bronze Age.

SH (Saturday, 21 June 1997): Wake up to terrible wind howling through the trees. We are in rescue mode now ... we must go on to the site whatever the weather. Put on a full set of waterproofs before leaving the caravan. Once walking on the Moor, Angus walks ahead ever chirpy ... almost too much for me this morning. ... Steve disappears ahead of me in a conspicuously pink waterproof. ... Dan blends remarkably well into the landscape with his purple camouflage gear. This morning is all about bailing out vast quantities of water from the trenches ... bucket loads and tea mug loads. Helen [trench supervisor of the Stone Row Terminal and Cairn 5] uses a plastic dustpan to great effect. ... All day the rain is unrelenting ... coming in great swathes. During our 'tea break' in H28 we stand like penguins, with our backs to the rain and heads bowed. Everyone remained ludicrously cheerful ... dancing to keep warm.

D. Sprout (23 July 1999): The thick mist still hasn't cleared ... we feel like grave-diggers disturbing the dead ...

North Stone Circle Trench Diary (9 June 1998): P.T.O. This page was too wet to write on.

The animals

A major problem at Leskernick was dealing with the local fauna.

SH (Friday, 19 June 1998): Arrive at House 39 to find a bullock on top of the spoil heap, determinedly chewing the wooden handle of one of our new box sieves. ... The Northern Circle has a cow happily sitting in the south side of our trench across the central whale-stone. Other cows sit contentedly on the turf, earth and stone stacks of our spoil heaps ... having utterly destroyed them yet again.

In addition to the intimidating long-horn cows, there were horses and

fig. 3:6 Working on the Leskernick excavations in June/July. Top row from left: trowelling vole-burrows; Gareth Spicer weaving a wheel-barrow amongst the rocks; Simon Smith and Mark Landymore sieving. Middle row: Sue giving site tour; Sue taking samples for pollen; inset – Cliff Sampson planning. Bottom row: Sue walking between trenches; Richard Hoyle moving stones; Dan King having a lunch break. Photos by: – from left to right – top row MST, FS and MST, middle row MST, FS, bottom row (including insert) FS and unknown.

sheep to contend with. They demolished our spoil heaps, turf stacks, and returfed excavation trenches. Four or five different designs of turf stack were tried to discourage these animals. On the hill, piling and stacking the turf amongst the clitter worked best. Down by the North Circle, the most 'effective' soil heap was one of hedgehog-like character that had the 'recycled' flag poles of the survey team sticking out of it at all angles. On the returfed excavation trenches, stones had to be placed on top of the replaced turfs (to be removed the following season, by which time the turfs were more secure).

The regime

There was some contention about the hours worked between the survey team and the excavating team. As far as the excavating team was concerned, the idea of an unregimented timetable was soon history – an unattainable luxury of the project's idealism. Digging is physically demanding, and needs to be *paced* to an agreed timetable otherwise the excavator wears him or herself out or under-performs. Our schedule of course included time for thought and debate. It was also important to timetable certain tasks. The weather conditions of the moor meant that once started tasks had to be finished or the archaeology would be lost.

SH (Wednesday, 28 May 1997): Today they stayed at H[ouse] 39 for tea; H[ouse]28 is just too far away for a short break. It puts the scale of the settlement in perspective, that such a distance seems too great after two rain-sodden hours of hard graft.

SH (Sunday, 9 June 1996): Within one week Penni and Wayne on the surface survey team have sketched the key elements of most of the 18 houses on the Southern Settlement. During the same time the excavation team have produced two pre-excavation house plans which replicate every visible stone. Wayne and Penni can now recount the broad characteristics of individual houses, and their method has speedily generated a familiarity with the settlement as a whole. Which method is more in key with experiencing the potentials and parameters of a Bronze Age world? Which method provides a database of a Bronze Age world for others to effectively engage with?

A sense of place

Although the excavations were in the same general landscape as the survey work, it is clear that each method provided a very different knowledge of, and familiarity with, the landscape.

SH (June 1998): This evening Mike W laid out his photographs of H23. Last week he went all around its trenches on his knees with the camera pointing down at the troweller's perspective. It took me ages to work out how on earth to piece it all together, yet those who had trowelled there recognised even the smallest stones. Working at one spot, eyes continually looking down in a trench simultaneously narrows knowledge but provides an intimacy and power of knowledge that separates those who work in a trench from those who visit a trench.

SH (Thursday, 6 June 1996): CG and I have now levelled from the stone row TBM to H[ouse] 39 and then H[ouse] 23. There is a 7 m change in height between the Stone Row Terminal and H[ouse] 23. This surprised us – it seemed so much more, as we foundered over the stones of the hill until we reached H23 with the Fowey valley steeply sloping away below. It reminds me of the situation of Mike ST and Ash's house plans (precise, clinical images) versus the elevation sketches (images more immediately appealing to the senses). ... Clearly, measured 'facts' do not always mirror perception. I asked CT (who yesterday evening complained about all of the walking which he was doing up and down the settlement) what he thought that the change in height between the stone row terminal area and H23 was – he answered '40 metres'.

SH (undated, summer 1999): I perceive the excavations as an inter-connecting whole with the information from one trench and season's work feeding into the next season's strategy and knowledge. Barbara and Chris see our trenches as fragmentary windows of detail in the overall story and verification of the surface survey's interpretation.

SH (Friday, 19 June 1998): Leskernick has become a landscape of 'taskscapes'. The landscape survey form asked participants to name the three most important places in Leskernick's landscape. Rather too many of the excavators wrote 'the tool store' as one of their choices. I think they misunderstood the question!

A sense of identity

In '*Experiencing the Past*', Shanks explores the characteristics of archaeology as a cultural practice, and specifically as a craft associated with the production of knowledge of the past (Shanks 1992: 172). In doing so, he focusses on the function, viability, and expression of archaeology as a discipline. The most overtly manual part of archaeology, namely 'excavation' is ignored in this exploration and is relegated to a small section in a wider consideration of 'archaeological poetics' (Shanks 1992: 183). It is, however, the excavation part of archaeology that is most strongly perceived as a craft by its practitioners, both in terms of attitudes to the work of excavation and in terms of the social and working identities that it nurtures. It also has the status of a craft in the romanticised public view of the archaeologists uncovering crumbling skeletons and fragments of pottery on still, sunny days, using small trowels and paintbrushes.

The process of excavation, particularly in difficult physical circumstances and distinctive conditions, nurtures a corporate group defined by its common purpose, skills, and knowledge. This is secured by knowing how to excavate a particular environment, an eye for 'things' such as layers that cannot be seen by the uninitiated, and knowledge of what to expect, such as the basic sequences below the surface. Such wisdom accretes. It can be taken to new trenches and used in subsequent seasons of excavation. This type of learnt knowledge, garnered through practice and experience, is similar to that acquired by apprenticed and skilled persons involved in manual craft – carpentry, building, decorating, and plumbing. Such crafts are all about construction, yet excavation is labelled as a destructive process.

Group definition is also created by the shared hardships. At Leskernick this included working in the wind and rain, which resulted in a particular interest in food that 'kept you going'. Cornish pasties, 'Jammy dodgers', and 'Hobnob' biscuits, nuts, blocks of dates, bananas, and the like all attained an unnaturally elevated importance.

Group definition also wraps itself around clothing and tools, which were used and created for special situations. These included Mike ST's design of large box-frame sieves (brought with him from another site), and his waterproof context sheet that he assured everyone he had tested in the bath (its chinagraph marking pencil melted in a rare moment of sunshine), and Chris D's golfing umbrella for writing up his trench diary in the rain. Cult shops for the purchase of digging clothes also emerged, such as the Clovelly Clothing Company in Boscastle for waterproof coats, trousers and boots. The Camelford charity shop had a particularly key role in providing clothes, it being cheaper to replace dirty worn clothes than paying for the launderette at the campsite. The latter resulted in Gary going around in trousers that were permanently too short for him. Some of this 'gear' became, or was perceived as, further markers of in- and ex-clusion. This included the wrap-around glasses and goggles which effectively kept the wind and sediment out of our eyes, particularly while sieving. To 'outsiders', these 'eye covers' made us look sinister and bizarre. Initial functionalism ultimately became a badge of 'craft', which was heightened by the non-excavators' violent dislike of them.

Then there is excavation humour. At Leskernick, this mostly centred around scrounging or stealing food, succeeding in secretly placing a banana skin in another person's waterproofs, and rain jokes. The personal gossip and sex lives of the excavators mostly passed me by, but took up a fair amount of space in people's diaries, and, by implication, their thought processes whilst on site. In retrospect, I realised that the tool store (an improvised enclosure of stones), where we gathered each morning, was a point of great social angst, as I sorted out who would be working with whom in each trench.

It is easy to lay the clothes, the regime, the specialist knowledge, and the organisational structure down to aggressive exclusiveness, small mindedness, inflexibility, and hierarchies. Alternatively, it is the by-product of a complex craft, which is undervalued. It is also not widely understood as a craft, because it is the result of the excavation that is published rather than the social circumstances of excavating. It is predictable that its practitioners react by focusing on 'badges of identity'. This sometimes defined itself down to the particular trench that a person was digging in:

Helen (12 June 1996, Cairn 5 Trench Diary): Gary has been 'baggsied' by the hut digging team … his singing talents will be missed.

Chris D. (June 1998, House 39 Exterior Trench Diary, pm): Louise to Gary's trench. He has not only pinched a member of my team but my pencil, rubber and trowel (and our survival Hobnob biscuits).

Such excavation communities are not deliberately exclusionary, but a particular sense of place, work, and purpose are almost inescapable in the cut-off environment of the stony slopes of Leskernick. Maybe the communities that we were excavating at Leskernick were not so very different in this respect.

Excavating on the moor

Our work has generated a specific methodology for excavating the environment of the moor. In particular, it involved thinking about the positions of stones, chemical processes, and the consequent development of the soil, and those things that are invisible (but implied by something else) or too small to see. At Leskernick, the latest phase of soil development took place after the abandonment of the structures. It is characterised by acidity – the result of high rainfall, acid bedrock, and the growth of acidic moorland vegetation. This soil development has produced distinct horizons (including multiple iron pans), which in places overlay Leskernick's Bronze Age features, and in places follow or line the features. Due to these processes, the non-stone features above the weathered granite bedrock (in Cornwall known as rab) have been rendered invisible. This particularly relates to shallow features, or the upper parts of cut features such as pits and postholes.

In addition, there is evidence of intense animal activity, particularly the numerous vole holes that both precede and succeed acidification. Even at the level at which they penetrated the rab, many of the features had been substantially destroyed by rabbit and vole burrows. For example, some 70% of the floor surface of House 39, and most of its postholes, were disturbed by vole burrows.

Reminiscent of Andrew Fleming's (1988) experience at Holne Moor, Dartmoor, these burrows often look like prehistoric postholes (burrow confluences) and stake-holes (individual burrows), so we had to check (excavate) each one of them. Most burrows eventually dived at strange angles, and thus distinguished themselves from the rarer archaeological features.

Our excavations indicate that the hill's surface was even stonier in the Bronze Age. Virtually all of the excavated stones on the hill either comprise, or are derived from, the clitter. This meant that excavation was extremely labour intensive, both in terms of stone moving and the need for very detailed excavation drawings. *Each* stone needed explanation as to whether it was humanly placed, or situated as the outcome of natural processes. The excavations have identified the systematic placement of houses, cairns, enclosure walls, and other structures with relation to the natural boulders on the hill. Both archaeological and geomorphological criteria were used to identify 'unnatural' versus 'natural'. These included the characteristics of the angle of rest of the stones (dip angles), and the axis of alignment of the stones (see chapter 9). Such criteria, of course, do not explain the prehistoric meaning of the stones, but do provide a way of investigating their prehistoric meaning by establishing what was pre-existing, 'god given', and ancestral from what was subsequent human embellishment.

D. Sprout (Wednesday, 27 May 1998 North Stone Circle Trench Diary, 3.50 pm): Mike and Sue have just been over for a 'discussion', which although very productive has pushed the photography back another 1.5 hours. ...

4.30 pm: feeling less anxious now Jeremy is here with the camera – It takes some time getting used to the pace of this site, but it is thoroughly understandable given the nature of the material and the geomorphological expertise that needs to be acquired. But ... it's a sunny day.

A very long journey at one spot

An excavation story cannot be told instantly. Compared to the work of the surface survey, excavating Leskernick seemed an extraordinarily slow and laborious process. Excavation was fixed at Leskernick for five years, whilst the survey team had completed their tasks at Leskernick after the first three years and moved on to surveying other settlements in adjacent parts of the moor. Excavation is laborious – excavation at Leskernick, with the vast quantity of stones that required planning and removing and the difficult excavating conditions, particularly so. And then there was the extra time taken by the numerous on-site discussions, which were part of our policy to feed knowledge and on-going interpretations between trenches and between the surface survey and the excavation. Our context-recording sheets, in a similar vein, were expanded to have sections for 'discussion', 'interpretation prior to excavation', and 'interpretation on completion of excavation' (Figure 3.7). It felt as if we were undertaking a very long journey at one spot.

In addition, there were the usual post-excavation procedures. Numerous bags of 'soil' needed to be wet sieved and floated for charred organic material, and numerous pollen, soil phosphate, and charcoal samples for radiocarbon dating from on- and off-site contexts had to be processed. To maximise the information provided by layer upon layer of planned stone, a great number of plans required drawing up. Finally, although Leskernick was not artefact rich, we had more than 200 finds to wash, examine, and perhaps 'weed'. Clearly, much of the information only materialised at the post-excavation stage. It is no wonder that excavation is often written up in such a pragmatic way. It is easy to become exhausted by all the detail that excavations generate and that we are duty bound to analyse and write-up in some form. Breaking the mould of a traditional excavation report format can take more time rather than less, and raises new issues that have to be addressed.

LESKERNICK - SURVEY AND EXCAVATIONS

CONTEXT RECORD

Site Code	Site sub-division	Context type	Context
LSW 99	A/T1	HORIZON	49

Interpretation *prior* to excavation (with date)

SOIL (JUNE 23rd).

Context description - *Sketch (plan, section) overleaf*

1. Compaction (friable, indurated etc.)
2. Colour
3. Composition/Particle size, percentage and support
4. Finds (pottery, stone, charcoal etc.)
5. Shape
6. Sharpness of boundary
7. Truncated
8. Other

FIRM SLIGHTLY YELLOW RED BROWN SLIGHTLY GRANULY SILT. CLEAR BUT DIFFUSE WAVY INTERFACE WITH (46). CLEAR INTERFACE WITH (15)/(9) DEFINED BY SEDIMENT-OLOGICAL CHANGE (17 IS MUCH LESS GRANULAR AND LARGELY STONE-FREE). DISCONTINUOUS OWING TO DISRUPTION BY BURROWING ANIMALS BUT VERY WELL DEFINED IN PLACES BELOW (9) IN WALL SECTION A. CIRCA 40MM DEEP. DIST-INCT FROM CONTEMPORARY PODZOLIZING SOIL HORIZONS. ONLY RECOGNIZED IN SECTION.

Stratigraphic matrix

44
49
46

Sampling strategy/ nos.

(33) PART SIEVED WITH (42) SAMPLES (33) B→E AND (39)

Interpretation on *completion* of excavation (with date) - *Discuss overleaf*

BURIED SOIL HORIZON (JUNE 23rd) / A-HORIZON.

Checklist

Drawing numbers	Plan NONE	Section L2
Photographs	B/W	Colour

Levels taken: Y/N | Reduced: Y/N | Transferred to plan: Y/N | Continuation sheet: Y/N

Annotated sketch

1. Dimensions
2. Physical relationships
3. Slope breaks
4. Matrix
5. Find/sample location
6. Clast support and orientation

N/A

Discussion

POSITION PROTECTED BY (9) ~~[illegible]~~, CLEAR HORIZON-AL MORPHOLOGY, ~~[illegible]~~ AND CLEAR RESOLUTION APART/SEPARATE FROM THE SILT-ING OF (9) INDICATE THAT THIS IS AN INTACT BURIED SOIL HORIZON. ITS PRESENCE BELOW (9) INDICATES THAT AT THIS POINT (9) WAS PLACED DIRECTLY ON AN ~~[illegible]~~ 'UN-ALTERED (O)LS.

Certainty (%) 80	Methods and conditions TROWEL, FINE, SECTION
	Initials MST.

fig.3:7 Leskernick excavations context record sheet (double sided), filled out for a buried soil horizon. Completed by MST.

Part Two

The Present *Past*

In chapters four to nine, we focus on the prehistoric landscape of Leskernick, trying to understand more about how people lived their lives and thought about their world.

This narrative can never be 'the truth', only an act of interpretation that winds its way around the archaeological material that we have retrieved. Our understanding of the past, and the processes involved in the retrieval and interpretation of the material, can never be neutral or divorced from the people who we are today – how *we* live, how *we* think.

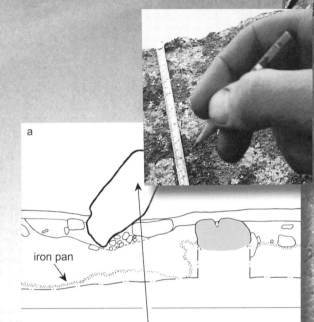

a

iron pan

North Stone Circle

b

Leskernick

The Search for Ancestors on the Moor

JAN FARQUHARSON

I see stones

I think of reed-thatch, sod fires, posts and ringbeams,
the lives of people who lived here, the hair on their faces …

I see stones

I dream of cattle, figures in file, thick hut-shadow, sooted women,
a boy with a stick, a man with meat on his short back,
fur-shod, self-conscious, unsure of his welcome,
a conclave of elders, bickering, parley …

I see stones.

I see stones, one edge meeting another,
upright, three stones together, a stone post fallen,
a backstone, bedrock, hearthstone, and stones pushed out of alignment
by turf weighted by stone, by water, turf and stone …

I see the stones of thirty huts scattered.

I pick my way where walls were.
I face the wind where hands and feet fretted.

We trouble this place with buckets and pegs,
tripods, stratigraphies and excavation,
the rational grope of theories and spades.

I climb to get away from sadness.

I climb the hill and the hill falls away around me.
The hilltop surges flat, is grass nibbled by sheep
who run and stop and stare, the cairn is broken …

I cannot climb any higher

The moor rotates before and behind me,
waved and flickering and nicked by rock.
I look for places, for accents, crinkles, habitation.
I look for what will arrest looking.

I cannot climb any higher

I see a windfarm and blueish space beyond
which has the appearance of a sea beyond this sea.

Skylarks, ponies, sheep, scurf the shoulders of decaying granite,
runkled sheets of bog and sod pare each other to the horizon.

I cannot climb any higher
I cannot people the sky

Chapter Four

The Old Sacred Places

The Story in Outline

The stones of Leskernick Hill were sacred, and in the second half of the second millennium BC as people began to build their houses and enclosures on the hill slopes, as they moved around performing their ordinary, everyday tasks, they did so in ways that reflected their relationship to the stones – to the ancestors and ancestral beings. People's actions and well-being depended upon the ancestral beings, just as the well-being of the ancestral beings depended upon people's attentive actions. It was necessary to select the 'right' stone, to build the 'right' way, to pay respect to the backstone within the house and to the field-shrine within the enclosure, to recognise and to respond to the sacred configurations within the clitter flows. It was probably also necessary to nurture and revere the older ceremonial places – the ones that were there before people settled the hill – the Propped Stone and Great Cairn on the hilltop, the stone row, and two stone circles on the moor below the hill. These ways of doing things were taken for granted, they were just part of how to 'go on' in the world.

Later it seems that some of the old places lost some of their significance and some may have been ceremoniously laid to rest.

Thus, before we turn to the story of the settlements, we need to look to the old sacred places that were created by people on the move – herds-people who came up on the moor for the summer pasture. And we need to go even further back, to a time before these herders placed their mark upon the landscape when gatherer-hunters, moving with the seasons between coast and upland, paused to pay their respects at special places across the moor. At Dozmary Pool, for example, hundreds of small microlithic flints have been found[1] (Berridge and Roberts 1986: 28–29; Jacobi 1979: 51–54), and large numbers of Mesolithic flint scatters have also been found along the eroding shorelines of the Colliford, Crowdy Marsh, and Siblyback reservoirs (Berridge and Roberts 1986; Trudgian 1977a, 1977b; see Tilley 1995 for further details of Mesolithic flint scatters).

We know from the ethnographic literature that in small-scale societies – both those dependent upon wild resources and those that, to a greater or lesser degree, depend upon domesticated plants and animals – the land is regarded as an ancestral creation and striking 'natural' features, be they mountain peaks, unusual rocks, caves, springs, lakes, rivers, bogs, or large trees, are sacred places Arnhem 1996; Bradley 2000; Carmichael et al. 1994; Feld and Basso 1996; Hirsch and O'Hanlon 1995; Tilley 1994; Ucko and Layton 1999). Thus, it seems highly probable that for the gatherer-hunters that moved around the moor, the hills and tors were significant and named places. The strange rock shapes would have been understood either as the petrified shapes of ancestral beings, or as the work of the ancestral beings or ancestors who sculpted the rocks and carved out the solution basins, created hiding places for themselves, places of entrance and exit, of activity and of coming to rest, of birth and death.

It is true that Leskernick is not one of the most dramatic places on the moor – it has no crowning tor – nonetheless its tabular outcrops and grey covering of clitter are easily identifiable. It is also a place from which it is possible to look out across a great sweep of territory. It would surely have been named by gatherer-hunter groups and have had its own particular stories woven around it.

In the third millennium BC, successors to these gatherer-hunters, people who had learnt to domesticate herd animals but who still depended a great deal on wild resources, moved with their herds across the moor along well-known and well-worn route-ways – trekking from coast to summer pasture. They would surely have been familiar with the earlier names and stories, would have built upon and worked with an understanding of a landscape already pregnant with meaning and ancestral power. As they began to leave their mark upon the landscape, we find that they built their rare long cairns below impressive tors and that, in two cases out of three, the higher end of the long axis is orientated towards the tor (Tilley 1995, 1996). We see them begin to build ceremonial enclosures around the two most impressive tors on the moor, at Rough Tor in the north-west, Stowe's Pound in the south, and De Lank in the west. Although these enclosures are, so far, undated, both Mercer (1981, 1986a: 52, 1986b) and Johnson and Rose (1994: 48) have noted the similarities between them and excavated Cornish examples of proven Neolithic date at Carn Brea and Helman Tor (Mercer 1986b). The long cairns may have been built by individual herding communities; the enclosures were probably the communal endeavours of many such groups. We may also – tentatively – add to these early monumental works the Propped Stone or Quoit on the top of Leskernick Hill. This Quoit, placed close to the great tabular outcrop at the top of the hill, mimics the natural propped stones found on the slopes below many of the tors in other parts of the moor.

Somewhat later, around the middle of the millennium (later Neolithic/Early Bronze Age), these people-on-the-move also began to build circles and stone rows on the lower ground, and, a little later, large hilltop cairns.

At Leskernick, we have the only radiocarbon date for a stone circle on the moor and it is a little earlier than our dates for the settlement (see below, and Table 4:1). It is true that the difference is not great and it is possible to tell the story somewhat differently and suggest that it was the people who settled the hill who built the Great Cairn and the stone row and two stone circles. For the moment, we are content to retain a small time lapse between the building of the stone row and circles by more seasonally mobile communities and the first settling of the hill.

In our version of the story, the people who settle the hill in the second millennium BC (Middle Bronze Age) would have acknowledged these constructions. Indeed, they probably settled at Leskernick precisely because these ritual places already existed or, rather, because the presence of these ritual places indicated that Leskernick Hill was an ancestral place of great and deep significance. The stone row and circles, Propped Stone, and Great Cairn were there because the hill was there, the hill was there – with its great tabular rock outcrops and its streams of clitter – because the ancestors or ancestral beings were there. It was a propitious place – a highly charged place.

The settling of Leskernick and of other clitter-strewn hillsides across the moor during the Middle Bronze Age means that people were living close to – alongside – the ancestral forces. This close domestic engagement with the stones has a counterpart in the obsessive attention lavished on the high places where the tors and ridges were increasingly ringed around by almost impenetrable ritual enclosures, and cairns were built up against and surrounding the tors. Whilst at the settlement sites people's engagement with the stones was, literally, built into everyday existence, the high places of the great tors were the set-aside places to which people from different parts of the moor, and perhaps even from off the moor, came together on high days and feast days.

We are running ahead of ourselves. This chapter is about the Late Neolithic/Early Bronze pre-settlement period at Leskernick, the time when people-on-the-move were beginning to leave their mark, both on the hilltop, and on the plain below the hill. It is time to begin to detail some of the findings from our excavations and surveys.

The Story in More Detail

The Hilltop

The Propped Stone (or Quoit)

There are no tors at Leskernick – nothing that immediately pulls the eye to the summit. But when one walks to the top of the hill, or if one looks up from the ford across the Fowey River, one sees that there are great tabular stones. These tabular rocks on the western side of the summit have been quarried in more recent times but with or without the quarry scars they are awesome – there is a stillness about them.

Although it is very difficult to date the Propped Stone, it seems as though, long before people started to build houses in among the hillside clitter, more mobile communities – people who followed their herds, and still probably depended heavily on wild resources – climbed to the top of the hill, and, close to the tabular outcrop, selected a long linear rock outlier[2] onto which they hoisted a huge roughly triangular slab, 2.8 m long, 1.8 m wide, and 0.3 m thick. They not only hoisted it up but they also propped it up at angle using three small boulders (Figure 4.1a). They thus created a peep-hole through which the horizon to the north could be seen. The positioning of the Propped Stone is extraordinary. On the longest day of the year, the dying rays of the midsummer sun shine through the peep-hole just before the sun sinks below the horizon (Color Plate 1). Moreover, from the Propped Stone the spiky silhouette of Rough Tor can be seen to the north west, and the long axis of this stone points towards Rough Tor and its summit cairns.

The Propped Stone is visible from long distances away to the south, from Codda Tor 1 km to the west, and from the southern end of the Buttern Hill stone row from the north. It is also visible on the skyline from the southern stone circle below Leskernick Hill and is just visible from the stone row terminal. It can also be seen from the western settlement compound. These constructions all postdate the Propped Stone but their siting suggests its continuing power.

Although it is difficult to precisely date, the weathering pattern on the rock and more particularly the residual 'cones' that remain where the prop stones have protected the base rock from erosion suggest that it is very old indeed. Pete Herring of the Cornish Archaeological Unit has argued on the basis of astronomical alignments with a possible long cairn to the north west of the Beacon and below Leskernick Hill that it is probably Neolithic (or even possibly Mesolithic) in date (Herring 1997). This makes it the oldest human construction on the hill.

fig.4:1   a) the Propped Stone or Quoit at the top of Leskernick Hill; b) the Great Cairn – much ruined.

The Great Cairn

Centuries, generations, went by. Still there were no permanent settlements on the moors, still people followed their herds according to the season. Slowly, a number of different monuments began to appear. At the top of the hill at Leskernick they built a Great Cairn. On the moor at the bottom of the hill they built a stone row and two stone circles.

Of the larger cairns on the moor nearly 80% are found on hilltops or on ridges – whereas nearly all (90%) of the small ones are in low-lying positions (Barnatt 1982: 85–86). Many of the large ones are associated with the tors, whereas at Leskernick the Great Cairn is close to – but out of sight of – the tabular outcrops and the Propped Stone. Many of them are highly visible on the skyline – the one at Leskernick would have been visible from many of the surrounding hilltops.

The Great Cairn at Leskernick is very dilapidated (Figure 4.1b). It was surveyed for the Ordnance Survey in 1976 and then again by Norman Quinnell for the RCHME in 1984.[3] Here is how it was described.

> ... a very ruined cairn with an overall diameter of 15 m & 0.4 m to 0.8 m high, in a hilltop position in an expanse of well grazed pasture and close to the large BA settlement of Leskernick. About 2.0 m within the perimeter a half dozen stones, paired and spaced, indicate a former retaining circle with a diameter of 11 m. A further 3.0 m within this there appears to be another circle cum retaining wall of inward-leaning slabs enclosing an area of 5.0 m in diameter. A shelter has been constructed in the NE quadrant. (Cornwall & Scilly Sites and Monuments Record: Small Entry Form. Compiler AHB 08/08/88)

The Great Cairn at Leskernick has not been excavated, but we know from other excavated sites, for example at Stannon Down (Jones 1998), Davidstow (Christie 1988), and Colliford (Griffith 1984), that such cairns were often multi-phased. The activities involved and the internal structures and the form of depositions are very varied but what is apparent is that, in the first place, these were open ritual and ceremonial sites. Often the ritual focus was a single stone or group of stones either occurring at the site or taken to it, and in a number of cases these ceremonial areas were enclosed and defined with stake circles and/or stone settings. The activities involved the lighting of fires, digging of pits, and the deposition of quantities of charcoal, lithics, and quartz.

Sometimes, too, but by no means always, there are cremated human bones placed in pits or urns. The charcoal deposits are almost always made up of mature oak. We might infer a chain of landscape signifers linking oak, quartz, and human bone, with fire acting as an agent of mediation and transformation. With fire, the green oak is transformed into black charcoal – wood whose life has been terminated – and human flesh into white calcined bones. These are deposited with white quartz, perhaps a material metaphor of the 'bones' of the land itself, to which living substance was being returned in a transformed state. In the process, both the individuality of trees and the human body was being reduced to ancestral substance with regenerative powers.

At a later stage, the Great Cairn is built over the ceremonial setting, sealing it off and creating a noticeable marker in the landscape that served to remind people of the activities that have taken place. Sometimes, at a later date, individual cremations are interred within the cairn. The cairn thus starts life as an area of heightened activity associated with hilltop and tor and then continues as a place of memory and perhaps pilgrimage.

On the Moor Below the Hill

On the moor just to the south of the hill are the remains of a stone row and two stone circles. There is also, very close to the terminal of the stone row, a large mound. The north circle and this mound are roughly in line with the Great Cairn on the hilltop, although it is out of sight.

This large mound poses a problem. If it really *is* prehistoric, it would be the only substantial low-lying mound on Bodmin Moor. It is much damaged, with a huge crater occupying the centre. There are no traces of kerbstones or retaining walls. We are strongly inclined to believe that its placement is fortuitous and that it is the result of much later mining activity. We would agree with the report of the 1984 RCHME surveyors:

> A disturbed mound measuring approximately 10.8 m by 10.1 m, with an average height of 1.0 m. The centre and south west side have been completely removed to ground level and there is no trace of a kerb or cist. It is composed primarily of peat although some small boulders are evident in the mound. It is situated below the extensive settlement of Leskernick, on the edge of a line of prospecting pits, each with their associated upcast mounds and would appear to be connected with that activity. It certainly cannot be accepted as a barrow. (Cornwall & Scilly Sites and Monuments Record: Small Entry Form, compiler AHB, undated)

We are rather aware that where this large mound is concerned we have rather abruptly closed off alternative interpretations.[4] Be that as it may, the mound remains but in the rest of this volume it makes no further appearance.

The Great Cairn on the hilltop and the stone row and circles on the moor below were built at about the same time – perhaps by the same people, or by their close predecessors or postcursors. Most stone rows and circles in southwest England seem to date to the Late Neolithic/Early Bronze Age (Barnatt 1980, 1982, 1989; Burl 1976, 1993; Miles 1975: 10–12). Our radiocarbon date from the North Stone Circle fits in well. It falls between 1750 and 1540 cal. BC, thus Early Bronze Age (see Table 4.1). Our sample comes from peat that either developed within or was back-filled into the hole from which the central stone in the circle was quarried, and although the peat could be of approximately the same date, it could also be centuries older. This is discussed in detail later in the chapter. Our date is suggestive but not conclusive.

Today, the stones of the stone row and circles are ruinous, indistinct, and grass covered. But even when they were first set up, they would have been modest. With the exception of the recumbent stones at the terminal of the stone row, hardly any are more than 0.5 m high.

The stone row was only found quite recently (Figure 4.2):

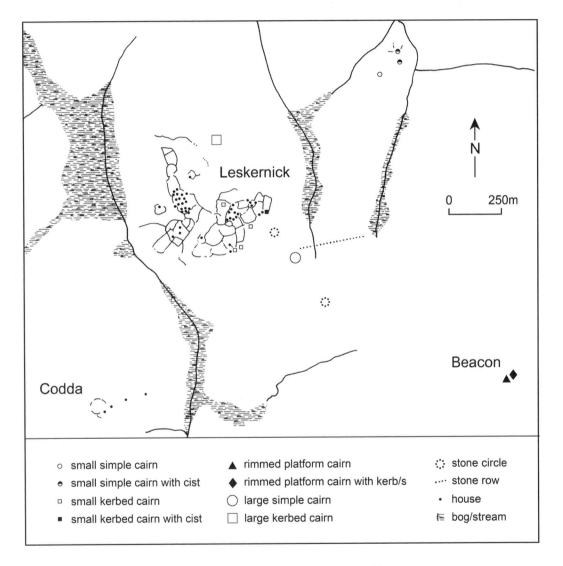

fig.4:2 Simplified plan of Leskernick showing the stone row, circles, and large cairn.

Table 4.1. Leskernick Radiocarbon Dates

All calibrated dates are quoted at 2 sigma and were calibrated using the CALIB programme of Stuiver and Reimer (1998).

Lab Number	Radio-carbon result BP	Calibrated date range (2 sigma)	Type of date	
Beta- 42321	3220 +/-50	1525–1375 cal BC	AMS	
Beta-125239	3100 +/- 40	1430–1265 cal BC	AMS	
Beta-164589	3320 +/-40	1430–1265 cal BC	AMS	
Beta-146722	3260 +/- 40	1670–1490 cal BC	AMS	
Beta-42322	2890 +/-50	1270–940 cal BC	AMS	
Beta-142324	3040 +/-50	1430–1265 cal	AMS	
Beta-142325	3110 +/- 50	1515-1305 cal BC	AMS	
Beta- 142323	2769 +/- 60	1030–810 cal BC	radio-metric	
Beta-164590	1440+/-80	cal AD 430–710 cal BC	radio-metric	
Beta-146721	3440 +/- 40	1750–1540 cal BC	AMS	

Material dated	Area of Site	Structure	Feature
oak charcoal	southern settlement	House 39	Old land surface on which the house wall was constructed
oak charcoal	southern settlement	House 39	Posthole
applewood charcoal	southern settlement	House 40	The ditch surrounding House 40
oak charcoal	western settlement	'Hut' 23	Old land surface on which the 'Hut' 23 wall was constructed
oak charcoal	western settlement	'Hut' 23	Linear gully inside 'Hut' 23
oak charcoal	western settlement	House 1	Pit at the back of the inside House 1
oak charcoal	western settlement	House 1	Posthole forming part of the post-ring supporting the roof
oak charcoal	western settlement	House 1	Hearth in House 1
bulk sample of charcoal	the corridor between the southern settlement and the western settlement	The 'Shrine Stone', also known as Field Feature 1	Hearth in front of the large lozenge-shaped stone (the 'Shrine Stone').
peat	ritual complex southeast of the southern settlement	North Stone Circle	Towards the base of the quarry pit for 'whalestone' that lies in the centre of the North Stone Circle

Peter Herring (1997): These sites [North Stone Circle and the stone row at Leskernick] were identified in the spring of 1981 when skirting Leskernick Hill ... while walking from Bolventor to record the deserted medieval hamlet on Bray Down as part of postgraduate research. ... They were found accidentally, or incidentally, as many archaeological discoveries are in upland Cornwall.

The stone row

The Leskernick stone row is unusual, partly because it is so modest, and partly because, of the seven rows that have been found on the moor, it is the only one in close proximity to a circle. The stone row is not directly aligned on either of the two stone circles but is roughly equidistant between the two. Today, the two circles and the row are intervisible, and we can be reasonably sure that this was true in prehistoric times. Pollen evidence suggests that the moor during the later Neolithic/Early Bronze Age was for the most part grass covered, with a few stands of hazel (see chapter 2).

It was the stone row and the circles that first drew Chris Tilley to Leskernick. His first impression was underwhelming:

CT (1994): I found myself trying to cross and re-cross the Fowey with some difficulty. Eventually I emerged from the 'newtake' land onto the unimproved moor. The first objective was to find the southern stone circle. I looked out for rocks emerging from the grassland and, following several false leads, found myself on the western slopes of the Beacon. I realised now that I was in completely in the wrong place and decided to locate the cairn that would give me an orientation and reference point for both the southern and northern circles, and the stone row. Working back from the cairn I found the southern and northern circles, eventually, definitely the worst preserved and inconspicuous of those I had visited on Bodmin Moor ...

The stone row is 317 m in length, orientated ENE-WSW and today terminates at a 'U'-shaped formation of three substantial, part turf-covered, recumbent stones. The rest of the row consists of 47 small, low, square-topped stones, mostly less than knee-height. The eastern part of the stone row is irregular. There are gaps, and clusters of stones lying off the axis of the align-ment. Approximately two-thirds of the way along the length of the stone row, walking towards the terminal, the row crosses a boggy area that has been modified by tin-streaming. The land then gently rises up to the terminal at the south west end, and the stones are more regularly spaced and maintain the axis of the alignment of the row. At the time the row was built, when the plain was mainly open grassland, the boggy area was perhaps a small stream marked by a tangle of tree and scrub. Perhaps this barrier created a degree of invisibility between the eastern less regularly aligned section and the west-ern section with the terminal setting.

Two questions arise: Was the disalignment of the eastern section original or was it something that the row had subsequently suffered? And, if it was original, was the topographic point at which the disalignment took place sig-nificant? It is only immediately after crossing the boggy area that, moving west towards the terminal setting, the tip of Rough Tor comes into view in the far distance, becoming more and more visually dominant as one approaches the terminal. It seems, therefore, quite likely that both the disalignment of the row up to this point, and the place at which it crosses water were, indeed, of great significance.

The tip of Rough Tor is also clearly visible from the southern stone circle and remains in view as one walks to the northern circle. It disappears just as one enters the northern circle. As we shall see, the importance of Rough Tor is signalled again and again in the configuration and orientation of par-ticular places on and around the hill. With its spiky, fugitive silhouette, its encumbrance of tor cairns and ritual enclosures, it was obviously a place of huge significance to the people of Leskernick. We shall return below to the relationship between the stone row, the circles, and Rough Tor and to how the sacred space of the stone row and circles might have been used.

Excavation of the stone row terminal

Of the eight stone rows found on the moor, five have taller stones or trans-verse-orientated stones at their southern terminal (see Figure 4.3). In contrast, the Leskernick stone row appeared to have a 'terminal setting' presented by a U-shaped configuration of three large, presumed fallen, stones at the west end. It was this setting that we focussed on in 1995. The choice was fairly obvi-ous: first, it was a small area – and we were a small team; second, it appeared to be an unusual stone setting; third, an interesting number of ritual and landscape features were visible from it; and fourth, it was situated between the stone circles and might be considered as a focal point in the overall ritual topography.

A small area excavation was chosen to maximise the possibility of reveal-ing the types of features and activities that might have occurred in the vicinity of a stone row terminal. These features included post-settings, the stone-holes of the now recumbent stones, evidence of human or animal burials or crema-tions, and artefact deposits.

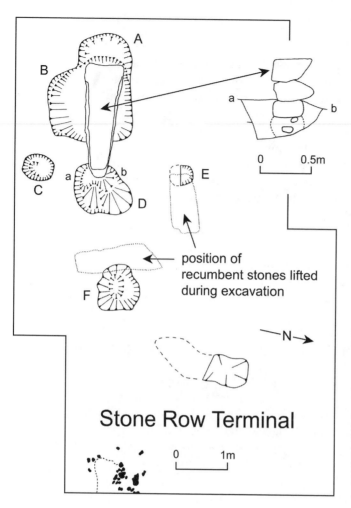

Stone Row Terminal

0   0.5m

0   1m

—N→

position of
recumbent stones lifted
during excavation

fig.4:3 Post-excavation plan
of the stone row terminal. A =
original stone-packed hole for the
great monolith that terminated
the stone row; B = pit dug around
the stone to dismantle it; C and E =
the stone-holes for putative outlier
monoliths; D = the stone-hole for
the penultimate monolith in the
stone row (possibly the recumbent
stone that was placed over E when
the row was dismantled); F = the
stone packed stone-hole for the
monolith that was dismantled
and placed across it. The stone
packing of F can be seen in Fig.4.4.
a–b = a cross-section showing the
stone column made to support
the top end of the pushed over
great monolith (to facilitated its
reworking, perhaps as a gatepost).
Field credits: drawn by HW and
Jane R.

*CT (1995): Sue has brought four of her own fairly massive 2"
grid pegs that form the initial basis of the grid. These seem
ridiculously thick and cumbersome to me, but I'm told they won't
be easily knocked over, or dislodged, unlike my own.*

*SH (1995): Ian and I set up the site grid, with Chris occasionally
holding the end of a tape with a lost look in his eyes. Having
got this underway Chris started setting up the fence around the
trench area. It amused me that the person who least liked the
'rules' of excavation had fenced us in.*

*CT (1996): There is a green baize door through the fence into this
interiorised little world. Highly incongruous in the middle of
nowhere, little figures huddling behind it, peering down at stone
and soil. The creation of another reality, dark and secret. Inside
the door there is discipline: you cannot smoke in there, there are
places one must not walk, lines, pegs, tapes, objects which should
not be disturbed.*

SH (1995): For me, the femaleness of the group was striking: Henry surrounded by Barbara, Gill, Cath, Helen, Mary, and Pippa.

CT (1995): I'm glad there are so few men. We can avoid the macho types who are so often attracted.

The results of the first season (a mere 10 days of excavation) were published as an interim excavation narrative, and we proposed a 'U'-shaped terminal configuration of three standing monoliths (Bender, Hamilton, and Tilley 1997: 164–65). The excavation of the terminal area was completed in 1996. Predictably, our understanding of the layout of the terminal area was transformed by the work of the second season.

The detailed findings from the excavation of the terminal stones will be published elsewhere.[5] Here, we have chosen to take the excavation of one small stone-lined posthole and have used our diary entries to give a feel of the hesitations and contradictions, the differences of opinion, the making and unmaking of interpretations. Most excavation reports airbrush out the way in which the daily process of excavation generates alternative site histories that are then abandoned, forgotten, perpetuated, or transformed. This 'forgetting' jettisons much that is of value to an understanding of both the site itself and the manner in which some conclusions and interpretations, rather than others, become the final report.

Diary of the excavation of one small stone-packed hole

SH (1995): It felt as if we were disturbing (mutilating) a landscape at rest (Figure 4.4; Color Plate 2).

SH Excavation Diary, Thursday 15 June 1995

With further trowelling [we found] a semi-circular area of mid-brown friable silt (Context 7) which continued into the western edge of the excavation trench at the point that it cut across the end of one of the recumbent stones. ... [Within this was the top of] a circle of fist-sized and bigger granite stones (Context 4) ... deliberately placed. ... Perhaps we had a stone-lined hearth? Or a cremation pit? But the stones were not affected by heat. Alternatively it might be a specially lined pit for the deposition of offerings: pieces of quartz, charcoal from non-local oak timbers.

... The uppermost fill (Context 5) within (and possibly encircling: we were not sure yet) the circle of granite pieces was all that was revealed. This fill was dark and of soft consistency. A new possibility emerged: we might have the post-pipe of a substantial rotted post, c. 0.30 m wide, which could be part of a post alignment preceding the stone row. Perhaps the terminal area had incorporated timbers as well as standing stones?

a

b

Stone
Row
Terminal

packed
stone-hole

survey
difficulties

fig.4:4 a) Packing stones in the stone-hole (see Fig 4.3 feature F) of the 'third to last' monolith of the stone row terminal. Note also that the monolith that originally stood in this hole was later placed transversally across the stone-hole. Scale 50 cm; b) cows dismantling a stone row flag. Photo: SH.

BB (1995): Spent the afternoon helping at the excavation. Henry mattocked, I shovelled and barrowed. Tiring and fairly tedious. Not much for the imagination to work on, though Pippa discovered that one of the recumbent stones was 6 ft plus …

SH Excavation Diary, Friday 16 June 1995

The edge of the cut (Context 3) in which the granite pieces had been placed was finally located. The cut was now seen to be wide of the outer edge of the packing by c. 0.20 m. This suggested a pit with an internal circle of stone pieces and not, as we had thought a post-hole with stone-packing. We now believed we had located the original stone-packed hole of one of the fallen terminals.

SH (1995): It was good to walk across the settlement and feel the freedom of moving through a landscape. The lack of ambulation in an excavation trench closes down some of the senses, and also concentrates others, slight changes in texture, compaction, sound etc. as the trowel blade scrapes along and slices through fills. The excavation trench seemed part of a secret world which could not be seen from the western settlement.

CT (1995): The excavation was proceeding at a snail's pace and I am longing to see what is at the base of the stones.

SH Excavation Diary, Monday, 19 June 1995

A section was created by removing the southern half of the fill. The edge of the feature was extremely difficult to define. The blueish fill of Context 5 (first thought to be a post-pipe fill) now seemed to be a shallow silting across the feature. Underneath this it gradually became clear that the fill (Context 12) within the circle of granite stones also continued for c. 0.10 m on the outside of the southern circuit, where it adjoined the compacted edge of a different fill (Context 10). On the south-west side of the circuit the compacted edge was seen to mirror the projected imprint of three of the granite stones, if their uppermost ends were sloped further backwards to meet it. This indicated that the granite stones had shifted. As the sectioning continued, the 'missing' stone from the granite circular arrangement appeared in the middle of the fill. Neither the movement of the stones, nor the position of the 'missing' stone, suggested that they had been caused by a fallen standing stone. The stone must have been carefully removed with the packing stones shifting marginally, and the one stone loosened from the circuit being placed (deliberately?) in the void left by the removed terminal stone. A new, and exciting interpretative possibility now emerged: a deliberate, but careful, dismantling of the terminal setting in the Bronze Age. This decommissioning of the site had been done in such a way as to preserve the essential character of the monument by: 1) only destroying its distant visuality, by taking down the conspicuous stones of the terminal setting; and 2) by selective disalignment of parts of the stone row only beyond a certain point – the boggy area marked by the leat created by later, post-medieval, tin-streaming.

BB (1995): There is a distinction between the excavation and the settlement work. The excavation, because it is destructive, has to be more detailed, more obsessional. There are other differences. About looking down in an excavation, as opposed to looking out. About the specificity of the small area under excavation: the 'box' that one has created, and that, if one is not very careful, is divorced from the multiplicity of nested scales of action, movement, thought, sight, understanding.

CT (1995): This is the first day I have spent most of the time on the excavation and it does provide some relief from shouting out 'Fowey valley and hut 20 straight out, Brown Willy and hut 24 to left'.

SH Excavation Diary, Tuesday, 20 June 1995

The difficulties of understanding the relationships between the fills in the stone-hole (Context 3) were further resolved by quarter-sectioning the remaining fill. ... It became clear that the stone-hole was surrounded by a ramp probably to help set up the stone, but the orientation of the stone-hole and its dimensions remained unclear.

CT (1995): Some of the rust that had been gradually accumulating on my new trowel was now worn away. I noticed how large it was compared with other trowels in use and was duly informed that all their trowels had started out this way. The more diminutive the size of your trowel the greater your status as an archaeologist since years of scraping were required to reduce the blade to an area little larger than a postage stamp. The trowel was a prized personal possession and a lengthy discussion ensued about the best place to carve one's initials, or name, on the wooden handle. This also would show signs of longevity – a sleek oiled surface produced by being pressed into the palm of a sweaty hand for months on end. Another quaint archaeological fetish. This ageing of objects, through appearance, and the clear relationship between use, time, and status reminded me very much of Kula *valuables but while these are given away it would be horrific for an archaeologist to give up a trowel as it was so obviously entangled with personal identity. I should have spent several days gradually filing down the blade of my trowel before the excavation commenced. But even if I had done that the handle would have given the game away. Taken to its logical extreme, the greatest status symbol of all would be to have no trowel at all. How foolish I had been to purchase one!*

SH Excavation Diary, Wednesday, 21 June 1995 *The excavation of the stone-hole was completed. ... Once the hole was entirely excavated it was possible to establish the original orientation of the long axis, west-east. The stone which it held would, therefore, have been aligned along the axis of the stone row. ... The weight of the stone had compacted the 'rab' and gave some indication of the shape of the base of the stone that had originally stood in it. This corresponded with the square-edged southern end of the adjacent recumbent stone. So the pointed end of the stone would have been the uppermost end. ... The section created at the point where this stone cross the ... ramp showed that a final silting (Context 5) and a turf-line (Context 1) had formed over the ledge/ramp before the stone came to be in its present position.*

Three interpretations are possible:

1. *The stone seals a Bronze Age turf-line which had already formed around it while standing;*

2. *During the Bronze Age the stone was dismantled and placed in some unknown location, and at some time after a turf-line had formed over the pit, the stone was moved to its present position;*

3. *The stone was dismantled in more recent times and the stone seals a 'modern' turf-line.*

CT (1995): The ignorant, including myself, are kept well away to minimise damage to certain areas.

SH (1995): I went down and looked at the trench where the turfing had been finished in my absence. The excavation hole was hardly visible. It, and I, felt lost in the landscape. ... The different axis of each terminal stone is interesting. It became too dark to think it through. It was a wrench to leave the place.

This, of course, was just part of the excavation process in the first year, and only the first part of the story. By the end of the first year, having located the stone-hole socket of one of the terminal stones, we thought it likely that the three terminal stones had formed a 'cove' or triangular space c. 2.6 x 2.6 x 4 m, with a stone at each corner. It seemed possible that the stones could have acted as 'backdrops', partly concealing, partly focussing attention on the activities performed within the setting. It also seemed that the approach from the northern stone circle would have been visually disrupted by the transverse orientation of two of the stones, and the approach along the stone row would have been blocked not only by a terminal stone on the axis of the row but also, beyond it, by another terminal stone placed transverse to the axis.

We were wrong. The following year, we extended our trench and found two more stone-hole sockets. Each one contained stone packing that would have served to support the upright. They matched the 'base' circumferences of the two remaining presumed fallen terminal stones that lie recumbent and visible within the present-day surface of the terminal area. One was the socket for the tallest (c. 2 m) 'Great Terminal Monolithic', and one for the 'Penultimate Terminal Monolithic' (c. 1 m). Together with the stone-hole socket we had found the previous year, these sockets were in a row – and they continued the line of the stone row. There was no 'cove'. The stones were placed in ascending height with the tallest, the Great Terminal Monolith, in the highest location (see Figure 4.5a). These three tall stones were more closely spaced than those of the stone row, and this spacing would have heightened the drama of their perspective effect. We also found possible evidence for two outlier monoliths situated one each side of the Penultimate Terminal Monolith. The evidence for these outliers comprised two small pit features, each with evidence of stone packing.

It is hard to get a sense of how people might have used the stone row. We surely need to envisage it as part of a larger sacred space encompassing both the row and the two stone circles. We can imagine the stone row as the sacred axis. The very fact that the stones are so modest – both here and elsewhere on the moor – suggest that they were not primarily erected to be seen at a distance. Although, having said this, the three terminal stones, which were considerably

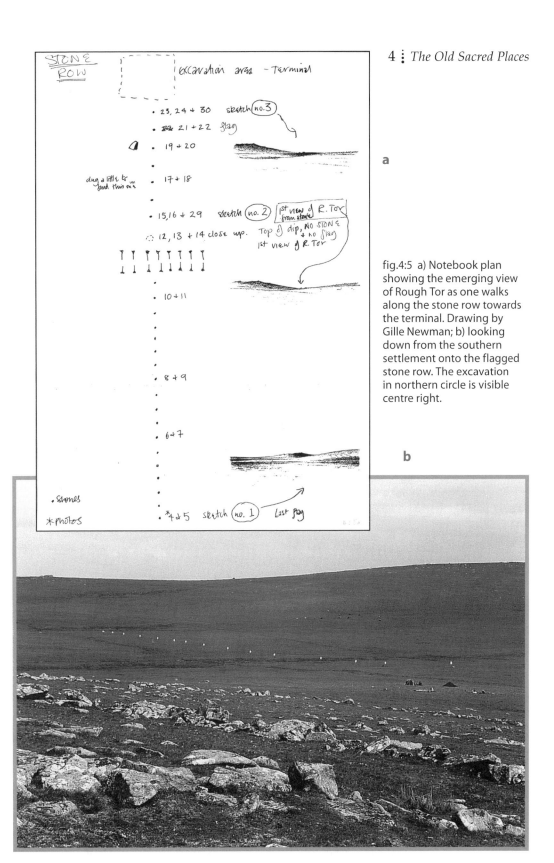

STONE ROW

excavation area — Terminal

• 23, 24 + 30 sketch no.3

• 21 + 22 flag

• 19 + 20

dug a little to find this one • 17 + 18

• 15,16 + 29 sketch no. 2 1st view of R. Tor from stone

12, 13 + 14 close up. Top of dip, NO STONE + no flag 1st view of R. Tor

• 10 + 11

• 8 + 9

• 6 + 7

• *4 & 5 sketch no. 1 Last flag

• stones
*photos

a

b

fig.4:5 a) Notebook plan showing the emerging view of Rough Tor as one walks along the stone row towards the terminal. Drawing by Gille Newman; b) looking down from the southern settlement onto the flagged stone row. The excavation in northern circle is visible centre right.

taller than the rest, would have been very visible across the moor. But perhaps more importantly, the stone row acted as a processional way through the landscape. Each part of the way carried its own meanings – the disalignment of the first part of the walk, the crossing of the watery place, the moving gently up hill towards the high terminal stones with the stone circles to either side. At the same time, the walk created a link in the mind of the participants with the other places within the wider landscape. Most specifically, the gradual emergence of the Rough Tor silhouette after the crossing of the water was a reminder of that most powerful of symbolic places within the moor (Figure 4.5a, Color Plate 4c). These, then, were stones by which to learn, by which to remember, by which to orient, and by which to think. All processes that required initiation and instruction. Such knowledge both empowered the individual or the group, and created and reproduced structures of ritual authority. The authority might not extend to other arenas of social life, but, whilst the rituals took place, whilst the knowledge was imparted and the offerings and libations were made, the authority of the ritual specialists would be unquestioned. One vitally important part of the ritual knowledge embodied in the stones, to be conveyed and selectively 'released' by the ritual specialists, was knowledge of the landscape and the spirit powers embedded in it.

It is not easy to create a sense of people in movement. Indeed, from the excavation trench it was hard to even see the line of stones because they were so small and overgrown. We tried to invigorate the stones by placing flags, sometimes red, sometimes white, alongside each knee-high stone (Figure 4.5b). Looking eastwards from the terminal along the row, beyond the point where it crossed the boggy area, the line of flags became interestingly irregular, unevenly spaced, with clusters that were off the main alignment. Some people went with the flow:

SH (1995): The flags drew our eyes out of the fenced-in trench and facilitated the consideration of wider sets of relationships between the 'trench' area, the rest of the 'ritual complex', and dominant focal points in the landscape. The waving flags made the 'trench people' feel part of a wider landscape. ...The wild horses were magnetically attracted to the flags and completely ignored our trench, which we had specifically wired to keep them out.

Others resisted:

A. Rennie (3 June 1996): On the way back to the cars I was somewhat bemused by the positioning of the flags along the stone row – not all of them seem to be at positions where stones are visible, and not all visible stones are flagged – so what is their

implicit/explict interpretation ...? It is currently 9.47 pm, so I am
NOT going to ask ...

The stone circles

Sixteen stone circles are known on Bodmin Moor. Those at Leskernick are
among the more modest ones. Only three of the other circles have been partially excavated and there are no radiocarbon dates. Our excavation of part
of the North Stone Circle and the solitary radiocarbon date we obtained thus
add considerably to the – meagre – sum of knowledge. Our date of 1750–1540
cal BC puts the construction in the Early to Middle Bronze Age (see Table 4.1).
As we have already mentioned, this is earlier than any of our dates from the
settlement, though not by much, and we therefore assume the circles and
stone row were built before people settled the hill.

The location of the stone circles below the hill and settlement area at
Leskernick is typical for Bodmin Moor as a whole. As elsewhere, there are
wide-ranging views of the surrounding hills and tors. The tip of Rough Tor
is clearly visible from the southern stone circle and remains in view as one
walks between the circle and the 'cairn' and stone row terminal. It disappears from view at precisely the point at which one enters the northern stone
circle.[6]

D. Sprout, North Circle Trench Diary (15 June 1998): Here is a
360 degree 'photo-shoot' of what we can see from the Northern
Stone Circle. ... [Starting Northwards and moving clockwise]
... Leskernick House 39 ... valley and the windmills of the wind
farm ... cows ... hills and green fields ... Brown Willy... and Gary
'enclosure walls' Trench Supervisor!

The two stone circles are c. 350 m apart. Both comprise low (some knee- ,
some ankle-high) unevenly shaped stones – quite similar in appearance to
those used to construct the stone row.

The southern circle, somewhat better preserved than the northern one, has
a diameter of 30 m and consists of 20–22 stones, with possibly originally as
many as 30.

Peat development obscures much of the northern stone circle (Johnson
and Rose 1994: 33). Its suggested size of c. 23 m diameter is small for Bodmin Moor. Of the 16 stone circles known from the moor, only Nine Stones on
the Altarnum/North Hill parish boundary, has a smaller diameter (Herring
1997; Johnson and Rose 1994: 31). The circle was 'found' by Pete Herring:

Peter Herring (1997) A cursory examination revealed an obvious ring of standing and fallen stones and stumps while a large whale-backed stone lying just north of the circle's centre was felt to be another possible upright ... 3.8m long which may have been either a particularly attractive moorstone around which the circle was built, or a standing stone.

Pete Herring (1997) suggests that 18 stones are securely part of the North Stone Circle and that between 9 and 11 are 'missing'. Our probing indicated the presence of several more peat-covered stones.

We, too, wondered whether the massive, 'recumbent' whale-shaped stone at the circle's centre was a fallen monolith, but its great size particularly in relationship to the small stones of the circle suggested that it was an earth-fast erratic. The incorporation of a dramatic moorstone within a circle indicates that specific 'natural' stones were given particular meaning.

Fairly soon we realised that things were more complicated – the earth-fast 'whalestone' could not be an earth-fast erratic because it lay at right angles to the main axis of the stone 'flow' of the hill. It must, at some point in time, have been moved.

Excavation at the North Stone Circle

We excavated two areas in the North Stone Circle. One trench was placed to enclose one of the stones of the circle's perimeter. The other was positioned across the central fallen/moved whalestone. In addition to giving us a section across the stone, the positioning of this trench reflected our knowledge that when one of the monoliths of the stone row terminal had been dismantled, it had been placed transversely across its stone-hole. The trench thus encompassed the likely position of the stone-hole for the large whalestone if it existed.

SH (Tuesday 25 June 1998): Today BB evocatively said to me 'You are finally wounding the hill', as she looked at our deep excavation trench across the central 'whalestone' in the North Stone Circle.

Our excavations (Figure 4.6) demonstrated that the whalestone had indeed once been an earth-fast field boulder, but that its orientation had been changed. A large pit had been dug around it and it had been levered out, stones being placed along the bottom of the cut to aid this process. It had then been placed, or came to rest, across this pit, at right angles to its original 'natural' axis. The fill of the large pit from which the boulder had been removed comprised mostly peat and it was this peat that provided the Early Bronze Age radiocarbon date (see Table 4.1). In addition to the peat fill, there were lenses and clods of rab. The presence of rab could suggest that peat was back-filled into the pit, as opposed to developing *in situ*. This scenario, together with the radiocarbon date, would indicate that peat had already developed on the moor below Leskernick Hill by the Early Bronze Age. On the other hand, the pollen profile from this peat appears undisturbed, which would seem to indicate that the peat developed *in situ*. In this alternative scenario, the rab clods must have weathered from the sides of the stone quarry hole at the time that peat was developing in the hole, and the digging out of the stone would then be just earlier than the date for the peat.

We have no evidence from the excavations that this reconfigured stone was ever set upright as a monolith. Its quarry hollow was either immediately backfilled or left as a watery hollow in which peat developed. The purpose of the exercise seems to have been to manipulate the stone into a more meaningful recumbent position. Pete Herring has remarked that, in its present location, it mimics the shape of Leskernick Hill as seen on the skyline from the centre of the north stone circle. Could the watery hollow have created a connection with the 'underworld' of the hill?

Perhaps one of the morals of this particular part of the excavation is that

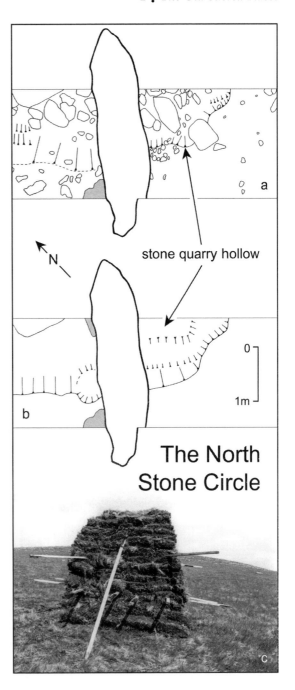

fig.4:6   The 'whalestone' in the centre of the North Stone Circle: a) during excavation. The 'whalestone' is at right angles to its quarry hollow, and there are stones in the lower fill of the quarry hollow; b) post-excavation; c) the turf heap from deturfing of the North Stone Circle – with stakes to keep the cattle off. Field credits: drawn by Justin R.; photo: JS-D.

fig.4:7 a) section, showing small 'propping stones', and b) excavation photograph of the excavated small stone on the southern periphery of the North Stone Circle. Field credits: drawn by Justin R.; photo: JS-D.

we make our best guesses based on what we think should happen – a central stone in the centre of a stone circle should, we think, either have stood upright, or have been a large earth-fast boulder. Our stories, until the excavation proved otherwise, did not include an earth-fast boulder levered out of the ground and then skewed round.[7]

SH (Wednesday 24 June 1998): A man and women arrived on the North Circle excavations today. … 'Oh, you've filled in the hole' they said. They had come up on Solstice night, and wanted to know if we had now found the stone-hole for the 'central standing stone' … which we had not. We are potentially destroying other people's narratives by finding things different to their imagination, or by simply not finding something which would resolve the issue.

The other stone excavated was one of the small standing stones that comprise the perimeter of the circle (Figure 4.7). This stone stood c. 0.7 m high in a peat-filled shallow hollow. It is possible that this hollow is the place where the stone was levered-up out of the ground. The stone lacked a deliberate stone-hole for its support. Instead, it had been propped up by a pile of smaller stones. As with the stone row terminal, this area had been tampered with at some time. It was also very evident from this trench that the 'stone-free' area of the ritual area had been a great deal stonier in the Neolithic and Bronze Age prior to the development of the peat cover across Leskernick.

Decommissioning the stone row

What happened to the stone row and circles and the Propped Stone and the Great Cairn when, in the Middle Bronze Age, people began to settle on the hill and build their houses and enclosures? The monuments would have been part of their story, part of their reason for being there. Perhaps they continued the ceremonies and still walked the length of the stone row on certain occasions, watched the sun set behind the Propped Stone on the summer solstice, lit beacons at the Great Cairn. We think that the corridor between the two settlements was a kind of processional way leading up to the hilltop. We note that there is an isolated very small house platform built close to the Propped Stone, and that even the most low-lying of the enclosures on the slopes below the southern settlement hold their distance from the stone row and circles.

But we also have evidence that the terminal setting was dismantled. What we are not clear about is when and how. The stone we excavated in the first year had been carefully removed from its stone-hole. It had been lifted out and placed transversely across its hole. But when? The stone was sitting high in the peat, which would tend to suggest that it was dismantled in post–Bronze Age times. On the other hand, peat had already formed in this area by the Early Bronze Age so that the dismantling could have occurred during the prehistoric occupation of the hill. It is thus quite possible that at some point in the Later Bronze Age, the people on the hill took down, with great care, one of the great stones from the terminal.

This version makes sense of the seemingly careful decommissioning, but ties in less well with the fate of the other monoliths of the terminal area. Let us examine the sequence of decommissioning more closely and, in particular, consider what might have happened to the two putative post or stone monolith outliers on either side of the terminal setting. It seems quite likely that their demise was intimately tied in with the 'felling' of the Great Terminal Monolith.

The Great Terminal Monolith – GTM – had been dramatically undermined by the displacement of its packing stones and deep digging around its base (Figure 4.3, at the western end of the excavation trench). It had then been pushed to the ground in such a way that its top end lay over the emptied stone-hole of the 'Penultimate Monolith' (the PM) – the packing stones within this hole having been pushed to one side of the cut and the PM removed. This removed PM may be the stone that at the time of the excavation lay recumbent across the stone/post-hole of the north outlier, and in this interpretative account, the PM had been yanked out immediately prior to the pushing over of the GTM (it would otherwise have been in the way

fig.4:8 Pete Herring replacing the tip of the Great Terminal Monolith. In the background the 'sculpted' Rough Tor spoil-heap.

when the stone was pushed over!). Within the fill of the dismantling pit quarried around the GTM lay a large granite block (c. 1 m 'tall') that was either a packing stone for the GTM or perhaps the 'missing' stone of the south outlier. Two large granite stones had been placed in the emptied stone-hole of the PM to prop up the top end of the pushed over great terminal stone. The tip of the great terminal stone had been smashed/broken off and lay adjacent to it (see Figure 4.8).

Along both sides of the GTM there were granite flakes, and these probably matched the faint, conchoidal flake scars on the sides of the monolith. Thus, it seems that attempts had been made to shape the stone. The granite flakes were fresh and unweathered, and their location within the peat makes it fairly clear that the GTM had, in fact, been dismantled in relatively recent times. In all probability, this ancient ritual stone had been knocked down and was in process of being turned into something as mundane as a gate-post, or a lintel for a door, window, or fireplace. For some reason, worked stopped, and the stone was never dragged away. A small reminder, perhaps, of the way in which things change their meaning and their use: yesterday's sacred stone becomes – or almost becomes – today's gateway or cow-scratcher …

fig.4:9 a) Matt and Henry bringing the mock-up of the Great Terminal Monolith on site; b) the 'stones' in place. The spiky tips of Rough Tor are just visible on the right-hand skyline.

If the GTM was only dismembered in fairly recent times, does it mean that it had, in fact, remained upright through for more than two millennia? Why, if it did remain in place, did the people of the hill decommission just one of the terminal stones? We don't know. We don't know what the people who finally abandoned their houses on the hill, or who came back less and less often, would have seen as they moved off across the moor and turned back for a last look.

Postscript

We added our own small postscript to the story of the stones. At first, we had thought of resetting them in their standing position, returning them to their former glory as revealed through excavation. No doubt, if we had done so, they would have fallen down fairly quickly, particularly because the cattle on the moor use the ritual area as a stomping and scratching ground. And, if we had, we would have scrubbed out part of the ambiguous history of the stones. As it was, official permission was not forthcoming and so, instead, we returned them to their pre-excavation locations, allowing them to tell a story of dismantling, interference – including our own – and slow elemental destruction … (Figure 4.9).

Chapter Five

Leskernick
The Southern Settlement

For generations, people had made their way across the moor to Leskernick as part of their seasonal movement with the herds. They had camped, on the hill, or at the foot of the hill, and had built the stone row and circles, the Propped Stone and the Great Cairn. But now, around three and a half thousand years ago, small groups decided to settle and to build houses. There was ample grazing on the hill and on the surrounding moor. There were stands of hazel and oak, and many and varied resources down by the river. A good place to stay. But more, a sacred place, a propitious place.

They built their houses on the hillslopes and chose the rockiest parts. To us, to live so tight up against the stones seems quite difficult – the ground is so uneven, so stony, so difficult to navigate. Why didn't they build below the hill, as at Rough Tor? But it seems that, for them, it was important to live in close proximity to the ancestors or ancestral beings. There was a reciprocity – they could nurture the stones and, in turn, the stones would care for them.

There are two important questions about this early settlement. The first, and more contentious question is did they stay on the hill the whole year round, or did they only come to the hill for part of the year? Our instinct, after five seasons on the hill, is to go for the first alternative and to suggest that the houses were lived in all year round. But, in truth, we cannot be certain, and we return to this question at the end of this chapter and again in chapter 18.

The second question is where did they choose to settle first? Was it on the west side of the hill, or on the south side? Or did they occupy both sides at about the same time? The hill is more densely covered with stone on the

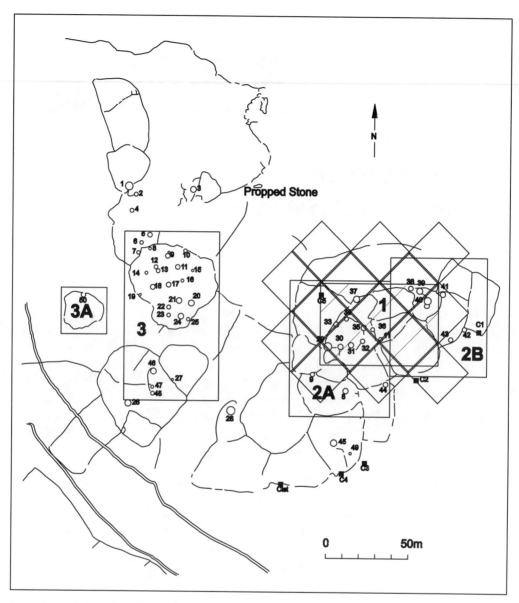

fig.5:1 Map of the Leskernick settlements and enclosures giving the positions of the more detailed plans.

west side, less so on the south. On the south side of the hill, the settlement would be in sight of the stone row and circles; on the west side of the hill, the Propped Stone would be in view. People settling the west side would be nearer the river, and to one, or probably two, springs. On this issue we hedge our bets and let them settle on both sides of the hill at about the same time. But as our earliest radiocarbon date for the houses comes from House 40 on the south side of the hill, we start there.

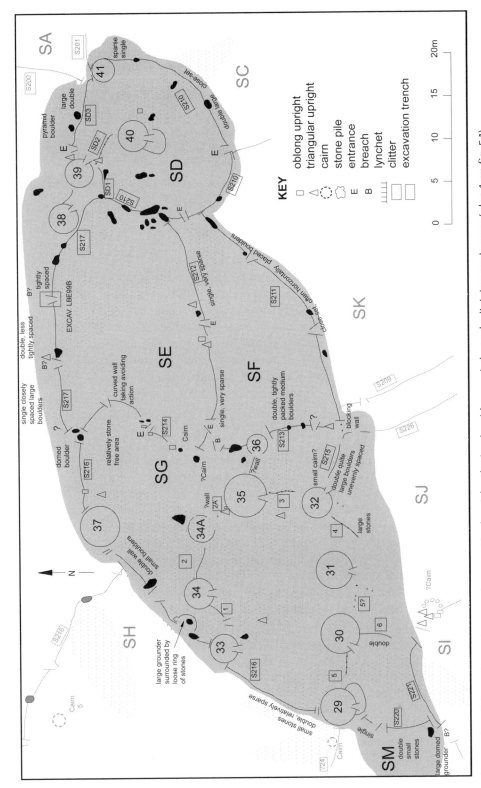

fig.5:2 Plan of the early southern settlement at Leskernick – the 'enclave', house circle, and adjoining enclosures (plan 1 on fig. 5:1). All survey settlement plans have been drawn by Jane Russell.

111

On the southern side of the hill

SH (Saturday, 15 June 1996): Walking back to the southern settlement from H[ouse] 23 I heard Kate singing while perched on a large stone in the southern settlement. For a while Leskernick's ruins became 'peopled' by a timeless child's song.

The eastern group of houses (Houses 38 to 41)

It seems probable that the little cluster on the eastern side of the southern slope – Houses 38 to 41 – were amongst the first to be built (Figures 5.1 and 5.2). In general, the southern hillslopes are much less stony than the western ones, but they chose to build in an area where there were large clitter blocks and a dense mass of stone. As always, we could offer a legitimate 'functionalist' explanation – they built where the stone was thick on the ground because they built their houses out of stone; they built on stony ground because that allowed the less stony ground to be used for grazing or cultivation. But this functionalism is always embedded in an understanding of what is appropriate and propitious. It was appropriate to make contact with the stone because the stone was the 'rock' of their belief. This was part of their functional understanding of how to go about things.

In this small cluster there are four houses. House 38, lying upslope from House 39, is very ruined. Both the inner and outer wall faces have been robbed. Its entrance almost certainly faced south-east. It seems to predate the enclosure wall that skirts its southern side, and it is also cut off by a small wall (SD1) from House 39, which seems to block access to its doorway (see note 5.4). It looks almost as though it was out of use – at least as a dwelling place – by the time House 39 was built. It could, therefore, be one of the very first houses to be built on the south slope.[1]

'House' 41, to the east of Houses 39 and 41, is in an even more ruined state. It's made of single boulder and slab construction and is unlikely to have been a domestic dwelling – it may even have been a cairn rather than a house (or it may have been a house that became a cairn). It, too, predates the enclosure walls that run up to it. It, too, may predate Houses 40 and 39.

Houses 39 and 40 are larger and more substantial, and House 40 sits centrally within the surrounding enclave wall (S 210; see Figure 5.2). The two houses lie very close to each other and are linked by a small wall. This wall runs over the ditch of House 40 and there is a radiocarbon date of 1670 to 1490 cal BC from the ditch. There are two radiocarbon dates for House 39. One, from the old land surface, is 1525–1375 cal BC, and the other, from an interior posthole, is 1430–1265 cal BC (see Table 4.1). Thus, House 40 would appear to

fig.5:3 Annotated plan and elevation of House 40.

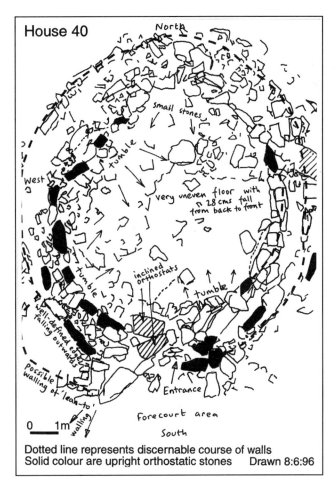

House 40

North

small stones

West

tumble

very uneven floor with 28 cms fall from back to front

tumble

inclined orthostats

tumble

well-defined edge falling outwards

possible walling of 'lean-to'

walling

Entrance

Forecourt area

South

0   1m

Dotted line represents discernable course of walls
Solid colour are upright orthostatic stones   Drawn 8:6:96

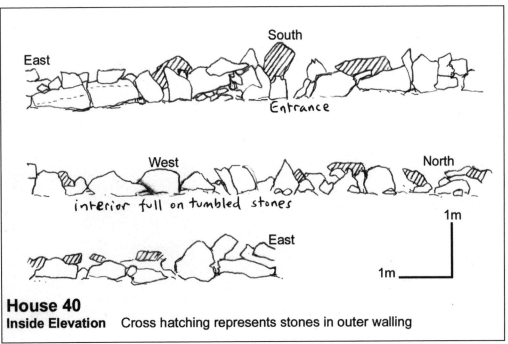

South

East

Entrance

West

North

interior full on tumbled stones

1m

East

1m

House 40
Inside Elevation   Cross hatching represents stones in outer walling

113

the radiocarbon date was obtained, seems to have functioned to protect the house from water and sludge washing down from the higher slopes above the settlement.

The house and its surrounding area are encircled by a substantial wall (S210). This is a very solid double wall built of large stones that, on its western side, rides over and incorporates some spectacular grounders.

CT (June 8 1996): The enclosure wall of the compound around 39 and 40 includes many large grounders including a perfect 'bench' with a view towards Brown Willy (Figure 5.4).

The northern edge is marked by a double wall of large stones (SD3) running between the ruined 'House' 41 and House 39.

House 39 is directly upslope and slightly to the east of House 40. The two houses were built so that the doorways faced south (House 40) and south-east (House 39). They look out towards to the Beacon with its summit cairns. But, perhaps more significantly, they – and probably House 38 – face directly towards the stone row with its large terminal stones and the northern and southern circles. Although these monuments can be seen from all the other houses in the southern settlement, these houses seem to be the only ones with a direct house-door orientation towards them. Just as the first houses on the western side lie within the orbit of the ancestral Propped Stone on the top of the hill (see chapter 6), these early houses acknowledge the ancestral stone settings on the plain below.

House 39

We excavated House 39. Like the Ur (the first, the grounding) house in the Great Compound of the western settlement, we found that a massive earth fast boulder (a 'grounder') served as its backstone. Here the archaeologists tell the story of the excavation of House 39 (Figure 5.5).

The house was chosen for excavation because its walls were the best preserved of the three main houses within the enclave (House 41 being an uncertain structure, see above). It also seemed likely that it would provide some details on the chronology of the founder settlement and more specifically, because of the wall that ran between the two houses, some stratigraphic evidence that would relate House 39 to the presumed founder house – House 40 (see note 5.1). Perhaps more instinctively we chose House 39 because its back wall included a dramatic, particularly massive backstone. It epitomised the relationship

fig.5:4 The bench stone within the encircling wall around Houses 39 and 40. From here there is a fine view looking west to Brown Willy. The Beacon is in the background.

that we had found in so many houses in that a prominent triangular or whale-shaped stone was placed in the wall directly opposite the house entrance. We wanted to discover whether these prominent stones were chosen and moved into place, or whether they were already 'in place' and the house was built around them.

House 39 was the first house that we excavated at Leskernick, and it took us three seasons (1996–98) to complete the excavation. During the first season we excavated the north-west quadrant, which incorporated the dramatic backstone. We approached this first season with a 'shopping list' of possible structural elements to look out for based upon our knowledge of other comparable moorland excavations of Bronze Age stone round houses, particularly the ones close by at Stannon Down (Mercer 1978), and, further afield, those at Holne Moor, Dartmoor (Fleming 1988). The list included the possibility of stone-covered drainage gullies under the house floors, stake divisions within the house – both found frequently in the houses at Stannon Down – and multiple phases of house construction – as at Holne Moor.

Such 'shopping lists' can generate false hopes and may mislead initial interpretations! During the first season, having only excavated

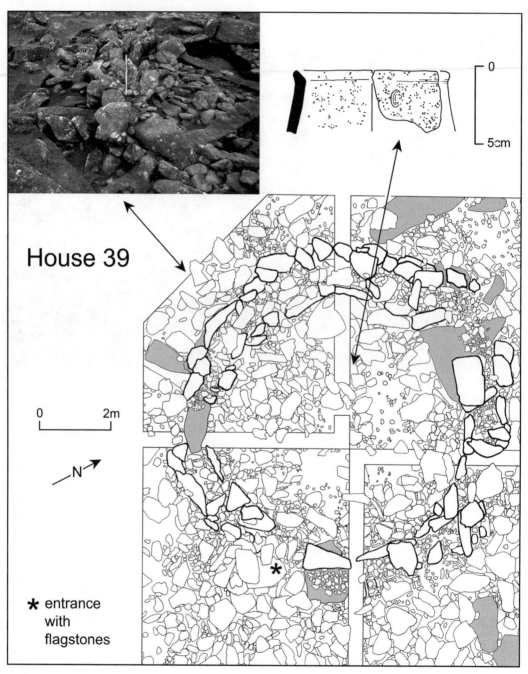

House 39

0   2m

N

* entrance
  with
  flagstones

fig.5:5 Plan of House 39 during excavation; photo showing part of the wall. Scale 2 m; the pot fragment came from towards the centre of the house from under a linear tumble of wall-stones, which initially looked like a drainage gully cover. Earthfast 'natural' stones are shaded, including the massive backstone (labelled on fig. 5.6). Field credits: drawn by Justin R.; photo: MST.

the north-west quadrant, we thought that we had a stone-capped linear gully close to the west baulk of the quadrant (Figure 5.5). At Stannon Down, six houses possessed such a feature and were interpreted as a drainage system that 'proceed[ed] in a "question mark" fashion around a large sector of the hut and out of the entrance' (Mercer 1978: 23). Alas – the feature in House 39 turned out to be a pseudo feature: there was no cut/gully discernible under the 'gully cover' and when the adjacent south-west quadrant was opened up in the following season, it became clear that the west baulk of our previous season had, fortuitously, followed the line of tumble from the wall of the house. The assumed 'gully cover' turned out to be part of a much more extensive tumble that extended into the baulk and across into the south-west quadrant. There was *no* evidence of a drainage system within House 39.

What we uncovered was a substantial, approximately circular, building with an internal diameter of c. 6.5 m. A house that could easily have accommodated a nuclear family *and* associated relatives. We certainly had no trouble fitting at least 10 excavators within the house at any given time. Such observation begs the question of whether there were internal divisions. Within the Stannon Down houses, Mercer (1978: 27) identified numerous stake-holes that were variously interpreted as hurdling screens, the bases of dressers and shelf arrangements, and the bases of beds, and evoked a cosy, cluttered world of Bronze Age house interiors. All the potential stake-holes within House 39 turned out to be vole burrows, so that we had to consider other possible ways in which the internal space might have been divided.

We shall return to this question. But, first, we want to consider the wall structure of the house. We found that some of the foundation stones of the circumference walling of House 39 had been fixed and levelled by being sunk into cuts made into the old land surface, but that most had been laid directly on the pre-existing land surface. Throughout its circuit, this walling was double-skinned and incorporated several distinct building techniques. There were stone-faced wall cells packed with small pieces of stone rubble at intervals throughout the wall circumference, there were – in all but the north-east quadrant – 'coursed' sections (flat-laid large stones generally on top of earth-fast stones), and, for part of the south-west quadrant, there were sections of abutting upright stone monoliths (large, elongated stones). In practical terms, these techniques adapted to, and accommodated, the pre-existing boulders on the hill. The resultant variation in the wall's visual appearance may also have been intimately associated with the different social, symbolic, and activity zones of the house's interior.

On its north and west (upslope) side, the house wall incorporated a massive triangular earth-fast boulder. This moorstone crossed the

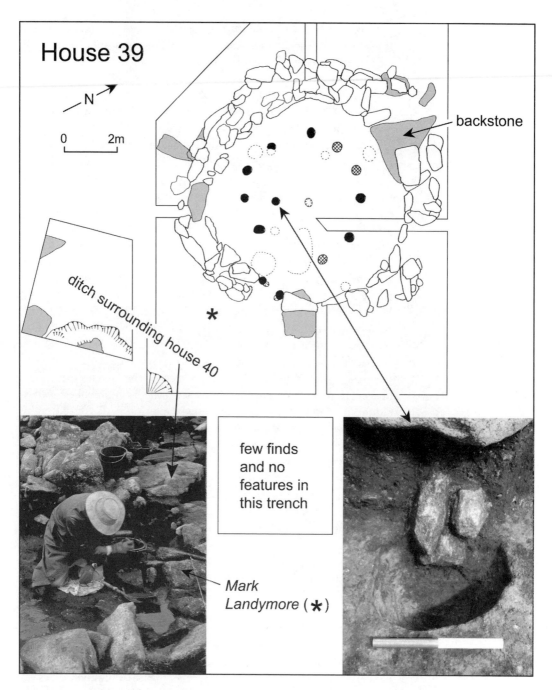

House 39

N

0   2m

backstone

ditch surrounding house 40

*

few finds
and no
features in
this trench

Mark
Landymore (*)

fig.5:6 Post-excavation plan of House 39 showing the circle of posts that supported the roof (scale on photos of packed posthole is 20 cm), and also the trenches excavated in front of the house. Mark is 'sponging-out' rainwater from the area in front of the entrance. Field credits: drawn by SA, MST, and Justin R.; photos: MST.

wall-thickness, effectively making this the 'ancestral' part of the house by physically binding it into the hill. It was also the stone from which the house walling sprung. It is just to the right of the dominant axis of the house, if this is taken to pass through the centre of the entrance.

Given the 'triangular' stone's great size, and the absence of any evidence for wooden cladding of the internal wall, such as was indicated by a ring groove just in front of the interior of the house wall at Site F, Holne Moor (Fleming 1988: Fig. 44), it would have been – even though located within the gloomy eaves' area – an imposing presence within the house, particularly when seated. On the other hand, when standing up it would have been the internal post ring (of 10 posts) that would have been more visually dominant (Figure 5.6). The posts are roughly concentric to the walls of the house and would have supported a conical roof of turf or thatch. The postholes from these posts penetrated the house floor to a depth of 35 cm and were stone-packed to keep the posts wedged in place. The posts may have been carved or decorated. They may have supported a ring beam from which the various objects that form the paraphernalia of household living were hung. Inside the post-ring, there was a central pit or unpacked posthole. Possibly this may have been a central support for the roof and would have dominated the view on entering the house. One of these postholes produced a Middle Bronze Age radiocarbon date of 1430 to 1265 cal BC.

There was one other stone-packed posthole in the south-west quadrant. This may relate to the management of interior space, being between the central feature and a post of the internal post-ring. These three posts thus formed a line that may have supported a crossbeam for an internal screen of textile, skin hangings, or wickerwork.

The floor was largely stone-free and lacked evidence of major stone removal, such as stone quarry holes. No doubt these floors would have had coverings, textiles perhaps, or skins, or grass/fibre matting.

A relationship between a massive 'natural' boulder like the one comprising the backstone of House 39 and a boulder-free area downslope was later observed in our excavation of Field Feature 1. It is *geomorphologically* explained by the largest hill boulders forming obstructions to the downslope flow of boulders under periglacial conditions. The clitter stream running along the north-east side of House 39 appears to have resulted from the channelling effect of the obstructive 'backstone'. Part of the wall of House 39 interfaces with this clitter stream, and the continuation of the clitter stream beyond the house forms part of the northern boundary wall of the enclave's enclosure.

In terms of the logistics of house building, prominent backstones correlate with stone-free areas, and thus provide arenas for house construction. Just as, as in the case of Houses 39 and 40, the resultant clitter streams around the sides of the prominent stones can provide the basis for enclosure boundaries. This, however, does not conflict with a 'logic of the cosmos' in that the well-being and protection of the household was ensured by the incorporation of prominent whale-stones or triangular stones as the 'backstone' of the house. That house construction is a question of cosmological as well as functional necessitude becomes apparent when we find that, in places on the hill where there are no suitable earth-fast boulders, the distinctive backstone is transported to the house and placed in position (see House 1, chapter 7).

The backstone in House 39 was opposite the entrance and the entrance was flanked by two postholes (stone packed), which indicate the presence of a covered entrance passage, or possibly a porch. No evidence of postholes were found outside the entrance gap to indicate a full porch extending beyond the house wall, but the surfaces immediately outside the entrance gap had been highly disturbed by animal burrowing and the evidence may have been destroyed. The entrance area was flagged, probably to protect the floor from the inevitable mud and erosion resulting from animal and human passage at a restricted point, and to visually mark the crossing of the house threshold. The rest of the interior was unpaved. Similar 'partial paving' occurs in Dartmoor hut circles (the old excavations at Holne Moor Site; Fleming 1988: Fig. 44).

In front of the entrance there was an effectively enclosed area. Looking out from the entrance, it is delimited on the right-hand side by the wall that joins House 39 to the back of House 40, and on the left-hand side by the clitter stream which the walling of the house is linked into. Originally, we thought that this 'courtyard' might have been a focal area for household activities. And, since we had not found a hearth inside the house, we thought that perhaps cooking and food preparation might have taken place outside. However the 'courtyard' was almost devoid of finds, and, indeed, the present day turf proved to mask a remarkably stony Bronze Age surface. Initially, the latter seemed to us to be a disadvantage in terms of the usability of the courtyard area. But, given the evidence of the substantial downslope wash of sediments that our excavations encountered in part the ditch of House 40, and our experience of rain-sodden days at Leskernick, we began to see an advantage in stony ground as opposed to trampled mud.

What can we say about activities, either inside or outside the house? The few portable finds came from inside the house, the house walling and from the 'old land surface' outside the house. These comprised some pottery sherds (of Bronze Age fabric and including the rim sherd from a jar) and worked and utilised stone (Figure 5.4). There were quartz pounders (interpreted as such on the basis of their end wear) – perhaps for pounding dry foodstuffs or for smashing granite or quartz. Most of the pounders were clearly not in their locations of original use. One was in the body of the wall joining House 40, one was in a posthole as a packer, and one was lying on the floor and either came out of wall rubble that had collapsed across the floor or was sealed by the collapse. Fragments of a beach pebble of metamorphic quartzite that seemed to have been used as polisher (perhaps for burnishing pottery or dressing leather) were found both inside and outside the house. Pounders were also found in the wall tumble of House 1 and Structure 23 in the western settlement. Both pounders and rubbers may have had a recognised secondary use as handy-sized wall and post packing. Interestingly, quern stones are recurrently associated with wall tumble at the Bronze Age settlement of Shaugh Moor on Dartmoor (Wainwright and Smith 1980: for example, in Houses 15 and 67). We can but muse on the potential symbolism of placing artefacts that had a life in previous households into the walls of new households and ritual structures. As such, it evokes a more widely recognised Bronze Age concern with signifying and conjoining artefact and household biographies (Brück 1999).

There were also some flaked flint and chipped quartz finds and these were the only portable artefacts with apparently meaningful distribution patterns. No flint was found within the interior of House 39. Instead, it occurred beneath the house walls (some of it therefore being earlier than the construction of the house), and, most abundantly, to the west of the wall joining House 39 to House 40. A flint flake was also found in the base of the ditch behind House 40. These flint flakes are not easily datable, but they would fit within a Neolithic or Bronze Age flint-working tradition. They are perhaps indicative of presettlement activity on the hill and also of possibly activity on the hill contemporary with Leskernick's settlements. Given that flint in any form must be an import to the site, the flint finds either signal contacts with nonlocal communities, or participation in wider interregional exchange networks. Leskernick as a whole produced two types of flint. That with traces of un-abraded cortex would have come from on or near Chalk strata, the nearest known source of which is Beer in Devon (over 100 km away). There are also flakes from flint beach pebbles. These flakes are from white-coloured (not patinated) flint, and possibly come from a Tertiary, rather than an active beach.

By contrast, the distribution of chipped quartz suggests an activity contemporary with, and centred, on House 39. There were quartz chips towards the centre of the interior of the house and both inside and outside the entrance. In contrast to the flint distribution, there were no chipped quartz finds to the west of the house, and none occurred under the walls where the flint was concentrated. Quantities of chipped quartz were also found associated with House 1 in the western settlement, and it would seem that quartz chipping was a significant activity, or by-product of an activity, which was carried out

slate with metal knife cut marks (from outside House 39)

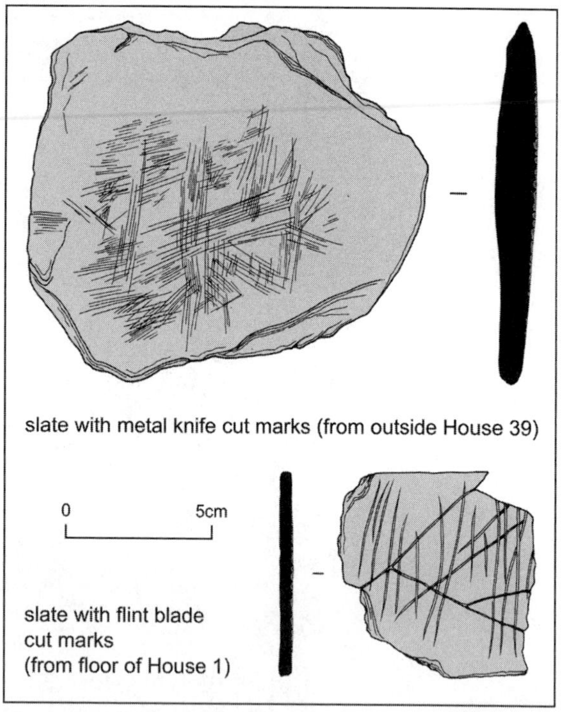

0   5cm

slate with flint blade
cut marks
(from floor of House 1)

fig.5:7 A piece of slate from House 39 with cut marks – perhaps made by a metal knife, compared with a piece from House 1 with possible flint cut marks. Drawn by Jane R.

at both settlements. We first began to think about this chipped quartz in context of House 39. Three options emerged: (1) the use of chipped quartz as an inscribing or cutting tool, (2) the production of quartz chips as a symbolic material, given that quartz 'pieces' and 'gravels' were a favoured material used in the construction of local Bronze Age barrows (e.g., locally on Davidstow Moor, Christie 1988: 54, 68; Tilley 1995), or (3) the unwitting accumulation of chipped quartz as a by-product of the damage sustained by quartz pounders when used to smash something hard such as cassiterite. These various options are discussed further in the context of House 1 (chapter 7).

We also recovered a piece of slate, about the size of a modern cup saucer, from just west of House 39. One face has a series of sharp criss-cross incisions (Figure 5.7). The cuts are thin, suggesting the use of a metal blade, and are consistent with a process of cutting something into strips, perhaps pieces of leather? The location of the slate does not directly relate it to House 39. However, given the association of a slate disc with Cairn 5 and slate finds from House 1 (also with incisions, but different to those described above), slate was certainly used by the Bronze Age communities of Leskernick. Although slate does not geologically occur on the moor itself, there are a multiplicity of locations on the edge of the moor (about a 45-minute walk away) from which it could be acquired.

Before we leave House 39 we can say something about the duration, and perhaps the end, of the occupation. There was no evidence that the posts of House 39 had ever been replaced, suggesting that the house had a limited time-depth of use. But scattered through the floor of House 39 were charcoal flecks and occasional larger pieces. These were consistently from oak. Oak may have been used for the posts of the house, and, initially, the possibility that the house burnt down occurred to us. This hypothesis had to be abandoned when, with further excavation, we discovered that the charcoal was only present in minor quantities in the postholes, and the packing stones themselves were not burnt. No evidence of post pipes (from the timber decaying below ground level) remained, which could suggest that on desertion of the house, the posts were removed rather than being left to decay *in situ*. In several cases, however, the packing stones were in upright positions suggesting that they had not been disturbed by the removal or scavenging of the posts. Several postholes were disturbed by animal burrowing, and this is the likely cause for displaced packing in some of the postholes. Thus, either the posts decayed *in situ*, or they were only scavenged for other purposes once their below ground-level wood had rotted and it was possible to harvest the posts without disturbing their packing. House 39 was certainly left to decay after its *initial* abandonment. There is no evidence of the systematic closing down of the house through the levelling of interiors with occupation debris and the hiding of artefacts as Nowakowski (1991) has noted for the settlement of Trethellan Farm in Lowland Cornwall.

It would seem as though the three or four houses in this small enclave were occupied sequentially, so that, at any given moment, there may have been no more than a single extended family living here – perhaps 10 or 15 people at most.

The circle of houses to the west of the enclave[3]

A few hundred metres west of the enclave there is a circle of houses – Houses 29–33 – and an outlier, House 37 (Figure 5.1). None of these houses were excavated and so we depend upon the survey to build up a picture of how life unfolded on this part of the hill.

We do not know exactly how enclave and circle related time-wise. Did two small groups arrive together and start building within hailing distance of each other? Or was there a small time lag – in which case, which place was settled first? What does seem clear is that some of the earliest enclosures run *between* the two groups of houses and pay heed to the enclave wall (S210) to the east and to the perimeter wall (S216/S214) associated with House 37 to the west. There is therefore a substantial overlap in time between the two groups. We imagine that they cooperated closely in the building of these enclosures and that the families involved were closely related.

You will note that we envisage that the houses were occupied by extended families. We have no real way of demonstrating the relationship between the people who lived in each of the houses. But bearing in mind the average size of the house, and comparing it with ethnographic examples (e.g., Guidon 1975; Preston Blier 1987; Waterson 1990), it seems reasonable to suppose that each house was built and occupied by an extended family, thus three generations and somewhere between 10 and 15 people. It is also seems likely that where houses are in close proximity the people who lived in them were closely related. In the circle of houses not only were the houses close to one another but they were joined by short stretches of wall.

On the other hand, just as further to the east, House 38 may have preceded the more substantial House 40 (and later House 39), so, in this more westerly grouping, there may have been a single household that predated the arrival of more numerous families. This would be House 37, which is upslope of and separate from the circle of houses. It is in very poor condition but originally it was a quite substantial double-walled building, 6.5 m in diameter. 'House' 34A, also off centre from the circle of houses, and also very robbed out, may have been an ancillary building. It is only 4–5 m in diameter and seems to be a single boulder and slab wall construction. We might even add a 'ghost house' to this first collection, for the perimeter wall (S216/S214) to the east of House 37 swerves as though avoiding a structure – perhaps of wood – of which nothing remains except the stone-free area (Figure 5.1).

This wall (S216/S214), encompassing the area (SG) downslope of House 37 and upslope of 34A may have been built at the same time as House 37. It starts at House 37, circles east to a large domed boulder and a large grounder and then swings south taking, as noted, avoiding action around something that was there but has now gone. There is an entrance through the wall of this curved section marked by an oblong stone and a recumbent stone, and towards its southern end there seems to be, first, a small cairn (2.20 m diameter) set between a fine oblong upright and a larger boulder,[4] and, second, a small grounder encircled by a cairn (also 2.20 m diameter).

Then – we surmise – more people arrive, probably six related families, and they build their dwellings in a circle downslope from House 37.[5] Perhaps at this point the earlier house and ancillary building were dismantled and some of the stone was reincorporated into the new houses.

The six houses are all built in much the same way. They are double walled with rubble fill. They have external wall-faces made of horizontal coursework that has often been partially robbed out, and they have better preserved internal wall-faces with fine large boulders or carefully chosen upright slabs that are often square or rectangular in shape. In several of the houses – Houses 29, 30, and 31 – orthostatic doorjambs mark the entrance.

BB (1995): I guess I had assumed that the doorways to the houses in the little semicircle would face into the central area, that people would come out and chat to their neighbours, watch the kids, chop the wood etc. in this communal space. My blueprint, I suspect, was a neat village green. But it wasn't like that.

With one exception, the doorways faced either to the south or south-east. They face out across the moor to the surrounding hills. In the distance, on the skyline, there are no dramatic tors, but cairns would have been visible capping every significant hill. In five houses, the entrance faced south with views down the Fowey Valley to, in the distance, Brown Gelly with its arc of five cairns (Figure 5.8a). House 32 faces east-south-east and takes in the same landmarks. Just one house, House 30, faces south-west looking out to Catshole Tor, Tolborough with its massive tor cairn, and Codda. Door orientation is not about easy access to your neighbour – people would have had to walk around their houses to talk and meet each other. Nor, in moving out of a house or between houses, is it about seeing the houses of the western settlement or the Great Cairn or Propped Stone on the hill top.

Although the houses have many features in common, House 35 is definitely the finest (Figure 5.8b; Color Plate 3a). It has an internal diameter of 7. 5 m and massive double-skinned walls (Figure 5.9a). It contains not only an oblong-shaped backstone, now recumbent, that would have stood to a height of 1.2 m and seems to have been set in a niche, but also two further niches, one inset in the middle of the eastern wall, the other in the western, both backed by prominent stones. Behind the substantial rounded grounder that forms the back of the eastern niche, a large piece of quartz may have been used as part of the rubble packing, and another large tooth-shaped white quartz stone now fallen into the interior of the house may have stood upright as part of the inner wall face. In this house the key architectural elements – entrance, backstone, and niche stones – are clearly aligned on the cardinal points. Outside the entrance is a possible small cobbled platform area.

This house, like all the others, appears to be well levelled into the slope – although, as we shall see, the excavation of 'House' 23 makes clear that this appearance of levelling may be fortuitous (see chapter 6).

The other nearby houses vary in size between 7 m and 5 m in internal diameter. Two have a backstone – others may have been robbed out at a later date. House 29 has particularly large stones placed in opposite walls and the same house contains an unusually weathered and gnarled orthostat. Another house – 33 – seems to have two internal niches in opposing walls.

In several of the houses internal subdivisions are visible. House 30 is divided into three; House 31 has a possible internal division running south-

fig.5:8 a) Looking southwards towards the Fowey Valley and Brown Gelly from House 29; b) wrapped entrance stones to House 35; c) 'House' 34 – a special house; d) a detail of 'House' 34 – Fay's private place (see p. 292).

west to north-east towards the centre of the house; House 29 has a possible west-east wall footing inside the doorway creating a small corridor that would have funnelled movement to the west. Two houses (29 and 37) have external annexes immediately to the west of the entrance area; one (31) has a possible annexe to the east of the entrance.

Many of the houses are connected by small walls made of single stones (see Figure 5.1; walls 1, 2, 2A?, 3, 4, 5?, 5A) – for example, Houses 29 and 30, and Houses 32, 35, and 34. The houses on the western edge of the circle – 29 and 33 – are also linked by an enclosure wall (S216), which then swings northeast and abuts House 37. The wall postdates all three houses.

One 'house' in the circle remains to be mentioned. House 34 on the north edge of the circle (Figures 5.8c, 5.8d, 5.9b). Even today it seems to be different from the rest. It is small (4 m diameter). Its interior is marshy with reed growth and glimpses of a cobble floor. The entrance faces south. What makes it strange is that the inner wall face is constructed of small stones, whereas the outer is made of very large distinctively and irregularly shaped orthostats. This is an inversion of the usual wall construction at Leskernick. There is also an unusual stone with deeply incised weathering lines criss-crossing the surface set in the northern sector. Its weathered surface faces outwards, its smooth surface faces in.

This particular type of weathering pattern on the stone, and the one in House 29, are found in none of the other houses on the hill. These stones would have had to be brought down from the great tabular stone outcrops at the top of Leskernick Hill where the stones are similarly weathered. The 'house' wall is irregular, differing markedly in width from place to place. It seems unlikely that it was ever roofed. In many ways, it resembles 'Houses' 14 and 23 in the western settlement and, like them, we suggest that it was an open-air circular shrine used by the people living in the surrounding cluster of houses. Just to the west of this special place there is a large grounder (G1), which seems to be surrounded by a loose semicircle of stones (Figures 5.2 and 5.11). These butt up against, and therefore come later than, the perimeter wall (S216) that runs north from House 33.

Unlike the enclave to the east, which is encircled by a substantial perimeter wall, these houses are more loosely encompassed by walls that form the edges of enclosed land – on the west side, wall S216 is part of enclosure SH, and on the east, S 213 is part of enclosure SF.

Although we know from excavation that there has been an enormous accumulation of earth and peat since the time the houses were built, it still seems possible to see obvious areas of clitter and equally obvious cleared ways in the area between and around the houses (Fig 5.2: SG). You get a feeling of where people could walk, and where it would have been difficult. This mirrors our findings in the Great Compound of the western settlement. Within the small clitter spread south of Houses 33 and 34 and south of House 35 there are some fine upright stones.

Another small enclosure was created to the south of Houses 29 and 30. On the east side it is defined by a small double-skinned wall (6) running south from House 30, on the north by the small wall between the two houses, and on the west and south by the walls of adjoining enclosures (S220 and S221).

Six houses; one shrine; a house that has fallen into ruin; a piece-meal perimeter wall. Six families. Sixty to 70 people – with another 10 or 15 across the way in the easterly enclave (Figures 5.2 and 5.10).

The enclosures

Meanwhile, they were beginning to build the enclosures.[6] We start with a general description of the enclosure walls, move on to the entrances, and then to sequence, and finally discuss what the enclosures might have been used for.

The walls

The walls took many different forms. The 1994 RCHME report said rather blankly:

> The majority of the walls are really linear heaps or banks of boulders and stone with some upright slabs and orthostats that link individual (or groups) of large natural boulders.

In reality, there is an enormous amount of diversity. In some cases, the walls do look 'heaped', but more often the stones have been 'placed'. The width may vary from 0.6 m to 2 m, and the height may again be no more that 0.5 or may rise to 1.2 m. They enclose areas that range from 0.25 to 1 ha. Some walls are skimpy and only a boulder wide. Some are carefully made, double sided with rubble infill. In some walls, the stones used appear rather amorphous in shape and size, but in many the wall is punctuated by stones that seem to have been chosen for their shape – triangular, oblong, or humped. The diversity, and the care taken in many cases, comes as no surprise, the walls would have been built both 'knowledgeably' and 'with attitude'.

The walls worked in conjunction with the major downslope axis of the clitter flows, and with the contour-following boundaries of clitter lobes. Sometimes the wall emanates from the clitter mass, sometimes it works to connect major clitter concentrations; often it 'hooks' itself between huge grounders. Sometimes these large grounders are re-marked by a pyramid stone propped against them. And often these grounders are used as enclosure corner stones.

Again, the functionalist could try and made a case that this close correlation between wall and clitter concentration is a way of minimising labour and maximising what is already in place. But the walls persistently take *un*-sensible alignments, suggesting, rather, that the walls were in a sort of dialogue with the stone, and that the location of clitter flow and lobe served to socially predetermine the division of space. We suggest that, although the enclosures accrete over time, they also demonstrate a higher order logic. That is, the pre-existing stony divisions of the hill provided an absolute and eternal order.[7]

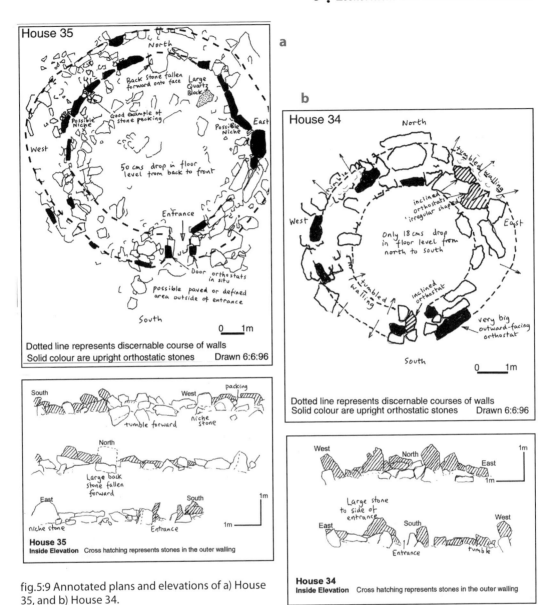

fig.5:9 Annotated plans and elevations of a) House 35, and b) House 34.

Moving between enclosures

We had hoped to be able to map entrances to the enclosures, to show something of the pathways that people used as they went about their daily business. But it was difficult because most walls had been breached in later times. Here is an example of some of the problems we faced. This entrance was in the northern wall of enclosure SE, a large enclosure that ran between the small eastern enclave with Houses 39 and 40 and the enclave further west with House 37 (Figure 5.1):

Excavation of a field entrance (LBE 99B) in wall S217

Having remarked on the difficulty we often had in distinguishing original entrances from later wall breaches – breaches that could signify Bronze Age modifications to the field systems, collapse of walls, or deliberate breakthroughs in more recent times – the large gap in wall S217, quite close to House 38, seemed a good candidate for excavation (Fig 5.2: LBE 99B). Even today, the wall is substantial and carefully constructed. It has something in common with the wall of the great compound in the western settlement and gives the feeling that it might have been built to emphasise the boundary of settled 'human' space. The wall is adjacent to, and mirrors, the line of a natural clitter lobe with many large stones, which, further to the east, is incorporated into House 39.

On either side of the 'entrance', the wall comprises a line of very large well-fitted boulders resting horizontally on the more or less stony old land surface. On the west side of the entrance, associated with the upslope part of the excavated wall, stood two stone uprights. The occurrence of similar stones elsewhere in the wall initially suggested *in situ* facing stones – ones that might have served to contain a rubble or earth infill, but the large size of the stones comprising the wall makes such stones seem superfluous, at least in practical terms. The idea that these may represent a displaced upper course, therefore, seems more plausible. A second course is clearly visible elsewhere in the wall and is 'implied' by a large pile of boulders downhill of, and resting against, the south side of the wall.

A superficial concentration of rubble downhill of the gap may – but not with any certainty – indicate that the gap was a secondary feature in the wall. There is no evidence of a gate structure.

A question-mark still hangs over the gap in the wall – a prehistoric entrance? A later breach?

The form of enclosure

In general, the prehistoric field systems on Bodmin Moor are curvilinear and accretional (Johnson and Rose 1994: 59). But coaxial field systems, found extensively on East Dartmoor (Fleming 1983, 1988) and, rather less often on South Dartmoor (Balaam, Smith, and Wainwright 1982; Wainwright and Smith 1980), are also occasionally present. These coaxial fields are laid out with a single dominant axis of orientation, in such a way that most of the boundaries run parallel to each other (Fleming 1994: 63). They give the impression of having been laid out at one time, or at least adhering to a preconceived 'master plan', something agreed by a community, or perhaps imposed by a community head (see also chapter 18). The more accretional nature of the enclosures at Leskernick and elsewhere on the moor seems to suggest greater household autonomy. On the other hand, our work at Leskernick suggests that there are conformities in the creation of the boundaries that perhaps respond to an overarching cosmology which dictates where the major boundary axes fell or could be placed.

The sequence of enclosure building

The southern slopes of Leskernick were enclosed over a period of time. The curvilinear fields radiated out from the enclave and the circle of houses, and then, later, further enclosures were added with, in some cases, isolated houses set within them (see chapter 8). Often it is quite easy to look at where one wall butts against another and to see which wall came first. But sometimes it's not so evident. An excavation may or may not resolve the issue. Thus, for example, to the eye, wall S207 of enclosure SC appeared to butt the southern corner of SA (Figure 5.11), but an excavation (LBJ 982) suggested otherwise. Although there was no physical keying or even sufficient evidence to prove a sequence of abutment, close examination of wall morphology made it reasonably clear that the downslope enclosure (SC) was built first. On the other hand, the excavation (LBJ 981) at the junction between the western wall (S218A) of the big enclosure SH to the west of the circle of houses, and the wall taking off to the north (S219) was unable to resolve which wall was built first. In the end, both the archaeologists and surveyors agreed, based on visual inspection of wall morphology, that probably the western wall came first.

What, of course, is even less clear is how much time elapsed between the building of adjoining enclosures or walls. Sometimes a series of walls may have gone up in quick succession, but then there might have been a long pause before another series of enclosures were built. And again, whilst the sequence *within* a parcel of adjoining enclosures may be reasonably clear, it is often much harder to ascertain how one such 'parcel' relates to another noncontiguous one. In what follows we have left out some of the inevitable 'possibly's' and 'perhaps's' but signal the really weak links.

This enclosure (SE) is big. The western end of its northern wall (S217) starts at the same great domed boulder and grounder that marked the corner of SG. At the eastern end, the wall takes avoiding action around House 38, or else the house had already been abandoned and the wall to some extent overrides it. This was the wall with the fugitive entrance (see above excavation of LBE99B).

The northern wall of enclosure SE is a strong close-set part single, part double-faced wall, but its southern wall (S212) is puny. It seems possible that, at some later date, the enclosure SE was enlarged to include the land to the south (SF) and that wall S212 was more or less dismantled. Perhaps the stones were used to make the fine closely packed double faced wall (S211). Alternatively, SE and SF were originally conceived of as one large enclosure and the puny wall was a marker line dividing it in two. The tightly packed double wall (S213) that marks the west end of the new enclosure SF also serves as a perimeter wall for the house circle. This wall, which incorporates 'House' 36 (a single slab and boulder construction that was probably a nondomestic adjunct to the house circle), was built as part of the enclosure rather than as part of the settlement.

There are 'positive lynchets' upslope from both walls S212 and S211 but, as we shall shortly see, these surface 'lynchets' may turn out to be something quite different.

As the circle of houses are built, two small enclosures are built radiating out from it (Figure 5.10).

The egg-shaped enclosure to the south of the houses, and the small enclosure

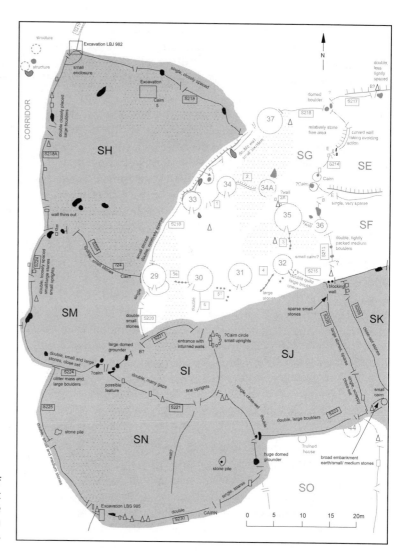

fig.5:10 Plan of enclosures to the west and south of the circle of houses (plan 2A on fig 5:1; key: fig. 5:2).

(SM) adjoining it to the west seem to have been built at more or less the same time. The egg-shaped enclosure (SI) incorporates the southern end of the clitter flow that extends downslope between Houses 29 and 30, and it also has one of the relatively few well-marked enclosure entrances on the hill. This entrance (E2) is marked by in-turned walls and gives direct access to the house circle. At the eastern end of the northern wall (S224) of enclosure SM there seems to be a small cairn, and, again, at the eastern end of the southern wall there is another possible cairn. If these cairns, and those on the perimeter wall (S217) to the east of House 37, and the small one alongside House 32, were used for burials, we might surmise that they date to a later phase of settlement when the house circle was abandoned (chapter 7).

fig.5:11 Plan of enclosures to south and east of the house circle and eastern enclave (Houses 38–40) (plan 2B on fig. 5:1; key: fig.5.2).

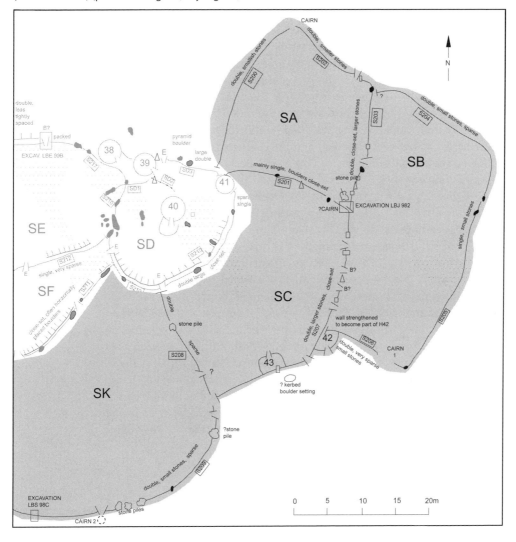

In quick succession, more enclosures are added.

Perhaps almost immediately, the big enclosure SH is added to the west of the circle of houses. Its eastern wall (S216), a relatively sparse double wall of small stones, delimits the western perimeter of the house circle. It moves between and butts up against Houses 29, 33, and 37. As we noted above (this chapter), a large flat grounder between House 34 – the 'open-air circular shrine' – and the wall is set within a loose semicircle of small stones that butt against the enclosure wall. SN is another substantial enclosure that butts against enclosure SM and the egg-shaped enclosure SI. As so often, a huge domed grounder marks the south-east corner.

Perhaps at the same time (Figure 5.11):

The large enclosure SK is built to the south of the earlier enclosure SF. Its eastern wall (S208) – double faced, with sparsely spaced stones – butts the House 40 enclave; its southern edge, beyond which the moorland stretches away, is defined by a robbed-out double wall (S209) of small stones. Probably at the same time, the land to the west of SK and south of the circle of houses is also enclosed (SJ), and between the two enclosures – SJ and SK – a drove-way is constructed. Its east side is formed by the quite substantial western wall of SK, its west side by a robbed-out skimpy wall, S226, within enclosure SJ. At the north end, a small double wall (S215) links the top of the drove-way to House 32. A gap between this wall and the corner of enclosure SF would have allowed the animals to move into the area around the house circle. This drove-way is one of those features that, like the pathway out of the Great Compound on the west side of the hill, allows the imagination to light up – it's not hard to envisage cattle or sheep jostling their way up and down the pathway between house circle and open moorland.

What makes this image more poignant is that, at a later date, the southern end of the drove-way was blocked by an earth and stone embankment and at its northern end by a small wall. The western side was also semi-dismantled. It seems as though, when the settlement retracted and the circle of houses were abandoned, the drove-way went out of use and was blocked off (see chapter 7) The building of a small cairn just outside, and blocking, an entrance in the southern wall of enclosure SK, is part of this same process of retraction and closure. 'House' 44, close to the bottom end of the drove-way, was probably not a house at all, but rather an animal pen used in conjunction with the drove-way. It seems to be U shaped and is about 5 m in diameter. It seems to predate the building of the sturdy southern wall (S223) of enclosure SR, which takes avoiding action around the back of it. (For an alternative interpretation, see footnote 7:8 pages 441/442.)

A little later:

Enclosures SA and SC were built to the south and east of the enclave wall around House 40. They were probably built at about the same time – first SC and then SA (Figure 5.11). The northern end of the western wall (S210) of SC seems to butt against House 41. On the southern wall (S207), a small U-shaped add-on of single boulder construction – 43 – is built up against the wall, its entrance opening northwards into the enclosure. Its back wall, which is part of the enclosure wall, incorporates one of several fine uprights that mark the enclosure wall at this point. The structure was probably an animal pen.

Enclosure SA is a relatively small enclosure. One wall (S201) seems to butt against House 41. On the northern corner, between two walls (S200 and S202), there is a small cairn (c. 3 m diameter) with kerbstones – particularly on the northern side.

And later again:

The last of the enclosures on the eastern side is built. SB flanks the earlier enclosures SA and SC. Like the southern wall of SC, the walls (S204, S205, S206) of this enclosure have been badly robbed out. In the short southern wall (S206), there is a cairn with a large upright in the centre and a kerb of small boulders. The wall sections on either side are particularly sparse and it seems likely that stones from the wall were used to make the cairn. This would mean that the cairn was built at a later time when the enclosure had gone out of use. A time when the places of the dead were, quite literally, imbedded into places of earlier usage and memory (see chapter 7).

Rather like structure 43, structure 42 is an add-on. Made of single boulders, it takes up the angle between two enclosure walls (S207 and S206) creating a triangular space. As part of this building, the western end of wall S206 was strengthened. The structure opens southwards and, again, was probably an animal pen or storage structure. Alternatively:

BB (June 23 1997) Pete [Herring] has a passionate commitment to medieval transhumance. He believes that the rectangular structure on the southern enclosure wall ['House' 43] and the house between the walls ['House' 42] and a few others are associated with this transhumance. Also the 'cairn' in House 26. It turns out that this is all part of a very romantic scenario, culled partly from Irish oral history, partly from a model of society in early medieval Cornwall. The young girls came up with the herds, and the young boys went up afterwards to collect the cheeses and … as one old lady in the Irish stories said, 'The valley rang with the sound of music'. As he talked, I could hear the penny whistles and fiddles![8]

Later still, a few more enclosures are built on the southern side of the hill, but these are associated with single houses and we shall return to them in chapter 7.

The use of the enclosures

The descriptive report for the National Monuments Record listing, supplied to us by Norman Quinnell as a typescript copy, and recorded for the Bodmin Moor Survey as described in Johnson and Rose (1994:14) was unhappy with the appearance of some of enclosures:

> Why some boulder covered areas have been enclosed is a mystery. Sheep will graze happily amidst boulders but cattle avoid the area. The fields vary in area from 0.25 ha to 1 ha and many are simply boulder fields. Some walls have been driven through dense boulder spreads where no amount of clearance would make any difference to the boulder layers.

In fact, our excavations show that even those enclosures that look relatively stone-free today were rough and stoney. So what were they used for, these stoney enclosures of variable sizes with clitter-orientated walls? Were they cultivated? Grazed? Were they, at some times of the year, hay meadows? What, if one stood in one of the door-ways, would the enclosures have looked like? *How did the people on the hill get by?*

Today, the walls look too low to have contained stock, and since the rubble associated with them is relatively slight it does not seem that they stood much higher in the Bronze Age. Of course, their height could have been augmented by hedges, but there is no pollen evidence to support the idea. Species such as Hawthorn or Blackthorn could not be separated from other members of the *Rosacae* species in the pollen samples, although it has to be admitted that the pollen of this family is relatively poorly presented. Alternatively, hurdling might have been used to increase the height.

Another possibility is that the walls were not there to keep things in or out, but, rather, to define holdings. Pete Herring notes that in medieval times on Bodmin Moor there were:

> Peter Herring (pers. comm., 4 December 1999): Low rickles of stones apparently cleared from cultivated land as markers of holdings. They were not stock-proof; in fact that was part of their design. Cattle could step over them when the field was down to grass and used in common. Temporary hurdle fences were used a lot in medieval outfields in Devon and Cornwall, but again strips and perimeters were usually also defined by low banks of stones. So we may want to see Leskernick's boundaries having temporary fences/hurdles when they were necessary. A bit like movable electrified fences in modern stock management.

On surface evidence, some of the enclosures have well-developed negative and positive lynchet systems abutting the walls and following the contours of the hill (see Figures 5.10, 5.11, and 7.19). In theory, these 'lynchets' could be the result of the uphill loss of sediments and the downslope accumulation of sediments dislocated by ploughing and soil creep. They could, therefore, indicate cultivation. However, excavations of two enclosure wall sections in the southern settlement suggest a rather different scenario (Figure 5.12). In both cases, the positive lynchet accumulation turned out to be a low bank of smaller stones placed against the wall face on the upslope side, and evidence of any sediment accumulation (colluviation) is lacking. These stone banks could be interpreted in a number of ways: the stones could have been piled against the walls during pasture and tree clearance; they could acted as ramps to direct animals out of the enclosures; or they might have had the opposite effect and formed unstable rocky piles that discouraged animals (specifically cattle) from climbing out of their enclosures (a cattle-grid effect). The excavations also showed that the negative lynchets were nothing to do with agricultural practice but rather the outcome of the contour walls following, and being built on, clitter lobes, thus creating a stepped effect in the hill profile on their downslope side.

This 'demolition' of the apparent lynchets might be taken to suggest that there was little cultivation and that the enclosures were mainly used for retaining animals and/or taking off hay. Alternatively, there may have been a much less intensive form of cultivation that did not lead to soil movement.

As far as stock-rearing is concerned, no bones were recovered at Leskernick, and it is therefore impossible to identify what animals

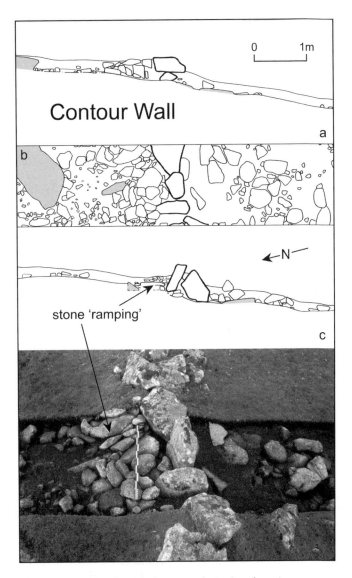

fig.5:12 Plan views (b, and photo – scale 1 m) and sections (a, and c) of excavated section across enclosure wall BSB, indicating that the suggested 'lynchets' were in reality stone 'ramping'. See Figure 1:4 for trench location. Field credits: drawn by ES; photographer unknown.

might have been kept in the enclosures. At Stannon Down, Mercer noted the absence of a preserved turf-line on the excavated land surfaces. He suggested that this indicated trampling by cattle or pigs, rather than grazing of sheep in pens (Mercer 1978). At Leskernick, alas, the voles and rabbits had been too active and there were no original land-surfaces preserved below the enclosure walls.[9] Pollen from the implied old land surfaces under house walls did, however, indicate that there had been woodland (oak and hazel), and that it was being cleared at the time of the settlement.

Importantly, none of the on-site pollen samples from Leskernick contain cereal pollen (although there is a very small amount in the Bronze Age part of the off-site pollen record). This independently argues against any extensive cultivation. Additionally, the presence of bedstraw (*Rubiaceae*), a ground-level spreading species, and ribwort plantain (*Plantago Lanceolata*), another pasture species, associated with the land surfaces preserved under house walling and floors of the houses in the southern and the western settlements argue for grazing.

So we postulate a mainly pastoral economy with some small patches of cultivation. Animals would have been kept in the enclosures and would, as well, have grazed beyond the settlement, down on the moor, up on the top of the hill, or on the northern flanks. We have the drove-road that leads away from the circle of houses in the southern settlement and opens towards the plain below the hill. The enclosures could also have been used to take off crops of hay for the winter.

Pete Herring somewhat tweaks our interpretation, wanting to give a little more importance to the patches of cultivation:

> Peter Herring (pers. comm. 4 December 1999): Remember the Burren, Aran, and even medieval Bodmin Moor. If machinery isn't a factor; if sowing, tending and harvesting were by hand; if sowing was not by broadcasting but individual, seed by seed. If a stony area had attractions for cultivators: micro-shelter for the germinating seed, and stones providing a form of weed suppression. If the plants were harvested by hand, even pulled up as they sometimes were in early modern Ireland, there would be no soil movement, hence no lynchets. Small allotments could be fenced ...

Permanent or seasonal occupation?

We circle back to the question we asked at the beginning of the chapter. With such a strong emphasis upon a pastoral economy, did people only live at Leskernick for part of the year? Did they take their herds off the moors in the winter months and return each summer, coming back not just for the pastures but for the rituals and celebrations associated with the stony places? Is it because Leskernick was only seasonally occupied that there's such a limited amount of portable material culture? And are the houses built so stoutly precisely because they are only occupied for part of the year and have to withstand the winter months without people being on hand to patch and repair? The excavators of Shaugh Moor on Dartmoor – where the houses are just as solid as those at Leskernick – believe that the economy was based on transhumance (Balaam, Smith, and Wainwright 1982; Smith et al. 1981):

> It is likely that pastoral agriculture was based at least partly on transhumance with the majority of herds and flocks moved to the lowland plain for winter quartering, culling etc. … If grazing pressure in some areas was as great as it is now … there seems no way in which herds could have been maintained in the Bronze Age, without transhumance, even if the climate was 1–2 degrees warmer that it is today. (Balaam, Smith, and Wainwright 1982: 257)

And in the ethnographic literature there are examples of well-built seasonal settlements. For example, the Vlahs (Aromâni) of the Balkans expressly built solid stone houses in the uplands to withstand the elements and the seasonal abandonment (Wace and Thompson 1981).

The alternative reading would be that the houses are *too* substantial, the ritual places and observances *too* complex, for this to be a seasonal place. The lack of hearths and the small amount of portable material culture could be due to the very poor conditions of preservation on the moor. People could have lived at Leskernick all year round, and they could have exchanged their wool and hides, their animals for breeding, draught, milk, and meat for fodder and other daily and winter requirements.[10] There may have been other activities – ones for which little or no traces remain – like leather working, or the exploitation of quartz, or tin extraction,[11] that extended the practicality of year-round occupation.

We have opted for year-round occupation, partly for the reasons just listed, and partly by comparing and contrasting the Leskernick houses and settlement forms with those from other parts of southern Britain. The argument in favour of permanence continues in chapter 18. But whichever way we tell the story, whether people lived at Leskernick all year round, or whether they returned regularly as the seasons came round, it was, in their cosmology, a place of huge significance. A place of deep attachment.

Chapter Six

The Western Settlement

Meanwhile, almost certainly overlapping with these developments, people began to settle on the west side of the hill. They had the Propped Stone on the hill top to their back, the view down to the crossing place across the Fowey River and up to the craggy hills, tors and tor cairns in front of them. ... After a while, they built a most impressive circular compound wall ... (Figure 6.1; see also Figure 5.1).

The Great House

On the western side of the hill the first houses were located in an area of dense clitter containing some of the largest and most impressive blocks on the hill. One such block, a huge whale-shaped stone, was incorporated into House 20 – the *ur* house, we surmise – and formed its monumental backstone. The house location, higher up on the hillside than any of the other of this earliest group of houses, meant that it was closer to the Propped Stone and closer to the great tabular outcrops on the hill top – closer to the ancestral powers of the hill.

It is a monumental house – 7.8 m north-south, 7.4 m west-east (Figure 6.2a and 6.2b). Its walls are up to 2 m thick, double faced, with lateral cross stones linking inner and outer walls and with rubble fill in between. The whale-shaped backstone is 4.2 m wide at the base and 1.7 m high, and the house walls seem to have at least in part ridden over it. A lot of the external wall facing seems to have been deliberately dismantled, but some horizontal stone course-work remains. The inner face is much more intact and is made of upright orthostats, including one fine triangular-shaped slab, almost a metre high, which in any other building on the hill would have served as a backstone but here is placed due north within the house wall.

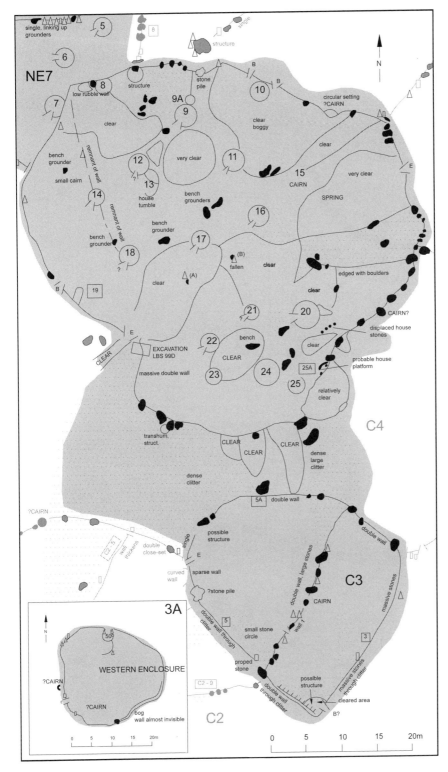

fig.6:1 Plan of the western settlement at Leskernick – the compound and the houses to the north (plan 3 and 3A on fig.5:1; key: fig.5:2).

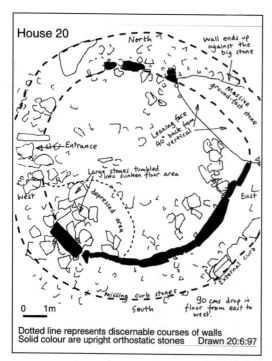

House 20

North

Wall ends up against the big stone

Massive ground-fast stone

Leaning face 40° back from vertical

Entrance

Large stones tumbled into sunken floor area

depressed area

West

East

External curb

missing curb stones

South

90 cms drop in floor from east to west.

0   1m

Dotted line represents discernable courses of walls
Solid colour are upright orthostatic stones   Drawn 20:6:97

fig.6:2 a) Annotated plan and elevation
of House 20; b) the whalestone and
inner wall of House 20.

North   East

Massive grounder 1·7m high
providing impressive back stone

South

Door jamb lying
on ground

south-west
stone

West   robbed out section   grounder

Entrance orientated
on Brown Willy

1m

1m

House 20
Inside Elevation Cross hatching represents stones in the outer walling

a

b

Other carefully selected stones are placed in the opposite wall, due south. The floor of the great house slopes steeply from east to west.[1] Initially, we thought this might be significant, the floor rising rather dramatically towards the backstone, but excavations in other houses suggests this steep slope is somewhat illusory and probably results from extensive tumble around the whale-stone, or perhaps from the construction of a stone platform immediately in front of this stone.

The entrance, defined by two fallen orthostatic door jambs, faces west towards Brown Willey and its summit cairn – the highest point on Bodmin Moor. It is the only house in the compound that is orientated in this way. The great house is very large: it could easily have accommodated an extended family of 10–15 people.

To the West of the Great House

There are several structures in a rough circle to the west of the great house – 'Houses' 21, 22, 24, 25, and 25A. They look quite different from House 20. They are smaller, between 5 and 6 m in diameter, with walls made of single or multiple boulder construction with no rubble core. Some of the walls incorporate earth-fast boulders, some have well-marked entrances. They seem more like cleared and levelled circular platform areas and perhaps originally the stone walls encircled wooden structures. Perhaps these structures were ancillary buildings to House 20 rather than dwelling houses.[2]

Within this eastern cluster there is one 'special' structure – 'House' 23. It is tiny, less than 4 m in diameter, and the central upright of the back wall is a very tall, thick, triangular-shaped stone, pointed at the top. This stone bears a rather close resemblance to the terminal stone of the stone row. As we shall see from the excavation findings below, it seems unlikely that this 'house' was ever roofed and quite likely that it was an open-air circular shrine structure, in which the arrangement of placed stones focused attention on the central upright. There are two associated radiocarbon dates (see Figure 4.1 and Figure 6.4). The first, from the floor of the structure is 1620–1430 cal BC (3260 ± 40 BP); the other, from a gully inside the structure, is 1270–940 cal BC (2890 ± 50 BP). These dates could indicate that this place remained in use over a long period of time, serving many different generations of Leskernick people.

The excavation of 'House' 23: A roofless shrine?
The locus of House 23

'House' 23 is positioned just inside the southern wall of the main compound of the western settlement, in front of the two largest houses (Houses 20 and 24). It is perched high above the impenetrable mass of spiky clitter that tumbles below the compound walling on the south-east side. Today, in spite of its small size (3.7 m diameter), the conspicuous 1.8 m high triangular stone in its walling makes it easily recognizable from a long distance. It can even be

fig.6:3 a) Mike Seager Thomas planning 'House' 23; b) the 'backstone' of 'House' 23, photos Ph-P.

distinguished from as far away as the hill across the Fowey Valley on which the Codda settlement is situated.

The excavations (Figure 6.4) show that there had been activity in the environs of H23 prior to its construction. They revealed a stake-hole immediately below an *in situ* wall stone. The hole was about 9 cm in diameter and 30 cm deep and had a pointed base. There is no evidence to suggest the purpose of the stake – it might have been used for something as mundane as an animal tethering post, or it might have been something more mystical such as a carved totem pole.

The structure of 'House' 23 (H23)

(Figures 6.3, 6.4; see also Figure 3.3)

H23 was an approximately circular stone-walled structure. The land surface sealed below the tumble from this wall had a date of 1620–1430 cal BC (Middle Bronze Age). This date doesn't tell us when the surface was sealed by the wall, although we know from the second date (see below, linear gully) that it would have been sealed by the Late Bronze Age or earlier.

There was no evidence of any postholes for roof supports. The triangular stone is considerably higher than the other stones in the wall circuit, and it would have required high walling and a large quantity of stones for it to be incorporated it into a roofed structure. The lack of sufficient accompanying wall rubble confirms that this did *not* happen. *H23 was therefore not a house.*

Prior to excavation, there appeared to be an entrance over a large flat earth-fast stone in the wall circuit, opposite the triangular stone. But in the course of excavation, minor stones only visible at the level of the turf became substantial stones across the 'entrance gap' on the inside of the earth-fast stone. We must now interpret H23 as a circular stone structure visually dominated by a tall triangular stone within the northern part of its circuit. In this scenario, entrance to the interior could only have been gained by stepping over the relatively low wall.

SH (Monday 7 June 1999): I went along to CT's and HB's caravan this evening. HB offered his spare waterproof trousers for a waterlogged excavator, which seemed a fine act! CT was in a particularly provocative mood about the excavators and snapped that we had deliberately reconstructed H23 to remove the impression of an entrance. CT has obviously been brooding about this for TWO years.

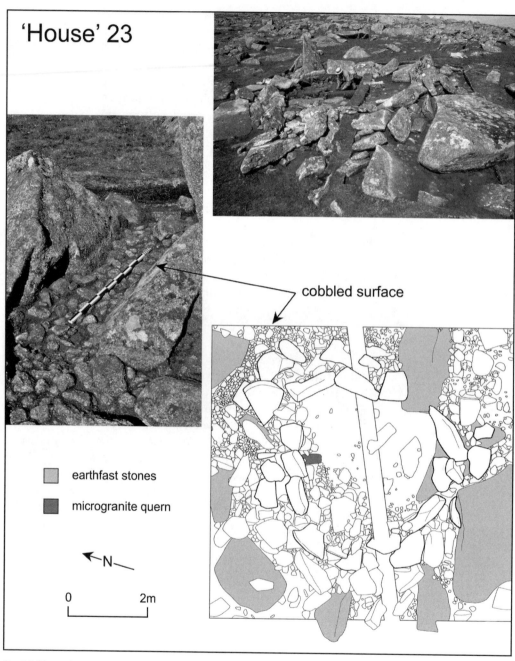

'House' 23

cobbled surface

earthfast stones

microgranite quern

N

0   2m

fig.6:4 'House' 23 in excavation. NB the cobbled surface (photo detail, scale 1 m) behind the 'backstone'. The 'backstone' (see fig. 6.4a) is the tall triangular stone behind the crouching excavator (topmost photo). Field credits: drawn by MST; photos: MST.

The inner face of the ruins of H23's walling was more continuous and had more remaining structural integrity than the outer. In particular, a series of near upright tabular boulders formed the inner face in the north-west circuit of the structure, and this part of the circuit also included the triangular stone. Some of these stones had visible sockets in the old land surface, implying that they had been dug in. To the east, the inner line of wall was continued by a series of more irregular boulders, and in the south-east part of the circuit the wall stones had been placed on top of flat earth-fast stones. To the west, outside the structure and on the slope of terrace, there was a mass of large mostly tabular boulders, which appear to be collapse from the wall. There were smaller stones between the wall skins.

The tall triangular stone is out of alignment with the circuit of the wall suggesting that it may be *in situ*, rather than a placed wall stone. Its upper end tilted outwards from the wall circuit and its base rested up against an *in situ* natural stone. Its near upright position can be explained by the pressures created by downslope sludging of periglacial clitter stones in the 'clitter stream' behind it.

SH (Tuesday, 18 June 1996): During my evening meal, MST came across to our caravan with a much-needed 'stone recording sheet', which he has made up for photocopying. It interestingly accounts for 'rod-shaped' stones, 'disc-shaped' stones, 'angular' stones, and so on, but does not have a box for triangular or whale-shaped stones. 'What about the triangular backstone in H23?' I asked. 'It's an angular rod', he replied.

Behind the triangular stone, and outside the 'house', there was a small area of cobbling. This cobbled surface was deceptively similar to the 'natural' slightly overlapping (imbricated) cobble-sized clitter identified elsewhere on site, but it was confirmed as cobbling because the soil horizon below it yielded a pollen profile in line with Bronze Age contexts from the site. The location of the cobbling between the wall of H23 and up against a large clitter boulder upslope indicates the existence of a regularly used passage way around that part of the site – one that must have become muddy enough to necessitate consolidation.

SH (Tuesday, 18 June 1996): Ceri dug a test pit to see how far the exterior cobbling at the back of H23 continued. Yesterday, in a rash moment of imagination, I had envisaged the whole of the western settlement being interlinked by cobbled ways and areas, but there was no cobbling in the test pit.

The linear trench in H23

(Figure 6.5)

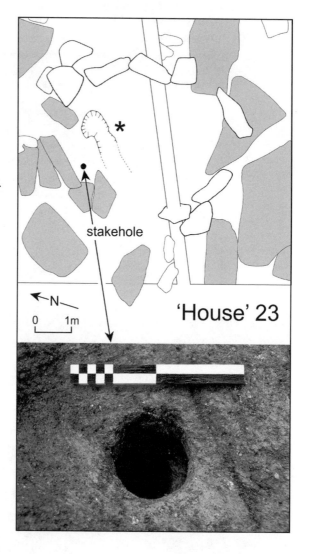

fig.6:5 Post-excavation plan of 'House 23' showing the unexcavated wall stones, 'natural' earthfast stones (shaded), stakehole (photo, scale 20 cm), and a 'linear trench' (asterisk) – perhaps for a ritual deposit. Field credits: Drawn by MST; photo: MST.

SH (17 June 1996): Two slabs of fine sandstone are now visible [later identified as microgranite] in H23's interior. ... CT wants them to be fallen 'menhirs', originally standing to one side of the triangular backstone. We currently interpret them as rubbing stones.

Inside H23, we found a linear cut or gully running approximately south-westwards from the triangular stone. Measured from the old land surface, it was about 20 cm deep and 40 cm wide. Downslope, it had been destroyed by rabbit burrows, but it had probably been about 2 m long. This gully contained two fills. Its upper fill comprised mostly granite rubble. In it lay two rectangular microgranite slabs (both c. 50 cm x c. 25 cm, and c. 9 cm thick), one of which turned out to be a quern-stone with its worn side face down. The lower fill comprised fine-grained sediments. The gully could not have been a covered sump or a drain because the lower fill supported the rubble. A radiocarbon date of cal BC 1270–940 (Late Bronze Age) was obtained from a small piece of charcoal from underneath one of the microgranite slabs. The gully could either be contemporary with, or later than, the wall of H23, since the upper fill of this feature abuts the inner north-west face of the wall. This, in turn, indicates that H23's walling is Late Bronze Age or earlier in date.

The positioning of this gully may be significant. Because we found nothing in the gully, and because it did not form an effective drain, it may well have had something buried in it that was organic and that rotted away. During the excavation, there was much discussion about the possibility of it being a grave cut for a foundation burial prior to the construction of the stone structure, and, as such, it was reminiscent of the grave cut for the poorly preserved remains of an extended male inhumation found under the hearth of one of the Bronze Age houses at Trethellan Farm (Nowakowski 1991: 45). The gully is long enough and wide enough to take a human body. On the other hand, it is not very deep (20 cm). Other forms of ritually charged deposits, such as libations or animal offerings, seem perhaps more probable. The backfill can be seen as a levelling exercise, which incorporated redundant settlement debris in its upper fill, included a large quartz hammer-stone, a burnt quartz hammer-stone, and the microgranite quern stone.

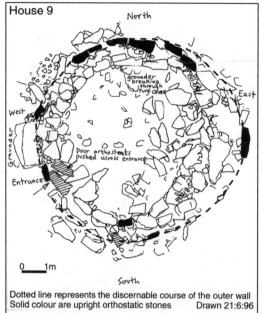

House 9

Dotted line represents the discernable course of the outer wall
Solid colour are upright orthostatic stones   Drawn 21:6:96

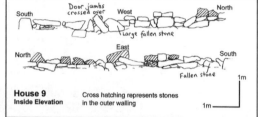

fig.6:6 a) Annotated plan and elevation of House 9; b) when the life of the house comes to an end, the door jambs are crossed.

b

The finds from H23

H23 not only had settlement debris incorporated into the fill of the gully, but it had a burnt rubber of microgranite in its walling and a burnt quartz pounder and several pieces of slate outside. These collectively suggest that H23, whatever its purpose, was built in a busy domestic part of the settlement. None of these finds are in their original-use locations and they probably do not relate to the active use of H23. It seems more likely that certain categories of settlement debris (e.g., querns and pounders) provided handy-sized stones for levelling disturbed areas or rubble for walling. Perhaps these essential daily working tools had a symbolism relating to the life of a community, and were deliberately incorporated into new houses and structures (see also Chapter 5, House 39).

A remarkable little structure?

There are few tangible clues to H23's function and it thus remains an enigma. Its lack of 'common sense' features suggests that it was a special place in front of a striking natural stone. It seems quite likely that during the Bronze Age this stone became a focus for ritual deposition (possibly a grave) and was incorporated into a circular structure or ring-cairn. For these various reasons, we have called H23 a shrine. This 'shrine' eventually began to decay and the circuit stones went through multiple stages of subsidence, indicated by some stones having more than one pressure-worn stone 'socket'.

To the rear of H23, sediments built up as a result of material being washed down from disturbed ground upslope of the structure. This suggests that there was intense activity upslope of H23. If it was a ritual structure, it was very much part of the daily life of the western settlement's inhabitants and it seems as though this part of the settlement continued to be intensively used into the Late Bronze Age.

The House Cluster to the North of the Great House

Perhaps a little later, a loose cluster of houses was built just to the north of House 20 (Figure 6.1). Like House 20, House 9, the largest house in this cluster, is upslope of the rest and on the edge of an area of dense clitter (Figures 6.6a and 6.6b). It is not as big as House 20, but it is substantial, with an internal diameter of 6.3 m. In this house, unlike most of the rest on Leskernick, the inner wall of the house is made of fine horizontal coursework, whereas the external wall is faced with tall and impressive uprights. The tallest and largest external uprights mark the northern and eastern cardinal points. The entrance faces south-west and seems to have been deliberately closed by pushing the door jambs in towards each other and placing a blocking stone in front of them (Color Plate 3b; see chapter 8). There is an external annexe constructed out of boulders.

The other houses in the cluster (Houses 11, 16, 17, 18, and 12)[3] are of varying sizes,[4] double walled, and often very ruinous. They were probably all domestic dwellings constructed and used around the same time, probably while House 20 and its ancillary structures were still in use. One small house (House 10, diameter c. 4.5 m) just north of the cluster is particularly depleted. The compound wall swings round it and it is possible that some of its stones were removed to make this wall.

There is one rather different structure on the western side of this house cluster. 'House' 14 is very small (3.2 m diameter) and again very robbed out. An unusually large and thin rectangular slab, 1.6 m long, now displaced and fallen, may have been the original backstone. The form of the house may originally have been quite similar to 'House' 23 with a large and impressive stone set opposite the entrance, and, like it, may have been an open air structure rather than roofed. Like 'House' 23, and 'House' 34 in the southern settlement, it may have been a shrine. Two cairns within the cluster probably date to a later phase (see chapter 7).

Because many of these houses are in poor condition it is often hard to discover the house door orientation, but where they can be discovered they, like all the rest in the compound except House 20, face south-westwards towards the Fowey Valley, the hillsides dotted with occasional settlements, and the skyline – the silhouetted tors of Catshole, Tolborough, and Codda, and the great spinal ridge of Brown Willy, all capped with tor cairns. The perspective on the landscape is thus entirely different to the one experienced from the southern settlement. These people saw the setting, rather than the rising of the sun. They lived in among the rocks, and the distant view from their houses was not of subdued rounded hills capped with cairns but of rocky outcrops surrounded by and built over with tor cairns.

It was also very different in that, as people moved around between the houses the great Propped Stone on top of the hill formed a continuous presence behind and upslope of their dwellings. With the exception of House 3 (see chapter 7, pp. 172–173), and the houses just outside the northern edge of the compound, these are the only houses on the hill from which it is visible. It seems highly likely that the first settlers chose to be located within its protecting orbit.

This group of dwellings could have accommodated around 30 people. So when the compound wall was built encircling the great house and the northern cluster, 40 or more people might have been involved in its construction.

The Great Compound

After a while, a massive wall was built encircling all these houses – the Great House with its ancillary buildings and shrine and the northern cluster with

fig.6:7 The substantial, finely constructed, wall just south of the compound entrance that leads to the spring and to the ford across the Fowey: a) pre-excavation with the ranging pole on the 'outside', downslope side, scale 2 m; b) pre-excavation from the 'outside' of the wall looking upslope to the wall and beyond into the settlement area; c) view b in excavation; d) detail of wall exterior during excavation and view c in a subsequent stage of excavation, scale 50 cm; e) the wall section removed showing the flat 'natural' stone at ground level on which the wall was built, scales 50 cm and 1 m. Photos: MST.

its shrine (Figure 6.1; Color Plate 4a). On the southern side of the compound the wall swings around 'House' 25A, whilst further round, on the north side, it takes avoiding action around House 10. The building of these houses thus predates the wall.

The compound wall is the most massive and distinctive wall on the hill. It is of double thickness with a rubble infill, and is visible from each and every house. On its southern side, it picks up and builds on the contours of the hill and links and rides over a series of huge earth-fast stones. Close to House 20, an enormous rock has been hefted on top of an even larger flat earth-fast stone. This, the most dramatic stone in the wall, is situated alongside the Great House – itself the only house in the compound that incorporates a massive earth-fast stone within its construction.

Below the wall on this (the southern) side of the hill, the ground falls away abruptly to a dense jumble of clitter. Looking up from below, this increases the awesomeness of the compound wall, and for someone walking across the moor towards Leskernick from the south the wall forms a strange dragon-toothed silhouette. On the northern side, the wall is less dramatic but it snakes its way through dense clitter and provides a contrast to the chaos of surrounding stone.

The compound slopes down towards the west, and in the western section of the wall there is a fine funnel-shaped entrance. The path from the compound leads out through this entrance down towards a small spring and then continues on towards a crossing place over the Fowey River. This is one of the most dramatically visible lines of movement within the settlements on the hill. It requires little imagination to see people walking down to the spring to fill their containers, taking their animals down to the river, setting out on expeditions to cut rushes, catch fish, trap animals, gather plant foods along the river banks, or trudging home with bundles of fire-wood.

CT (19 June 1995): After tea we ... started looking at and following some of the enclosure boundaries rather than simply walking across them. In one we found a superb gap with an evident track that led directly down out of the western settlement area to a ford across the Fowey. This must surely have been a place for bathing, washing and gathering during the Bronze Age. ... This little discovery, right at the end of the afternoon, brings the whole project and settlement area alive for me once more.

Just to the east of this funnel-shaped entrance, a small part of the compound wall was excavated (LB S99D). Here, the wall was made of carefully chosen square blocks, tightly fitted together, and, as further round to the south, it falsely crests a steep clitter slope to achieve rampart-like properties (Figure 6.7). Given the builders' apparent concern to create a neat outside wall face – more so than anywhere else on site – it is surely at least in part a strategically placed social statement. It would have been highly visible, highly impressive, to people making their way from the surrounding hills to the river crossing place and thence to the settlement.

There is a substantial build-up of earth (9 cm) against the back of this wall, and this, in conjunction with the build-up around the back of 'House' 23, suggests that there was a lot of activity within the compound resulting in heavily trodden areas, eroded land surfaces, and downslope accumulation of sediments. Although today's peat deposits and accumulations of earth disguise the stony nature of the compound interior, it is still possible to see cleared corridors within the compound – still possible to imagine the people who lived in the compound walking uphill from the river crossing place, past the spring, through the entrance, and up the main corridor between the two groups of houses – the one with House 9 as its focus; the other with the Great House 20 (Figure 6.1). This pathway runs up to a stone setting that consists of a single upright surrounded by what must originally have been a small boulder circle. It continues to another large (now fallen) orthostat upslope to the east. Standing at the compound entrance, this orthostat would have stood out against the skyline. Beyond this orthostat, a boggy area may have contained a spring and provided another source of water. Upslope of the boggy area there is a smaller entrance within the compound wall.

Between Houses 24 and 23 and immediately upslope and east from House 20 there are relatively stone-free areas that seem to have been cleared, and there are others close to the houses in the northern part of the compound. Perhaps the ground had been cleared to create small garden plots.

There are also numerous flat bench-like grounders within the compound and those close to the houses would have provided convenient seating and working areas (see plan). One such grounder, for example, is linked by a low wall to the entrance area of House 17.

There are no dividing walls within the compound, only a few short wall sections – one, for example, connects House 18 and Structure 14 and then extends from Structure 14 to the compound wall near to House 7. Another short stretch links the annexe of House 9 with the compound wall, making its way across a particular dense clitter mass.

A couple of small structures, 8 and 19, were built up against the wall of the compound. They are rough looking and could have been used for storage or animal shelters, or they could be transhumance shelters dating to a much later period (P. Herring, pers. comm. 12 April 1999).[5]

Not only was the compound much in use, but we suspect that there were small cleared plots at the foot of the boulder-strewn slope below the southern wall of the compound. Here, as the clitter spread levels out, there are well-defined clearances. Here again, we can imagine people from the compound planting, gathering, talking …

BB (23 June 1997): Pete's [Pete Herring's] notion is that, at first, in both the southern and western settlement, the occupation was seasonal. Then they tried a little cultivation. When it worked, they settled. Later the settlement grew smaller.

CT (14 June 1996): Pete maintains that the western settlement was a pastoral summer occupation, claiming that it would not be suitable to live there during the dark winter months. You would simply trip over the stones in the long dark nights and break your necks! But I simply don't envisage it as a summer site for herders.

Enclosures South and West of the Great Compound

With some hesitation, we suggest that as part of the early settlement of the western side of the hill, the people built two large enclosures (Figure 6.1). We hesitate because they could also have been built somewhat later.

The first of these walled enclosures (C3) – a neat semicircular affair – lies south of the massive clitter spreads and the small cleared areas below the Great Compound. Its northern edge is marked by a double wall (5A) that curves round and runs over a number of large grounders; its eastern wall (3) is built of massive stones and, as it moves south, runs through clitter. The southern edge is marked by a double wall (5) that, again, runs through clitter along part of its length. A skimpier north/south wall (1) divides the enclosure in two.[6] Was the enclosure built to keep animals in – or, perhaps, out?

> Pete Herring (pers. comm., 12 April 1999??) Could it be an exclosure rather than to 'hold animals'? Keeping animals out, not in. In those early days when, as you rightly say, I saw the western settlement as pastoral, I imagined the main enclosures as designed to keep animals out rather than in.

To the west of the Great Compound entrance and the spring is a roughly circular enclosure that is somewhat similar to the semicircular enclosure (Figure 6:1 3A). There is a very small structure just inside the enclosure on the north side that could have been used for storage or as a place to keep a few animals.[7]

Houses Just North of the Great Compound

Just to the north of the wall of the Great Compound there is another small group of houses (Houses 5 to 7 with House 4 a little further north) that may represent a budding off from the compound settlement (Figures 6.1 and 7.3). In one of these, House 7, the compound wall actually forms the back wall of the house (Figures 6.1 and 7.3). These houses are all modest in size (5.7 m, 4.7 m, 4.2 m, and 4 m respectively), double walled, and appear to be levelled into the slope. Two (Houses 5 and 6) face west; one (House 7) faces south-west. House 4 is too dilapidated for the orientation to be clear. One, House 5, has a large grounder incorporated into the back wall opposite the entrance, whilst-Houses 5 and 7 both have orthostatic door jambs. In addition, House 7 has an external step. Below House 7, a small wall extends to the compound wall and between it and the house entrance is a small cleared area. House 6 has a large bench-like grounder to the south-west of the entrance, providing a fine seat; House 7 has a large low grounder to the north of its entrance; and to the south of House 5 is a massive kerbed grounder.

We end the first instalment of the story at this point. We accept entirely that we cannot be sure of the order of things. This is our best guess and it might easily have to be changed if and when more excavation takes place. Indeed, even with the archaeological information that we have already garnered from the hill, we could tell the story differently. For example, close to, and west of, this northern outlier of houses there is a particularly well-constructed enclosure wall (wall 1) running north/south (Figure 7: 3); there are also many small structures and segments of wall in the dense clitter to the east and north of the houses. We have assumed that these were not built at the same time as the outlier and that they tie in with the later construction and use of House 1. House 1, which was excavated and which we shall talk about it at some length in the next chapter, has radiocarbon dates of 1430–1205 cal BC, 1515–1305 cal BC, and 1030–810 cal BC. Two of these dates overlap with both H23 inside the great compound and with H39 over on the southern hillslope. We could, therefore, quite legitimately concertina the developments on the hill and have most things happening at much the same time. Or, using the same dates, we could draw the sequence out a little. We have opted to do the latter – thus, when the story opens again in chapter 7, a few generations have come – and gone.

Chapter Seven

Time Goes On

Introduction

In the last chapter we settled for two kernels of original settlement, one on the south side of the hill with the small 'enclave' and the house circle, and the other on the west side with two groups of houses enclosed within the Great Compound and another just outside and close up to the north wall of the compound. We suggested that there were probably a couple of large enclosures associated with the early western settlement, and that on the southern side there was a radial accretion of enclosures. It seems likely that these developments occurred over a few centuries and that we are talking about maybe eight families or so on the south side, and something similar on the west. Perhaps between 100 and 200 people.

This chapter takes the story forward. It covers several more centuries, several more generations, and spans, in conventional terms, the later Middle and Late Bronze Ages. The process of building, abandonment, sometimes further reuse, and then gradual withdrawal are complicated. We do not pretend that we have understood all the subtle ordering of events. We can see, for example, that on both the western and southern hillside, people began to build isolated houses within their own enclosures. There were six or so such houses. But we are not sure whether these houses existed alongside the earlier closer set households, or whether the latter had gone out of use. We rather think that they had, and that what is happening is a change from rather separate settlements on either side of the hill to a community of individual households encompassing both sides of the hill. This community is bound together by the perimeter walls that mark the edge of the settlement towards the hill top, and by the corridor that wends its way from the bottom of the hill towards the hill top and the Propped Stone. It is a community that continues to define itself in terms of its relationship to the stones – stones that are part of the house or enclosure walls, or that relate to the tabular outcrops near the top of the hill, or that are picked out from among the clitter spreads.

We can watch the everyday processes of house and wall maintenance – see the continual attention required to strengthen or alter these structures. We can witness the life cycles of house and field, the diverse states of use, shoring, dilapidation, scavenged depletion, and deliberate slighting and closing down. Sometimes we see the formal decommissioning of houses, and sometimes we believe that the houses of the living became the houses of the dead.

And then, perhaps already starting in the Middle Bronze Age and definitely within the Late Bronze Age, we chart a process of more radical decline – enclosures on the lower edges of the settlement go out of use and often become liminal spaces – places for the dead, places of memory. In one instance at least, we seem to see the way in which, in the last stages of occupation, the Leskernick community begins to break up. House 1 begins to crumble, is perhaps temporarily abandoned, and then, within the Late Bronze Age, is reoccupied in a much more make-shift way. If this pattern is more widespread across the hill, it would suggest that the settled households have packed up and gone, and instead some fraction of the community, perhaps herdspeople, return on a more seasonal basis to make use of the summer pastures. Eventually, at some time in the Late Bronze Age, even this activity is no longer viable, the human beings depart and other animals and plants reclaim the settlements.

We are aware that this chapter is very detailed. Our excuse, if one is needed, is that it is only through what Clifford Geertz has called 'thick description' that we can begin to suggest something of the complexity of people's lives and their encounters with the material world (Geertz 1973). We hope that in charting the intricacies of house and wall structure, of clitter forms, of 'cairn' and 'stone pile', we will allow the reader to appreciate the give-and-take between people's understandings of how the world should be, and their continuous day-to-day or more long-term reappraisals and negotiations, the ways they find to cope with the contingencies that arise. There is a biographical depth to the story of each and every house and enclosure, and there are many different ways to take things forward. The people of the hill both reproduce and negotiate what is meaningful to them and thus subtly change their relations to each other and to the world around them. Their world view structures life, but it is created through their individual actions and is therefore always in motion.

Pete Herring (pers. comm., February 2004): Think of the seasons
and the life cycles ... the rites de passage ... How differences in
health, character, the competence of individuals, are also part of
the story. Think about more transitory things like the weather
and wild animals, and domesticates and birds.

We are going to take you on a tour of the hill. This time, we start on the
western side of the hill, move north, then south-west, then south. But remember, in this later period of settlement, the people of the hill were probably one
interrelated community.

At the end of the chapter, we briefly return to some of the more general
questions concerning sequence and causality. Relationships beyond the hill
will have to wait until chapters 16–18.

The Western Side of the Hill
Within the Great Compound

A striking feature of the houses in the Great Compound is their ruinous
state when compared to the houses in the southern settlement. In particular,
many of the stones that make up the external skin have been robbed out or
displaced. We think that much of this destruction occurred during the later
Bronze Age and that many of the houses were decommissioned during the
time when the more isolated houses were being built and lived in.

The dismantling of these houses was partial. It was not so much an act
of destruction as one of transformation. Perhaps some of the external orthostats were taken away and used as foundation stones for some of the isolated
houses creating a sense of continuity with the past. Sometimes, as with the
Great House 20, the outer orthostats were removed and piled up outside the
house. In one or two cases the house was symbolically closed. House 9 – the
second of the big houses in the compound – had its door jambs crossed and
a blocking stone placed in front of them (Figure 6.6b). Other houses either
had their external wall kerb removed and/or their centres infilled with displaced orthostats and rubble. Thus, in House 18, close to House 9, much of the
interior was covered with slabs including a large number of small triangular
shaped stones set upright. Perhaps in this way the house was returned to
'nature' – the house stone returned to clitter.

In some cases, the houses may have been reused and may have become
houses for the dead. The surface evidence is not very clear, but it seems as
though a few houses may have had cairns built within them or may have been
dismantled to create a cairn nearby. For example, 'House' 14 – the house shrine
– has been much disturbed. It may have been 'closed' and then partially dismantled to create a small cairn 4 m downslope (Figure 7.1). This cairn, 4 x 3 m,

has traces of a kerb infilled with small stones and incorporates a very weathered stone that may originally have been an orthostat in House 14. 'House' 22, one of the ancillary buildings alongside the great house (20) may also have been transformed from house to cairn. It is filled with larger and smaller slabs except for a small clear area just inside the doorway. And again, Structure 8, a small oval single-wall structure built up against the north wall of the compound, contains two cairn-like structures inside its tumbled walls, one in the north-east part of the interior made of small stones with the remains of a kerb abutting the compound wall, the other formed out of the remains of the western wall.[1]

We propose the conversion of houses to cairns with some caution. As we shall see below, excavation can indicate alternative scenarios, as do the recent excavations on Stannon Down.[2]

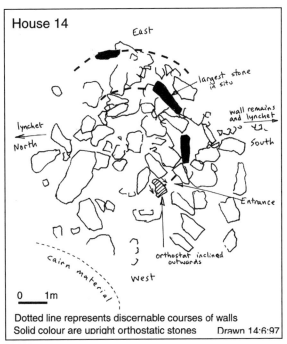

fig.7:1 Annotated plan of House 14.

North of the Great Compound

We have talked about the small cluster of houses (4 to 7) that seem to be part of the earlier settlement (see chapter 6 and Figure 6.1). House 4, which lies a little to the north of the others, has been robbed-out and is very dilapidated. The concentration of tumble in the northern part of the house may mean that the house was reused to make a cairn around a central orthostat that had originally been an internal wall slab.

North again is a large isolated house – House 1 – with two associated enclosures. And to the west and upslope of House 1 is another large and rather special house – House 3. A substantial and well-made perimeter wall (1) runs north/south between House 1 and the north edge of the Great Compound wall (Figures 7.2 and 7.3). It skirts to the west of the small house cluster (4 to 7) built alongside the compound wall. We think that this wall is later in date than the cluster and forms part of major ritual focus associated with the dense clitter mass that extends downslope from House 3.

We shall look first at House 1, then turn to House 3, and then move to the complex ritual working of the clitter mass and to the construction of the fine perimeter walls, both the westerly one just mentioned, and the long northern perimeter wall.

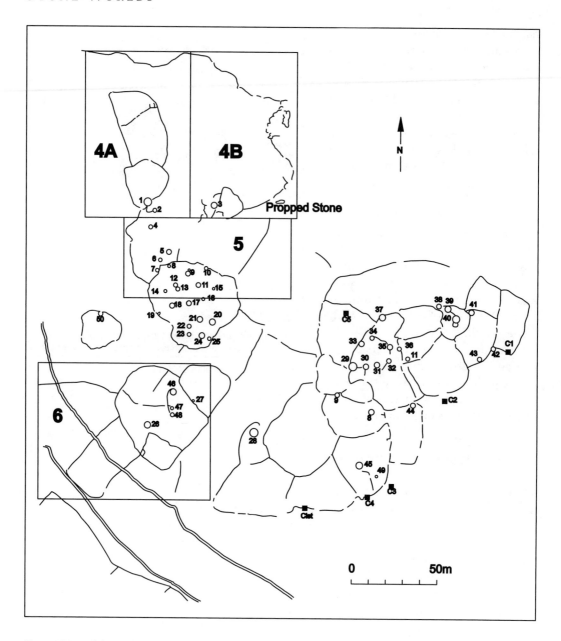

Fig. 7:2 Map of the Leskenick settlements and enclosures giving the position of the more detailed plans.

House 1
(Figures 7.2–7.8)

House 1 is the most northerly house at Leskernick and has a smaller building (House 2) alongside it (Figure 7.5). Both are sited on relatively clitter-free,
sloping ground with spiky, jumbled clitter masses both up- and downslope of

them. From outside the house, looking across the Fowey, Brown Willy seems omnipresent. Perhaps it was this setting that made the excavators feel that House 1 was much calmer and less windswept than House 39 in the southern settlement.

House 1 was very large (measuring about 12 m across), but because of the experience gained in the excavation of House 39, it took much less time – a single five-week season – to complete the excavation. The strategy used was to leave some areas unexcavated whilst exposing a sufficiently large area to get an understanding of the posthole configuration, the entrance area, the different types of floor surfaces, and any artefact distribution patterning that might be retrievable. The baulks were positioned to answer specific stratigraphic questions, irrespective of how bizarre their configuration would look on the excavation plan. One particular question concerned the large rubble pile that dominated the uppermost side of the house. The surveyors had earmarked this as a possible house-cairn. There was also an area around the front of the house that seemed very suitable for outdoor activities, so this area and the one behind the house were also excavated.

Life of – and at – House 1
The beginning of House 1

One of the last features found during the excavation of House 1 may well have been among the first features created by the original inhabitants (Figures 7.6 and 7.7). It was a large oval pit at the back of the house, opposite the house entrance. It was under the flagged floor of the house and thus predated its earliest occupation phase (see below). It was filled with clean rab, suggesting that the cut had been made and then immediately back filled with the material dug from it. We propose that it was a deliberately dug hole in which something organic, something that left no trace in the acid environment of Leskernick, was buried. Given that elsewhere in southern and south-central Britain, Middle and Later Bronze Age houses and their enclosures were often associated with small-scale votive deposits (Barrett, Bradley, and Green 1991: 225), we surmise that the oval pit contained a foundation deposit for House 1. The size of the hole suggests something quite large, perhaps a slaughtered animal, or even the remains of a human ancestor.

Living in House 1

The house was subcircular, and its floor the natural slope of the hill. The shape and slope of the house challenges the notion that Bronze Age houses had level floors and true circularity. Such norms should be seen as regionally specific. They are based on the post-built round houses terraced into the chalk downs of south-central Britain. Elsewhere, things may have been done differently.

163

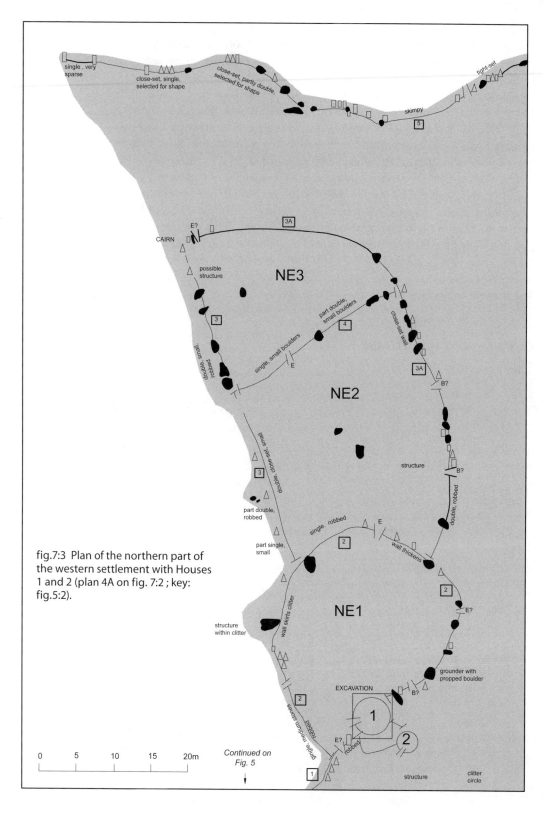

fig.7:3 Plan of the northern part of the western settlement with Houses 1 and 2 (plan 4A on fig. 7:2 ; key: fig.5:2).

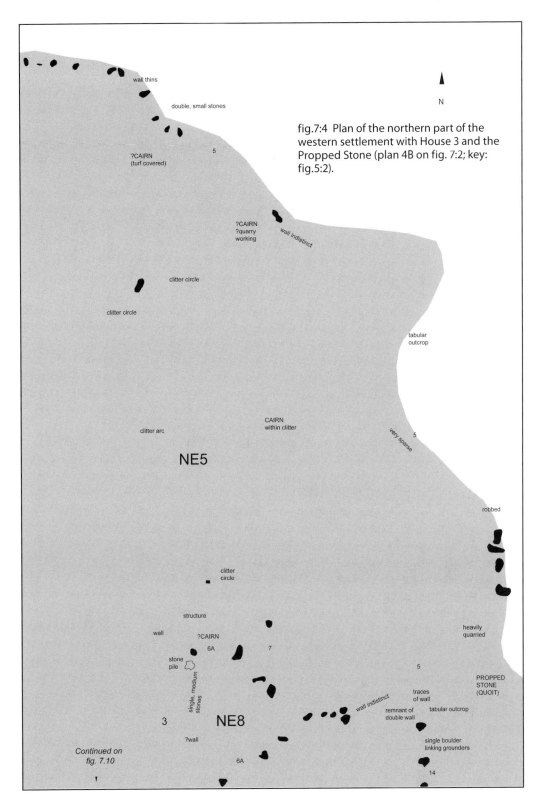

wall thins

double, small stones

?CAIRN
(turf covered)

5

fig.7:4 Plan of the northern part of the
western settlement with House 3 and the
Propped Stone (plan 4B on fig. 7:2; key:
fig.5:2).

N

?CAIRN
?quarry
working

wall indistinct

clitter circle

clitter circle

tabular
outcrop

clitter arc

CAIRN
within clitter

very sparse

5

NE5

robbed

clitter
circle

structure

wall

?CAIRN

heavily
quarried

6A

7

stone
pile

single, medium stones

5

PROPPED
STONE
(QUOIT)

3

NE8

traces
of wall

tabular outcrop

wall indistinct

remnant of
double wall

?wall

single boulder
linking grounders

Continued on
fig. 7.10

6A

14

165

fig.7:5 Aerial photograph of northern part of western settlement. House 1 is on the southern edge of the circular enclosure. The elongated enclosure running north is very visible. Northwards again is the snaking perimeter wall. To the southwest are the tabular outcrops on the hill top, and centre south is House 3. Kind permission of the RCHME.

House 1's wall comprised an inner and an outer skin of large boulders mostly packed with smaller stones. The wall skins included vertical orthostats and horizontal coursed stones. For the most part, this walling lay directly on the pre-existing land surface. The Sites and Monuments' Record indicated that the house entrance was on the south-east side, but on closer inspection this gap proved to be the result of wall collapse. In fact, the entrance of the house was located at the lowest (downslope) part of the wall and was orientated west-south-west, looking out towards Brown Willy. Just as at House 39 in the southern settlement, the old land surface in this entrance area comprised several very large flat ground-fast boulders (Figure 7.8).

The precise site of House 1, unlike those of House 39 and 'House' 23, lacked a suitable grounder for use as a backstone (Figure 7.6). Instead, a large tabular stone and a smaller triangular stone were placed opposite the entrance. Additionally, the height difference between the front and the back of the house, with the upslope back being more than a metre higher than the downslope front, gave greater visual importance to the back of the house, and possibly to those who occupied or used that part of it.

There was a stone-free area in the centre of the house that included a number of shallow cuts where the floor surface had been evened-out by the removal of stones. We imagined this to be the working and/or entertaining hub of the house, with a floor covering of skins, textiles, and dried vegetation. Outside of this central area, the floor was 'hard', being flagged with flat boulders of local stones (Figure 7.8). These flags had been laid around the posts that supported the roof, and they continued up to the house walls – thus below the eves of the roof – and to the flat clitter boulders that comprised the entrance area.

The postholes for the roof support measured up to 35 cm across and were evenly spaced about 1.5 m from the inner skin of the house wall (Figure 7.7). They were presumably linked by a ring-beam, which would have spread the load of the house roof. A packed posthole close to the centre of the house may have supported an internal partition, if the post that it contained was linked with one of the roof support posts by a textile or hurdle screen (Figure 7.7). We have a Middle Bronze Age radiocarbon date from one of the postholes (cal BC 1515–1305) and another similar date, cal BC 1430–1205, from a shallow (?storage) pit at the back of the house, against the wall.

Close to the front of the house there was a small pit with burnt stones but no charcoal (Figure 7.7). The feature perhaps provided heat, or generated purifying sauna-like steam when doused with water, with the stones having first been heated elsewhere. Quantities of charcoal recovered from the sediments across the house floor may indicate that there were surface hearths for cooking somewhere within the house interior, but these have left no other trace. It is perhaps worth noting the general dearth of hearths across the moor.

House 1

entrance area

backstone

cairn/revetment

fig.7:6 House 1.
Photo: MST.

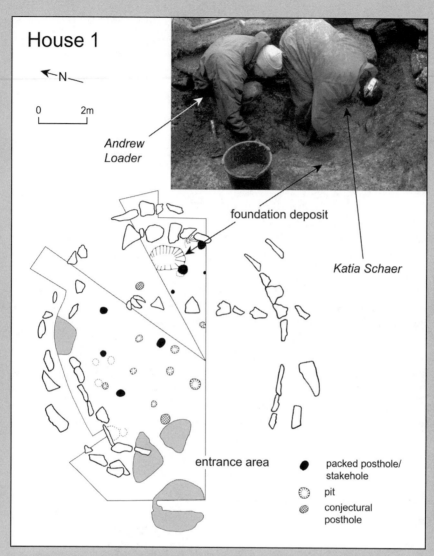

House 1

N

0   2m

*Andrew
Loader*

foundation deposit

Katia Schaer

entrance area

● packed posthole/
   stakehole

⊙ pit

⊛ conjectural
   posthole

fig.7:7 Excavation at House 1 showing the pit that might have held a foundation offering. Field credits: plan: SA; photo: MST.

Activities within and around House 1

Artefact finds from the house floor and the ancient land surface outside the house included struck flint and quartz, slate (often incised), a small quartz boulder battered on one side and best interpreted as an anvil, stone pounders, and a few sherds of Middle Bronze Age–type pottery.[3] The spatial distribution of this material implies the existence of internal social and/or functional zoning within the house. The sparseness of finds from the flagged area – which would have acted as a 'finds trap' – might indicate that it was used for sleeping and storage. Most finds came from the stone-free area in the centre of the house. The chipped quartz, pottery sherds, and slate pieces were wholly concentrated within the post ring. If this area had been covered in skins and textile, it would have been a place where small objects could easily have been lost. Outside,

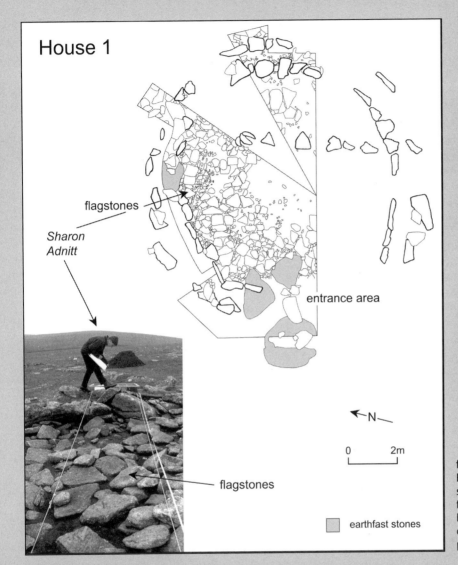

House 1

flagstones

*Sharon
Adnitt*

entrance area

flagstones

←N←

0   2m

earthfast stones

fig.7:8
Excavation plans
showing the
flagged floor of
House 1. Filed
credits: plan: SA;
photo: MST.

downslope of the entrance, there was also an abundance of chipped quartz. As at House 39, there was a complete absence of finds from behind the house.

The incisions on the slate from House 1 are broad, and mostly comprise groups of parallel lines (Figure 5.7). As with the slate from outside House 39, this suggests that they were used as cutting surfaces. Slate does not occur naturally on site (see House 39), and its deliberate import might mean that people in the household needed something that provided a flat surface that allowed precise cutting activities. They might, for example, have been used for cutting leather. The broader width of the incisions on the House 1 slate suggests that the people in House 1 were using flint rather than metal blades as cutting tools.[4]

The quartz chips, which were found inside and in front of the house, are similar to those recovered from House 39. They do not appear to be usable tools in their own right (although the possible role of chipped quartz in ritual depositions has been discussed in the context of House 39). The quartz chips are perhaps associated with the same activity as the three quartz pounders and the quartz anvil. The anvil and the two pounders came from inside the house – one of the pounders had been broken and then reused, and the other was very large. Fragments of another pounder were found in front of the house. The quartz chips could have been waste from the disintegration of quartz anvils and pounders which were being used to break down some unknown hard material. Given the evidence for postmedieval tin-streaming close to Leskernick hill, it seems possible that this 'unknown material' was cassiterite (tin oxide); alternatively, it may have been cassiterite associated with quarried or eluvial vein quartz.[5] Either way, cassiterite is absent from our excavated finds. This is not particularly surprising because the cassiterite would have been carefully curated and exchanged off site. As suggested earlier (see chapter 5, House 39), it seems highly likely that the exploitation of tin did occur at Leskernick, that it was an important and valuable resource, and that we have underestimated the role of tin exploitation in sustaining the upland communities of the southwest (Ballam, Smith, and Waintwright 1982; Johnson and Rose 1998: 48; Penhallurick 1987).

> The tin industry has underwritten the farming economy for centuries in those areas of the country where farming has always been hard, and this may have had a long ancestry. (Johnson and Rose 1998: 76)

The death or repair of House 1

SH (8 June 1996): During the afternoon, I spent some time with CT who is fast developing cairnitis. He showed me 'House 15', which I agreed did look more like a cairn than a house. The possibility of numerous cairns within the western settlement provides new dimensions – do ruined houses mimic cairns or are 'dead' houses converted into cairns?

SH (16 June 1996): Arrived back at our caravan to find that CT had left the English Heritage Bodmin Survey volume conspicuously opened at a page filled with cairn profiles. I have a sinking feeling that the western settlement has now wholly metamorphosed into a cairn-field. Spent the rest of the evening in the bar.

SH (21 June 1996): Just before lunch once more I went around the western settlement with B and CT, ... several of the 'cairns' were to the side, not the middle, of the interior, including that of House 1.

It has been suggested for the Bronze Age lowland Britain that rites of artefact deposition and breakage were used to mark the end of a building's life. This act of closing down a structure included the placement of artefact-rich levelling layers across the house floor, and the breaking up and burying of household possessions (Brück 1999). Prior to excavation, we thought that the 'cairn' across the back of House 1 might be part of a closing-down process. We envisaged that when a house was left, or its final occupant died, it was transformed into a cairn, and thus into a metaphoric dead house.

Our excavation suggests a more mundane explanation of the piled stones. It seems that the back walling of House 1 had a built-in weakness. As a result, a major wall collapse occurred. The excavated evidence suggests that the occupants of the house attempted to shore up this collapsing wall. On the one hand, a substantial posthole was dug in against the back wall. This would have been too far under the eves to serve as a roof support, and was probably a shoring post. On the other hand, they piled up stones outside the back of the house, on top of a collapsed skin stone and the packing stones that had spilt out from it, to act as a brace to the internal shoring (labelled as 'cairn/revetment' in Figure 7.6). For once, we catch a glimpse of the maintenance required to keep a house in good heart.

Several hundred years later, during the final gradual decay of the house, more walling collapsed into an area that was by then defined by an internal division (see below), and coalesced these various elements of ruination into a cairn-like feature. Such an interpretation is less evocative than the idea of transforming dead houses into cairns, and begs the question of how to interpret the cairn-like piles associated with other houses in the western settlement. Irrespective of whether other 'dead' buildings were purposefully transformed into cairns or whether, through decay, they merely metamorphosed into something cairn-like, they would have created potent visual forms of abandoned homes.

Beyond repair: House 1 in the Late Bronze Age

The excavation of House 1 points to two distinct occupation phases. First, there were the people and their offspring who built the house, lived in it, repaired it, and eventually abandoned it. Second, later on, but still within the Bronze Age, a stone partition comprising a line of stones was placed across the floor of the house, and the back area was reoccupied. The partition cuts across the earlier activity area with its associated incised slates and pottery sherds. Within the partitioned back area of the house, a hearth partially overlays the fill of a posthole belonging to the post-ring, suggesting that its new occupant(s) modified the house after it had lost its roof and the supporting posts had rotted or been taken away. The hearth produced a Late Bronze Age date of cal BC 1030–810.

The exact nature of the partitioning at the back of the house is difficult to ascertain. We found no postholes nor any additional rubble to suggest that the partition might have been the base of a wall. It is possible that the structure had a skin or textile lean-to roof, supported and raised on one side by the old house wall and fixed to the ground on the downslope side by the line of stones that mark the partition. Perhaps by this time the settlement was being used purely on a seasonal basis and the occupant was a shepherd. Certainly the lean-to area would have been uncomfortably small for more than one or, at most, two people.

To the south of, but not touching House 1, lies House 2. It is only 4.7 m in diameter but is quite elaborate. It is double-walled, has a small triangular backstone opposite the south-west facing entrance, a larger stone – now slumped forward – due east in the inner wall and another, roughly similar in shape and size, in the western wall. This certainly looks like a small dwelling house and, given its proximity to House 1 and the fact that the two houses are linked by a small roughly square open area enclosed by boulders and grounders, we imagine that the occupants of the two houses were closely related.

To the north of House 1 in an area where the clitter thins out there are two large enclosures that clearly relate to the house (Figure 7.4). The first, built alongside the house is a well-made, more-or-less circular enclosure (NE1). The south-western end of this enclosure wall (2) seems to butt against the north end of the western perimeter wall (1) that runs down to the Great Compound.

To the north, and attached to the circular enclosure, is a very large, roughly rectangular enclosure. This enclosure was subsequently subdivided by a fairly flimsy wall (4), with roughly two-thirds lying to the south (NE2) and one-third to the north (NE3) of the divide.

BB (15 June 1996): I went with Henry and Matt around part of the enclosure of house 1. They've done a good job. ... What is very striking is how similar their enclosure walls, in this northern section, are to mine in the southern one. What does this say about the connections and chronology?

The Shaman's House (House 3), the mini-tor, and the Clitter Lobe

Higher up the slope, above House 1, lies an exceptional building, House 3. Unexcavated, we leave it to the survey team to describe it (Figures 7.9a, 7.9b, 7.10).

Leskernick Survey Team (16 August 1997):

This house is one of the most northerly at Leskernick. It is peculiarly isolated and set high up the slope and levelled into it. It appears to be circular in form but is in fact very irregular in plan. The internal diameter west to east is 7.8 m. The walls, rather than being truly circular in form, consist of straight lines of coursing with curved joins. The southern half of the house appears to be almost triangular in plan.

The entrance facing west to Rough Tor on the horizon is marked by two fallen orthostats. South of the entrance a large grounder has been incorporated into the wall.

The walls vary in thickness between 1.1 and 1.3 m. The south-west section of the house wall appears to run up to another large grounder marking the edge of a dense clitter mass immediately to the south of the house. The southern wall is built up against this clitter mass, which extends to the 'field-shrine/mini tor' 10 m to the south (see below).

The internal wall face is made up entirely of a horizontal coursing of well-chosen slabs. Between outer and inner wall there is a rubble core and traces of cross-slabs indicating a cellular construction. No backstone survives. The stone coursing of the eastern wall is particularly well constructed. There is much tumble derived from this wall in the upslope eastern sector of the house. External wall orthostats are either missing or slight.

Internally, there are traces of a dividing wall running north-south to the middle of the house. This would block a view of the inner back wall from the entrance and a view out of the doorway from the back of the house.

Outside the house, in front of the entrance, there are traces of a low platform or annexe, semicircular in form, 3.5 m long west-east and 6.5 m north-south. Garrow Tor, with its extensive settlement areas, and Rough Tor and Brown Willy are visible from here: a window onto another world.

The Shaman's House? This is, of course, a conceit, a fantasy on our part. One based on its relationship to hilltop, clitter mass and the distant pinnacles of Rough Tor. Situated high on the hillside, it is the only house at Leskernick from which, looking straight out through the doorway, Rough Tor is visible. Situated high on the hillside it is the nearest house to the Propped Stone and whilst the Propped Stone peephole can be seen from the Great Compound and from the houses adjoining the compound to the north, House 3 has a unique aspect onto it – it becomes a large precariously leaning stone (Figure 7.10).

Another unique feature is the small 'invisible' enclosure (NE8) at the back of the house (Figure 7.10). This small cleared space is out of sight of *all* the other houses. But the Propped Stone is in view, and, from the south east corner of the enclosure, a rather scant and sinuous wall (5) snakes up through the clitter to fade away just below it. North of the Propped Stone, wall 5 takes off again and becomes part of the northern perimeter wall of the western settlement. It is a very particular wall, to which we shall return (p. 177) – suffice to note how one end is tethered to House 3.

There are other things that mark House 3. Circa 25 m to the south of the house, in an area of dense clitter, lies what we have called the 'mini-tor'

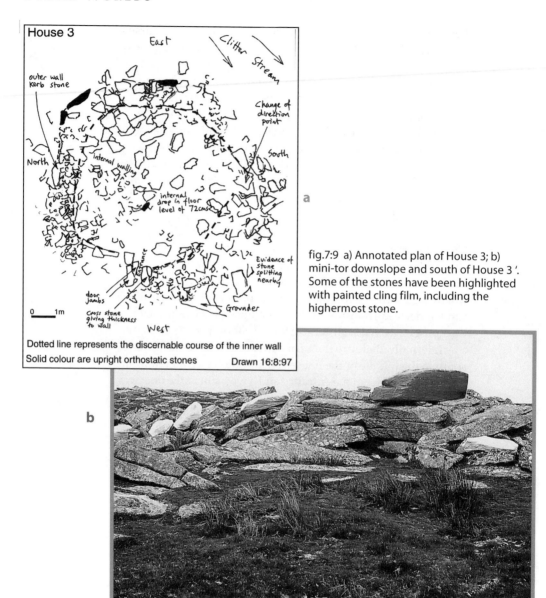

House 3

East

Clitter Stream

outer wall
kerb stone

Change of
direction
point

North

internal walling

South

internal
drop in floor
level of 72cms

Evidence of
stone
splitting
nearby

door
jambs

Cross stone
giving thickness
to wall

Grounder

West

0   1m

Dotted line represents the discernable course of the inner wall
Solid colour are upright orthostatic stones   Drawn 16:8:97

a

b

fig.7:9 a) Annotated plan of House 3; b)
mini-tor downslope and south of House 3 '.
Some of the stones have been highlighted
with painted cling film, including the
highermost stone.

(Figures 7.9b and 7.10). This is a very large earth-fast boulder topped by a
great boulder. It looks like a scaled-down tor and was, we think, an important place. Approaching from below, the area in front of this mini-tor seems
to have been cleared and delimited, some of the adjoining clitter has been
reworked and there is a small cairn. Behind it, some of the clitter also appears
to have been reworked. This is one of the areas on the hill where the line
between the gravitational forces of nature and the work of human beings is
hard to tell apart (see chapter 9).

In the great lobe of clitter that extends south and west of House 3 and the
mini-tor down to and into the Great Compound and to the houses (4–7) just to

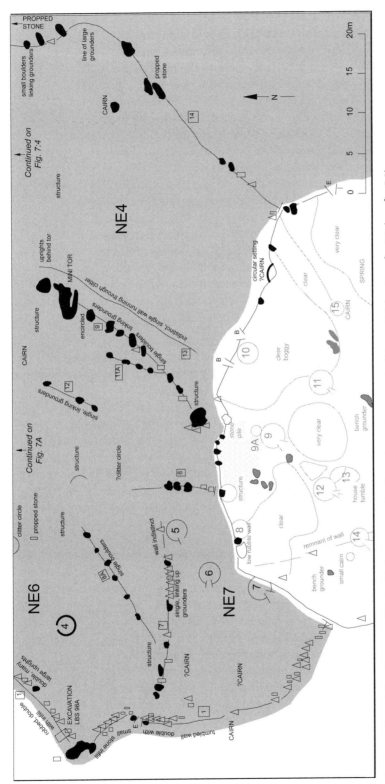

fig.7:10   Plan of the clitter area filled with fragments of walls and structures west of House 3 (plan 5 on fig.7:2; key: fig.5:2).

175

the north of the compound, there is a mass of short wall sections that seem to create links between House 3, the mini-tor, and the compound (Figure 7.10).

One such wall (9) runs southwest from the mini-tor, moves between a series of large earth-fast boulders, and terminates close to the north edge of the western compound wall at another large earth-fast boulder around which the clitter has been reworked. Two other sections of wall (12 and 13) parallel this one and seem to create a track through the clitter. Again, they work their way between numerous grounders. Further west, still within this mass of clitter, a short section of wall (9) runs north from the Great Compound wall. It fades out and, forming a rough arc, there are three or four rough circles and one squarish structure. This last lies just below House 2. West again, and still within the clitter lobe, are traces of further small wall sections – one of which (8A) terminates against one of the rough circles.

And then downslope and to the west of Houses 4–7, as the clitter mass thins out, there is the particularly distinctive rubble-filled double wall (1) already mentioned (p. 157). It is marked by a number of fine uprights, oblong and triangular. Its southern end butts against the northern wall of the Great Compound. It then arcs its way northwards until a dramatic switch-back takes it north-west to a couple of very large earth-fast boulders. Eventually, it again swerves north-east to end close to House 1.

SH (June 1998): Gary sectioned the perimeter wall 1 (Figure 1.4 BSA). It was coursed, the wall stones being in horizontal layers using earth-fast clitter boulders as foundation stones, and faced on either side with orthostats. It is here that we first observed the intimate relationship between walling and clitter. This boundary wall not only incorporated in situ boulder lines along its linear route, it also took 'unsensible' kinks to lasso particularly dense clitter clusters.

It does not seem too fanciful to suggest that the dense mass of clitter between House 3, House 1, and the Great Compound was of great ritual importance to the community. It connected these places; it was filled with dense associations and symbolic importance; and it was worked and reworked in many different ways. House 3, the one we call the Shaman's House, stood at the eastern upslope end and was perhaps the locus of calendrical and fertility rituals. The distinctive perimeter wall 1 stood at the western downslope end and marked both the physical and symbolic closure of this ritual arena. As we have noted earlier, the location and alignment of major clitter clusters and 'streams' often appears to predetermine the division of space and rather suggest that many of the lines of enclosure were agreed upon at a communal, rather than a household, level.

The northern perimeter wall

An *extra*-ordinary wall (5) marks the northern edge of the western settlement (Figures 7.2, 7.3, and 7.4). It begins just above the Fowey River and runs west/ east upslope until it touches the great tabular outcrops on the hill top. On the hillside north of the wall, there are no further houses or enclosures. This section of the wall loops its way between the clitter masses, riding over grounders and between clitter lobes. The stones have been chosen with care and are often triangular in shape. Moving east, it clambers past a cairn marked by uprights, loses itself in a dense clitter mass, and then moves upslope to the great tabular outcrop – a powerful landmark – and stops short.

BB (21 June 1997): We were up close to the laminated cliff outcrop. It's blotched with large grey lichen spots and has a particularly powerful feel about it. We found a sheep's placenta among the rocks. Up here, it was damp and blowy and intoxicating.

On the south side of the outcrop and within an area of heavy quarrying, the wall starts up again and straggles southwards across the top of the hill through an area of reworked clitter and along a line of large grounders towards the Propped Stone. As we noted before (p. 170), from below the Propped Stone a scant wall (5) then snakes westwards and downslope through the clitter to end up against the small enclosure (NE8) upslope of the 'Shaman's House'. Another, very ruined section (14), moves south downhill from the Propped Stone, veers south-west, and comes to rest against the wall of the Great Compound (Figure 7.10).

Even today, this is an almost magical wall – linking river, clitter, grounder, cairn, tabular outcrop, Propped Stone, Shaman's House, and compound. In many ways, it seems similar to the northern wall (S237) of the southern settlement (p. 173). There is a strong sense that these two walls, demarcating the edge of a territory – real or symbolic – were built at much the same time and by people who were closely related. As we have suggested before, by the time of the building of the walls the communities on the western and southern sides of the hill were one – they were the people of the hill.

Although there are no human markings to the north of the wall, there are numerous cleared plots and also cairns to the south, between the wall and the enclosures attached to House 1.

HB (Monday 10 June 1996): A series of cleared areas become increasingly visible as the sun lowers in the afternoon. I suggest that they are probably very early fields. The area also has a large number of cairns (one particularly nice one with very stylish kerb stones).

BB (15 June 1996): [Matt and Henry] showed me a fine shrine stone with a pyramid boulder in front of it. There seems to me to be no doubt about the juxtaposition of pyramid stones and large whale-stones or oblong stones.

What happened beyond the perimeter wall? Was the area at the top of the hill, with the Great Cairn and the Propped Stone, a sacred area, separated by the wall from the everyday business of the hillside settlements?

ML (1996): This wall takes in a lot of large grounders and connects with the natural outcroppings of the top, runs along the rim and dips down to cut off the Quoit [Propped Stone] and the cairn from the western settlements. It's almost as if the top of the hill was divided off as a sacred or ritual space.

Or was it sacred but not set aside. Is it, again, our notion of what is 'right' that requires solemnity and silence in high places? Perhaps it was both sacred *and* busy:

> Pete Herring (pers. comm., 4 December 1999):
>
> The separation of high ceremonial from everyday lived space may be questioned. If the land beyond the perimeter was, as seems reasonable to assume, also rough grazing, it may have been busier, more 'everyday' than many of the other enclosures. There may have been sheep, cattle, pigs, etc., out there, with herds-people watching and guiding them while many of the walled enclosures will have been nearer home, but much quieter. Like the hay meadows close to modern Cornish farms which apart from the June hay-saving, are unvisited and unconsidered.

South of the Great Compound

The enclosure just south of the Great Compound

In the last chapter, we suggested rather tentatively that two semicircular enclosures were built to the south and west of the Great Compound (Figure 6.1) and formed part of the earlier settlement. We think that, somewhat later – but how much? – a more irregular area (C4) was enclosed between

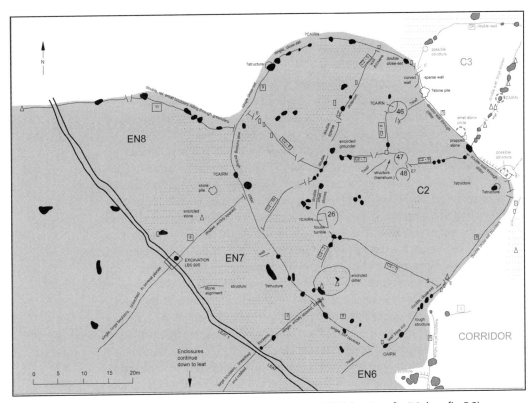

fig.7:11 Plan of the south-western enclosure with Houses 26 and 45 (plan 6 on fig.7:2: key: fig.5:2).

C3 and the Great Compound (Figure 7.15). Its long eastern wall (2) has the same north-east/south-west orientation as wall 3 of the semicircular enclosure and together they form part of the western edge of the great corridor. The north end of the wall – which forms the north-west corner of the corridor – is marked by a group of very large grounders. From these grounders, the northern edge of the enclosure (wall 2A) takes off, runs between a series of large grounders, and comes to rest against the wall of the Great Compound. To the west, the enclosure fades off into dense clitter within which there are a number of cleared areas (see p. 155).

The subdivided south-west enclosure

One of the extraordinary things about working on the hill is the way in which, while the houses seem to retain a structural integrity that sometimes makes it hard to finger temporal distinctions in house style or building methods, the configurations and relationships between houses and enclosures are much more variable and visible (Figures 7.2 and 7.11). Thus, there was the Great Compound that surrounded the early settlement on the western side of the hill; there were the enclosures large and small that radiated out from the enclave and circle of houses on the southern side; there were the two big enclosures that fanned north from House 1; and there was the Shaman's

179

House with no more than a small 'secret' compound, a situation replicated as we shall see in House 28. There were also small cleared plots.) The south-west enclosure (C2) is different again and, rather like the Great Compound, it emanates a feeling of bustle and movement, of people and animals (Figure 7.11). There is room for small hay fields, for holding pens and small cultivated plots. But, as always on the hillside, this sense of everyday life is wedded to a particular way of being in the landscape and of being linked to the ancestral stones.

The C2 enclosure is large and contains at least two houses. It butts up against the earlier semicircular enclosure C3. The perimeter walls are substantial. The eastern wall (9) is almost linear, a double-faced wall incorporating a number of earth-fast boulders along its course and terminating at its southern end at a large earth-fast boulder and a cairn. This eastern wall lines up with the eastern wall of the earlier enclosure (C3) and the more irregular wall of enclosure C4 further to the north; together they define – indeed create – the western side of the great corridor that lies between the western and southern settlements and makes its way up the hill towards the Propped Stone. This eastern wall is also one of the few perimeter walls with a well-marked prehistoric entrance marked by two uprights. The entrance, halfway down the length of the wall, permits a coming and going between the two houses in the enclosure and the great corridor.

Within the enclosure are two very separate houses, 26 and 46 – the structures to the south of House 46 are probably ancillary buildings. The enclosure is relatively stone free, but there are clitter build-ups – one almost in the centre of the enclosure, the other in the south-west corner. What makes this enclosure so remarkable is the way in which it is divided by numerous small walls and the way in which these walls relate to the clitter concentrations, with the central jumble of clitter acting as a focal point.

BB (11 June 1997): At the centre point of the south-west compound the clitter mass seems to contain a triple structure. Downslope there's a depression with little markers in it; then upslope there's a cairn of stones; and then upslope again an encircled boulder. It's from this complex clitter mass that the walls radiate out.

Within this clitter there are a number of small – ambiguous – structures, similar to those found in many other areas of clitter on the hillside. What is unambiguous is that from this complex knot of clitter four or five small walls radiate out (see Figure 7.11). These slight walls divide the enclosure into smaller areas. One of the walls (C2-7) extends east from the clitter to House 47; another runs due south and probably ends at House 26. These walls thus create a link between the clitter mass and the two houses.

BB (10 June 1997): These walls, which on the survey look disconnected and fragmentary and that I had thought were almost ritual markings radiating out from the clitter mass, are, in reality, both ritual and functional. They take their being from the clitter mass but, as well, they serve to divide the compound into [smaller] enclosures.

The other clitter mass, in the south-west corner of the enclosure, has again been reworked to create a small semi-circle of stones around a couple of fine pyramid stones. Here, rather than walls radiating from the clitter, two small walls (C2-1 and C2-2) plus sections of the enclosure perimeter walls (9 and 5) encompass it.

This is not the end of the small walls. As the plan (Figure 7.11) shows, many start or end close to one of the houses. Some of the small enclosures thus created are relatively stone free; others have mosaics of clitter and open ground. There also seems to be a positive and negative lynchet on either side of part of the southern wall (but see p. 137). There is a strong sense of a space that is being intensively used.

To the south and west of this patchworked enclosure two, possibly three,[6] large rectangular enclosures (EN8 and EN7) angle away. Their southern reaches have been much destroyed by two latter-day leats. These long enclosures are rather reminiscent of those stretching north of House 1.

So – who lived in the patchworked enclosure and used the fields that fanned out to the south and west? There are two households – Houses 46 and 26. House 46, with two ancillary buildings ('Houses' 47 and 48), is in the northern part of the compound; House 26 is further south.

House 46

House 46 is a substantial double-walled building with an internal diameter of c. 7.3 m. The floor slopes markedly. The house has been much robbed out and transformed and it is hard to know the precise entrance orientation, but it probably faced due south. Opposite the putative entrance, set almost due north, there is a triangular stone set in the inner wall kerb. The entire western part of the interior is filled with smaller stones and rubble and this rubble extends outside the house to the south. Low, vertically set stones appear to define a kerb and this, like House 26, may be an example of a house that is later transformed into a cairn.

A low wall (C2-8) runs from the western side of this house south towards the two much smaller houses, 47 and 48. The walls of these have been very depleted. Perhaps these structures were decommissioned and the stones taken elsewhere.

Close by, on the further side of the enclosure wall 5, is a small structure built up against the enclosure wall in an area of dense clitter. It is a small rather ill-defined roughly oval structure made of small fist-sized stones.

House 26

Leskernick Survey Team (14 June 1995): The estate agent's dream (Figure 7.12). Entrance south looking down valley and towards Brown Gelly. Very large hut, double-faced walls. Annexe to right of entrance. Free area around the back of the hut. Large rectangular stone opposite entrance. Very fine internal semicircle of slabs to right of doorway. Slabs and rubble covered area to left could demarcate an earlier hut?[7]

House 26 is built a little distance away to the south-west. House 26 is a *big* house (8.6 m internal diameter). It seems to be well levelled into the slope. It has double walls that are up to 1.5 m thick. The entrance faces south. A

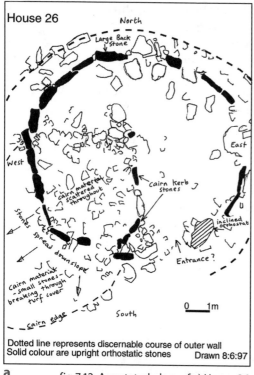

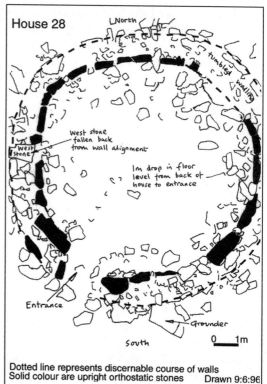

fig.7:12 Annotated plans of a) House 26 and b) House 28.

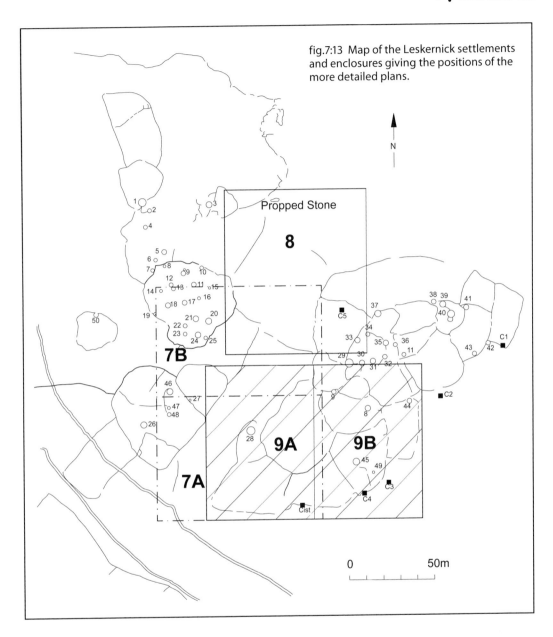

fig.7:13 Map of the Leskernick settlements and enclosures giving the positions of the more detailed plans.

large, rectangular, distinctively shaped backstone (height 1 m, breadth 1.2 m) is positioned in the back wall opposite the entrance. The external orthostats of the house have been robbed out, whilst much of the internal face has been left intact – a common feature of the houses in the western settlement of Leskernick. A pile of some of the dismantled orthostats lies one metre to the north-west of the house wall. The western part of the house interior consists of a pile of larger and smaller stones with traces of a kerb on the eastern and northern sides. The house thus seems to have been decommissioned and transformed into a cairn. A pile of smaller and larger stones extends

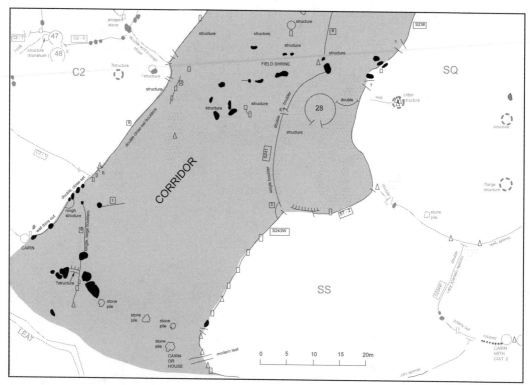

fig.7:14 Plan of the southern part of the corridor including House 28 and the Shrine Stone (plan 7A on fig.7:13; key: fig.5:2).

beyond the cairn-like structure outside the house, downslope to the south-west. There is no structural evidence in this external accumulation of stones to suggest that it might have formed an annexe to the house or that a later structure; was built outside the house. Most probably the pile results from subsequent robbing of the cairn.

Were the two households contemporary? We have no way of knowing. The fact that the small internal enclosure walls link the houses, might suggest that they overlapped in time. But of course the enclosure walls could have butted against empty buildings. And if the houses were transformed into cairns, would the enclosure have gone out of use? Or is this assumption that activities would have drawn back from the houses of the dead yet again one of *our* assumptions? Might the sheep continued to have cropped the grass around the houses, and people moved to and fro, acknowledging but not avoiding the ancestral places?

The corridor

The corridor has been mentioned several times in passing (Figures 7.13, 7.14, and 7.15). It is in many ways pivotal to the (*our*) story of the later settlement

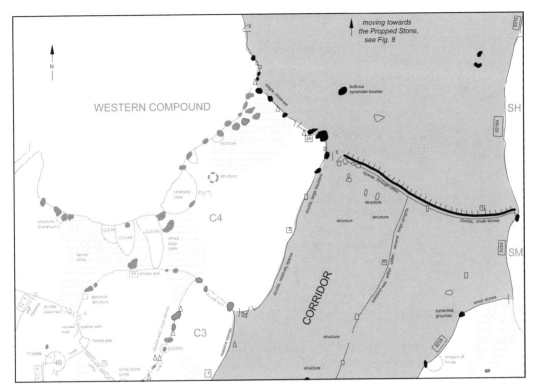

fig.7:15 Plan of the northern part of the corridor (plan 7B on fig. 7:13; key: fig.5:2).

on the hill. Its western flank, as we have seen, seems to have been created by aligning the eastern perimeters of three enclosure walls (9, 3, and 2). The eastern side is less tightly marked. On the one hand, there are the rather wavery walls (S238, S224, and S218A) that mark the western edges of the enclosures on the south side of the hill – walls that relate closely to a long lobe of clitter. On the other hand, it is possible that the corridor was more narrowly defined, in which case the eastern edge is marked by the faint traces of wall 6 (Figures 7.14 and 7.15). Alternatively, this wall divided the upper end of the corridor. Upslope, the northern end of this wall peters out close to a thin east-west wall (1) that defines the top of the corridor. At its southern end, wall 6 seems to end – or begin – at a large earth-fast boulder just north of an important field shrine. As we shall see, this same earth-fast boulder also marks the northern point of the 'Shaman's Compound'. This compound and House 28 sit at the bottom east side of the corridor where two lobes of clitter coalesce – the one carrying wall 6, the other the western walls of the southern enclosures.

This processual way is not just a bounded trackway, it is filled with structures, and so, despite Pete Herring's caution, we remain wedded to the idea of a very significant processional way.

A note of scepticism

Peter Herring (pers. comm., 12 April 1999): ... I, in my functionalist mode, can happily see the relatively ragged eastern edge, formed by the perimeters of successive, accreted enclosures, running where it does not out of respect for the old ceremonial passage, but because this is roughly the edge of the relatively stone-free ground on which the southern settlement is established. The clitter which you see as significant may to a functionalist be seen as not worth enclosing. ... Could the corridor effect be partly illusory? Another product of the map?

Walking in procession

Let us imagine it is a processional way and that people are walking up the hill. Across the southern neck of the enclosures are a string of small – and one large – stone piles. The most easterly one, below the compound of House 28 and close to, but outside enclosure SS, is very large – 5.90 m diameter. It has a wide perimeter wall of small stones – particularly marked on the east side. There are two small uprights in the western section of this perimeter. The centre seems somewhat hollowed out. Is it a cairn, or perhaps the remains of a ruined house? Or, third possibility, is it a ruined house, with, on its west side, an off-centre cairn, approximately 2.4 m in diameter? Perhaps the two small uprights are part of the cairn-like structure.

These stone piles line up between enclosure SS downslope of the Shaman's Compound (see Figure 7.14) and a distinctive group of grounders on the west side of the corridor. These grounders are marked by a small walled structure and by stones placed upright, including one particularly large pyramidal stone (Figure 7.16a).

The fact that people are moving uphill is important, not just because of places encountered on the way, but also because things – features – seen from below are always more impressive:

> Pete Herring (pers. comm., 12 April 1999): Is it worth exploring ... whether most stone features look more impressive from below? They will more often be against a skyline or the light, less often lost against the spreading land which you usually see from above. But people will also have had to come down from the Quoit [Propped Stone]. Is the movement to a ceremonial/ritual site more significant than movement away from it? Anticipation and excitement more important than satisfaction or completion?

a

b

fig.7:16 a) The pyramidal stone at the southwest end of the corridor. Cling film and white paint;
b) moving towards the Propped Stone the full panoply of Rough Tor comes into view;
c) platform at the top of the corridor close to the weathered rock. Line of stones leading from the platform and pointing to Propped Stone or 'Quoit' with cling film and paint'.

c

They move up the hill, past the grounders, through a relatively clitter-free area to a band of large clitter and grounders. Among the grounders are a number of circular structures. And here, close to the northern edge of the Shaman's Compound, is the 'field shrine' – a huge lozenge-shaped grounder (3.8 m long, 1.2 m high, and 0.9 m wide) with a small pyramid stone and a small platform in front, and another rough structure behind (Colour Plate 5).

We assumed that the structure was a later, post–Bronze Age, creation – probably a shepherd's shelter. We thought that the platform was prehistoric. On excavation, it turned out to be a ring of self-supporting stones filled with in-washed sediment (chapter 8). Underneath was a hearth and nearby a single flint flake. It all looked promising. But a radiocarbon date from the hearth gives a much later date – it was early medieval (430–710 AD). Perhaps it was built and used by the person who built the shelter at the back of the stone.

Does this mean that we have to abandon the notion that this place was sacred in prehistoric times? Or do we say that, although the excavation shows us that at some much later date – perhaps at the time the rough structure was built on the other side of the stone – people built a hearth and then a small stone setting, this does not – cannot – rule out the possibility that at some much earlier time people stood in front of this stone, performing their rituals, leaving their offerings? Do we emphasise the impressive nature of the stone, its relationship to the corridor and to House 28, and the way the back of House 28 lines up both with the shrine stone and Rough Tor? Do we say that the fact that it was used later suggests that not just prehistoric people but other people – including ourselves – have been drawn to this place and to this stone? In chapter 8, we offer a cautious archaeological interpretation, but, for the moment, we won't abandon our story.

Further up again, on the western side of the traces of wall 6 the ground is stone free until, just before the thin east/west wall 1 across the top of the corridor, there is a spread of small grounders with a number of small structures. Meanwhile, to the east of wall 6 there is another cleared way that extends from the Shaman's Compound (House 28) north to the east/west wall 1.

The people moving uphill reach the thin wall that defines the northern end of the corridor (Figure 7.15). The narrow entrance through this wall is close to the western end. Beyond this entrance is a dramatic bulbous 2 m high pyramid stone (Figure 7.15).

From the entrance, the pyramid stone blocks the view of the Propped Stone on the top of the hill, but then, having passed the pyramid stone, first the top of the Propped Stone and then its window come into view. But before reaching the Propped Stone there is another, smaller, propped stone, and, walking between the pyramid stone and this stone, the entire Rough Tor ridge is revealed in all its enormity and power (Figures 7.16b and 7.17). This propped stone has very deep solution hollows on its top and eastern face – they are exactly like those found on the top of the great tors (at Rough Tor, Tregarrick Tor, and elsewhere). There are no other well-developed solution hollows at Leskernick, and it seems quite possible that this stone was brought from elsewhere.

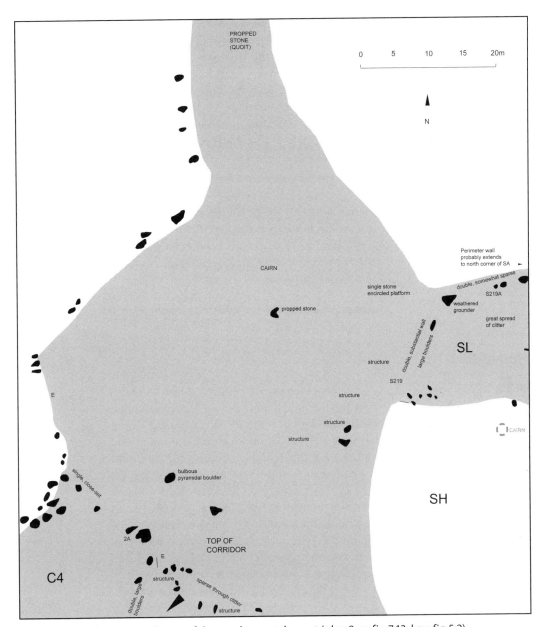

fig.7:17 Plan of the area northwest of the southern settlement (plan 8 on fig.7:13; key: fig.5:2).

Beyond the small propped stone is a large low cairn, and 20 m to the right is a 5.2 m wide circular platform structure – a clear space ringed by small boulders (Figures 7.16c and 7.17). It might have been the remains of a small cairn, or it might have encircled a wooden structure. From this structure a low line of stones extends for about 10 m. It is directly in line with the great Propped Stone and seems to arrow in its direction. It is also in line with the particularly striking weathered stone that marks the north-east corner of the corridor and the beginning of the perimeter wall (S219A) that springs from it and circles the southern settlement. It may be that the short section of wall is all that remains of a wall that once linked the weathered stone and the Propped Stone and was part of the great perimeter wall that extended from the Fowey River on the west, up to the tabular outcrops, down to the Propped Stone, across the weathered stone and then – probably – across the top of the southern settlement to the corner of the furthest north-eastern enclosure (Figures 7.13 and 7.17).

BB (16 June 1997): Tony, Henry, and Wayne have found a small low stone circle south of the Quoit [Propped Stone]. Then Wayne notes that a line of stones leads off from it pointing directly towards the Quoit. Like an arrow, a sign, moving the eye and the action Quoit-wards ...

House 28

House 28 is a 'special' house – the counterpart, we believe, to House 3 high up on the slope to the north of the Great Compound (see Figures 7.14 and 7.18). House 28 and its rocky compound jut out into the corridor, and House 28 lies close to the impressive field-shrine within the corridor. The compound that surrounds House 28 is contained within a mass of clitter. Had the house been built only 30 m or so downslope, it would have been in a more or less clitter-free area.

The compound seems (but unfortunately the abutment is less than clear) to have been added to the very large enclosure (SQ) lying to the east: the eastern wall (S238) of the compound is part of the western wall of the enclosure. The western wall (S241) of the compound is made of large boulders, sometimes single, sometimes double, and terminates at its northern end at an enormous earth-fast boulder – the same one that defines the end of wall (6). The northern neck of the compound is open but heavily strewn with clitter. Within the south wall of the compound (ST2) there is a wide entrance, but since a positive lynchet lies right across it, this may be a later opening associated with the building of the additional enclosure (SS).

House 28 is monumental. With an internal diameter of 8.5 m and double walls up to 1.4 m thick, it is the largest house on the southern hillslope and the second largest on the entire hill. Within the house, the floor slopes markedly from north to south. It is similar, in both size and construction to House 26 in the enclosure to the west of the corridor. Some of the external wall orthostats are robbed, tumbled, and displaced, particularly on the western side of the house. A quantity, including the door jambs, appear to have been piled up to the south-west of the house entrance next to the compound boundary. The internal wall orthostats are well-chosen tabular rectangular or square shaped slabs. They are much larger and more impressive than those that survive in the external wall face. The backstone is rather small, c. 0.7 m high, and roughly rectangular in form with a tapering top. The largest and most impressive rectangular slabs are placed opposite each other in the western and eastern sectors of the wall.

The entrance to House 28 faces south-west towards the Fowey Valley and Catshole, Codda, and Tolborough Tors. From the back of the house, Rough Tor comes into view. The back wall of the house also lines up with the field shrine close by within the corridor.

House 28 mirrors House 3 in many respects. Both are large, isolated, and set amidst dense clitter. Both have small adjoining compounds. Both are close to important field shrines. House 3 lies just below the Propped Stone; House 28 marks the southern end of the corridor leading towards the same propped stone. They can be seen as structural inversions of each other. House 3 is located high up on the hill to the north; House 28 low down the slope to the south. House 3 has its compound above it, House 28 below it. The field shrine associated with House 3 is to the right (south) of the entrance, that associated with House 28 is to the left (west) of the entrance. From the doorway of House 3, one looks directly up and out to Rough Tor. From the doorway of House 28, the view is to Catshole, Codda, and Tolborough Tors and down the Fowey Valley. It seems likely that both houses were in use at the same time, and that both were the focus of ritual and ceremonial acts. Perhaps they were both shamans' houses.

The southern side of the hill

An extraordinary wall

And so to the southern side of the hill. Although, for the purposes of the 'tour' we have distinguished between the western and southern sides of the hill, this is only for descriptive purposes. We repeat again – in this later part of the story the people of the hill were one people. One of the things that, to us, makes this very clear is that just as there had been an *extra*-ordinary wall that bounded the northern side of the western settlement (see p. 177), so there was an *extra*-ordinary wall that defined part of the northern edge of the southern settlement. Taken together, these walls mark the boundary between the places of habitation and the hill top with the Propped Stone and Great Cairn and the northern hillslopes.

The walls (S219 and S219A) to the north of the southern settlement, are dramatic (Figure 7.17). The western section is a substantial double wall made of large boulders. At its south end, it butts against enclosure SH; at its north end it runs up against an enormous rugged grounder with unusual horizontal striations (Figure 2.2b). Here, it changes direction and runs eastwards (S219A). The wall becomes sparse and moves jerkily between three more very

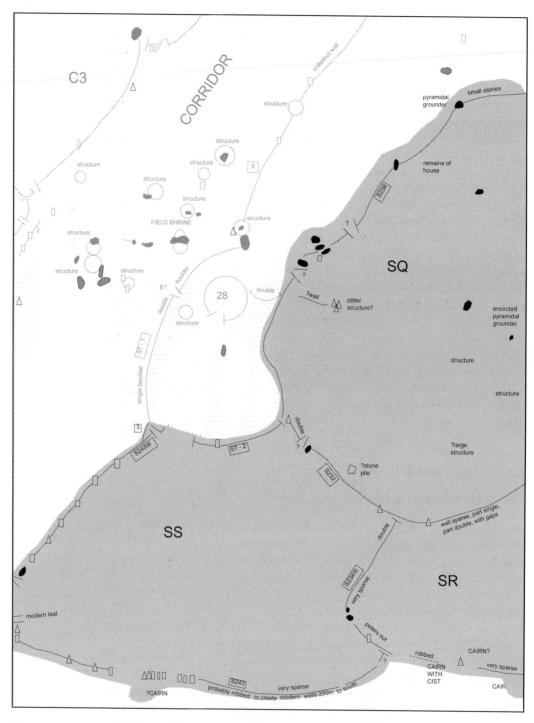

fig.7:18 Plan of area southwest of southern settlement (plan 9A on fig.7:13; key: fig.5:2).

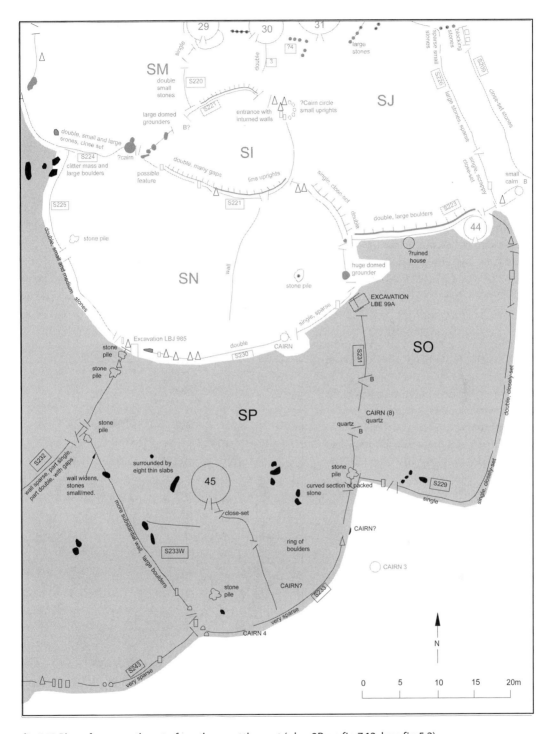

fig.7:19 Plan of area southeast of southern settlement (plan 9B on fig.7:13; key: fig.5:2).

large grounders. Two of the three are further marked by a pyramidal upright. The wall then *seems* to end abruptly – but there are possible traces swinging right round the northern edge of the settlement. It may originally have linked right across to the corner of the furthermost enclosure to the northeast (enclosure SA).

Within the large area thus enclosed (SL), there are great spreads of clitter. There is, however, little evidence that this clitter was reworked, and this is true of virtually all the clitter on the southern side of the hill.

Another late enclosure

As on the western side of the hill, so on the south several more large enclosures were built. What distinguishes many of these is that we glimpse both the time of construction and the time of retraction. They are built and then, some time later, they go out of use. Or rather they change use. For, again and again, what we find is that the southern boundaries of these fields, the ones furthest downslope, the ones nearest to the stone row and circles, become a liminal zone – a zone for the placement of the dead. Small cairns were erected on or alongside the enclosure walls. Often they include stones taken from the enclosure walls. When first mounded up, their fresh stones and earth would have been very visible to everyone as they moved around the southern hillside or out on to the plain. The lower slopes become a place of remembrance.

One of the new enclosures (SQ) (Figure 7.18), is close to House 28 (the 'Shaman's House') and its stone-filled compound. On its western side, above the Shaman's Compound, the enclosure wall (S238) makes its way through a thick clitter spread, riding over earth-fast boulders along the way. It forms a substantial, somewhat irregular part of the east side of the corridor.

This particular enclosure seems to cradle a long history. Upslope within the enclosure, are the remains of a circular house structure. It is in a very ruinous state and it is not clear whether it butts the enclosure wall (S238), in which case it postdates the enclosure, or whether it is slightly overridden by the enclosure wall, in which case it would predate the enclosure. Downslope, in the south-east section of the enclosure,

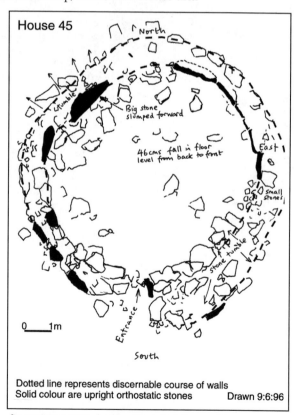

fig.7:20 Annotated plan of isolated House 45.

House 45

North

Big stone slumped forward

46cms fall in floor level from back to front

East

small stones

Entrance

Stone tumble

crumble

South

Dotted line represents discernable course of walls
Solid colour are upright orthostatic stones   Drawn 9:6:96

0 ___ 1m

there are the remains of several small circular structures – perhaps used for storage – which again may be coeval with, or earlier than, the enclosure. Then, in the south-west section, there is a clitter structure marked by three small uprights, while along the southern wall (S232), which is sparse and part single, part double in width, there are several stone piles. Because the wall has been quite badly robbed, these could be part of later (medieval or postmedieval) stone removal activities. Alternatively, some of them may be small cairns. What we seem to glimpse then is, first, the construction of the enclosure in an area already in use, and then its abandonment and the redefinition of the southern boundary as a suitable place for the burial of the dead.

House 45 and its enclosure

To the east of House 28, they built another house, one that sat within its own large enclosure (Figures 7.19 and 7.20). Like most of the isolated houses, it is a substantial double-walled building. It has an internal diameter of 8 m and the floor appears to be levelled into the hillslope. The entrance, with one orthostatic door jamb still in place on the eastern side, faces due south and from it the view extends down the Fowey Valley to the summit cairns of Brown Gelly. As with House 28, the external wall orthostats – still mainly in place – are more modest than the internal ones. The stones are smaller, less distinctive in shape and horizontally rather than vertically set. The most impressive are in the south-west sector where they emphasise the entrance area of the house. The inner wall is made of well-chosen rectangular-shaped slabs. There may have been a small annexe to the east of the entrance.

A slight wall within the enclosure runs southeast from the house down to the enclosure wall. Downslope of the house, and to the east of this wall, there is a tiny structure that consists of a circular ring of boulders. There is no discernible entrance, and it seems to be little more than a platform that probably footed a small ancillary structure.

The enclosure (SP) that surrounds House 45 is substantial, and, as in the neighbouring enclosure SQ, we seem to witness both its construction and its demise, for along the southern perimeter wall are a number of 'cairns'. Again, some of these will have been created much later when the perimeter walls were robbed and breached. But others are definitely prehistoric. One of them (Cairn 8) seems to have a perimeter kerb on the north-west side and larger sparse kerb-stones on the eastern side. There is a small internal mound (3.5 m diameter) with a reasonably defined kerb. There is also a quartz boulder within the eastern arc of the perimeter kerb and another outside the south-west perimeter kerb. Another cairn (no. 4, diameter 2.60 m) lies on the southern wall (S233). It has a marked kerb, particularly on the south side. It appears that the wall was semi-tumbled at the time the cairn was built.

The enclosure also contains a number of substantial grounders, at least one of which appears to be marked by small uprights. There is also a curved section of small packed stones that may have formed part of another cairn.

BB (20 June 1996): Going round the lower enclosures of the southern settlement, we're finding many cairns – often in the field walls. Today, in the enclosure of House 45 we have at least a dozen in the walls and some more in the field. What are they for? Burial – perhaps. Prehistoric clearance – but why bother when you could just shove the stones up against the wall? Perhaps it is 'clearance' in some more meaningful way – clearing the stones respectfully? Using the small piles to mark places or to ring places – to keep things in or out. Hard to say, but the word 'cairn' does not tell us much. If we're not careful we close prematurely on a possible multitude of meanings.

Excavation of an 'entrance' between enclosures SO and SP

There was a 'gap' (BEA, Figure 1.4) in the cross-contour wall between the enclosure/field of House 44 and that of House 45 (Figure 7.19). The wall comprised a single course with large tabular blocks. Smaller, well-fitting elongated, and triangular-shaped boulders fronted the upslope (north) side of the wall gap. The apparent continuation of a foundation course across the gap suggested that the gap was a secondary feature and that the rubble to the east of it was derived from it. Nonetheless, the gap appears to have been created *before* the development of the blanket peat and was perhaps therefore a secondary modification of the original wall.

Adjoining enclosures

Beyond House 45 and its enclosure, to the east and to the southwest, further land was enclosed (Figure 7.19). To the east, the enclosure SO took in land from below the old circle of houses. It seems that these houses were no longer in use, and it was perhaps at the time of this late enclosure that the old droveway that went up to the circle of houses was taken out of use. Its western wall was more or less dismantled, and the southern end was blocked by a wide bank of orthostats and small stones. The stone pile at the east end of this blocking may have been created much later when the bank was breached, or it may be another small cairn (3.6 m diameter) for there are some possible kerbstones.[8]

On the west side of House 45 and enclosure SP another enclosure (SR) went up. And then SS with access to the Shaman's Compound through the new entrance in the compound wall (ST2).

The walls of both these enclosures have been heavily robbed. All that remains of the southern edges of SR and SS are sparse walls (S233, S243) with a number of small uprights, a couple of possible small cairns, and a small cist located in a completely robbed-out section of wall S233.[9] It seems very likely that much of the stone was carted a short distance across the moor and was used to build Leskernick Farm.

Conclusions: Questions of Change and Abandonment
The time of the isolated houses

At the beginning of this chapter, we said that we were not sure whether the isolated houses overlapped in time with the earlier house clusters. If they did, then we are talking about an increase in the number of people on the hill, if not then a quite radical decline.

Now that we have been round the hill and looked more closely at the different elements of settlement, we can pull things together and see whether we get any closer to an answer. Let's look first at the south side of the hill – what evidence can we produce?

- Probably around the time that the large isolated House 45 was built, the drove-way went out of use and it became part of one of the new enclosures. As the drove-way directly linked to the circle of houses, this dismantling could mean that these houses had been vacated. Or it could simply mean that there were changes in the way livestock was being handled.

- The two radiocarbon dates from House 39 in the enclave fall within the Middle Bronze Age. They are somewhat earlier than those from the isolated House 1 on the west side of the hill. This could mean that House 39 went out of use before or during the main occupation of House 1.

- We might have expected that if the house clusters had been abandoned during the lifetime of the settlement on the hill there would be evidence of formal closure or decommissioning. But there is none; the house walls have remained relatively intact right through to the present.

- A more ambiguous line of evidence is the biography of two of the (assumed) earlier enclosures (SK and SB). There are small cairns along the eastern and southern edge of enclosure SK. There is also a cairn (no. 2, 2.40 m in diameter) that lies just beyond the southern wall and almost blocks an old field entrance. The placement of this cairn would suggest that the field entrance, and probably the enclosure, were no longer in use. In the southerly wall of the nearby enclosure SB, there is another, very fine, cairn (no. 1). This one is 3.35 m in diameter and seems at least in part to be built from stones from the wall.

These early enclosures may have been abandoned around the time that House 45 and the new enclosures were being built, and the mounds covering the dead could have been created along, and out of the old walls that contained memories of earlier times, earlier activities.

But, equally, their abandonment and transformation into places of the dead and of remembrance might have happened in the later Bronze Age. It may have been part of a more general retraction in land use when the 'new' enclosures around House 45 also fell into disrepair.

We have to admit that although we *think* that the houses in the enclave and the circle of houses on the southern side of the hill went out of use at the time the isolated houses were built, we are by no means sure.

Things are rather different on the western side of the hill:

> The houses within the Great Compound are much more ruinous than those on the southern slopes, and it does look as if some were formally decommissioned. It even looks as though some were reused to house burial cairns.

If the western Great Compound was abandoned at the time the isolated houses were built, then the overall numbers on the hill may have declined. If, as well, the clusters of houses on the southern side also went out of use, the drop in numbers becomes quite stark. We estimated 100–200 people on the hill at the time of the more clustered settlement; now, if the six or so isolated houses each harboured (for the sake of argument) an extended family of around 10 people, there might be no more than 60 or so. The figures are, of course, fairly arbitrary; what is important, and remains open to question, is whether, at the time of the isolated houses, the community was witnessing growth or decline.

The slow withdrawal in the later Bronze Age

> *BB (23 June 1997): Pete's [Peter Herring] done a wonderful set of maps showing the growth of the settlement and then the retraction. He thinks that the cairns on and close to the southern wall come after the wall has gone out of use. In other words they date to a time when the field system was retracting. A few lonely people still left behind, building their cairns, referencing themselves on the older memory-filled walls. 'It's a sad story', said either Gary or Helen.*

We have talked about the abandonment of the lower fields on the southern side of the hill. We have mentioned in passing innumerable small 'cairns', sometimes more cautiously described as 'stone piles'. In most cases, without excavation it is extremely difficult to distinguish a 'cairn' from a 'pile'. We have talked about houses going out of use and sometimes being reused. Again, without excavation, it is often hard to distinguish whether the destruction of house occurred during the Bronze Age or very much later. It is salutary to compare the detailed life history of House 1 that emerges from excavation from the interpretations of, say, the houses in the Great Compound or Houses 26 and 46 that are dependent upon close survey work.

To be clearer about the final stages of prehistoric occupation, we need to also take in account some of the later activities on the hill and their material imprint:

- We know that medieval herds-people returned to the moors and camped out with their herds during the summer months (Herring 1996). They often built rough shelters alongside enclosure walls or perhaps, on occasion, camped within the earlier houses.

- In medieval or postmedieval times, people from the settlements on the edge of the moor also made their way to the hill in search of stone – for building, gate-posts, mill-stones, and so on. Many of the stone piles found along the southern length of the enclosure walls will have been created by these later stone-seekers – by people sorting and discarding stone in their search for what they wanted, or piling up stones to create entrance ways for their sledges or carts. It may be that these people were the ones who removed the fine, smooth, rectangular doorjambs and threshold stones from many of the houses in the Great Compound of the western settlement – stones that would have made excellent gate-posts or lintels. They may have dismantled the easier-to-get-at outer walls of the houses in the compound. On the other hand, it seems strange that these later stone-seekers should focus on the western rather than the southern settlement, when the western settlement involved a more difficult journey, taking carts or sledges over very uneven and heavily clittered land. Why didn't they concentrate on the houses on the southern side of the hill? Yet, these are the ones that remain relatively intact. Following this line of reasoning, we think it quite possible that much of the destruction in the Great Compound of the western settlement took place in prehistoric rather than later times, and that the later stone removal took two main forms. Those people who wanted smaller building stone attacked the more accessible (lowest and most southerly) field enclosure walls and, in the process of dismantling and sorting, created small stone dumps, many of which are found in the vicinity of the small Bronze Age cairns. Those in search of larger stones suitable for splitting to make gate-posts or mill stones, made their way upslope, avoiding the major concentrations of smaller-size clitter, and quarried the large, more tabular stone. In fact, rather than attacking the old houses, the people involved in quarrying seem to have avoided – even perhaps respected – them. Thus, for example, traces of post–Bronze Age stone-working activities occur in the immediate vicinity of House 39 in the southern settlement and House 3 in the western one, but in neither case does the activity impinge upon the houses. It may be that medieval and postmedieval people still, through legend and folk stories, acknowledged and respected the work of their forebears.

- Tin miners drove leats and a hollow way through the most southwesterly enclosures and largely destroyed them.

- The people who built Leskernick Farm 200 m across the moor almost certainly used the stones from the southern walls of the settlement for their buildings and walls.

- More recently visitors – including servicemen during the last war and ourselves – have destroyed things.

CT (2 June 1998): ... We spend all morning examining the clitter in the western settlement. We notice five soldiers hiding up by the rocks to the north of the Quoit ... with radios and all their equipment. This is the first time soldiers have been on the hill while we have been working. ... but traces of their activities always litter the hill each year – stones dislodged out of the houses and walls, bullet cases, flares, burning, food wrappers ...

Based on the above, we are inclined to believe that much of the destruction in the western settlement is prehistoric rather than medieval or post-medieval. We posit a two-stage prehistoric retrenchment. First, overlapping with the construction and use of the isolated houses and the new enclosures in the later Middle or Late Bronze Age, was the closure and sometimes reuse for burial cairns, of houses in the western Great Compound and perhaps the abandonment of the southern house clusters and some of the associated enclosures. And then, in the later Bronze Age, there was a retraction of many of the new enclosures (and perhaps some of the earlier ones), and their reinvestment with meaning as places for the dead. Gradually, the settlement emptied. If House 1 is illustrative of a more widespread tendency, then it seems that there was a period when the family households packed up and moved away, leaving just a few members of the community who continued to return during the summer months to mind the herds. Then, sometime before the beginning of the first millennium BC, even they stopped coming.

There came a time when the hill was deserted, no-one stooped to enter the houses, or made their way around the fields or down to the crossing place on the river. No-one stopped to pay their respects at field- or house-shrine, or buried their dead below the small cairns. No-one marked the special days by wending their way up the corridor to the Propped Stone or Great Cairn or down to the stone row and circles.

Why did the prehistoric people leave?

Why did they, and all the other people that lived on the moor, move away? Partly, no doubt – as others have said before us – because the weather appears to have worsened (van Gell et al. 1996), though we cannot be too certain of cause and effect (Gearey et al. 2000). What we have found is that there is an increase in heather and ferns in the pollen diagrams relating to the period after abandonment. This suggests a decrease in grazing – but this may not necessarily be due to climatic deterioration. Additionally, evidence of a worm-sorted soil on the floor of House 1 sealed beneath stone from its collapsed wall indicates that its final collapse took place prior to acidification and the development of overlying peaty soil.

Although environmental factors must have played a part in the decline in settlement on the moor, it is worth reiterating that almost certainly, intertwined with these environmental changes, there were social and economic changes that made life on the hill less viable. But for once our imagination runs dry – and we leave this story for someone else to tell. ... We leave Leskernick with the last of the herders and their animals trudging across the moor with the herds, turning to salute their stone world.

Chapter Eight

The Shrine Stone

The Surveyors Speaking

In the last chapter, the corridor that ran between the southern and western settlement figured as an important element in the story of how the hill was occupied, used, and conceptualised (see chapter 7). It linked the two settlements; it formed a processional way between the bottom and the top of the hill.

Much of this corridor is filled with a massive jagged clitter stream and, as it makes its way downslope, the stones become more and more densely packed and more and more upended until they terminate against an immense upright lozenge-shaped boulder. This boulder's shape is unparalleled elsewhere on the hill. On the upslope side, up against the boulder and among the upended stones, is a small rough structure – the sort of thing that we associate with later medieval transhumant occupation of the site. Downslope, there is a smaller, flat triangular stone resting against the boulder, and in front of this is a small circular platform of stones (1.4 m diameter). The area in front of the boulder and the triangular stone and platform is conspicuously stone free.

To us, the great size of the stone and these features downslope of it suggested that this stone and its setting was a place of great symbolic importance. We believed that stories, myths, and rituals would have been wound around the great stone and that offerings would have been placed on the platform in front of it. We believed that the location of the isolated House 28 within its stony enclosure was connected to this stone. This stone added emphasis to our sense of the ritualised everyday world of the people on the hill. It also made us realise that our detailed survey would have to extend beyond the obviously created structures of house and enclosure to the much less obvious and seemingly natural clitter flows that coursed down the western and south-western sides of the hill (see chapter 9).

In our second season of work (1996), we named it the Shrine Stone, and on the eve of the summer solstice, we made our own offerings of joss sticks and a corn sheaf. In the third season, we wrapped the huge lozenge stone and the triangular slab stone in cling-film and painted the cling-filmed lozenge white and the triangular slab poppy red (Colour Plates 5a and 5b). The additional layerings of contemporary meaning gave the shrine stone increased significance, and it became more and more important that the area in front of the shrine stone be excavated. Probably more than any other feature on the site, this particular excavation was driven by the phenomenological bent of the project, and, although the archaeologists recognised that it had to be done, there was a not unreasonable reluctance on their part to use hard-pressed resources and increasingly circumscribed time to excavate a natural feature outside the settlement enclosures with a small platform in front of it that could as easily have been modern as prehistoric.

The Archaeologists Speaking

In 1998, a 5 m x 3.5 m trench was opened up against the downslope of face of the lozenge-shaped stone and blandly allocated the excavation code of FF1 (Field Feature 1) (Figure 8.1).

In the first instance, the excavation clarified the geomorphological processes that had formed the clitter patterns on the hill. Even before the excavation, the geomorphologists had insisted that the relationship of the lozenge-shaped stone and the dense collection of upended stones immediately abutting it upslope were wholly characteristic of the slumping of boulders under periglacial conditions. The compaction of this 'boulder flow' against the massive, immobile lozenge-shaped stone had caused the upending of the stones. Additionally, the great size of the stone had forced the clitter flow to divide to either side of it, with the result that the area downslope of it remained substantially boulder free (see chapter 9). Nonetheless, it did seem possible that there might have been some deliberate clearance of the area in front of the stone in order to create a ritual arena. In excavation, the surface was confirmed to be a wholly natural construct comprising small cobble-sized, slightly overlapping, clitter stones (the substratum over which the larger boulders had rafted downslope), patchily filled with silty material.

During the time of the settlements, the surface of these stones might have had a cover of moor-land vegetation, or, if the vegetation had been eroded or removed, there would have been a cobble-like effect. After two weeks of working on FF1, it also dawned on us that the shape of the pyramid slab resting in front of the lozenge-shaped stone exactly matched a negative scar on the front of the lozenge-shaped stone. Clearly, a slab-like chunk of the lozenge-shaped stone had at some time fractured off as a result of frost action. Thus, the lozenge-shaped stone had a 'god-given' arena-like setting.

What of the circular platform downslope of the stone? Well, it turned out not to be platform but rather a small ring of self-supporting stones that

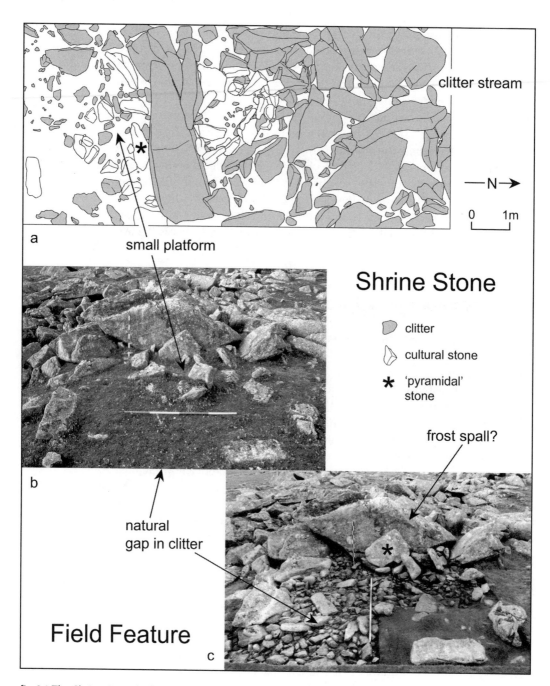

clitter stream

—N→

0   1m

a

small platform

Shrine Stone

clitter

cultural stone

* 'pyramidal' stone

frost spall?

b

*

natural gap in clitter

Field Feature

c

fig.8:1 The Shrine Stone before (a and b) and after (c) excavation.

had filled with peat and in-washed sediment (Figure 8.1). No doubt, offerings could have been placed within this. Partly underlying the ring's western
edge was a small hearth (c. 30 cm diameter, c. 15 cm deep), which had been
cut through the clitter and was filled with charcoal-rich silt. A few cobble-
size pieces of pink-coloured burnt granite lay on, or in, the clitter in front of
the platform, and also around and in the hearth. Clearly, the lozenge-shaped
stone had been a focus of activity before the construction of the stone ring. A
single flint flake (of Neolithic or Bronze Age date) lay in front of the platform.
This flint cannot date the ring structure or the hearth because it has no stratigraphic relationship with either, but it confirms at least some prehistoric use
of the clitter zone between the settlements. The hearth is 'old' in terms of its
stratigraphic relationships, and the stone ring had peat abutting and filling
it, which elsewhere on the settlements appears to have developed after their
abandonment. This seemed to indicate that the hearth and the stone ring are
both of considerable antiquity.

The size of the hearth was big enough to cook on, to boil a pot of water
on, and to provide some warmth. It is, of course, the dramatic setting of the
hearth that suggests that it was more than an 'everyday' fire, and the subsequent construction of a small stone ring on the same place suggests some
time depth to the activities that centred on the lozenge-shaped stone. Our
excavated results do not offer any certain explanation as to the role and function of the lozenge-shaped stone and its associated features. We can only
speculate on the nature of the activities that took place in front of it, but the
setting inspires the idea that they were not mundane.

Conclusion

We were happy with these findings. We were not so enthusiastic when the
radiocarbon date for the charcoal from the hearth came through: 430–710 AD.
It would seem that the hearth and the stone setting had nothing to do with
prehistoric Leskernick and had more to do with the rough structure butted
up against the back of the stone.

All that this tells us is that there was medieval activity around the stone
and that neither survey nor excavation could find any *physical* evidence
– except for the one flint flake – that the prehistoric people of Leskernick
had also used it. If they did, they left no evidence that would be preserved
down through the centuries. If they left their equivalent of the joss stick or
corn sheaf, or a libation in a wooden or leather container, the evidence disappeared long ago. As for their actions and their words, these have gone with
the wind …

Chapter Nine

Nature, Culture, Clitter[1]

Chris Tilley and Sue Hamilton
working with Stephan Harrison
and Ed Anderson

Introduction

We were beginning to get worried. It was one thing to discover large centrally placed backstones in many of the houses, or to recognise that certain large stones had ritual importance, but now, as we surveyed the clitter streams, we seemed to be finding slight, human, modifications amongst the stones. A circle here (Figure 9.1a), a row of stones there (Figure 9.1b), stones piled on each other. It was getting hard to know where, quite literally, to draw the line (see Table 9.1). More, as we climbed amongst the giant clitter formations below Rough Tor, we were uneasily aware that many of the rock masses, although they were 'in place', looked very like megalithic monuments. We needed, yet again, to deconstruct the taken-for-granted divisions that we were still slipping into between nature and culture. As part of this rethinking, and, to be honest, because we needed some reassurance from 'specialists', two geomorphologists were invited to Leskernick – Stephan Harrison and Ed Anderson.[2] As they bounded over the site, they began to look increasingly excited and worried.

The following chapter was written by Chris Tilley, Sue Hamilton, and the two geomorphologists. In the version of this paper that appeared in the *Journal of Material Culture*, the voices of the anthropologist, archaeologist, and geomorphologists were homogenised – they attempted to speak as one. In retrospect, it seemed much more straightforward to allow their distinctive voices to come through in certain parts of the chapter.

fig.9:1 a) Wrapped stone: circle (no. 30 on fig. 9:6) in the clitter – a roughly circular arrangement of slabs within a central depression in a hollow within a clitter lobe to the west of some large and impressive grounders. There is at least one internal arc of stones (diameter: 6.5 m north-south; 3.5 m west-east). Some possible side-set slabs around the northern and eastern sides of the depression define an area 14 m north-south by 6 m west-east. Reinvestigating the wrapped stones with the geologists suggested that about half of them could be accounted for through solifluction processes, the rest involved the human inhancement of a natural pattern; b) pyramid stones on wall 6 pointing towards Brown Willy.

In Unison

If God created the world, Linnaeus was able to claim that *he* ordered it. A distinction between nature and culture is one of the key building blocks of modernist epistemologies and has been central to anthropology and archaeology in various ways. In cultural ecological approaches, nature is regarded as determining or shaping and constraining human action requiring an adaptive cultural response. Alternatively, in structuralist and symbolic positions, nature may be regarded as a kind of void or a blank slate on which societies, more or less arbitrarily and contingently, impose meaning, order, and coherence. The roots of culture may be regarded as residing in nature, or nature is referred to as a cultural construction. Both of these approaches accept the nature/culture distinction. The only difference is the relative weight given to either side of the binary opposition. It has, characteristically, been rather easier to make these kinds of blanket statements than to specify and justify what is actually meant by them. The central paradox is that nature may be the product of a constructional process; it is also a precondition for this process to take place at all. In a curious way, it is then both present and absent in culture (Collingwood 1945; Descola and Palsson 1996; Ellen 1996; Horigan 1988).

In this chapter, we want to examine the relationship between 'nature' and 'culture' by focussing on the human modification of the clitter flows primarily at Leskernick but also further afield on Bodmin Moor. We begin with a series of geomorphological criteria for distinguishing between 'natural' and humanly modified stones. We then move on to consider archaeological evidence for stone movement and/or placement. Finally, we attempt to provide an interpretation of modified clitter masses, leading us back to challenge the very nature/culture distinction with which we introduced our analysis. Our argument is that whilst we can acknowledge that the distinction between a stone that has been moved by human agency and one that has not is important for interpretation, this does *not* necessarily make that stone more, or less, culturally significant. The result is a paradox that can never be resolved: in research and interpretation, we both require a distinction between culture and nature *and* need to abolish it!

The Geomorphologists
Stephan Harrison and Ed Anderson

Clitter is a rather evocative Cornish term used to describe extensive boulder and stone spreads that lie downslope of upland tors on the granite hills of the county. The term has also been applied to similar deposits in other areas of the world. It is assumed that they formed as a result of the large-scale frost shattering of the tors and the downslope movement or mass wasting of the shattered material during periglaciation. In the past, there has been much debate about the nature of the climatic conditions under which the tors formed (Linton 1955, 1964; Palmer 1967; Palmer and Nielsen 1962; Palmer and Radley 1961), but the status of the clitter spreads does not appear to have been questioned.

The age of the tors and clitter is problematic. Linton's (1955) two-stage hypothesis of tor formation required the initial deep weathering of granite during subtropical (probably Tertiary age) conditions, followed by the stripping of the weathered material during periglacial periods. In this view, tors are pre-Quaternary in age, whilst the clitter developed during repeated cold periods within the Quaternary. The alternative hypothesis, championed by Palmer and co-workers, required a single cycle of periglaciation involving the extensive, large-scale frost shattering of the tors and the removal of the blocks downslope by mass-wasting processes (mainly solifluction). In the absence of deeply weathered *in situ* rock on Leskernick Hill, the one-cycle hypothesis seems a more likely explanation for the development of the tors on the hill.

Large-scale modification of the landscape by periglacial processes ceased at the end of the last cold period (the Younger Dryas: 11,000–10,000 BP), and since then geomorphological processes have not modified the clitter or tors to any great extent. However, the tors and exposed bedrock have been subject to minor freeze-thaw processes and chemical weathering, and recent peat development and vegetation growth have obscured some areas of the clitter.

The prevailing view amongst geologists, geomorphologists, and most archaeologists is that the tors and clitter are the products of nature and amenable to geological description and explanation, requiring no reference to culture and meaning.

The Anthropologist (CT)

Today, people are fascinated with the dramatic and weirdly weathered shapes and sculpted forms of the tors endlessly reproduced in photographic images of Cornwall. They are part of the cultural construction of locality and place. We can plausibly infer that ever since the first human encounters with the granite uplands of Cornwall, the tors have been invested with enormous cultural significance as landmarks, orientation points, and places inscribed with stories, myth, and meaning (Tilley 1995, 1996). Nobody made the tors, and we can readily acknowledge that they are natural formations invested with cultural meaning – an overlay of culture on nature. But what of clitter? Clitter does not carry the same kind of contemporary cultural baggage as the tors. A jumbled pile of stones sometimes resembling the products of a quarry rarely provides a picturesque image. Clitter, unlike tors, never features in postcards or snapshots. Where it does, it is by default as an adjunct to a photograph of the tors. In conventional wisdom, the clitter masses, like the tors, are a product of natural processes. Just as nobody sculpted the tors, nobody piled up and spread out these stones. Although people have been interested in the tors because of their inherent aesthetic qualities and dramatic and impressive forms, nobody, other than geomorphologists, has been interested in clitter. For archaeologists, clitter has simply been seen as a useful source of building stone: a natural quarry.

The Geomorphologists

If we are to consider the possibility of cultural transformations of clitter, we need to set out some geomorphological criteria for identifying them. But first we need to think about the appearance of natural unmodified landscapes.

One: solifluction

The most common periglacial process affecting frost susceptible sediments is solifluction. This is a mass wasting process by which stony material is moved downslope at velocities of the order of 1–7 cm per year. Hillslopes affected by solifluction tend to be concave in form and soil depth may thicken considerably towards the base of the slope. Flow of the top metre or so of material during solifluction is initiated by the freezing of fine-grained wet soils followed by thaw-induced instability leading to mass wasting. Freezing of the ground draws water to the freezing front, allowing ice lenses to develop. This increase in ground volume results in frost heave. During thawing of the ground, the excess water cannot be expelled efficiently from the soil, and the consequent stresses are transferred from intergranular contacts to porewater pressure (Ballantyne and Harris 1994) with an associated decrease in frictional strength. This means that the water pressure increases until particles are no longer in contact with each other. The process is most effective when the soil is composed of fine sand or silt-sized particles. Finer or coarser materials inhibit the development of ice lenses during freezing, and solifluction will not occur in these sediments.

The implications of solifluction for the archaeological identification of cultural structures are threefold:

1. The process creates a characteristic spatial arrangement or macrofabric to the deposit in which elongate stones are aligned with their long-axes (a-axes) in a downslope direction parallel to the direction of the flow vector. Such flows also result in clast[3] imbrication where their long-axes dip into the slope whilst maintaining their downslope a-axis macrofabric (see Benedict 1970, 1976 and Figure 9.2a).

2. Solifluction can only occur in frost-susceptible soils (Harris 1981). Where the soil matrix is either too fine or too coarse for solifluction to occur, another process must be invoked to explain clast orientations and/or movement. The sandy silty nature of the soils on Leskernick Hill, exposed during excavation, are highly likely to be frost susceptible.

3. Such mass-wasting processes are very old and have not occurred to any significant extent in upland areas of southwest England since the Younger Dryas. By implication, a solifluction layer – resulting from periglacial activity – will not occur above a Mesolithic or later cultural horizon.

> Chris: Here we're in an area where there are large, kind of deep fissures within the rocks – almost like mini caverns or cave-like

structures that may have been of interest to the prehistoric people. And one of the things we were thinking about at Rough Tor the other day was that you could imagine excarnation practices, people stuffing bones within the fissures. … I'm just wondering how these kind of fissures or holes occur – they always seem to be high up.

Stephan: The reason you don't get them downslope is probably because, as you go downslope, the solifluction layer, or the slope wash layer, gets thicker so that fills in all the holes. The reason why you get them in certain locations, like the one we're standing at here, is because if you've got lots of rock breaking up, you get an awful lot of frost heave, an awful lot of movement, and the rocks are prised apart; therefore, you get the fissures between the blocks. So they're an entirely natural phenomenon.

Two: frost heave and clast displacement

In areas where large clasts are abundant (e.g., in clitter fields below tors) frost heaving, frost sorting, and clast displacement may have occurred by a variety of processes (Figure 9.2a). The a-axes of elongate clasts may display high dip angles (up to perhaps 80 degrees) as a result of large-scale frost shattering and frost heave and may thus mimic standing or placed stones of a cultural origin. However, for this to occur naturally, several conditions must be satisfied:

1. 'Standing boulders' are unlikely to occur in isolation since intense cryostatic pressures are required to elevate them. These pressures require the presence of other large stones. The depth of burial in soil determines the pressures required to elevate the clast. It follows that shallow burial requires large cryostatic pressures.

2. Although standing boulders may occur on flat and gently sloping ground, they are unlikely to survive rapid mass movement on very steep slopes (greater than 30–40 degrees).

3. Where 'standing boulders' occur as a result of mass-movement pressures, they have a distinct pattern comprising groups of 'standing boulders' separated by groups of boulders with lower dip angles. The separation of different flow regimes on slopes, and the differing response of elongate clasts to these regimes create this pattern. At the downslope edge of topographic hollows, flow is retarded and stones stand up (Hooker 1998). On convex hillslope segments, it accelerates and stones lie down.

Chris: The other thing that strikes me of interest here is the focus of stones in this depression. If you go a little way up to the north, west or east, they're hidden. It's only when you come across them in this depression that you can see them … which suggests … that [it was a] secretive place to which people could have been led – knowledge

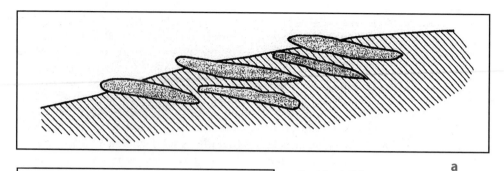

a

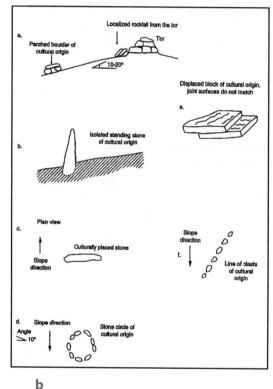

b

fig.9:2 a) Side-way view of a stony deposit that has undergone solifluction. The clists are imbricated and dip upslope whilst their long axes are orientated in a downslope direction b) distinguishing cultural landscapes on the basis of geomorphological criteria.

that could be easily kind of guarded and controlled. But how does a depression like this form?

Ed: These stones have obviously come from somewhere. You need to find a scar in the landscape from whence they came. Looking up the slope towards the east, there is a bedrock outcrop that could mark their origin. ... The fact that these stones have very high dip angles suggests that the dominant movement has been vertical, so I would suggest that the depression itself was created by the frost heaving of the stones upwards. ...

It may be just imagination, but some of these reedy plants suggest that the ground around is very damp. Now if you have a damp area due to an underground spring, that would accelerate the frost heaving because you have an additional supply of water. So that could be a clue! Yeah, I think essentially this is rock that has been frost shattered due to enhanced water supply.

Three: perched boulders and rockfalls

In many archaeological sites, boulders are found perched on top of one another or on the top of bedrock outcrops. In a geomorphological context, such

212

arrangements imply three things: (1) the perched blocks have been deposited as a result of rockfalls from bedrock masses upslope; (2) they have been deposited by avalanches; and (3) they are *in situ* and the result of weathering out of corestones from a larger bedrock mass.

However, rockfalls require the presence of a steep source area, such as a cliff, and the slope in front of the cliff must be steep and long enough for the debris to gain sufficient kinetic energy to travel horizontally. Although determination of whether a perched block has been emplaced by rockfall is site specific, and therefore can only be achieved in the field, it is clear that perched boulders, when found on low-angled slopes and at considerable distances from cliff faces or on hillsides with no backing cliff, must be cultural relics.

> Chris: Can we just go over and look at what we call 'the Monkey Stone' and have a discussion about that?
>
> Ed: Look at the arrangement of joints on this perched block – they are discordant with the arrangements of joints on the block it stands on. So it's obviously been placed here by human activity. It's aligned downslope. It seems to be aligned parallel to the long access of the large block it's lying on as well. Maybe there's some symmetry that the people that placed it wanted to highlight. It must have taken an extreme effort to do it – it's approximately 2 m by 1.5 m, weighs somewhere in the region of 8 to 9 tons.
>
> Stephan: Yeah, I agree with Ed when he says that it's probably been placed, because at the very back of it, underneath it, there are small stones which couldn't have got there … by weathering, and they certainly couldn't have got there by any other process.
>
> Chris: We found many examples of big blocks with … smaller stones … underneath them, and I wonder to what extent, when you get something like that, it could it occur by accident?
>
> Stephan: If you've got stones underneath very large boulders, there's no geomorphological process that creates that. And it's just been pointed out by Wayne that the amount of power it would require to move a big block weighing eight, nine, ten tons, with the friction involved … is beyond the wit of most human societies at that time, I guess. So the way to do it is to put small rounded boulders underneath it and then you can just roll it along. … So I guess this is maybe how they did it.
>
> Chris: I suppose an interesting contrast is the stone immediately behind the Monkey Stone … on the same line, which I would say is definitely kind of in place.
>
> Ed: Again, the best clue to look for is the joint – if the joints of the upper block match the joint pattern of the lower block – which they don't! … I think it's been moved approximately 85% in an anticlockwise direction.

Chris: So, in fact, in this case we've been … much more cautious than we needed to have been. … For the first time!!

Four: stone circles and polygons

There are periglacial processes that may form stone circles and polygons. These include frost sorting (without the presence of permafrost) and large-scale frost wedging, which implies permafrost development. The former process creates small (less than 1 m in diameter) stone circles in the uplands of present-day Britain (e.g., Ball and Goodier 1968, 1970; Ballantyne 1986), whilst large-scale permafrost development may create large circles (perhaps up to 5 m in diameter). Hence, large, naturally formed stone circles in the landscape can only be attributed to intense ground freezing, probably during periglacial periods. So far, these have not been found in the British Isles. All natural stone circles degrade to form stone stripes on ground sloping more than 5 degrees (see Goudie and Piggott 1981; Tufnell 1985). The implications of this are that stone circles are likely to be cultural if (1) they are larger than 1 m or so in diameter and/or (2) they are on sloping ground. Straight lines of clasts may occur on steep ground because of frost sorting, but these lines are generally composed of small debris.

We now move to *cultural transformations* (Figure 9.2b).

Elements of a landscape must be considered to be of cultural origin if they include:

- Perched boulders on gently sloping ground or near hilltops.

- Isolated standing stones or standing stones whose buried portion is only a small proportion of the total length.

- Elongate clasts whose a-axes are at right angles to the dominant flow vector during mass wasting.

- Large-scale circular patterns in stone streams or stone circles on steeply sloping ground.

- Grooves on rocks found on bedrock or other rocks which are not parallel to the bedding planes or where the joint surfaces of the perched block are not aligned with joint surfaces on the resting block.

- Straight lines of large clasts, especially when these are oblique to the slope angle.

Chris: We're standing directly beneath what we call the mini-tor, which is the only major granite outcrop in Leskernick Hill, and immediately to the west of this area we have an area that appears to be cleared. So, one of the first questions is whether this actually is a cleared area.

Ed: One of the striking things about [the largest] block is that it's not particularly well jointed. The joints are subhorizontal and are about a metre to a metre and a half spaced, which could be the reason why you

214

have an area [that is] relatively debris free in front of it. It could be joint control, in the sense that either side of it, the joints in the granite are more closely spaced, which makes it more vulnerable to frost shattering.

Stephan: I'd put forward an alternative view. ... This block could actually be protecting the area in front of it. ... I suspect there probably has been solifluction here [and] then all the clasts would go round this block. ... This was a braking block, so it's almost like a negative wake in front of it.

Ed: The theory that Stephan proposed, that debris is flowing either side of this braking block is slightly spoilt by the fact that, behind the braking block you seem to have a build-up of debris, where on either side you haven't because it's simply flowed downhill. So, well, I think it is striking how this large braking block is formed, because it's not closely jointed and that's a factor that explains why it hasn't frost shattered and subsequently moved.

Chris (standing behind the mini tor): Well, here you can see the remains of a wall that's coming down, ... and what we were wondering about was these slabs here that appear to be kind of wedged in round the back of this very large outcrop – as if they've been placed there to ... demarcate or enclose the back of this small tor.

Stephan: I would say that certainly ... one or two of the clasts that ... have very high dip angles appear to be natural, but I think there are others that are sort of perched on top of them, supported by them, I would suggest may well be cultural. Yeah, I think you could argue for a cultural origin of the clasts standing up now to the south of the block.

Chris: What they may be doing here then is, basically, enhancement, possibly of a rather minimal nature, of a feature that was already formed here. Something was recognised so they were just altering a few stones to make ... the pattern they recognise in it clearer.

Ed: You haven't said much about the big block on top of the massive stone outcrop. I mean, one of the things that occurs to me when looking at it from down below is that it's actually been rotated through maybe about 15 degrees, so that, in fact, it looks more cultural than natural. What thoughts on that?

Stephan: I think this has been moved. ... I don't think it's *in situ*. I don't quite know what criteria I use to make that decision, but it doesn't fit right. That's my own personal feeling.

Ed: The fact is that it's a very large block, it probably weighs something in the region of five or six tons, and it's in a very unnatural position, sitting on top of a large granite block – I can't think of any physical process that put it there. Nothing behind it – so where does the momentum come to actually push it there? ... Yeah, ...I'd say that it's been culturally modified.

The Anthropologist

Leskernick Hill, whilst completely lacking major tors and cliffs and with only small areas of exposed bedrock, is incredibly stony. It appears in the distance as a distinctive *grey* whale-backed mass.

The clitter masses on the hill take two main forms. Lower down the slopes there are linear streams or stripes of material, varying between 10 and 20 m in width and up to 100 m or more in length separated by comparatively stone-free areas covered with peat and turf. Higher up the hillslopes, the clitter masses are often denser and more irregular in form, a generalised spread with differential densities of stones rather than more regular bands of material. The clitter masses consist of some extremely large boulders (up to 5 m or more in length and weighing many tons) and many smaller stones with dimensions of 1 m or less. These clitter masses were plotted on the map of Leskernick (on the basis of aerial photographs) by the RCHME, together with the houses and walls. The different densities of the clitter were indicated by stippling, and all the individual very large boulders were mapped and are readily discernable by a user of the map in terms of shape (see Figure 1.4).

In the first two years of our surface survey of the hill, we ignored the clitter, considering it to be entirely natural. Instead, we recorded, planned, and excavated obvious cultural features: the stone row terminal, houses, walls, and cairns. In the process of doing this, we became more attuned to the stones on the hill. We began to note a series of connections between the *de facto* cultural constructions and what we had previously regarded as 'natural' stones. Thus, large 'grounders' or earth-fast stones were incorporated in the houses; the enclosure walls variously ran up to, incorporated, included or linked other large grounders and different clitter masses in a seemingly 'illogical' and 'irrational' fashion. Some large 'natural' boulders appeared to have stones placed around them. Others appeared to have had stones removed away from them, thus in two very different ways enhancing their presence and significance in the landscape.

As we became more familiar with the larger and more impressive stones on the hill, we tentatively identified some as being of especial significance and referred to them as 'field shrines' – possible offering places and sites of minor ceremonies, part of the rituals of everyday economic and social life. Although we were willing to grant such cultural significance to large and impressive stones on the hill, we still regarded the clitter masses as natural. As we searched out the larger stones on the hill, trying to understand which ones were 'significant', the clitter merely got in our way …

But slowly we began to rewrite our story. We began to see that it was an artefact of our *own* modernity that Bodmin Moor in general, and Leskernick Hill in particular, appeared to be more 'natural', or in some way 'closer to nature', than the chalk downlands of southern England that were an obvious palimpsest of thousands of years of human activity. In British culture, chalk is to granite as the domestic is to the wild. Yet, nothing could be further from the truth. *The appearance of Leskernick Hill today is the result of its fashioning as cultural artefact.* As we have seen in earlier chapters, there are almost 3 km of compound and enclosure walls, 50 houses and structures, over 100 larger and smaller cairns or stone piles, two stone circles, and a stone row over 300 m long.

The amount of stone moved on and below the hill during the Bronze Age was thus truly enormous. And we know that these people were capable of moving not just smaller stone blocks but massive stones requiring teams of people, rollers, and levers. In this sense, when we look at Leskernick Hill we see nothing that might be described as 'natural' or untouched. Stones were cleared from enclosed areas and used to build the houses, walls, cairns, and monuments. Stones must have been removed from the clitter masses, thus transforming their character; stones cleared to create pathways, clearings, and fields may have been dumped in clitter masses. So, on purely *a priori* grounds, we have good reason to think that the clitter, rather than being left untouched as 'natural' form, has been culturally transformed.

Culture in the clitter

We can take the cultural nature of clitter a step further. Eventually, in the third year of our research, having investigated the houses and walls, we started surveying the clitter. In the first instance, we surveyed it because it lay *within* the field boundaries and might contain obvious cultural features such as cairns.

As soon as we started surveying the clitter masses with as much attention to detail as we had surveyed the walls and houses, we started finding structures. During the 1997 field season, we identified about 40 clitter structures on the hill (Table 9.1, p 229 and Figure 9.7). By these, we refer to patterned arrangements of stones within clitter stripes or masses.

We used the following criteria to identify these structures:

- Morphology: the structures we identified are generally circular or semi-circular in form, none are perfect geometric forms.

- Size: this varies between 1.5 and 20 m in diameter.

- Overall stone orientation or angle of rest: the long axis may be either vertical or leaning.

- Shape: generally thin 'artifical'-looking slabs with regular sides, often rectangular or square in form, and always contrasting with the other stones in the clitter.

- Spacing: some degree of regularity in spacing between the stones in the cluster but, as with the shape, this is usually approximate.

- Viewing angle: any of these structures were meant to be seen from below, looking upslope.

- Stone size: frequently a contrast, or anomaly, is evident between these stones and the surrounding clitter.

Suddenly, the clitter masses appeared to us to be no longer amorphous, random masses of natural stones that had moved by themselves; instead, they seemed to be the ordered intentional product of human agency. The heaviest concentration of these clitter structures is in the corridor separating the western and southern settlement areas on the hill (see Figures 7.14, 7.17, and 9.7). The rest are in the western settlement area (see Figure 7.10). There are none in the southern settlement. No clitter stream or clitter mass of significant size is without such structures, although they are differentially concentrated. For the most part, they consist of approximately circular or semicircular rings or arcs of stones situated within the clitter masses. All are small, usually 5 m or less in diameter.

In some cases, the stones simply define a 'space' that is entirely cluttered with other stones, and the stones defining this 'space' are themselves surrounded by more stones. There are no clearings, no openings, no paths, no stone-free areas. In other words, we are identifying roughly circular or arc-like patterns of stones within an overall ground or field of stones. In about half the cases, the structures encircle a central boulder, or radiate out from a central boulder, curving downslope in a semicircular arrangement. In no cases are we dealing with perfect geometric forms: the circles and arcs are irregular. These structures are, quite literally, hidden in the clitter and can often only be seen from within the clitter mass or standing immediately outside of it. As soon as one moves a few metres away or alters the tilt of one's head, or the angle of view, these structures are instantly lost and have to be rediscovered (Colour Plates 6, 7, and 8).

The Archaeologist (SH)
Scales of engagement

Excavating on Leskernick Hill involves learning to 'navigate' in this world of stones. Approximately 400 m² of the hill have been excavated. As archaeologists, our understanding of the natural and architectural elements of Leskernick's stony landscape is articulated down to the level of the detailed description, planning, removal, and interpretation of individual stones.

There are various scales of engagement. When Leskernick Hill comes into view from a distance (from the south side), it immediately appears to be an extremely stony hill. Coming nearer, it is possible to distinguish long stony lines, some of which are the wall boundaries and divisions running up and down and around the hill. Eventually, one focuses in on the circular stone walls belonging to its numerous Bronze Age houses. These images have to be picked out of the clitter. From this outsider's point of view, it is possible to formulate the gross patterns of what is humanly constructed, but it is as if one is constructing a map without having to decide, stone by stone, what to put on the map.

Once inside the settlement, the scale of the houses is such that a meaningful wall circuit can be comprehended at a glance. By contrast, the boundary walls and clitter begin to shift out of focus because they are too big to be viewed as a whole. Then there are the stony 'cairns', many of which are quite small and discrete and seemingly merge into the clitter. These prompt a series of questions such as are they burial cairns, or clearance cairns, piles of 'raw material', or clitter agglomerates? The possible origins of the clearings and spaces between the stones also seems increasingly problematic. Particularly dramatic stones, for example, are visually emphasised by the existence of stone-free areas around them. But *are* these stone-free areas clearings or products of geomorphological processes, or a combination of the two? Overall, there is a sense that the particular scale at which the eye focuses on the patterns alters the accommodation, recognition, and questioning of the common-sense constructs of 'natural' and 'cultural'.

In excavation, *each* stone 'demands' a history. We are challenged to classify, describe, and make decisions about which stones are humanly placed and which are *in situ* at a series of macro and micro levels. We offer two examples of archaeological investigations of features encompassed in the nature/culture discussions of the geomorphologists and the anthropologist. The first a cairn, the second some sections of enclosure wall.

One: clitter cairns

Cairn 5, approximately 2.5 m in diameter, was built in a liminal position on the western edge of the southern settlement within a discrete concentration of surface clitter (Figures 5.2 and 9.3). Although the RCHME describes it as a kerbed cairn (Johnson and Rose 1994, Figure 28), its status became increasingly ambiguous as excavation proceeded. The roughly circular piled 'cairn' stones in fact enclosed a void, subsequently naturally filled with in-washed silt (Figure 9.3, deturfed). The original constructed configuration would have been (1) a ring of elongated stones (Figure 9.3: excavation stage one, upper course) on top of (2) a 'base' of smaller, squarer stones (Figure 9.3: excavation stage 2, lower course), over (3) a natural base of elongated clitter stones 'rafted' on a natural surface of overlapping imbricated clitter cobbles (Figure 9.3, post-excavation/natural). There was no central stone-built cist or other mortuary evidence. The sole small find was a flat piece of shaped slate (possibly a pot lid) from the clitter surface under the 'cairn' ring.

Architecturally, the construction had actively transformed a lobate flow of large boulders into a circular configuration – a vortex that with time and increasing silting and vegetation growth mutated into something that looked like, but was not, a kerbed cairn.

Two: clitter walling

From the results of surface survey, it was evident that the enclosure and boundary walls of Leskernick link with large, apparently 'in place', boulders and surface clitter concentrations. No single wall building technique was used, but in each specific case a structural dialogue was apparent between the wall and the clitter.

219

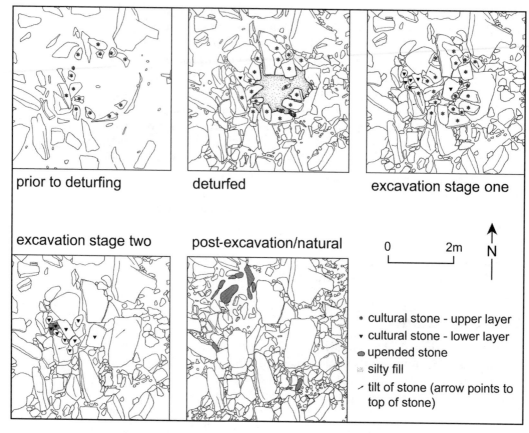

prior to deturfing

deturfed

excavation stage one

excavation stage two

post-excavation/natural

0 2m

N

* cultural stone - upper layer
▾ cultural stone - lower layer
● upended stone
▨ silty fill
⌐ tilt of stone (arrow points to top of stone)

fig. 9:3 Clitter Cairn 5 showing the sequential stages of excavation. Field Credits: Plans JR and HW.

Five boundary walls were sectioned by the excavation (BSA-BSE, located on Figure 1.4). Two of the excavated walls, BSA and BSE, cross the contours of the hill and incorporate the lines of downslope clitter flows (BSA: Figures 9.4 and 9.5). Three of these walls – BSB, BSC, BSD – follow the downslope limits of contour-hugging clitter lobes (BSB: see Figures 5.12 and 9.6; BSC: see Tilley, Hamilton, and Bender 2000: Figure 9; BSD: see Figure 6.7). Two walls were coursed (BSA: Figures 9.4 and 9.5; BSC: see Tilley, Hamilton, and Bender 2000: Figure 9), the wall stones being in horizontal layers, using earth-fast clitter boulders as foundation stones. BSD was partially coursed (Figure 6.7) and is discussed in more detail in chapter 6.

In the case of BSB and BSC, smaller cobbles and boulders lay against the inner (upslope) northern face of the walls and may have created a form of ramping (BSB: see Figures 5.12 and 9.6; BSC see Tilley, Hamilton, and Bender 2000: Figure 9 and chapter 5 this volume). BSA was additionally faced with orthostats (Figures 9.4 and 9.5), and BSB was constructed of a line of orthostats that had been placed between earthfast boulders within the clitter (Figures 5.12 and 9.6). These various construction techniques might be regarded as a form of adaptive variability, minimising construction effort by maximising the use and characteristics of stable *in situ* clitter stones in the

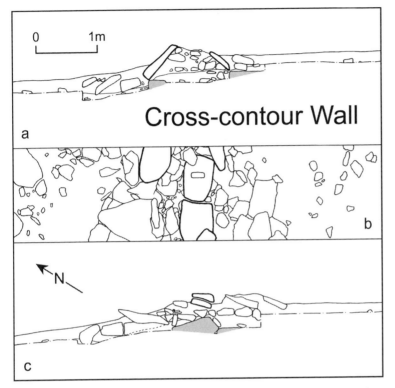

Cross-contour Wall

fig.9:4 Cross-contour wall in excavation trench BSA – the wall crosses the contour of the hill and incorporates the line of downslope clitter. Field credit: Plan and section ES.

fig.9:5 Photo of excavated section across enclosure wall BSA (camera facing north east) showing: n = *in situ* natural boulder; up-side-down triangle = stones of coursed wall; O = wall orthostats; * = wall rubble. Scales 50 cm and 20 cm long. Field credit: photo J S-D.

walls. However, to make these links, the walls persistently follow alignments that cannot be explained in terms of practical, functional, or utilitarian considerations (e.g., in the vicinity of BSA, Figure 1.4).

The excavation at BSD (Figure 6.7) encompassed part of the markedly more impressively constructed wall that surrounds the major housing enclave of the western settlement. This wall is unlike any of the other boundary walls excavated – particularly with respect to the careful selection and fitting of

fig. 9:6 Photo of excavated section across enclosure wall BSB (camera facing west): n = *in situ* natural boulder, O = wall orthostat. Rubble packing of wall to the right of the 20 cm scale. Scales, 20 cm and 2 m long. Field credit: photo J S-D.

its stones. It is fronted by tabular boulders placed upright (the downhill face of the wall). Behind this face, angular boulders mixed with *in situ* clitter rest directly on the old land surface with a course of horizontal tabular bounders on top. This south-facing wall section again follows a clitter lobe, but here the overall intention is to encapsulate the clitter formation within a dominant cultural image.

Overall, the wall excavations indicate that the hill was even stonier in the Bronze Age. Many of the earth-fast boulders incorporated in the walls are hidden below today's turf-line (which is several centimetres higher than the Bronze Age land-surface). The excavated surfaces around the walls revealed clitter no longer evident on the modern surface. Thus, the inhabitants of Leskernick chose to inhabit, even in their field systems, an extraordinarily dense world of stones, the major axes of which formed the *basis* of their bounded space.

The Anthropologist, the Archaeologist, and the Two Geomorphologists

Chris: So we're standing by the clitter mass … just to the south of the shrine stone excavation [and close to House 28] and we've identified at least three stones that we think are possibly – on the basis of their small, thin, slab-like appearance – cultural. And again … these stones fill the hollow (Figure 9. 7, structure 4).

Sue: The two largest cling-filmed boulders, I think are … moved by humans. But the one which … my hat is on, the smaller of the three … looks perfectly natural to me.

Chris: [Stephan,] I have to pin you down … can you just spell out why you believe those are placed – those two stones?

fig. 9:7 Map showing location of identified clitter structures on Leskernick Hill.

Stephan: Well, the northern-most one is resting at a very steep dip angle – it's resting against another tabular clast. The dip angle doesn't appear to be related to imbrication against another stone … [and] it's not associated with other boulders that have the same dip angles, so it can't be a frost sorting or cryostatic pressure phenomenon. And the one in the middle, similarly, to get these to have such a steep dip angle you've got to have them in association with other clasts or in the frost-sorting position.

Chris: Why just these two stones?

223

Ed: It seems to be to elongate the stripes. We seem to be standing in an area that is relatively … boulder free, and it may be my imagination but I can see a slight circular pattern that these stones have, by their position, enhanced. So, it's a circle-like structure at the centre of a clast-free zone, which is bounded by two elongated stripes. And upslope is a large blocking mass of boulders with a circular stone pattern.

Chris: What always struck us about clitter structures in this area is that they were very near to this rather isolated house (28), with this very dramatic lozenge-shaped stone [the shrine-stone] just to the north of it. So there's a nonrandom association, as it were, between a very …. special house and this lozenge-shaped stone and this series of clitter-structures above and below it.

Interpretation and Conclusion

It might be claimed that every stone and clitter mass on Leskernick was significant to the prehistoric inhabitants but this would be a rather unhelpful generalisation. Some stones were clearly more important than others, and the interpretative problem today is deciding which ones. This is particularly difficult in the case of large unmodified and unenhanced stones not incorporated in any cultural structures. In the case of these stones, our criteria for identification can only be subjective: we have a hunch or feeling that they were important because of their size, shape, and location along pathways. Born out of our own practice and engagement with the stones, our own sense of place as we wind memories and expectations around the hill, we have become more aware of surface, angle, layout, shape, and texture. Perhaps this contemporary experience of the stones meshes with the way the stones were experienced in the Bronze Age. But we would not want to make this claim. All we can hope to do is to rework and re-present the stones of the past in the present.

We have not found it easy to find words to describe these often fugitive structures; we have found it still more difficult to represent them adequately. Photographs, whether taken from the air or the ground, simply show more or less indistinguishable rocks; conventional archaeological plans drawn from a bird's eye viewpoint are equally unhelpful. In the end, the most vivid way that we found was to cover the stones with cling film and then to paint them. Only then did the patterns become more accessible (see Figure 9.1).

The clitter structures are simple constructions. They require no more than the levering up of some of the stones to emphasise them and differentiate them from others. In most cases, they have hardly been moved from their original positions. They were formed, then, by (1) choosing stones of suitable shapes and dimensions; (2) altering the original angle of rest; and (3) enhancing naturally occurring arc-like or circular patterns in the clitter by adding or removing a block here or there.

In some cases, almost identical patterning is achieved by geological rather than human action. We suggest that this *ambiguity* is not accidental. It is intended, it is part of the original cultural meaning of these places.

Chris: There are couple of stones I'd like to show you over here [north-east of the Shrine Stone] that we're intrigued with because we think they are pointing to Brown Willy. ... We cling-filmed them previously – this one, and that one over there ... If you kind of stand behind them and look from that angle, they seem to be pointing towards Brown Willy and its summit cairns (Figure 9.1b).

Stephan: Yeah, but there are also other stones nearby that are also pointing in the same direction. And there are other stones to the left of that. ... I don't think they're cultural.

Ed: It could be related to frost heaving. Stephan's mentioned that there are one or two stones also pointing in the same direction. But they're only one or two stones, and it does seem to be quite significant that the long axis of this boulder is dipping exactly ninety degrees to the overall dip of the slope. Equivocal!

Stephan: Yeah, I agree it's equivocal!

In most small-scale societies, the attribution of life and a soul to inanimate objects, most commonly through anthropomorphism, is a basic part of human conceptualisations of the world. In animistic systems of thought, natural beings are endowed with human qualities: boundaries between nature and culture collapse, becoming thoroughly ambiguous. The nonhuman world is thought of in the same manner as the human world. Continuity between culture and nature is asserted, and social categories are used to construct models of nature.

We believe that the people of Leskernick Hill regarded the stones as animate sentient beings, the very opposite of a modernist belief system in which the stones are regarded as inanimate objects to be exploited at will. As animate beings, the stones become subjects rather than objects, and possess a personality, an essence, a spiritual and moral power. The stones almost certainly have ancestral significance either as physical embodiments of a generalised ancestral spiritual essence or in terms of individual ancestors and events and stories connected with them. They contain forces exogenous to human will but forces that can nonetheless be pacified, tapped and controlled. The stones, as subjects possessing internal essences, require respect and reverence. They can have a protective function guarding the population of the hill and be potential sources of evil and danger.

The people at Leskernick would be intensely aware that through moving the stones and altering their configurations to create houses, walls, etc., they were doing violence to their hill, a violence necessary for life and sustenance. There would be morally right and wrong ways to engage with the stones. Altering the clitter, simply by modifying it, could in this light be viewed as an act of atonement. In altering the clitter, people were *merely materialising its own essence* (i.e., displaying the properties, powers, and potentials it contained within itself). People were not so much making the circles as drawing them out from amongst the stones: revealing a cosmic patterning, the circle, and a transcendent order lying beneath surface appearances – a jumbled chaos of stone.

There is a reiterative circular patterning within the clitter, a patterning that is repeated over and over again on the hill, and beyond. The post-hole circuits in the houses at Leskernick are circular, the houses are circular, they built stone circles, the cairns are circular, Leskernick hill itself appears to be circular,[4] and the hill is ringed with a circle of cairns on the top of other hills surrounding it in the landscape. The prehistoric architecture and its relationship to landscape are circles within circles within circles, and these circles encompass relationships both between the living and the ancestral dead, and between the people on the hill and those living elsewhere on the moor. Building circles was a re-presentation and materialisation of cosmological ideas.

In the most general sense, building circles for living in and building circles in the clitter are two facets of the same process that, to borrow a term from Appadurai (1996), we can refer to as the spatial production of locality. The arrangements of stones on the hill are part of a spatio-temporal technology of localization involving sentiment and feeling, local knowledge, and local subjects. Building houses and building clitter structures both objectifies local knowledge and forms a fundamental element in the production and reproduction of local subjects – that is, skilled and knowledgeable agents. The material structures and spaces that people created were skilled social accomplishments that acted recursively in the production and reproduction of persons through the production of meaning and value. A sense of locality was being imagined, produced, and maintained through moving stones and moving past stones on the hill and through ritual acts in and around them. Through engaging with the stones, people made themselves, physically and emotionally, creating an attachment to place. An understanding of stones was both integral to their cosmological beliefs and to an understanding of themselves.

The stones on Leskernick are differentially visible. Leskernick is entirely different when seen from a *fixed* point of observation (e.g., a house doorway) or from a *mobile* field of vision and experience (walking a path). We have tended to neglect the latter and need to keep experimenting with movement between places. The fact that structures and stones come in and out of view as one moves around the hill and are visible for long distances or are hidden, like the clitter structures until one is very close up to them, is part of their meaning and the way in which they fit into the hill. Compared with a house, the clitter structures appear more like shadows or spirits.

The ambiguity also works at another level. When one first starts to look hard at clitter, the eyes hurt, the stones begin to swirl: a pattern is no sooner seen than it is lost. The stones appear to be an ever-changing kaleidoscope of forms. Such effects would be ideal in inducing the trance-like states that are so important in shamanistic experiences and their capacity to mediate between this and other worlds. It is no accident that on Leskernick the majority of the clitter structures we have identified are concentrated in the vicinity of the large isolated Houses 3 and 28 (see Figure 9.7) located, when compared with the others, in liminal positions amongst the densest areas of clitter on the hill. Thus, the clitter structures form an intimate part of the ritualised making of connections between the ancestral stones and the living people.

Postscript

Chris: So do you think that recognition of that modification alters the way you as geologists would think about these rocks and think about this hill? Does it complicate matters, or how might it change things?

Stephan: It completely changes my perception of all clitter fields now, and it does complicate things because we use things like dip angles and orientation of clasts to determine past processes and therefore to determine past climates, and if it can be shown that a significant number of the clasts that we see on this hill have been moved by humans then obviously it questions our interpretations.

Chris: Would you agree that a lot of the things that we've seen have been ambiguous, I mean they might be natural, they might be cultural, they might be a combination of the two? One is always having to make interpretative decisions about these things and their relationships. It strikes me, thinking about this anthropologically, that this very ambiguity is part of the meaning and significance of these things. That basically, to them, there was no distinction between nature and culture, it was a seamless web, a kind of continuum from a house that was obviously cultural to a clitter mass that has a much more ambivalent status. So, this kind of ambiguity, rather than being a problem that in a modernist mind set we always think it is, in fact was part of the way they created cosmological meaning in the world.

Stephan: (chuckle) Yes, I think I agree with that!

Ed: Could you say it again! Chris was saying are any things ambiguous here, and of course I guess that there's no way of differentiating between what is cultural and what is natural in at least 50% of what we've seen – so that adds to the interest of the work you're doing!

Stephan: We talk about the chaotic nature of this landscape – I think actually the landscape is really quite ordered, even by natural processes. There is a definite asymmetry to the clitter development on this hill. On certain parts of the hill the clitter is well developed, and on certain parts it isn't. It's well developed along freak joint structures and … there's a lithological control, and there's probably a periglacial control as well creating structures, creating whirls and vortices, and creating imbrication. So, I think the clitter is quite ordered anyway, and then human beings have seen that order and tried to interpret it.

Table 9.1. The clitter structures on Leskernick Hill

(for distribution, see Figure 9.7)

About 40 in number, these have only been identified by surface survey in the corridor separating the two settlements and in the western settlement area. They cluster in the corridor and in the vicinity of House 3 in the western settlement (i.e., they appear to be associated with the

The Corridor

St 1. A semicircular arrangement of boulders linking two grounders and a single boulder wall to the east. Dimensions: 4 m W-E, 5.4 m N-S

St. 2 An encircled grounder approximately 2.8 m in diameter

St. 3 An encircled grounder 2.5 m in diameter

St. 4 Three uprights in a hollow in the middle of a clitter stream

St. 5 Circular structure behind and upslope of Shrine Stone 28. A ring of small stones demarcates a hollow 1.6 m in diameter

St. 6 Semicircular arc of stones 3 m in diameter (W-E) in front of and downslope from shrine stone 28

St. 7 Small circular structure 2 m in diameter

St. 8 Small circular structure 2 m in diameter

St. 9 Small circular structure 2 m in diameter

St. 10 Encircled grounder 2.5 m in diameter

St. 11 Encircled grounder 2.3 m in diameter

St. 12 Semicircular arc linking grounders 3 m in diameter

St. 13 Circular arrangement of stones 3 m in diameter

St. 14 Semicircular arc of stones with grounder as a focus 3 m in diameter

St. 15 Circular arrangement of stones 2 m in diameter

St. 16 Circular arrangement of stones in a depression with a slab as a focus 2 m in diameter

two special, isolated and liminal Houses 28 and 3). Figure 9.7 shows their distribution. Some of these are undoubtedly natural features in which stones have not been moved or displaced by human agency. In other cases, the clitter has clearly been modified and enhanced.

Clitter structures in the western settlement

St. 17 Stones partially encircling large, low, flat grounder 2.5 m in diameter
St. 18 Line of façade-like stones running up to and encircling the back of the mini-tor in front of which there are arcs of stones
St. 19 Just to the east of House 2 forming a kind of 'annexe' to it: a cove-like hollow in the grounders 3 m in diameter N-S and 4.8 m in diameter W-E
St. 20 Stone facade at the head of the clitter mass. The thin, virtually upright slabs protrude out as if a long spring line
St. 21 Encircled grounder later reworked as millstone and broken

St. 22 Semicircular arc of facade like stones behind a grounder: like 20 and along the same line at the head of the dense clitter mass upslope
St. 23 Façade-like arc of thin upright slabs at the head of the clitter mass like 20 and 22. These all form a discontinuous line
St. 24 Large square flat grounder 3 m long W-E, 3.6 m long N-S, with three stones propped against it on the N, S, and W sides and another two on top at the E side of the block
St. 25 A circular arrangement of stones 2 m in diameter
St. 26 Arc of stones above or upslope to the E of a large grounder 2m wide and 2.9 m long

St. 27 Cairn-like structure with central upright 2 m in diameter
St. 28 Arc of stones around the back or upslope of two large grounders 2 m in diameter
St. 29 Small circular arrangement of thin slab-like stones around a small central depression 2 m in diameter
St. 30 Large roughly circular arrangement of slabs within a central depression in a hollow in a clitter stripe above (E) of very large and impressive grounders consisting of at least one internal arc of stones 3.5 m in diameter (W-E) and 6.5 m (N-S), with side-set slabs around the northern and eastern sides of the depression defining an area 14 m in diameter (N-S) by 6 m (W-E)
St. 31 Semicircular arc of stones on the southern edge of a clitter stripe 3.5 m in diameter (N-S)

St. 32 Circular cairn-like mass of small stones in the middle of a clitter stripe 4.5 m in diameter (N-S)
St. 33 Encircled low, flat grounder 1.8 m long and 0.9 m wide
St. 34 Encircled low, flat grounder 3.5 m in diameter
St. 35 Small circle including some thin, flat stone slabs in the middle of a clitter stripe 2.5 m in diameter
St. 36 Circular cairn of large clitter blocks 3.4 m in diameter from which walls subdividing the enclosure radiate out

St. 37 Approximately circular deep depression in a clitter stripe surrounded by large grounders, 2.7 m in diameter. In the centre are upright clitter slabs resembling a graveyard
St. 38 Encircled upright 1.4 m high now at the base of a windblown hawthorn tree 2.5 m in diameter
St. 39 Encircled grounder in a hollow in a clitter stripe 5 m in diameter
St. 40 Large grounder with a clear area in front (downslope). The southern end has traces of an arc of stones 3 m in diameter
St. 41 Circle of stones at the end of a large, low flat grounder, 2.2 m in diameter

Photo Essay

Moving in Procession across Brown Willy

– A Narrative –

The dramatic stepped spinal ridge of Brown Willy rises to 420 m. It is the highest point on Bodmin Moor and in Cornwall, and one of the most memorable, distinctive, and impressive landscape features and topographic points of reference on the moor. From the south or the north, it appears as a huge grey pyramid. From the west and the east, its distinctive profile appears as a series of four great craggy steps rising gradually to the north. Although slightly concave in form, the profile of the ridge on the western and eastern sides is particularly steep, appearing to rise up at an angle of 45 degrees to the ridge top. The ridge acts as a formidable topographic barrier to movement across the north of Bodmin Moor from west to east (or vice versa). Dominating the western skyline from Leskernick and the eastern skyline from Rough Tor South and Garrow Tor, it visually blocks all views across the moor further to the west or the east creating distinctive worlds on either side of it.

Compared to many other hills across Bodmin Moor, there is very little evidence of prehistoric settlement around Brown Willy. It seems, rather, to have been a ridge that was communally used by people from the surrounding settlements.

Although there are no prominent outcrops on the top of the ridge, there are two substantial summit cairns, one at a higher altitude than the other. As there is undoubtedly an association on Bodmin Moor between height and spiritual power, the 'correct' path of movement between these cairns, and along the ridge as a whole, must have been from the south to the north, a rite of passage and symbolic transition from the world of the living to the world of the ancestral dead associated with the cairns.

It is on the far southern slopes of Brown Willy that this narrative begins.

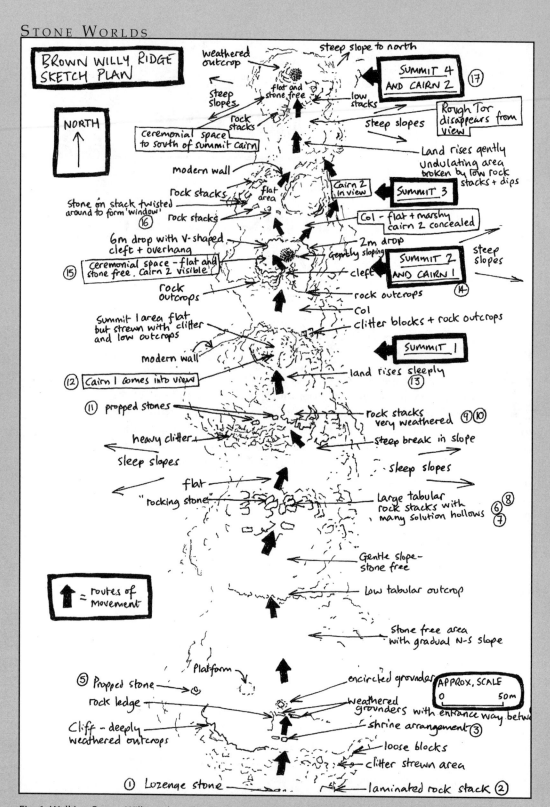

Fig. 1 Walking Brown Willey ridge. The numbers refer to the places from which the photos were taken.

First encounter

At the southern end of Brown Willy about 1.3 km due south of the summit, and on the 310 m contour, there is a 1.5 m high upright lozenge-shaped stone that has distinctive weathering patterns on its surface and is very prominent (Photo 1). This has been placed and set up at the base of a linear clitter stream consisting of large, flattish tabular blocks leading upslope to the north. To the west there is an area of dense clitter, to the east an isolated stack of deeply weathered tabular rocks, the lowest on the southern end of the Brown Willy ridge (Photo 2). To the south the land slopes gently away to an extensive marshy area separating the Brown Willy ridge from Butter's Tor and Pridacombe Downs. To the north of the lozenge-shaped stone, 58 m up the slope, there is an exposed west-east linear rock face 2 m high and increasing in height to the west to a height of 3 m or more (Photo 2). There are numerous fissures and cave-like hollows in this rock face at the western end and deeply weathered lines. Set on top of this rock outcrop, 14 m to the north, and in an approximate north-south alignment with the lozenge-shaped stone, is a V-shaped 'shrine' consisting of a very large lozenge-shaped block 2.8 m long and 1.3 m high and an irregularly shaped grounder somewhat resembling in form an Easter island statue, 2 m wide and 2.7 m high. The lozenge-shaped block rests on an exposed granite platform and appears to have been placed here and kept in position by a wedge of smaller stones at its base on the northern side. The two stones frame the lowest summit peak of Brown Willy looking to their north (Photo 3) and Carburrow Tor in the far distance, looking to the south. They are very prominent from the ridge to the north, from the Catshole settlement and tor area, and are visible from the western settlement area at Leskernick.

Moving on

North of these stones there is a small boggy depression 26 m wide whose northern end is marked by two distinctively weathered grounders with west-east weathered surfaces through which there is an 'entrance' way 3 m wide (Photo 4). On the western side of the depression there are low deeply weathered outcrops, on the eastern side a slight wall of small stones and clitter blocks. Fifteen metres north of the entrance there is an encircled grounder. Thirty-five metres to the north-west there is a circular single boulder platform 8.5 m in diameter constructed from *in situ* clitter blocks and placed stones. Skylined to the west is a distinctive propped stone, a rectangular block 1.5 m long and 0.6 m high resting on a grounder (Photo 5). Below it and downslope to the west there are at least six more propped stones in the clitter. Thus, the southern end of Brown Willy has an entire complex of monuments and structures and 'natural' features of markedly different form.

North of the 'entrance'

North of the 'entrance' between the heavily weathered grounders the ridge rises very gently to the north and is virtually stone free for another 180 m until one arrives at a west-east outcrop of low tabular blocks with diagonal weathered crevices and fissures. The stone free slope continues to rise gently for another 97 m to where a series of

233

massive tabular granite blocks outcrop. These are a very prominent feature of the Brown Willy ridge when seen from a distance from either the west or east (Photo 6) and in their rounded forms, shapes and dimensions contrast markedly with the rest of the rock outcrops on the ridge to the south or the north. An 'entrance' way between outcrops to the west and the east encourages movement between them. Ahead are another series of higher and more massive tabular rock stacks through which one must move to the right (east) in order to walk through a 28 m–long 'corridor' between them.

On the top of these tabular rock stacks, but invisible from below, are a series of deep circular and oval-shaped water-filled solution hollows on both sides of the route of passage. The largest of these is 0.9 m wide and 0.3 m deep (Photo 7). They contain numerous loose quartz crystals. One of the most massive of the blocks to the left makes a gentle rocking motion as one walks across its top to look down at the solution hollows on its surface.

The first clitter-strewn summit

The first clitter-strewn summit of Brown Willy is now directly ahead (Photo 8). For another 60 m there is a virtually flat and almost stone-free area until the ridge begins to rise up steeply in an area strewn with numerous clitter blocks of moderate size and a series of heavily weathered rock outcrops 3 m high on the southern side with particularly deep crevices on their western faces. These contrast markedly with the smooth rounded surfaces of the tabular stacks with the solution hollows below (Photo 9). To the west of these rock stacks there are two propped stones. One is a very weathered block with the weathered face positioned so as to face downslope to the south and be visible from this direction (Photo 10). The other stone is a thin smooth slab propped up on a grounder. The weathered propped stone marks the point at which the Rough Tor ridge to the north of Brown Willy disappears from view.

Above the propped stones

Above the propped stones the slope rises up more gently and is littered with small clitter blocks for another 62 m until one encounters another fissured and heavily weathered west-east rock outcrop. One must now climb up and through a series of stepped rock stacks and very weathered rocks forming 'terraces' to the very top of the first summit at which point the large cairn on the second summit area becomes visible to the north with the Rough Tor ridge beyond. The top of the first summit area is strewn with small clitter blocks and has deeply incised and weathered rock stacks on its eastern side. The cairn ahead is sky-lined from here (Photo 11).

Into the col

After walking across this area for 27 m the land plunges down deeply into a col separating the two most southerly summit areas. Both sides of this col are marked by rock outcrops over which one must climb passing across an almost stone-free 30 m-wide west-east passage way between them. On the southern side of the col a modern transverse wall runs up to the rock stacks from the west and east. The cairn on the second summit area is perched above a series of deeply incised rock outcrops visible below it from the south (Photo 12). Passing across the col and moving upslope the cairn goes out of sight.

Movement towards the cairn is now funnelled

Movement towards the cairn is now funnelled through a 3 m wide cleft in a series of deeply weathered rock stacks to the west (left) and right (east). These are up to 2 m high and block out any views of the surrounding landscape (Photo 13). Finally, one must climb over the northern end of the rocks to reach the cairn sited 20 m away to the north. Climbing over the end of the cleft the cairn above dominates one's view, even though the wider landscape is again becoming visible to the west and to the east. Walking up to the cairn, Rough Tor appears once more on the skyline to the left.

Standing on the top of the cairn

Standing on the top of the cairn, a panoramic vista over the moor explodes. In a few steps, one moves from a close-up view dominated by the cairn to a wide open view across the moor.

The top of the second summit is completely bereft of stones apart from those comprising the cairn itself. These stones are remarkably uniform in size without any visible large blocks. The presence of the cairn, and the lack of other stones, contrasts greatly with the rough littered surface of the lower summit top.

Today, the cairn is 19 m in diameter and up to 1.8 m high with a central depression. It is situated on the drum shaped, flat-topped rock outcrop of the second summit. The rock outcrops below it are steepest to the west, where they rise to a height of 6 m. The drop on the eastern side is much gentler, only 2 m. On the western side of the outcrop there is a deep V-shaped cleft with deeply weathered rocks with a small overhang where some shelter is possible from the wind and rain.

The cairn is positioned to the right or on the eastern side of the flat summit area. To the east of the cairn, the land begins to shelve slightly until the break created by the rock outcrops, but to the west and south and north of the cairn there is a flat area 17 m wide extending to the rock outcrops on the western side (Photo 14).

Looking north from this cairn, the top or fourth summit area of Brown Willy and its cairn is masked by the third summit. This suggests that the exact positioning of the lower summit cairn is very specific. It was deliberately sited so that the upper summit cairn would remain invisible when approached from the south. However, when one stands in the middle of the stone-free shelf of land to the west of the cairn, the top summit cairn becomes visible between pairs of rock stacks to the south and south-west (Photo 15). Assuming that a view of the northern higher summit cairn was significant in terms of ideas of transition and a south to north passage from the lower to the higher part of the ridge, the space for ceremonial activities around the lower summit cairn would have been to the south and west of it.

Moving north from the second summit

Moving north from the second summit, the land drops down to another col, separating it from the third summit.The top summit cairn soon falls out of view as one passes through a small cleft between rock stacks to left and right. We pass over a small flat wet area to reach another series of rock outcrops 55 m away (Photo 16) and once again, the Rough Tor ridge falls out of view. The outcrops, dropping steeply to the west and east, are again very weathered with deep crevices. Moving on, the land to the east continues to fall away very steeply, whilst, to the west, there is a flattish shelf of land bounded on the western and southern sides by a series of weathered stacks with tabular plates some of which have slipped off. One of these appears to have been repositioned so that it is now aligned transversally to the bedding planes of the rocks below it creating a space or 'window' along the ridge top to the north.

Moving north again

Moving north, the top summit cairn comes into view again as one passes to the right (east) of the higher of the rock stacks on the third summit area. The summit cairn is now directly ahead. The passage to it entails walking gradually upwards over an undulating area broken up by rock stacks and dips creating a series of broken spaces on the ridge top. Thus, the passage from the third to the fourth summit area is significantly different from that between the first and the second or the second and the third, and entails a downward movement over a col before climbing up the ridge once more. On entering the highest summit area, the Rough Tor ridge comes into view once more and is revealed sequentially from the south-west to the northeast ends (Photo 17)

The cairn, now 15 m in diameter and 3.2 m high, is built up against a series of exposed weathered rock stacks on the western side beyond which the land drops away steeply. There is no evidence here of modern restructuring of the cairn, and it would seem that these rock outcrops, which could easily have been covered by the cairn material, were deliberately left exposed. On its northern side, the cairn extends down to a series of flat outcrops. Beyond these the land drops away steeply. To the east of the cairn there is a very weathered low rock exposure after which the land drops down precipitously. South of the cairn there is a large flat stone-free area, 45 m long and 49 m wide, the only possible space for ceremonial activity. Ceremonies would thus be conducted facing the cairn with the Rough Tor ridge visible beyond it to the north.

The conceptual difference and visual contrast between the two summit cairns on the Brown Willy ridge was of the utmost significance. The lower cairn is entirely 'cultural' in form, wider and lower. One must pass up and over rocks to reach it but it occupies a summit space devoid of all but its own stones. In contrast, the upper cairn, at the ridge end, incorporates the weathered rock outcrops as the very core of its structure.

As we move from south to north along the Brown Willy ridge what is really striking is the manner in which 'natural' features replace 'cultural' constructions. The shrine, propped stones, platform, and encircled grounder are all encountered at the southern end of the ridge. Apart from the two propped stones beneath the first summit and the stone slab twisted round to form a window to the west of the third summit, we encounter a landscape seemingly unmodified apart from the construction of the deliberately contrasting cairns, each of which plays off cultural form, notions of place, and contrasts in topography in a different manner. The reason for this would appear to be obvious. There was little reason or necessity to further modify the top of one of the most evocative and powerful ridges on Bodmin Moor whose power and mystery was derived from the sleeping powers of the rocks themselves, their forms, constellations … the appearance of the ridge at a distance. The cairns merely enhanced and served to emphasise what was already there. They act as cultural markers in a spiritual passage to the roof of the world and the end of the ridge where an entire panorama was revealed across Bodmin Moor, north and south to the sea, and beyond.

Part Three

The *Present* Past

In the next chapters, the emphasis shifts to different ways in which we, in the present, engage with the past. Chapter 10 introduces the two sociological chapters; chapter 11 discusses the practice of archaeology; chapter 12 is about the way in which archaeologists and anthropologists interacted with the place and the landscape; and chapter 13 presents the creation of art installations on the hill.

Beyond
Britain
England
Cornwall
Bodmin Moor
Leskernick Hill

Chapter Ten

Introduction to the Sociological Study of the Leskernick Project

Introduction One: BB, SH, and CT

We have not finished talking about prehistoric Leskernick; we want to pause to consider our contemporary interactions with the hill and with each other. It will be abundantly clear by now that our interpretations are subjective. Like all interpretations, they are filtered through variable contemporary understandings of the past, of landscape and of social relations. We have no choice: we can only ever attempt a contemporary reworking of the past. So it seemed to us that it was important to try and understand more about our relationship and attitude to landscape, material culture, and other people. It also seemed important to pick apart the sociology of the group enterprise that we undertook at Leskernick. We were using specific archaeological and anthropological techniques. These were not just adjuncts to our endeavours and our interpretations, they were affected by them, and affected them. There has been relatively little study of how practice and interpretation work off each other, and this lacuna seemed worth addressing. We asked two anthropologists, Mike Wilmore and Tony Williams to come on site and to undertake these studies.

Mike Wilmore and Tony Williams both studied in the Department of Anthropology at University College London (UCL). It would be fair to say that their (unequal) relationship to at least two of the project directors probably acted as a constraint. But perhaps this heightened their determination to retain their autonomy. As we began to edit the book, we made suggestions to the two authors – but they were only suggestions and they were by no means always accepted. The directors and other members of the team admit to embarrassment at some of the things that they were seen to have said and done but accept that once Pandora's box is opened, there's no way to shut it.

Introduction Two: Tony Williams and Mike Wilmore

> A satisfactory explanation for the various trends in Anglo-American archaeology must incorporate a sociological analysis of the way the discipline is structured here [in the U.S.A.] and in England, the way knowledge is produced, and the purposes to which it is put. (Kohl 1993: 19)

Kohl is not suggesting that sociology is the *sole* means of analysis, simply that it is an important component. Before we begin, we must be clear about both the potential rewards and limitations of sociological analysis.[1] We are certainly not claiming that we can perform some sort of strange alchemy whereby the lead of sociology will be turned into the gold of archaeological knowledge. These sorts of alchemical experimentation have occurred in the past, most notably with Durkheim's attempt to establish sociology as 'an independent source of philosophical truth' (Gell 1992: 13); but as far as we are concerned, the problems of archaeological epistemology and reasoning must be solved from within the boundaries of the discipline itself. Sociology can offer diagnoses, but cannot serve as a remedy for problems in archaeological theory or practice.

These chapters are, therefore, not strictly speaking *about* archaeology – meaning the body of theories and ideas about the past that are based upon the analysis of material cultural remains – rather, they are about the process of *doing* archaeology, in its diverse incarnations, in the messy context of the 'real' world. Our goal is to provide an empirically informed critique of a particular archaeological undertaking through which a whole collection of archaeological consciences and consciousnesses, moralities and identities can be delineated. These are identified in the 'folk lore' of the discipline through the application of the sorts of distinctions between archaeologists identified by Shanks and McGuire:

> In the theoretical arena ongoing debates pit processualists against post-processualists, scientists against humanists, evolutionary theory against history, and an interest in generalizing against an interest in the particular. Many scholars have a difficulty in moving from these polemical controversies to the doing of archaeology; they are plagued by doubt as to the relationship between theory and practice. There is uncertainty about how to connect academic archaeology, rescue archaeology, and cultural resource management, or how archaeology should relate to the public interpretations and uses of the past. Witness the lack of dialogue and institutional connection between academics and fieldworkers. (Shanks and McGuire 1996: 75)

Contradictions within the social structure and organisation of archaeology as it is practiced within the context of the Leskernick Project and, perhaps, more widely within archaeology in late 20th/early 21st–century Britain tend to reify, but do not create, these distinctions between different theoretical and methodological positions in archaeology.

To attempt such a task on the basis of fieldwork and research focussed upon one very small fraction of contemporary archaeology is ambitious. Moreover, since the Leskernick Project was deliberately formulated by its directors to be of a novel and innovative character, there may well be some question about how representative it is of archaeological theory and practice. We are not claiming that it is 'representative,' but are suggesting that the approaches we have taken, and the insights we have gained, will be germane to the discipline as a whole. We are also happy to admit that there is much about the project that we do not know for many quite obvious reasons. Any claim to objectivity in sociological analysis based upon the adoption of a position of panoptic omniscience is, and always will be, a total fiction.

Our place in the scheme of things

When we were asked to participate in the project as 'site sociologists', our brief was minimal. We were to focus on the project as it played itself out at Leskernick and the nearby campsite. We were not concerned with the work that occurred 'off-site', although we did, on occasion, sit in on meetings at UCL. The directors spelt out, in very general terms, two main objectives. One, the exploration of the social contextualisation and dynamics of the fieldwork practice, and, two, the study of how people involved on site – including not just practioners but visitors – engaged with the landscape and how their sense of identity and of belonging, or not belonging, were manifested materially. There was no specificity about how we were to proceed or about who was to do what. We decided to divide the labour along very general lines and were keen not to allow too rigid a separation between the reseach themes so that overlapping interests might be worked through from different methodological perspectives.

Mike Wilmore joined the excavation team early on to participate in physical work on site, to look and listen, and to ask questions. In particular, he looked at the ways in which archaeological fieldwork is articulated through discursive and nondiscursive means; that is, through the practical 'doing' of archaeology as much as through talk about how or what things should be done. He was interested in the potential interrelationship between these practices and the personal biographies of the project members. To explore this, and bearing in mind the restricted time available for research, he also used a short questionnaire that asked respondents to give, amongst other things, details of their education, employment, hobbies, and household circumstances, alongside questions about their involvement in archaeology.

Tony's involvement with the sociality of the project focussed on the phenomenological experiences of the project's members in terms of their attitudes and perspectives towards the place in which they were working and (temporarily) living. In short, he attempted to understand more about the experience of 'being there', about the participants' varied perspectives on the place in which they were engaging with the past, and about the way in which places become resources of power, identity, and authority for members of the project.

As the field sociologists, we were in a somewhat anomalous position, wavering between being 'insiders' and 'outsiders'. This ambiguity was exacerbated by our both being connected with the Anthropology Department at UCL. One of us – Tony Williams – had been a student in the department; the other – Mike Wilmore – with a background in both archaeology and anthropology – was in the throes of an ethnographically orientated PhD that had nothing whatever to do with Leskernick. Our informants were thus often friends and colleagues, teachers and students, and the dialogues we conducted ranged from face-to-face interaction, through diaries, e-mail, telephone conversations, and some of the participants' academic writings. We readily accept that there is no way in which the 'normal' distinction between the sociologist or anthropologist who reports, and the population who is reported on, could be maintained.

Although our emphasis was upon fieldwork practice and daily routine, it will become clear in the following chapters that these practical endeavours were reiteratively textual – from funding applications, through annotated maps, context records, surveys, exhibition materials, diaries – the list is endless. It is through their texts that authorative claims and counterclaims are made by the Leskernick practitioners; just as it is through our texts that we lay claim to a degree of sociological understanding. We can claim no privilege – our attempts at sociological objectification lie alongside and work with the cultural objectifications that play a key role in the life of the people we are discussing. These people also include you – the reader – whose presence must be acknowledged if we are to realise the full scope of the Lesknernick project in our sociological analysis. We expect you to answer back.

A note on using diaries

With only limited time available for fieldwork, much ethnographic detail has been retrieved from participants' diaries that were written at the site directors' request. The use of informants' diaries is fairly common in anthropological research, providing a 'document of life' tracking the contemporaneous flow of public and private events (Plummer 1983: 170). Written mainly in private, the diaries are, in most cases, the result of individual authorship and share much in common with a memoir – presupposing an audience.

AA (day 2 1996): It's quite an odd thing writing a diary you know someone is going to read, yet I feel this is really just an extension of my usual diary – minus the gossip.

241

SR (29 May 1997): The diaries add an extra element to the social aspect of the dig, everybody is aware of them and many times people have said, for instance, 'Don't put that in your diary' because they are aware of the signficance of some events and conversations which will probably be recorded in people's diaries.

CT (13 June 1966): I am more and more convinced of the importance of diaries and it is becoming increasingly evident the manner in which the diary keeping is itself structuring the social relations: what can and cannot be put in, by whom, when, where and how.

MST ('Caravan Diary', 4 June 1996): HW said something interesting today, the caravan diary is like big brother. There are two reasons for this, one, we don't want to say too many 'interesting' things, in that case we would be writing all the time, and, two, because we don't wish to hurt anyone. The latter point is emphasised by CG and AR in particular. In particular, they like SH and don't want to distress her, she having formed a close personal attachment to the site.

The project diaries are valuable research tools because they provide unprompted details of unobserved behaviour.

MST (21 May 1997): His [TW's] questions, though normative, give you the opportunity not to be normative in reply. If the intention is to draw out the questionee, they are the best sorts of questions, for they allow full rein to his ego. This is good socio-anthropological practice. 'What on the hill is natural, cultural, ambiguous?' he asks. 'Position, shape, weather, geology, relationships; domesticates, us; vegetation (peat), the horses, the ruinous state of the settlement etc.' I answer. Very fancy. The trouble is I would never have thought this if I had not been asked in the first place. Our unprompted diaries have far greater validity.

The excerpts not only reveal useful detail about the accumulation of archaeological knowledges but also chart patterns of mobility and sociability amongst the participants. Each participant's diary can, however, be read as considerably more than a straightforward narrative account of their involvement in the fieldwork at Leskernick. The familiar tropes of diary writing, in particular conformity to a chronologically arranged account of the time of fieldwork, creates a bounded spacio-temporal account that can limit their potential usefulness for an understanding of how the writer is enmeshed within diverse sociocultural fields (Bourdieu and Wacquant 1992). One of the members of the survey team paused to consider the strengths and limitations of his own attempt at diary keeping:

Ian (December 1997–January 98): This diary was written-up in December 97/January 98 several months after the third season (my second) on the Leskernick hillside. The original script was written always very late at night – the very last thing to do. No matter how tired or drunk I was it was the final act before lights out. Sometimes the handwriting became very flamboyant and therefore difficult to read. Writing it late at night meant that the whole day had to be recalled. I think this is why certain structural events feature prominently – the journey into Camelford; who travels in the car; the cooking of food. These events become the framework for the day remembered onto which more reflective ideas are placed. The process of writing up the original script brought forward all sorts of additional memories and thoughts to those actually noted. In this way the diary is double-layered. The first remembering at the end of each day and a second memory in the writing-up many months later. In this way the diary which follows has become a more vivid fiction – a fragmentary personal account.

From our point of view, the limitations imposed by the 'bounded spacio-temporal account' could be offset by disrupting the diaries' narrative flow. Rather than look at each diary as a self-contained entity, the analytical technique used was one of literal deconstruction. Each diary was plundered for references to a set of topics that defined some of the key characteristics of the sociocultural fields and subfields that concerned us in our research. The collation of thematically linked and cross-referenced diary excerpts forms a useful adjunct to the more familiar methods of sociological research – participant observation, survey, and interview – because it focusses attention on contrasting interpretations of and reactions to events, whilst allowing us to search for patterns amongst these reactions.[2]

More will be said about the use of diaries in the next chapter; suffice to say that the use of diary exerpts presents a number of ethical as well as methodological problems. The extracts used in the next two chapters have had minor errors in grammar and spelling corrected. In some cases, punctuation has been added where this was necessary to clarify the substance of the extract. In a few cases, diary extracts that might cause offense were not used, even where they might prove useful to the argument.

Chapter Eleven

The Book and the Trowel
Archaeological Practice and Authority at the Leskernick Project

MIKE WILMORE

Introduction

The Leskernick Project is embedded within the hierarchical structures of academic life. However, although social relations between the project members reflect this fact, the archaeological fieldwork is also characterised by strong bonds of 'mateship' that originate from the collective experience of working conditions that are often extremely difficult. In apparent contrast to the academic concerns of the project, the participants lived for a short time in a liminal space free from many of the concerns of day-to-day existence. But this contrast is more apparent than real because, as with other instances of liminality that are constitutive of rites of passage, one of the goals of participation is the achievement of new status through processes akin to rebirth (Turner 1967: 95). This status clearly relates to the position of each practitioner within the field of academic archaeology and it is towards this domain that we must look to identify the cultural materials through which both liminality and formal order are structured in the context of the project.

A problem of authority

One of the aims of the Leskernick Project was to question the working traditions of archaeology and develop different ways of organising fieldwork. The diaries written by project members in the first year speak of the hopes and disappointments that surrounded their desire to create new ways of collaboration:[1]

Barbara (in Bender, Hamilton, and Tilley 1997: 169, 172): There was a time, at the beginning, when Chris [Tilley] said 'Everyone must do everything, we must all excavate, survey, go up on site. We must all be familiar with everything because then there'll be an egality of knowledge'. [But] we're trapped in the hierarchy of knowledge: however much we try to democratise, we nonetheless end up validating and invalidating the perceptions of the students and subtly appropriating them.

Henry, an anthropology undergraduate who later became a survey supervisor (in Bender, Hamilton, and Tilley 1997: 172): I was also learning about the supposedly non-hierarchical nature of the project. What we had was a good and creative discursive process but at the end of the day there was a latent hierarchy that usually became manifest around tea time. This is not a bad thing as obviously those with more knowledge and experience are bound to have a certain authority over those who are basically students.

These entries introduce the question of how authority was distributed amongst the members of the project team. My concern is with authority in three interrelated senses – authority as the power to command, authority as expertise, and authority in the related sense of authorship. According to Frank Kermode (1981: 87), 'authority doesn't normally raise the question of authority,' because by doing so it draws attention to itself and risks undermining the unspoken assumptions about the right of a person or group to speak on behalf of others. Much of the dynamic social interaction of the Leskernick Project derived from the project directors' decision to raise the question of authority in relation to archaeological practice.

Any appreciation of how authority is manifested within archaeological practice is predicated upon understanding how archaeological knowledge is constructed through the creation of texts.[2] Archaeological practice is obviously not entirely textual in form – indeed, more than most academic disciplines, it involves large amounts of physical labour. Nonetheless, it is dominated by textual practice, because status within the discipline ultimately accrues to those who create texts.[3] These texts may include diaries, context records, and project/site reports as well as works of synthesis that place the results of a project in the context of the overall prehistoric (or historic) record and archaeological theory.

The Leskernick Project offered an excellent environment in which to discuss these issues, because one criterion for people's involvement in fieldwork was that they take on an authorial role by completing a diary describing their work and thoughts during their stay in the field. The intention of the project directors was to create a record of each participant's reaction to the processes and environment of their fieldwork.

Chris [Tilley]: The basic idea was that we would record the process of discovery that would be as significant as writing some kind of report. See how ideas develop and so on; and out of that the idea of the trench diaries was developed to try to cope with this.

Mike [Wilmore]: Were the personal diaries conceived in this sort of way as well?

Chris: The personal diaries were conceived as partly that, but also to do with the fact that, you know, there are individual persons here: Why are they doing it? What do they think? What do they understand? So. it is also part of the sociology; people expressing their opinions about what they were doing and what they thought about. This was a way of thinking about another dimension of it [the project].[4]

Each participant would narrate their own experience and, as Barbara hoped, provide 'anthropological detail on how such situations play themselves out, and the very variable perceptions of what is going on depending on where the person is socially (gender, age, status) situated' (Barbara: 'Post-1996 Season Thoughts').

The creation of these diaries was contentious. Writing a diary placed a considerable burden upon the project members, many of whom had never previously done such a thing. Apart from the time and physical effort involved, it often forced people to inscribe complex emotions and thoughts. The semipublic nature of the diaries was also a problem. Although all participants were required to complete a diary, the circulation of the complete corpus of diaries was restricted to the three project directors and the two project sociologists. This had two effects. First, the project participants knew they were 'on the record', as the following quotation shows.

Mike ST, an excavation supervisor (e-mail to the author, 19 September 2002): Both ethically and practically the key to my and my fellow sociological 'guinea-pigs' involvement in the Leskernick project was our knowledge that we were on the record. Outside archaeological fieldwork, we did not have to say – or do – anything, and, provided that you represent it honestly, we cannot object to its honest attribution.

Therefore, the diaries were subject to considerable self-censorship prior to being handed over to the project directors. Second, certain project members refused to comply with this discipline, either by refusing to complete a diary, producing a deliberately banal diary, or by using techniques such as the production of a coauthored, 'caravan' diary to circumvent problems of disclosure. In addition to this, the compulsory completion of texts by student fieldworkers, which were then handed over to the directors of the project, was seen by many participants as similar to the normal, hierarchically ordered routines of academic life, even though the directors' expressed intention had been to 'open-up' the project to a multiplicity of voices.[5]

When I came to write this chapter, my first instinct was to use pseudonyms for all project participants apart from the project directors, on the grounds that this would afford them some degree of privacy. However, this decision was opposed by many of the participants whose identities I sought to disguise on the grounds that this was tantamount to the appropriation of their original texts. Mike ST expressed this in the e-mail from which I have already quoted:

Just as inconsistencies in the characterization of the site will jar, misrepresentation or incorrect interpretations of our characters will be clear to the reader; while our presence thoughout the text, maintained through the consistent use of a single set of names, should help the hold the narrative together. Pseudonyms, however, are unacceptable. Their imposition would be a breach of faith on the part of the project directors. By removing our real identites from the site narrative and preventing us from mounting any sustainable challenge to its interpretations, they would be acting contrary to the project ethos as represented by them to us.

I have therefore restored the original first names of all participants and included initials of surnames where necessary to distinguish amongst participants with the same names.[6]

The organisation of the Leskernick Project
Vertical and horizontal distinctions

Chris (14 June 1996): Sadly, we live in a split community. There is an absolute social divide between the diggers and the settlement people. The diggers created it from the outset and they maintain it. They are not part of the spirit and romance of Leskernick, only partially within the bubble of the hill. They listen to football matches on their radio while digging, still part of the outside world. Out buying Chinese take-aways, in pubs in different places (settlement people rarely go beyond the campsite). The digger lineage are more outsiders than insiders. This is why they will never be able to understand, or comprehend, the power of the stones.

The project organisation involved both a 'vertical' hierarchical organisation and a 'horizontal' division of labour, the latter based upon a distinction between project members who were primarily excavators – 'diggers' – and those who were primarily surveyors – 'settlement people'. This horizontal distinction was the subject of repeated, often anxious, discussion between project members and was constantly referred to in their diaries. For good or ill, people used it to explain to themselves the problems and tensions within the Leskernick Project:

Gary, an archaeology undergraduate later to become a postgraduate student and excavation supervisor (6 June 1996): It quickly became apparent that a certain amount of friction had occurred between those excavating and those working on the field survey. From what I can gather a gulf was starting to emerge between the two camps. Which camp will I be placed in? Neither I hope!

Henry (17 June 1997): I do regret the lack of any anthropology students. I was surprised by what I see as the rudeness of some of the excavators today, but it doesn't bother me much. The two sides of the project are now such separate entities I no longer expect us all to be sharing our time. However I do find it quite sad that it has to be like this.

This discourse was clearly a part of the 'common sense' of the project, a characteristically 'Leskernick' way of speaking, and, as such, rather than offering us an explanation of the project's social dynamics, it is something that requires explanation.

Project hierarchies

In common with most archaeological projects in the United Kingdom, the Leskernick Project had a three-tier system of fieldwork organisation, with the least people at the top and the most at the bottom. The project directors were the apex of this pyramid, followed by the project supervisors; the fieldworkers were at the base. This is a functional distinction and a model of organisation familiar to most archaeologists. It is, however, a much simplified ideal model of archaeological organisation and most, if not all, archaeological projects show some variation.

This tripartite system, based upon the separation of responsibility for collecting, recording, and interpretating data, forms part of any large archaeological project. But other contingent factors sometimes blur these divisions.[7] For example, within a commercial archaeological unit, the economic context of the unit's work, including the need to tender competitive bids for work, requires that costs be kept to a minimum (see Pryor 1995). The introduction of multitasking and the employment of those with a flexible skill base parallel those in other sectors of the economy (see Harvey 1989: 117–97).

The Leskernick Project was situated within a very different socioeconomic field and was academic rather than commercial in its practice. The main sources of funding were the British Academy and, to a lesser extent, University College London, and the project participants were involved, with only a few exceptions, in academic institutions, as lecturers, researchers, or students.[8] Although the financial resources available to the project could not match those available to commercial archaeologists, the project had one valuable resource that is chronically short in commercial archaeology, namely time. The Leskernick Project received a relatively long-term funding commitment from the British Academy, and the fieldwork site was not threatened by imminent destruction. A degree of flexibility and variation over the years in the organisation of the project was possible, therefore.

Perhaps the most significant characteristic of the project organisation was that it had three directors. Initially, the directors were optimistic that they would be able to maintain a flexible set of fieldwork practices through the sharing and free transfer of labour between different tasks. There would be no middle tier of supervisors, and the role of director would be brought closer to that of the ordinary fieldworker. Theirs was, in essence, an egalitarian and nonhierarchical vision of fieldwork organisation. In the first year of fieldwork, this was attempted and the acknowledgment of the existence of a collective 'project team' in the first publication (Bender, Hamilton, and Tilley 1997), along with the diary comments of some participants, provides evidence of some, albeit limited, success.

Andrew, an anthropology undergraduate (Day 2 1996): The non-hierarchical system works well here, but I prefer some amount of instruction just to save time from continual discussion about pointless (to me!) matters ...

Matthew, an anthropology undergraduate (June 4 1996): It is nice to be involved in a project where the opinions of everyone are considered valid, rather than [just] those with notable reputations.

Henry (11 June 1996): It was nice how we had so much discussion last year. OK we never got away from hierarchy but a lot of barriers were taken down and there was a genuine sharing of ideas.

Barbara (1995): We're trapped in the hierarchy of knowledge: however much we try to democratise, we nonetheless end up validating and invalidating the perceptions of the students and subtly appropriating them. We are nervous of their interpretations. However much we accept the subjectivity of knowledge and the reflexive nature of our interpretations, we want to finds ways of validating our findings. The students are less inhibited, they look at 'interesting' rocks or potential structures and surmise their meanings. We back off – if we aren't careful anything might become 'meaningful'! It was only towards the end [of the season] that we felt safe enough to incorporate some of their discoveries into what seems like a more coherent understanding of Leskernick's stone world. There is an inequality. It was something we talked about a lot, and we didn't resolve it.

In retrospect, however, the small size of the initial group and the fact that the bulk of the first year funding was provided by the directors from their own incomes meant that few other alternatives were possible. By the second year, when external funding from academic institutions became available, differences between the directors over the allocation of resources to the various constituent parts of the fieldwork became apparent. This centred in particular on Sue's need to enlist excavation fieldworkers, primarily recruited from amongst the student body at the Institute of Archaeology, as well as more experienced archaeologists to supervise this larger body of fieldworkers. Accommodation costs, salaries for professional archaeologists, and excavation tools for use by the expanded workforce meant that the excavation component of the fieldwork was allocated a far larger proportion of the total budget than the survey.

In the first instance, the directors tried to circumvent this imbalance by keeping the total number of people involved in the project to a minimum. However, by the third season of fieldwork (1997), there were considerably more people involved in the excavation than in the survey, and the demands of the excavation in terms of manpower meant that very few of the excavators were able to spend time doing survey work. By the fourth year of fieldwork, attempts to keep a degree of parity in numbers between the excavation and the survey were abandoned, and Sue, the director in charge of excavation, decided to recruit as many fieldworkers as she felt were necessary to complete the excavations.

Although it would be wrong to overemphasise the long-term impact of these disagreements, they undoubtedly created some tension between the project directors. In 1997, one of the excavation supervisors commented on this issue in somewhat stark terms:

> *Comments reported in author's own diary (29 May 1997): Without the excavation component of the project funding from the British Academy would not be forthcoming. The implication of this is that Barbara and Chris are exploiting the excavation and by extension the excavators to further their own agenda.*

This comment undoubtedly surprised some members of the surveying team. One of the surveying directors, although admitting that the excavation was an important component in the grant proposal, suggested that the grant was awarded because of the project's theoretically 'ground-breaking' ideas that, in her opinion, primarily emanated from the anthropologists. The same notion is succinctly stated in the following diary note:

> *Chris (12 June 1996): There is a danger of settlement survey ideas sprinting way ahead of any possibility of being linked in with ideas governing excavation.*

The debate over resources was complicated by the fact that the administration of the grant proposals and the monitoring of the project expenditure was undertaken by the director most closely involved in the excavation side of fieldwork.

> *Chris (4 June 1996): Sue comes and starts doing accounts. Apparently Barbara and I have already spent beyond the fixed budgets she has devised for us and will be financially penalised after this if we buy anything else.*
>
> *Barbara (24 May 1997): Sue has really managed everything so far. Chris and I have been very passive. It's just that the dig has a life*

and a timetable of its own and so it gets underway without any help from us. ... But, of course, it's much more than that. Sue put in all the grant applications. It's as though Chris and I, having always operated solo, continue to do so despite everything. But at least I got round to thanking Sue the other day. I guess, from her response, that she has been feeling rather put upon.

As is so often the case, issues about money and resources got tangled up with more theoretical questions about procedures and aims, and the original desire of the project directors to collaborate as closely as possible during fieldwork was tacitly abandoned by the end of the third year. This in no way implies that collaboration between the project directors did not continue. Indeed, it is significant that away from the site of fieldwork, during meetings at the directors' university to discuss the publication of the project's findings, overt conflict between directors was, in my experience, nonexistent.

Divisions of labour

At both ends of the project's hierarchical organisation there was some cross-over in the horizontal order, that is in the types of fieldwork undertaken, although there was always a bias to one or other side of the labour division. In the case of the directors, there was both the freedom and the necessity for discussion of matters relating to the project as a whole and necessary collaboration in interpretation and writing. For the fieldworkers, most of whom were students, there was little formal reason why they could not cross between the excavation and the survey, but, in reality, once someone had become established in one area they rarely moved across the divide.

Fay (24 June 1997): With a little trepidation, fed by comments and ribbing last night and this morning about my 'defection' and a little uncertainty as to what I might be doing, I found myself very much at home and excited trying to find structures within clitter. It made such a difference to raise my eyes from an excavation trench and explore the site, this freedom of vision inspiring new thoughts and ideas enabling a more holistic approach to the site, its surrounds and what the aspirations of our work here are.

Steve, an archaeology undergraduate (23 June 1997): We had a little 'tour' of some of the cultural stones in one of the clitter streams. Very interesting. I'd like to know more about what the survey team's been up to, but it's a bit late now.

It is not surprising that fieldworkers who were recruited to the project from the Institute of Archaeology or through prior association with Sue became closely involved with the excavation, whereas those recruited through the Department of Anthropology or through association with Barbara and Chris tended towards the survey.

Group solidarity and feelings of friendship between students and lecturers in the fieldwork situation were expressed by both the archaeological and anthropological students:

Henry (6 June 1997): Once we are on Bodmin Moor there is something that ties and binds us all together – our 'conscious collective' [sic] – that is our desire to interpret the remains of the ancient community, the enjoyment of bringing life back to the stones. ... Our survey team is small and we all share the same relative understanding of what we are doing. There is a shared passion between us that I feel goes beyond academic interest. This is the quality that we bring to this project, we are free with our ideas, people think aloud, disagree or agree.

Stuart, an archaeology undergraduate (29 May 1997): Never before have I socialised with one of my lecturers or teachers and I am used to seeing them in college/school time only. ... I guess I expected the more important members of the project to distance themselves from the 'diggers' but this is not the case.

In contrast to the top and bottom of the hierarchy, an increasingly impermeable barrier came to exist at the supervisor level of organisation.[9] Although only those involved in the excavation at this middle level were (following archaeological convention) actually spoken of as 'supervisors', certain individuals performed a comparable function in the conduct of the survey fieldwork. In the first two seasons, these individuals taught less-experienced fieldworkers how to conduct and record the survey work. By the third season, mainly because of frustration on the part of the directors with inconsistency in the execution of site records and the unwieldy nature of survey groups above a particular size (normally about three to four people), the survey team got smaller. A restricted core of experienced people carried out the bulk of the work in conjunction with the two 'surveying' directors. Just as the excavation supervisors never helped with the survey, these experienced surveyors never excavated.

The differences between excavation and survey were often described by those involved in the survey in terms that contrasted the dynamism of the latter with the conservatism of the former. Common contrasts included stasis versus movement, an inward or downward focus of attention versus outward or upward focus, discovery versus nondiscovery, and the freedom to discuss methods of analysis, representation, and interpretation versus a restricted, proscribed methodology that discouraged unwarranted interpretation. The following exchanges relate to the particular issue of how the stone should be drawn:

Wayne, a volunteer member of the survey team working in adult education, who was later to become a survey supervisor (5 June 1996): A grenade exploded concerning [our] methodology and its relationship with the work [of] Mike – who was producing a superb technical excavation drawing. His work was using a different mind-set to ours. Our purpose was different. Both were relevant to their purpose but fundamentally different. We seemed to get over this by agreeing to do our own sketch plan of Hut 23, not as an alternative to Mike's but to complete the record in the manner in which we had been recording the other huts.

Barbara (6 June 1996): Sue's base-line is archaeological 'exactitude' and an encoded way of doing things – planning, etc. 'Anyone', Sue says, 'looking at Mike's ground plan would be able to read it'. 'Anyone', of course, is anyone with the right training and knowledge. For most people it would be quite meaningless. Ours, on the other hand, are instantly readable.

Sue (9 June 1996): On the Southern Settlement Wayne and Penni [an amateur archaeologist and survey volunteer] gave an outline of their 'rapid' planning methods for the house interiors. Within one week they have sketch-planned the key elements of most of the 18 houses on the Southern Settlement. During the same time the excavation team have produced two pre-excavation house plans which replicate every visible stone. Wayne and Penni can now recount characteristics of individual houses – their method has speedily generated an intimate familiarity with the settlement as a whole. Which method is more in key with experiencing the potentials and parameters of a Bronze Age world? Which method provides a database of a Bronze Age world for others to effectively engage with?

Those involved most closely with the excavation tended, not surprisingly, to reverse the contrasted polarities. For them, surface survey created only a superficial understanding of the material remains of the past, whereas excavation with its meticulous attention to such things as soil structure and stratigraphic relationships was able to provide a clearer understanding of people's actions in the past. This understanding, they insisted, does not simply appear fully formed from the soil beneath the turf line, but is developed through discussion and cooperation amongst the excavators within the frame-work of the accepted methods and techniques of archaeological excavation. The negative points made against excavation by the surveyors were, as the following diary excerpts show, largely seen as its essential positive features and any lack of subjectivity or discussion was more apparent than real.

Sue (14 June 1996): At lunchtime Chris and Barbara came to see me about Gill's [an anthropology undergraduate] crystal from H23. Mike has refused to accept it as a small find – could have predicted this since it is not a foreign stone and it is not a humanly produced artefact. For Mike it is technically no different to a mica fleck or a bracken root. During the morning Ceira had recovered a similar, but less attractive quartz crystal from topsoil of H39, and Gary had pointed out a granite block in the H39 tumble which incorporated several such crystals. After lunch I went over to H23. Penni and Mike were the only people working there. I mentioned the quartz crystal to Mike. He determinedly refused to small find it, but in due course a compromise was negotiated, namely that it is a narrative find ('NF') which would be plotted on the plan as such, i.e. something that has contributed to trench discussion and consideration of the structure's interpretation. A white garden tag was duly marked up as 'NF' and nailed into the ground at the 'find spot'. Mike is satisfied because 'NF', in his opinion, stands for non-find.

These overt distinctions being made about interpretations and methodologies are, however, often balanced by statements that point out the similarity between, or convergence of, the methods used by surveyors and excavators.

Chris (June 1995) (in Bender, Hamilton, and Tilley 1997: 165): The excavation was dominated by technical procedures, a rhetoric of recording. In the settlement work there was no obvious starting point or procedure to follow, no standard context sheets. But we rapidly tried to create standardisation in recording and got very concerned if things were not being done in the 'right' way.

Chris (June 1995) (in Bender, Hamilton, and Tilley 1997: 165): There was this strange thing about temporality. In the excavation people seemed to be doing the same thing all the time, yet they were recording and doing different things every day. In the settlement work there seemed to be continuous variety, yet we were doing pretty much the same thing all the time.

Sue (15 June 1996): After lunch talked to Barbara and Chris. They had been checking some of the settlement sketch-plans and have noted discrepancies ... all very time consuming and casting some doubt on the completed sheets. Barbara said that we really needed 'professional' trained sketch-planners which reminds me of my original plea for competent people on the excavation. The requirements of our separate methodologies are beginning to replicate each other.

It is also obvious that participants' descriptions of each other's work often bore little resemblance to reality. Surveying tended to be carried out extremely systematically once the initial methodology had been refined in the first two fieldwork seasons. Equally, excavation, portrayed by some as the rigid application of a set of inflexible rules, involves the practitioner in a continuous hermeneutic process both as an individual in relation to the conditions of the particular archaeological environment and in discussion with other practitioners. Jane, a professional archaeologist and friend of Sue who regularly visited Leskernick during the fieldwork season, described her impressions of this process of discussion:

Jane (17 June 1996): The moving of a [recumbent] standing stone ... was debated for a while – and the actual removal from its fallen position took less time than the discussion – but that's archaeology for you! Adapting to the archaeology – so different from Sussex – is taking a while – understanding the stone alignment, its possible destruction and then trying to make sense of the evidence, whilst the debates go round and round takes getting used to! At least problems and ideas are chewed over, with all sorts of ideas discussed, assimilated or thrown out as necessary (this gives most people a chance to put forward their ideas and hear those of others).

Finally, the following excerpt from my diary regarding a conversation with a mature student from the Institute of Archaeology working at Leskernick in 1999 summarises these points neatly because (much to my initial surprise) he reverses the polarity of the stereotypes of excavation and survey:

(19 June 1999): After finishing our meal the table fragments. I talked with Ken [a mature student, archaeology undergraduate]

about his involvement in the Leskernick Project this year.
He's spent more time with the survey this year than last. I'm
flabbergasted when he says that he is impressed with the
systematic nature of the survey when compared to the excavation.
The survey has a set form of recording he says whereas the process
of excavation tends to involve many more ad hoc decisions about
what to do next and how to interpret what is found.

The persistence of a distinction between excavation and survey during the time of fieldwork at Leskernick cannot, therefore, be explained in terms of a radical differences in methodology. Nonetheless, for many participants such a difference was assumed to exist and was used to explain why the ideals of cooperation with which the project started were not borne out in practice. Like the discourse about horizontal hierarchy, these explanations should be regarded as Leskernick 'folklore', part of the 'common sense' of the project, and as noted above, behaviour that requires explanation rather than something that is itself explanatory of behaviour. This explanation requires an examination of the role that the Leskernick Project played in the educational life of the project members.

Liminality

Fieldwork as a rite of passage

The first report on the Leskernick Project published in the Proceedings of the Prehistoric Society (Bender, Hamilton, and Tilley 1997: 175–76) concludes with the following list of acknowledgments:

> Acknowledgments: The project team was: Phil Ableson, Gill Anderson, Cath Baynton, Barbara Bender, Alan Benn, Henry Broughton, Sue Hamilton, Mary Hinton, Jason Hutter, Pippa Pemberton, Chris Tilley and Helen Wickstead. Ian Grieg helped us set up. Figures 4, 6, and 8–11 were drawn by Jane Russell. We are grateful to Mrs Dowton and the Commoners of Leskernick for giving us permission to undertake the project. Peter Herring, Nicholas Johnson and Peter Rose of the Cornish Archaeological Unit gave us much support and allowed us to borrow equipment. Dave Hooley of English Heritage gave us much encouragement. He and Peter shared their knowledge of Bodmin Moor with us. The quotations in the account are taken from the personal diaries of the team, written during the project.

The notes to the survey map of Leskernick were written by Martin Fletcher. The southern stone circle was first found by the Archaeological Division of the Ordnance Survey in 1973 and published by John Barnatt (1980). The northern stone circle, and the stone row, were discovered by Peter Herring. Peter pointed out the significance of the 'Quoit' on the top of the hill to us, and predicted the setting sun would shine through it on the summer solstice, which we were able to watch.

Part of this paper was presented at the Prehistoric Society Conference in Dublin in September 1995 as part of a joint paper written by Barbara Bender and Mark Edmonds on *The Ritual of Daily Practice*. We would like to thank Mark for his contribution and comments.

Table 11.1: Geography of Participation in the Leskernick Project

Project Participants	Place
'The commoners of Leskernick'	Leskernick Hill
'The project team'	Bodmin Moor
'The Cornish Archaeological Unit'	Cornwall
'English Heritage'	England
'The Ordnance Survey'	Britain
'The Prehistoric Society Conference in Dublin'	Beyond the United Kingdom

If we examine this text, we see that it is structured according to principles of a time-geography (Giddens 1985) mapped onto the broader spatial and temporal form of the Leskernick Project. The geographical elements of this participatory structure are summarised in Table 11.1 and Figure 11.1 below.

The temporal elements of this time-geography are more difficult to represent in schematic form. But it is notable that the acknowledgments indicate not only a changing geographical scale, but also a changing temporal scale. The latter moves between the limited and occasional 'moments' of the fieldwork season in which the total fieldwork team were involved to the longerterm involvement of various specialists to, finally, the directors who were involved throughout the duration of the project.

These spatial and temporal elements of the project organisation correspond to Anthony Giddens's notion of 'regionalisation' (Giddens 1985). 'This,' he says,

> should not be understood merely as localisation in space, but as referring to the zoning of time-space in relation to routinised social practices. Thus a private house is a locale which is a 'station' for a large cluster of interactions in the course of a typical day. (Giddens 1985: 272)

Not all participants were granted equal access to each region within the time-space of the total project, but, at the same time, certain regions were sites of what we might describe as high intensity action. The fieldwork season[10] was, through its place at the start of this list of acknowledgments and at the heart of the time-geography of the project, foregrounded in the project's presentation. This foregrounding was manifested in various ways during the project – through the restriction of the diaries to the fieldwork season and through the formal presence of sociological observers and other visitors at these moments in the life of the project.

Figure 11.1: Geography of participation in the Leskernick Project[11]

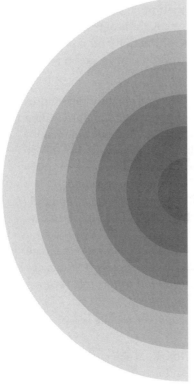

Beyond

Britain

England

Cornwall

Bodmin Moor

Leskernick Hill

Routinised social practices are creative of, as well as created by, systems of organisation and authority. The symbolic and functional characteristics of the fieldwork season at Leskernick can be understood as a *liminal* point within the project participants' educational development. The 'micro-situation' of the fieldwork was inextricably enmeshed within the 'macro-situation' of the higher-educational field that provides the encompassing sociocultural context of the Leskernick Project.

Liminality is an analytical term derived from Van Gennep's work on rites of passage and subsequently developed in Victor Turner's influential ethnographies of Ndembu society (Turner 1967). 'Liminality' describes a state of being that is outside or marginal to normal social categories. Although admitting that liminality reached its 'maximal expression in small-scale, relatively stable and cyclical societies, where change is bound up with biological and meteorological rhythms and recurrences rather than technical innovations' (Turner 1967: 93), Turner maintains that Van Gennep's three-fold model of ritual processes involving separation, transition, and incorporation is a widely applicable sociological model.

Sociality, according to this model, consists of two contrasting characteristics – social structure and communitas – that work in unison to maintain and reproduce society:

> Between incumbents of positions in secular politico-jural systems there exist intricate and situationally shifting networks of rights and duties proportioned to their rank, status, and corporate affiliation. There are many different kinds of privileges and obligations, many degrees of superordination and subordination. In the liminal period such distinctions and gradations tend to be eliminated. (Turner 1967: 99)

The ritual practice of the liminal period creates the conditions within which the participants' previous position within the social structure can be obliterated. For a time, the participants exist in a state of free association with their fellow participants. After this period of liminal sociality, which Turner came to call communitas, the participants are reintroduced into social structure, but in new positions with new rights and duties, rank and status.

This is not the place for a long exegisis on liminality, but we may note, following Morris (1987: 253), the following important facets of liminal sociality:

1. It is a time of ambiguous status for the participants of rites of passage during which normative sociocultural categories and classifications are dissolved. This dissolution is often brought about through 'role reversal or a suspension of normative obligations'.

2. There is often a period of seclusion during which the initiate is separated from normal life.

3. There is a stress on the absolute authority of the ritual elders. Such authority is moral and ritual rather than secular and is seen as expressing the 'common interest'. It is linked to secret, esoteric knowledge.

I have already described some elements of sociality at the Leskernick Project that correspond to Turner's notion of social structure, that is, the formal organisation of the project that derives its authority from within the academic field. The next section considers some of the liminal social practices observed and discusses whether they perform a similar function of disarticulating and then rearticulating the individual participant within the social structures of the academic field.

A place apart
Liminality and the experience of participating in the Leskernick Project

> *Chris (12 June 1996): Over the past few days there have been grumblings about how long it takes to walk to Leskernick, particularly when we are carrying water containers, food, toolboxes, etc. Wayne in particular has wanted to drive to site. Christel's [a mature student, fine art undergraduate working with the survey] jeep would be ideal for this: it could be used for what it is actually meant for – off-road driving, and she is prepared to drive it up every day. But I hate the idea. Leskernick is all about transitions: camp-site to the edge of the moor, walking across the moor. It all develops a sense of liminality, a daily and repeated rite of passage.*

Certain adjectives are used throughout the diaries of the participants to describe the fieldwork site. Leskernick and its environs are (in descending order of frequency) magical, eerie, mysterious, special, enchanted or enchanting, fantastic, calming, different, electric, enigmatic, extraordinary, impressive, intoxicating, nightmare[ish], powerful, sacred, strange, superhuman, unique, and weird. More than simply different, Leskernick is fetishised and becomes an animate entity in its own right (see also chapter 12). Sometimes this fetishism is inspired by the rapidly changing weather of the moor:

> *Dan, an archaeology undergraduate (11 June 1997): The mist returned to the hill in late afternoon. It swooped up the valleys with rapidly moving flanking tendrils of dense mist which seemed to be alive. They sort out and envelop the hill, reclaiming it,*

261

letting us know our time here is only finite. This seemed almost meant to give us impetus to leave, however, when this was not enough it started to rain.

Henry (11 June 1997): As we began to walk to Leskernick we were shrouded in mist. It did not take long before I realised I had no idea where we were. I was simply following everyone else. Everyone was following everyone else. No one knew where we were or in which direction to go. We stood around trying to locate ourselves in the invisible landscape. Everyone seemed to think that we should go in different directions. It was very damp, my feet were sodden and I began to feel cold. Eventually we came to some agreement and we gradually found our bearings. If I had been on my own I think I would have got completely lost. A useful reminder, perhaps, to have respect for the moor and its changing moods.

Sometimes stones and weather become nightmarish:

Chris (19 June 1996): I am desperate to escape from Leskernick and be on my own. I feel absolutely exhausted mentally and physically. The stones have finally taken their toll and by the time I finally leave, around 9 p.m., the stones have taken on the dimensions of a kind of nightmare. I am sick and tired of them and their contemporary community. The weather is turning, a thunder storm blows up and it begins to pour with rain.

As each participant struggles to convey their experience of this landscape, he or she resorts to a vocabulary that distinguishes between the otherworldly character of the fieldwork site and the 'normal' places where he or she has come from. This is not just a vision of separate landscapes: it is a difference that is physically experienced. The following extracts convey some of the ways in which this difference is felt – Leskernick is described as a place where emotions, thoughts, and even the fundamental ontological realities of time and space are quite different to other places.

Barbara (6 June 1996): Driving home last night, dead tired, it took about fifteen–twenty miles before home/college swam back into focus. It is very strange how that world recedes and the other world, in which the present is pricked through with the past – this stone, this enclosure-opening, this house – takes over.

Jane (20 June 1996): The stone terminal looked good – the rain had helped. We took the fences down and the site instantly became part of the landscape – Chris was right about fences shutting off the site. Mike then completed the day by fitting a small block to the top end of the standing stone and it was obvious that it had been broken off – the fitting together of the stones gave a much better shape to the stone's profile. Mike, at last, began to return to our world.

Fay (8 June 1997): Enjoyed the walk up to the Quoit which seemed to centre the site for me. Until then it felt as if it was floating and shape shifting. This feeling was probably due to the unfamiliarity of the site and the shifting patterns on the land created by the clouds and light. I wonder if I will feel the same about the Quoit in a few days?

Wayne (10 June 1997): Bodmin [town] was grim. Wet, almost deserted and closing. Then to Safeways. Inside the shop we all wandered around like the Stepford Wives – tired, completely dazed at the riches before our eyes and totally unable to comprehend what it all meant. It was as if our world on Leskernick had a reality unconnected with that which we were experiencing in the aisles. An experience completely alien to that of the hillside. Two worlds apart.

Fay (18 June 1997):I am having vivid dreams of the soil acoustics, earth hues, rain textures, skyscapes – I feel more part of the land, more integrated with it.

London, arguably the ultimate urban environment, is the 'Other Place' to which Leskernick is contrasted, but is less a real place than the participants' conception of quotidian urban experience. Leskernick itself is, therefore, largely understood in imaginative terms (see Said 1995). As Raymond Williams (1993) argues in his study *The Country and the City*, the Industrial Revolution and changes in land-ownership combined to bring about the movement of the majority of the population into towns and a corresponding discourse eulogising the countryside appeared in English literature and politics. Descriptions of Leskernick as 'magical,' etc., can clearly be interpreted in this way. The liveliness of Leskernick is invariably contrasted with the deadening effect of life in the 'grim', 'polluted', and, for the duration of fieldwork, 'alien' town.

But the participants' descriptions of this separation also suggests that this discourse does not exist solely in the emphemeral realm of thought and language, but is experienced both physically and emotionally. Thus, it contributes to the embodiment of each participant. Leskernick is not simply manifested as liminal through symbolism that represents it as a place apart from the normal situation of the participants' lives; its manifestly different presence leads to personal transformation.

Using some of the participants' own words, we can summarise the experience of liminality at Leskernick in terms of the three aspects highlighted by Morris. First, the liminal period is a time of ambiguous status. This, to a large extent, is brought about through role reversal.

Part of the ambiguity may arise from a sense of 'not-belonging':

> *Henry (12 June 1996): Everyone has been delegated a job. Roles have been assumed by people and today I feel a little out of place. There is not the flexibility of last year. The archaeologists are very professional in their outlook and a divide of us and them type is very apparent. Because of this I begin to worry as to where I would fit in – what would my role in all this be?*

Partly this may be the result of the sudden intimacy between participants of demonstrably different ascribed status:

> *Chris (12 June 1996): I keep considering whether I should stay in a tent next year rather than indulging in the luxury of a caravan. It is this obsession I have with avoiding power and hierarchy. But it is impossible. Last year I camped in a tiny tent with all the others but still stood accused of being hierarchical. What if I slept naked outside?*
>
> *M. [name not given in diary], an archaeology undergraduate (2 April 1996): From feeling quite apprehensive … about coming to Bodmin – about 'fitting in' – about perhaps feelings of inferiority of intellect and so on, I feel quite comfortable with things (and people).*
>
> *Anna, an anthropology undergraduate (Day 7 1996): I don't quite know if I like knowing them [Barbara, Sue, and Chris] as ordinary people or whether I would have preferred to have continued a teacher/student relationship. You get to know their faults as well as the good aspects and so they no longer sit on the pedestal you have placed them.*
>
> *Matthew (2 August 1996): I was disappointed with the lack of organisation and apparently missing hierarchy (unless one is God it is useful to know one's place in the scheme of things, if anything this allows us to gauge how much we should rebel).*

And part may occur through the dissolution of 'normal' boundaries between work and leisure, expert and nonexpert, student and teacher:

Wayne (7 June 1997): Although the next three weeks is work it is also three weeks away from work. A holiday which isn't. [...] I have brought my Dorset long barrows research stuff including a whole load of books which I feel I must have to hand ... just in case!

Henry (16 June 1997): I'm working with Barbara on the same patch in a way that I think both she and Chris would like the whole project to work. While we did not agree on everything we are prepared to listen to each and reach new ideas through our conversations. The work we did today was really good and it proved that you don't always need a hierarchy.

It is quite obvious that the next element of liminality, the seclusion of participants from normal life pertains to fieldwork at Leskernick. Not surprisingly, then, this was the subject of frequent comment either as a subject of note itself, or in terms of the journey to and from Leskernick, or because of various factors that struck the participants as abnormal and that therefore implied this separation.

'caravan diary' – Mike (27 May 1997):

Chris D. [a mature student, archaeology undergraduate]: One day blurs into the next.

Chris G.: He feels disconnected from the world, like he's floating away.

Chris D.: It's the lack of reference points outside archaeology.

Barbara (10 June 1997): Watched the news with the Conservative Party election results. Very interesting, a wonderful send-up of the upper classes. Nice to break out into the world for a moment.

Sue (11 June 1996): Although it was raining, the excavation team tried going up to site first via Buttern Hill and then via Westmoor Gate, but we soon gave up. Instead, we went to Camelford and settled in a newly-opened coffee shop. It felt surreal sitting in our wet, muddy clothes at a pink-clothed table and having coffee served in gilded cafeterias.

Wayne (9 June 1997): Barbara seemed a bit horrified that I should want to have a mobile phone with me as apparently I had said something last year about not having such things on site. I can't remember but it sounds like the sort of thing I would say.

Another manifestation of this seclusion was the way in which the group often became the totality of each participant's social life during the course of fieldwork. As a consequence, people who were not project participants came to be regarded as 'outsiders':[12]

Stuart (1 June 1997): Today has been the worst possible day and I have ruined my hard work and my relationship with the rest of the group. I didn't make it back to the caravan park last night or early morning and woke up with a blazing hangover and therefore missed a day's work at the site. I'm disappointed and annoyed with myself as I have let down Sue, Mike and the rest of the group and most of all myself. I now feel isolated from the rest of the group.

Chris (14 June 1996): At Leskernick I am part of a different community and another world in which the wider outside world becomes irrelevant. Normally I am interested in the news. While at Leskernick I couldn't care less about politics, the state of the world or anything else. I am inside this hill. This is the reality. The outside world becomes a fantasy. A kind of ritual reversal in which the king, for a day, becomes low and is pelted with rotten tomatoes. We have our own Leskernick conversations and thoughts here. Anyone coming to visit us from the outside can't really take part in the conversations or the sociability of the group. They are inevitably left on the margins even if we try to speak to them or make them welcome.

The final aspect of liminality is the stress on the absolute authority of the 'ritual elders'. Unlike the other elements of liminality, this aspect is more difficult to apply to the Leskernick fieldwork experience. Morris suggested that 'such authority is moral and ritual rather than secular and is seen as expressing the "common interest", the elders reflecting the axiomatic values of the community' (Morris 1987: 253). But, as we have seen, there were significant disagreements during fieldwork – that is, during the period that we are describing as liminal – over what these interests were, thus authority was open to contention. There are frequent references to the imparting of esoteric knowledge, the sacra of the project, by senior members to their juniors, but there is no necessary agreement as to what these sacra consist of. This question of ritual authority is of great importance and forms the subject of the next section.

Making archaeology – making archaeologists

One implication of the vertical structure of the project is that participants at each level of the hierarchy learn something from those above. Even some of those who are nominally at the top (i.e., the directors), referred on occasion to their own 'lowly' position in relation to the knowledge of 'experts' who came to Leskernick. The diary excerpts that follow are arranged in order of the project hierarchy with the observations of a director coming first:

Barbara (23 June 1997): I said goodbye to Peter [a professional archaeologist and specialist advisor to the project]. I felt very humble, almost tearful. It felt that although, undoubtedly, we're breaking new ground in terms of a ritualised landscape and much else beside, there's so much that we haven't really understood in terms of how people lived, and how they built up their Leskernick worlds. And where these things are concerned I feel my knowledge is very superficial compared to Peter's.

Ian (15 June 1997): In the afternoon we went around with the geomorphologists and they confirmed our suspicions that many of the stones in the clitter streams had been moved – reorganised. Brilliant! If this is the case then the implications about how we read the landscape could be radically transformed.

'caravan diary' – Mike (10 June 1997): I believe Sue has confidence in my work now. I have not thought about this before, but on reflection I find it very flattering: it warms me and it boosts, in a way that has positive implications in the field, my own self-confidence.

Tony [Williams] (25 May 1997): Chris, Barbara, Mike [Wilmore], Stuart, Lesley [an archaeology undergraduate] and myself detach ourselves from the group in order to receive our long awaited induction to the site. Slowly we amble towards the hill as Chris unfolds the story of Leskernick.

Henry (16 June 1997): Tony had asked us to take one photograph that summed up one's 'sense of place' here at Leskernick. I have found it really difficult to decide what to take. Every idea I had seemed to miss something. The more I thought about this I decided that it was going to be necessary to include people in the photograph. My sense of place here is something that has come about through my relations with various people – most importantly Chris and Barbara. But where to take the photograph? I wanted to have some kind of foreground and background with Chris and Barbara standing somewhere that

would tie together some of my feelings about Leskernick. [...]
Eventually I went for the Shaman's Hut with a nice background of
Rough Tor.

Christel (19 June 1996): Barbara and Chris got into a discussion
about what is natural and what is artificially constructed.
Barbara considers two huge grounders on top of each other as
an artificial construction, while Chris sees this as one grounder,
weathered along a linear fracture, so that the stone appears like
two stones, placed on each other. I am too inexperienced to have
an opinion.

Steve (11 June 1997): Talking to Sue has made me feel more a
part of the project than just one of Chris's [Chris G's] 'diggers'. She
has a wonderful sense of what will engage each of us, she knew
I would get a lot out of watching the stone moving. It was like
somebody had pressed my 'go' switch.

Such statements, which demonstrate the communication of authority from 'higher' to 'lower' participants within the project, mask the horizontal tear-line between 'diggers' and surveyors across which such communication rarely occurred. To understand this 'tear line', we need to pay attention to the ways in which authority, the power to command, is manifested through its two predicates – expertise and authorship.

It might be thought that hardships in relation to archaeological fieldwork refer to the physical labour involved in excavation and the unfamiliar experience of working outdoors in often testing environmental conditions. These are, of course, important and certainly play a part in people's decisions about whether to pursue archaeology as a vocation. But the hardships I wish to highlight centre upon a different kind of labour with different pressures that are commented on in a well-known manual on excavation techniques:

> The director must resist pressure to over-excavate, to go from
> one site to the next, piling up a backlog of reports which will
> seem to grow as it recedes in time. Only thus can he fulfil his
> academic responsibilities to the site and his moral obligation to
> all those who have worked on it. (Barker 1982: 227).

These concerns are touched upon in one of the project director's diaries:

Chris (14 June 1996): During the afternoon Wayne, Christel,
Marylyn and I go and record house 20 in the western settlement
and nearby house 17. Marylyn notes how our activities are
genderized. Wayne draws the site plans and elevations while

Christel measures. I fill in the interpretation sheet and dictate to Marylyn who writes. But this is also a question of knowledge and skills. Wayne is a superb artist and very quick. I simply couldn't do his job, nor can anyone else. My knowledge of the houses is considerably greater than Marylyn's and I have to write the report. I didn't really realise how I was taking over and dominating the hut recording. This embarrasses me. Should I write down what Marylyn says even if I deem it to be inaccurate?

It is axiomatic within the discipline of archaeology that excavation without publication is little more than wanton destruction; this is a key feature of a recognisably archaeological *morality*. Not publishing an excavation would betray the people who helped during fieldwork, future generations for whom the site no longer exists, and the people of the past whose remains have been disturbed. For Barker, this burden rests upon the shoulders of project directors, who bear the ultimate authorial responsibility for the expression of this *common interest* in the archaeological record. But this obscures the collaborative processes through which a fieldwork report is written. At Leskernick, most people were both authors and fieldworkers, fully enmeshed within the practical manifestation of this archaeological morality. The text-based, academic practices of archaeological fieldwork must be considered if the distinctions and disagreements between project members are to be understood.

In general, text-based practices differentiate between the directors who write the material that will be published, the supervisors who write the material that will not be published but that forms the site record used by the directors, and the fieldworkers who make almost no written contribution to interpretation. Of course, in most fieldwork situations the division of labour is not so clear cut. Thus, at Leskernick, the directors complete records of excavation and survey and so duplicate the role of the supervisors in this respect. Partly this is because of the restricted number of people involved in the project, which meant that people had diverse responsibilities. The reverse situation also occurs, and some of the supervisors will contribute to project publications.

Many of the fieldworkers are students at the Institute of Archaeology, and their involvement in the project is part of a compulsory fieldwork requirement. Each student has to complete a formal report on their fieldwork describing his or her own involvement in the project and its archaeological background. It is not so much the students' actual fieldwork that is assessed as their textual account of the fieldwork. In a curious way, the students' and the directors' use of texts are similar, because both use written reports of fieldwork to communicate with an expert audience that simultaneously assesses the quality of the archaeological work carried out and the qualities of the person carrying out that work. In both cases, progress through the discipline is at stake:

Henry (17 June 1997): Sitting in the caravan on my own gave me time to reflect on my own position to the project. Since deciding to start an MPhil I am now taken more seriously. Although I hadn't noticed myself, a number of people have remarked on how much more confident I am. I certainly feel much more comfortable this year. Last year was difficult at times as I wasn't involved with academia and was having a horrid time in London working in a wine shop. I think that some people thought that coming to Leskernick was just a holiday for me. It was certainly an escape. I had to prove myself last year which I found annoying.

'caravan diary' Mike (undated postscript): Eric [a mature student, recent graduate of Institute of Archaeology and excavation supervisor] is doing an MA now, Helen has deferred hers and I have been refused funding for mine. All this seems terribly predictable and terribly ironic to me. Big Foot [Chris] is now a professor. Ash, who was with us last year, and who is doing an MA, read a recent piece by Barbara. 'It was surprisingly good,' he said with a smile.

Barbara (22 June 1997): Quick talk with Chris about the geomorphologists. An interesting conundrum. [...] Chris [felt that ...] we should tell them not to do an independent survey but to survey the things we thought were interesting. But, I said, that means they have all our information, and could, presumably, still publish 'their' survey. Moreover, for me, the interesting thing was to see what they surveyed, what they thought was important, what they saw, and how they interpreted it. And how that differed from our perceptions. My sense was that the only point of friction was their independent publication.

Ceri, an archaeology undergraduate (30 May 1997): Went to the bar on the campsite in the evening, got a bit worried as I suddenly realised that Sue had just come back from an examiners' meeting. However Sue claims she's a 'fair marker'.

My diary (15 June 1997): On tour students ask few questions, Fay in fact rarely looks up from her field notebook where she is documenting what Sue says in very neat handwriting.

There is reciprocity involved in this process, as the 'senior' project members obviously have an obligation to tutor those lower down the hierarchy in the various skills involved in archaeology – both the processes of excavation and survey and how to record and write about the data retrieved. The following quotations, all except the first taken from the diaries of Institute of Archaeology students who worked at Leskernick during the 1997 season, show how highly regarded the excavation supervisors were, both for their own skills and for their ability to pass on those skills:

Ash (15 June 1996): I've learnt how much I still have to learn about digging. I'd dearly love to have the opportunity to improve/ develop these skills. … A couple of years … is the length of time I'd need to become a good digger. I'm stunningly impressed by Mike's practical skills and carefully thought out approach to all aspects of digging and recording and very impressed by Chris G's and Sue's ability to rapidly take in, process and analyse evidence – especially when I find it difficult to even see the contexts.

Lesley (30 May 1997): Chris [G.] takes Ceri and me through the context sheets and stratigraphy. I learn more in an hour from him, than I do in a whole day at Boxgrove. He also tells us what to put in our field notebooks. This trip has been an excellent learning curve. Have learned so much just from talking to Sue, Gary and Chris [G.].

Steve (9 June 1997): Sue has said before the project that each trench has its own character and it's certainly true. The trowelling technique that Helen required of me was very different from what had been required by Chris [G.] the day before. That was also true of Mike's 'hut' 23 in the afternoon. There's an awful lot in the way of soil changes in that structure and it takes quite a bit of concentration to get to understand what you're seeing. Mike's great though, he makes a point of telling you what's going on in the soil and what you're looking for.

An interesting distinction exists between the sorts of excavation skills taught by the supervisors and valued by the student fieldworkers, which were often described in terms of the inculcation of a craft or métier by the supervisors (see Shanks and McGuire 1996), and the text-based and discursive skills valued by those involved in the survey. For example:

Tony (26 May 1997): She [Helen] wants to DO archaeology, not just think about doing it. It is her craft, she explains. She takes pride in the knowledge that she, and others, are working within established parameters, carrying on the traditions, sweat and toil of her predecessors.

Although the pedagogy involved in excavation privileged observation and the repetition of the processes carried out by the supervisors, the survey work required each fieldworker to learn through discussion or even by challenging the supervisor's work, even if the ultimate decision lay with the most senior person present. Partly this reflects the contrast between the destructive processes of excavation, which requires a high degree of discipline amongst those involved to ensure that the archaeological remains are recorded with maximum precision, and the nondestructive survey work, which leaves the archaeological record intact to be reexamined by those who follow on. But it also reflects different perceptions of the role that the liminal moment of fieldwork plays within the academic development of different participants.

Texts are less the product of a predetermined functional division of labour (between excavator and surveyor) than the currency through which this division is made manifest and through which the relationships between people in different structural positions within the field are mediated. The double sense of the term 'field' as it is used here, meaning both the place where excavation and survey take place (fieldwork) and the sociological sense of 'a network, or configuration, of objective relations between positions' (Bourdieu and Wacquant 1992: 90), helps us understand how the social relations that we observe at Leskernick are ultimately situated within and structured by the academic field which encompass them. To understand the conflicts and friendships, the agreements and disagreements that punctuated the fieldwork, we have to recognize the way in which the project members' participation in this rite of passage contributed to their (re)articulation within this academic field.

Thus, it could be argued that both the appearance and function of liminality are present within the Leskernick Project because the special qualities of the space and time of fieldwork contribute to the transformation of the participants' being. Crucially, it is the functional aspect that is often missing from analyses that seek to use liminality as an element in the interpretation of social behaviour. It is not the case that the period of fieldwork associated with the Leskernick Project is *like* the liminal period of a rite of passage, but rather it *is* the liminal period of a rite of passage.

This is an important distinction. The connected theories of liminality and rites of passage were originally developed from observations made in small-scale societies, in situations in which it was assumed that there was some degree of agreement between people about the norms of social structure. But, as we have seen, the formal organisation at Leskernick – its social structure in Turner's sense – is split along both vertical and horizontal axes. These axes are important to our analysis because they provide status positions between which participants aspire to move. The liminal period of fieldwork contributes towards this movement. The horizontal distinction between the excavator-archaeologists and surveyor-anthropologists signals a potential disagreement over what criteria should be used to control movement between positions within the hierarchy. More particularly, it signals the ambiguous relationship between authority vested in the development of expertise based upon excavation as craft and authority derived from the attainment of academic capital through the production of texts. It is this ambiguity that generates the schism within the structure of sociality of the project.

The book and the trowel

A project at war with itself?

The following diary extracts describe some events surrounding an incident that occurred in the course of the 1997 fieldwork season.

Chris (13 June 1996): He [Wayne] had come here to excavate but immediately got more interested in surveying. He doesn't need to accumulate brownie points, show he is a proper archaeologist by digging. His trowel will remain in the bottom of the rucksack. Mine, as usual, is accumulating stratified rust deposits somewhere. At least Wayne knows where his trowel is.

Mike (7 June 1997):Chris D.: '[Bourdieu] is used as a symbol of power by those who read it and pretend they understand it.' I use Outline of a Theory of Practice as a coffee pot stand

Mike (15 June 1997):Tony came in yesterday to photograph our private space. He saw my Bourdieu. 'Good book,' he said buoyantly. It is not a good book, it is my coffee pot stand. Tony is a prat. He asked me today when he could interview me. I said, 'After work.' 'But then it eats into my personal time,' he said. 'Well if you don't think it's important enough, don't bother,' I said. 'Of course you're important,' he replied. 'You're an integral part of the project.' Clearly we value our work here differently. When we – the excavating team – are on site, the anthropologists [surveyors] have just got up and are cooking bubble and squeak. When the sociologists work, it is at the expense of the excavation. I on the other hand work all day, on and off site. Good book indeed. Page 72: Structures and the Habitus, paragraph one ... Bollocks.

Wayne (24 June 1997): After lunch we go up to House 23 to Mike who says farewell to his trench by ceremonially placing his copy of Bourdieu's Outline of a Theory of Practice in the bottom. Sue picks the book up only to discover it was all wet. Mike had pissed on it. Chris came up and decided to neutralise Mike's gesture by burying his trowel alongside. Here were the two faces of modern archaeology being sealed together forever. I photograph the event. A small cairn is constructed over the artefacts by Mike and Chris before the serious back-filling starts. I think Mike was slightly caught off guard by Chris's quick response. There was even some comment from him, Dan and Angus [student excavators] about the wasting of a good trowel. I said something similar in respect of him wasting a good book.

Henry (24 June 1997): Mike the excavator had finished his hut and was going to back-fill today. He has found very little apart from a small stake hole and what appears to be a hearth. ... He had decided to bury a copy of Bourdieu's Outline of a Theory of Practice before back-filling the trench. I went over to the trench to see this, to find Mike urinating over the book. I was shocked at this. While I thought that burying the book was slightly amusing, pissing on it seemed out of order. He knew that Bourdieu's work had been quite a strong influence in much of the thinking by the anthropologists on the project. Was this an act of vengeance? I was disappointed. I thought that Mike had been much more amiable this year and had hoped that he was taking our work more seriously. Chris buried his trowel next to the book unaware what Mike had done. They built a little cairn around these offerings and Mike's 'staff' (for that is how he refers to Angus and the others who have been working on his trench) began to back fill.

Henry (27 June 1997): When I woke up it was time to go to Barbara's caravan to say farewell to everyone. Barbara's husband was there and lots of food had been prepared. I ended up next to Mike who said that he did not like my diary of last year and was generally rude to me. I told him that as he had not even bothered to write a proper diary last year and that I had heard that he wasn't keeping one this year he should keep quiet.

I asked him why he had pissed on Bourdieu and I said that I thought it was a bloody stupid thing to do. Why was it that he went around with that silly scowl?

He got very angry with me and began to shout. 'How dare you question my involvement with the project?' He said that he thought the survey team was basically lazy and half hearted. 'Where were you when it was pissing with rain?' he shouted as he walked out.

This incident is a 'social drama', a moment of action that concentrates and makes obvious a 'society's basic value systems and organisational principles' (Gledhill 1994: 127), because it encapsulates both the hierarchical relationship between director and supervisor and the divide between excavator and surveyor. In accordance with aspects of liminality discussed above, it involves actions and reactions expressed in ritualistic terms or contexts. The liminal period is brought to a conclusion through rites that are symbolic of both the experiences that have been endured and the sociality fostered through those experiences. The fragmented sociality of the project meant that both the rite of burial and the caravan supper eaten at the end of the 1997 season performed neither of these functions with particular success.

Mike's burial of his copy of Bourdieu's *Outline* was clearly intended to be a private act, performed in the 'backstage' area of his place on the hill (Goffman 1990). At the same time, by transferring the defiled book (already demoted to coffeepot stand) to a more public space through its burial in the excavated house, Mike attempted to create secret knowledge.[13] His actions can be interpreted as an example of back-stage resistance as described by Goffman or akin to De Certeau's (1988) 'tactics of the weak'. Seen from this perspective, it was not so much the symbolism of the simultaneous burial of a trowel by Chris that 'neutralised Mike's gesture', but rather that he had to reveal his secret knowledge of what he had done to the book.[14] Equally, the attempt to stimulate some sense of communitas through the staging of a meal to celebrate the conclusion of the fieldwork season in one of the surveying director's caravan failed when an argument ensued between two of the project supervisors.

Mary Douglas, in her classic work *Purity and Danger*, has observed that:

> When the community is attacked from outside at least the external danger fosters solidarity within. When it is attacked from within by wanton individuals, they can be punished and the structure publicly reaffirmed. But it is possible for the structure to be self-defeating. This has long been a familiar theme for anthropologists. Perhaps all social systems are built on contradiction, in some sense at war with themselves. But in some cases the various ends which individuals are encouraged to pursue are more harmoniously related than in others. (Douglas 1970: 166)

The social drama highlights how the basic value systems and organisational principles of this particular society, the 'artificial community' during the fieldwork season, were, like the societies examined by Douglas, built upon contradiction. This is the third and most important aspect of the social drama. The choice of the book and the trowel by each of the main participants represents the strained nature of their individual relationship and their own personal feelings of antipathy towards each other. But, at the same time, as symbols, they reflect a broader set of collective representations of the relationship between the different forms of cultural capital through which the academic archaeological field is constituted.

Conclusion

Bourdieu, the author of the much-abused book, has noted that the variation in the exchange rates of different forms of capital is probably one of the most important factors influencing an individual's ability to achieve success and influence within any social field. Each field, constituted through this relationship between different forms of capital, is a field of force or power. In modern societies, education forms the most important field of power through which dominant meanings and, therefore, notions of the appropriate rates of exchange between forms of cultural capital, are inculcated, reproduced and, occasionally, challenged (Bourdieu 1984, 1988).

This analysis of the Leskernick Project is a case study of the operation of the educational field. Here, the period of archaeological fieldwork was, amongst many other things, the liminal period of rites of passage within higher education experienced by undergraduate, post-graduate and established academics. Liminality, however, by temporarily removing some of the barriers that separate these different members of the educational hierarchy, allowed inequalities that exist between the different forms of cultural/educational capital to come to the fore. Inevitably, rather than fostering communitas or unity of purpose, liminality in this context led to open disagreement and the fragmentation of the artificial community created by the fieldwork situation.

As with most liminal rites, the Leskernick experience was often uncomfortable, sometimes confrontational, and occasionally grotesque in its manifestation. But, as Veena Das has stated, 'if liminality poses dangers, these are not only the dangers of darkness but also the dangers of blinding light' (1990: 131). I would argue that this light illuminates some previously unspoken of corners of the archaeological field and leaves us with a clearer understanding of the context within which our disciplinary practices are evolving.[15]

Acknowledgments

The primary debt of all anthropologists is to the people with whom they lived and worked. I would therefore like to put all the Leskernick Project Team at the head of my list of those who should be thanked. Barbara Bender and Tony Williams, in particular, have been immensely supportive whilst I worked on this project, both during our time in Cornwall and whilst writing this chapter. Spencer Hall read and commented on an earlier version. Harriet Wilmore has given me support whenever it was needed and I could not have completed this work without her. Any errors in this chapter are my responsibility alone.

The Dig

Leskernick, Bodmin Moor, 1997

Jan Farquharson

1

Post modern times – empiric facts are dry.
	We're worming into something. That's the plan,
	and it allows us to be near the sky
and feel that we – well, relatively – can
	find truth out on a wide sun-simmered moor.
	Here is our team, modern ungendered Man.
We're off to dig a trench below the tor.
	And feeling small's the point. The great blue day
	up here highlights us like our ancestor –
enhanced dots on a screen, mere pawns to play.
	The landscape is the meaning, evidence
	of how they must have thought and felt, *we say.*
Now context is all the truth. And it makes sense
	when cups aren't rinsed, our post-processualist
	won't dig, Alan won't wash, Dee's on the fence,
and Jane's in love with Una. ... We get pissed
	and talk till dawn, enquirers loosed from cages.
	But it's alright – we dig, therefore exist.

277

2

We are exact with stones. Stones are the pages
    of this hill's book. We read them, bent like crones,
    lifting the turf and peat from close-glued ages,
and dust them, disarticulated bones
    of a once-living labyrinth – quoins, butts
    and cyclopean hearths, primeval thrones,
enclosures, cairns, the footings of granite huts …
    The Bronze Age really changed how this hill went.
    It seems they left no weapons, beads or pots
but that's alright, the stones were what they meant.
    We trowel the hardpan layered over them,
    we sift the grey grit patiently, intent.
But what comes up is always shape and room
    for more stones – cracks and gaps we have to weigh,
    to plot, to heave against our brains. No tomb.
No hoard. No bones. We're only here today
    to thumb the texture of forgotten lives:
    this is a cowshed, this a cobbled way …

3

And yet we think their gods arranged the tors,
    and come to see what little gap would be
    between such gods and mighty ancestors
who moved the stones, so know their hierarchy,
    dreaming our sandwiches. … And no surprise
    if there are tears, or if we can't agree.
And it's alright. Here come inquisitive eyes –
    the former schoolmaster with silver hair,
    some children at his elbow nibbling fries;
four learned locals careful not to stare;
    the man from Heritage, our Mr Big;
    a potter and a poet (funny pair)
who ask bright questions about 'the dig'.
    We keep a layered silence, bucket and trowel
    tilted towards our work, attend the rig.

Una explains the meaning of it all.
    'Here's the long stone', she says going pink, 'and here
    the sun came through the slit, we think, to fall
on something that was once, maybe, quite clear'.

4

And it's alright, it's fine, though rain casts gloom
    and numbing mist envelops curious man.
    On through the drift! … We ritually inhume
a trowel, backfill the trenches, pack the van. –
    Another year's dig done. Subdued in grime
    we bump the trail from site to caravan,
and grab a beer cold as ourselves, and climb
    like front-line veterans flushed with success
    into our bunks to celebrate our time.
And what of her, that small archaic princess
    sleeping above us on the night-spelled moor,
    her bones still buried in the stones that press? –
Fat question. Time has locked us to the tor
    and squashed us in the book of joy and grief.
    Something, no wider than an open door,
has shown its face, advancing out of brief
    failed dreams of past becoming – brighter, more clear
    for us than unitary fixed belief.

Chapter Twelve

Where Worlds Collide
The Past in the Present at Leskernick

Tony Williams

Introduction
Landscapes, place, and past

Small wonder that archaeologists regularly develop a special affection for the sites they excavate and record. Working in a particular landscape engenders a feeling of intense familiarity, even identification, with a setting replete with names, memories, and historical associations. What is surprising is to find that within much academic discourse this sense of place, encounter, and experience is usually ignored in the final publications. As Bradley argues, 'the demands of academic writing set us on another course and we suppress our subjective response in favour of description and documentation' (Bradley 1995: 38). It has been convincingly argued – in other chapters in this book and elsewhere – that archaeology can never be a self-contained objective activity because it can never be divorced from the values, judgments, motives, and beliefs of those involved (Shanks and Tilley 1987). If this is so, the time is right to explore the complex and meaningful relationships that archaeologists create with the landscapes that they excavate, survey, and record.

I shall take as given that people attribute meaning to everything that exists in the material world; that different individuals or groups attribute meaning in different ways at different times (Bender 1993; Hirsch and O'Hanlon 1995; Tilley 1994); and that a sense of place derives from feelings that develop out of both personal experience and wider sets of social, economic, and political structures (Giddens 1981: 69; Rose 1995: 88). Places or locales provide some freedom for social action, but not total freedom, as rules and resources – 'structure' – both enable and constrain what people think, say, and do. Thinking about place as 'facilitating' leads us to Hirsch and O'Hanlon's (1995) argument that landscape involves a relationship between the foreground ('the way we are now') and background ('the way we could be') of social life. These concepts, they argue, cannot be divorced from a number of mutually reinforcing concepts, namely:

foreground actuality ↔ background potentiality

the way we are now ↔ the way we could be

place ↔ space

inside ↔ outside

image ↔ representation

(After Hirsch and O'Hanlon 1995)

The concepts 'are moments, or transitions possible within a single relationship', and the polarities penetrate each other so that the 'way we could be' becomes, albeit temporarily, realised in the here and now of everyday experience (Hirsch and O'Hanlon 1995: 4).

This chapter focuses on the nature of archaeological activity from the point of view of its practitioners' engagements with places and with each other within places. It reinforces the idea that archaeology is a social practice that involves statements and interpretations about the past, place, and landscape that can never be divorced from present-day concerns. By attempting to understand the nature of the encounter and experience that contemporary practitioners enjoy with the physical remains of the past, we begin to reveal the background 'noise' that instructs much of what they do.

Transitions

Modernity to moorland

In the following sections, some of the complexities surrounding the concept of landscape and place are explored through images, experiences, and understandings of Leskernick Hill and its environs as conceptualised by project participants. The analysis begins with a journey.

Each morning, at more or less prearranged times, participants gathered together to travel in cars to one of two 'punctuating points' on their journey to Leskernick Hill. One of them, Westmoorgate car park, lies at the end of a rough tarmac lane and marks the north-eastern entry point onto Bodmin Moor.

There is little indication from the main road that the car park exists, such is its *ad hoc* nature. Along the narrow winding lane, various obstacles –

including cattle grids, chickens, horses, and the occasional walker – need to be negotiated, and, on arrival, cars have to be carefully parked. Wooden fence and stone wall enclose the area on all sides, and at the farthest end of the car park, marking the access point onto the moor and the world of Leskernick beyond, is a five-bar gate. Not unusually, the gate acts as a barrier to animals wandering off the moor but, at the same time, it also assumes a structuring location and physical threshold for people. Just as a garden gate marks the boundary between public and private domains, the Westmoor*gate* accentuates the symbolic division between two worlds, the imagined wilderness and heritage of the moor and the mundane domesticated world 'beyond' it.

Both Lang (1989) and Eliade (1959) have drawn attention to the way in which doors and gates embody human experience and reflect subjective life through the accessing and disclosing of aspects about the world, so that movement through them is akin to a movement between two worlds. For many participants, Westmoorgate car park marked a major transitional point in the daily journey to and from the hill. When asked to describe where they considered the 'world' of Leskernick to end, over one-quarter of project participants (predominantly surveyors), claimed Westmoorgate as a defining location.

Although the surveyors named Westmoorgate, certain excavators named the car park at Bowithick, situated a few miles away, which marks the second popular point of entry onto the moor. As the project progressed, it became clear that groups of surveyors and excavators were using the two routes to Leskernick Hill fairly exclusively. Occasionally, student excavators would walk to site from Westmoorgate simply because they had had to travel in surveyors' cars. One diary entry, written by an excavation supervisor, illustrates the importance of 'sticking' to the 'right' route:

Mike, excavation supervisor: I am disappointed that Old Chris and the rest of the excavation team have elected to approach the hill from Westmoorgate, not the more attractive Bowithick route.

Such was the importance of demarcating alternative routes that, amongst the excavators, the Bowithick route was renamed the 'Hamilton route' after their excavation director, Sue Hamilton, who used it almost without exception throughout the duration of the project. In the following diary entry, a surveyor clearly values the Bowithick, or 'scenic' route as he calls it, quite differently from the excavation team.

Henry, surveyor: We decided to park in Bowithick which means walking what is termed the "scenic" route to Leskernick. It is the

fig. 12:1 a) 'Dinosaur Park'. Photo by Sue, excavation director; b) 'The embracing stone'. Photo by Penni, excavator; c) 'Planning'. Photo by Justin, planner.

> *longer and hilly walk. There is also a stream and a few gorse bushes, the occasional tree. For some people these factors make it more "scenic" – a nicer walk. In fact I do not like this approach ... it is not the way to see Leskernick Hill.*

Sheltering behind aesthetic valuations, excavators and surveyors became embroiled in a space/time movement drama. Paths structure the experience of the places they link, helping to establish a sense of linear order; consequently, the alternative paths served to establish and maintain a cohesion within and a division between the two groups. Although photographs taken by project participants are discussed in detail below, it is worth noting that Sue Hamilton, the excavation director, chose to photograph part of the 'Bowithick route' as her most significant place on or near Leskernick Hill (Figure 12.1a):

> I called it Dinosaur Park because the rocks look like ones in a film set – too manicured. The photo shows the way I approach the site each morning. It's at the limits of the moor and marks the beginning of me thinking about the moor. The photo has the stones in it and two people rest against the stones and that makes the point that I don't walk onto the moor alone.

Imagining Leskernick through language

Boundaries are drawn to serve the interests and identities of particular groups. They are expressions of power; they impart a sense of belonging – or not belonging. Inevitably, by demarcating an inside and outside, boundaries draw upon meanings located in the spaces beyond them.

> local (village)
>
> regional (county)
>
> national (English)
>
> supranational (European)

To assess how boundaries can play an intimate part in the construction of identity, participants were asked to provide examples of landscapes or locations they felt 'comfortable' in. The responses might determine at what 'scale' participants construct elements of their own identities. Most often, participants used a regional example: 'Sussex', 'The woodland and downland of south-east England', 'The South Downs'. These images of place contain ideas about 'Englishness', rootedness, and belonging and may sometimes be aligned to patriotic and nationalistic 'structures of feeling' (see Hooson 1994; Palmer 1997; Smith 1986). However, a sense of belonging does not necessarily have to mean identification with the familiar or domestic, and a number of respondents described foreign destinations: 'France', 'Tuscan hills', 'Mt Monserrat, nr. Barcelona'. Others claimed quite alien environments to be their most comfortable places: 'desert', 'empty wilderness (moorland, deserts)', 'remote, unpopulated landscapes (moorland)', 'wilderness'.

The unsettled, harsh and unpredictable landscape of the 'Other' stands in contrast to the idyllic images of rural English landscapes. Notably, only males chose the exotic, alien environments; this seems to accord with the masculine ideal of 'conquering' unknown, harsh environments. The desire to display an experience or knowledge of the global, or of sites that represent 'alternative' interests and meanings, may also relate to the individual accumulation and demonstration of 'cultural capital' (Bourdieu 1984; Merriman 1989).

To elicit an initial sense of place at Leskernick, participants were asked to record their perceptions using adjectives. Given that landscape, at least in the Western tradition, is closely related to 'pictorial images', of 'seeing' and representing the surface of the land in particular ways, it is not surprising that respondents often referred to Leskernick as 'isolated', 'enclosed', and 'cosseted'. These types of adjectives carry a sense of boundedness and are perhaps part of a process of establishing differences between project members and others – locals, visitors, and non-visitors. Other adjectives referred to proportion: 'small', 'vast', 'spacious'.

> shape – 'curved', 'rounded', 'irregular'
>
> size/proportion – 'small', 'vast', 'spacious'
>
> texture – 'treeless', 'rocky', 'rugged'
>
> enclosure – 'isolated', 'remote', 'enclosed', 'contained', 'open'

It may be that different perceptions of proportion relate to participants' previous exposure and prior knowledge of Leskernick. Colour, on the other hand, which we may assume has psychological import (Dittmar 1989), was hardly mentioned: 'monochrome', 'grey'. Respondents often used romantic adjectival terms to describe Leskernick: 'deceptive', 'beautiful', 'rooted', 'fascinating', 'enigmatic'. Some participants (mainly female) combined the romantic with the quasi-mystical: 'eerie', 'eternal', 'secretive', 'enigmatic' (see Wilmore, chapter 11). With their deep interest, even fascination with the past, we might have expected archaeologists to identify with the remains of human activities in the Leskernick landscape. However, very few participants used adjectives that related to human activity in the past or present:

> archaeology – 'Neolithic', 'ancient'
>
> land use – 'pastoral'
>
> buildings and settlements – 'ruined'

Adjectives provide a useful starting point to assess initial responses to landscape but their communicative value is limited. Participants were therefore asked to provide a narrative-based description of Leskernick in up to five sentences:

Concise physical descriptions of colour and size

Female student: It is small from the outside, looking on – but is big looking out. An enclosed world surrounded by barren hills.

Impressionistic descriptions with no archaeological references

Female student: A beautiful, special place situated on the side of a hill viewing a landscape of surrounding hills and valleys where one can find tranquillity, serenity, and peace.

Descriptions of topography and archaeology

Male supervisor: A (probably) Bronze Age settlement of around 50 round houses coating (with the associated infield system) the south and west facing slopes of a gentle hill in the centre of Bodmin Moor, Cornwall.

Highly imaginative interpretative descriptions

Male survey site director: An isolated grey and green stony hill set in the N part of Bodmin Moor. A hill on which the stones, their sizes and shapes, textures and forms were appropriated and symbolically empowered by those who lived there in two small villages. A hill in which the domestic and ritual were intimately linked to a sense of place and a wider cosmology of circular form involving ritual practice, burial, and domestic space.

Broadly, there are four distinguishable, though overlapping, levels of description provided by participants. The degree of interpretation offered seems to relate to the degree of archaeological knowledge and consequently the degree of confidence in describing the human activities at Leskernick. The most imaginative archaeologically based narratives, conveying inter-pretations of ritual and symbolism, were provided by the site directors and supervisors; the least imaginative, focussing on the settlement and other structures, were provided by student excavators.

When asked directly how their own activities as archaeologists changed the character of Leskernick, the majority of participants agreed that they did effect a change. On the one hand, there was a 'temporary' change associated with the excavation: 'more noise and activity', 'temporarily peopled'. On the other hand, there was a perception of a more permanent and long-lasting change that seems to be related to the physical alteration of the landscape. When viewed in this way, excavation activities were sometimes seen as negative:

Male survey site director: Excavation is very intrusive and destroys the hill.

Male student excavator: It doesn't change the place at all, apart from the damage excavations cause.

But, on the whole, the excavation and surveying activities were seen as a legitimate means to knowledge for the benefit of others:

Male excavator: Brings it back to life and draws people to the hill.

Female excavator: We make it a living place.

Male surveyor: Gives new identity through activity and publication.

Finally, respondents were asked how their perception of Bodmin Moor had changed whilst they were participating in the project. Students and less archaeologically experienced project members refer to visible scale and environmental factors, whereas experienced archaeologists and site directors refer to an increasing knowledge of the archaeology.

Student excavators

Smaller than expected; It has grown smaller; It has become a mosaic; It has become more familiar.

Site directors and professional archaeologist

Male survey director: It changes every year. I acquire a more intimate knowledge of Leskernick.

Female survey director: From bewilderment and nonseeing to a sense of place and human materiality and thought that – still – is always slipping away, mysterious, very present-past.

Female excavation director: Better understanding of the morphology and archaeology of the moor, and how it relates to the rest of Cornwall, Devon, etc.

Male professional archaeologist: Added more detail to knowledge about Leskernick, but not to a great extent.

As a discursive social practice, archaeology produces knowledge that is inseparable from power (Foucault 1979: 27). For the directors, perhaps more so than for the students, the moor becomes a potential resource of academic and cultural (archaeological) capital. Implicit in the directors' descriptions is an emphasis on the difficulties presented by the archaeological remains of the hill. Their ability to grapple with these difficulties rebounds to their academic credibility.

Imagining Leskernick (and the self) through image

> Seeing … establishes our place in the surrounding world; we explain that world with words, but words can never undo the fact that we are surrounded by it. (Berger 1977: 7)

Through language, words attempt to capture the essence of some 'thing', although they can never really fully succeed. It is, therefore, interesting to move from the word to the image.

In the act of viewing, people situate themselves vis-à-vis the image they view, thus taking on a particular relationship to the things being viewed. During the Renaissance, the term *landscape* became associated with a particular genre of scenic painting using linear perspective (Cosgrove 1984; Thomas 1993:22). The concept of landscape came to imply a distance or separation between viewer (subject) and scene, vista or view (object). The modern archaeological gaze that uses maps, photographs, and other visual tools for depicting the environment is firmly rooted in the emergence of this particular way of seeing that privileges sight over the other senses.

This archaeological 'gaze' is illustrated by the RCHME Leskernick site-map that represents an objective, simultaneous, and totalising image of the place, one in which all the features (houses, walls, enclosures, etc.) are laid bare for scrutiny and examination (Figure 1.4). The fixed relationship that the map implies firmly locates the viewer outside and above the scene being depicted: a bird's eye view rather than one grounded within the landscape topography (Barrett 1994; Ingold 1993: 155; Thomas 1993). Despite various 'experimental' attempts to depict the archaeological trench in a manner more sympathetic to the human experience at Leskernick Hill, 'conventional' black and white photographs and planned drawings remained the primary representations.

To elicit a more intimate visual sense of place, every member of the project team was asked to photograph something evocative, significant, or meaningful on or around Leskernick Hill. Because photography has the capacity to deal with the banal and the emotion of everyday experience, it was assumed that elements of participants' ontologies might be subtly revealed within the single 'snapshot'. Although much attention has been lavished on the photograph as text, or on the conditions of use that determine their meanings, the emphasis here is switched to the 'creating' of that text by the project participants. The production of a text that articulates a sense of place and past is both enabled and constrained by structures of power. Photography was such a potent constituent in official representations of Leskernick that the 'inappropriate' use of cameras challenged the conventions of archaeological enquiry and even the integrity of certain archaeologists themselves:

The Propped Stone wrapped in gold,
photo: Jeremy Stafford-Deitsch

Midsummer sunset behind the Propped Stone
(Quoit) at the top of Leskernick Hill 1995

a

b

C2 a) The largest of the monoliths at the stone row terminal. Pastel: Jan Farquharson; b) Craddock Moor stone row, photo: Jeremy Stafford-Deitsch

C2

C3 a) Doorway orthostats of House 35 framing the view towards the summit cairns of Brown Gelly in the distance; b) the crossed jambs of House 9

a

b

a

b

C4 a) flagging the Western Compound wall; b) flags following the course of the far northern wall of the western settlement. Photo: Jeremy Stafford-Deitsch; c) Leskernick stone row looking towards Brown Willy. Note the water course (now a leat) that crosses half way along

C5 a) the Shrine Stone in the Corridor between the southern and western settlements; b) 12 hours later, after a storm

a

b

c

d

C6 Leskernick clitter structures (see fig. 9:7, p. 223): a) and b) structure 24 within a dense band of clitter; c) clitter structure 38 in the area south of the southwest enclosure and House 26; d) the clitter mass in the centre of the southwest enclosure from which half a dozen small walls radiate

C7 a) stone setting Trehundreth Downs, western Moor;
b)Tregarrick Tor Cairn;
c) encircled grounder, Craddock Moor;
d) Codda spiral.
Photos: Jeremy Stafford-Deitsch

a

b

C8 a) orthostats
demarcating stones
with solution basins,
Tregarrick Tor;
b) 'Shrine', Carneglos Tor;
c) solution basin,
Elephant Rock.
Photos a) and b):
Jeremy Stafford-Deitsch

c

C 9 Peoples' favourite places:
a) Gary: 'The Detective';
b) Chris: Rough Tor;
c) 'Me' by Dan, photo taken
by Tony Williams

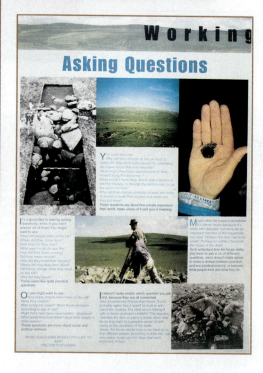

C10 Boards from the Stone World exhibition.

C11 a) Showery Tor at the northeast end of Rough Tor ridge; b) Stowe's Pound Tor stacks and enclosure wall; c) Kilmar summit stack; d) Hawk's Tor East. Photos a), b), and c): Jeremy Stafford-Deitsch

C10

a

b

c

d

a

b

c

C12 a) Elephant Rock on the southern side of Beacon; b) Sharp Tor, isolated rock stack to the west of the summit with, in the foreground, a rock with large solution basins; c) Hawk's Tor East, summit stack with eroded solution basin. Photos: Jeremy Stafford-Deitsch

Extract from author's fieldwork diary: After lunch I visited Mike's [male excavation supervisor's] trench and suggested to everyone that they begin to think about a significant feature of the landscape (people, views, places, anything) and I would give them a camera to take a picture of it in a few days time. Mike immediately interjected by refusing to allow pictures of 'his' trench being photographed while it was being dug, claiming that it would compromise his 'professional integrity' if the photos were ever seen by his peers.

Photographs do, of course, have their limitations because they are unable to reveal all of a person's feelings, impressions, and understandings about a place, especially the way those feelings change. Although a camera is often taken as an eye, it is no more than that. However, the photographer controls the composition and arrangement, and the inclusion or exclusion of particular objects, all of which invoke an ideologically constructed image of place. The image, moreover, reveals not just the photographer's representation, but the social relations that underscore the image. Thus, the landscape is not simply 'out there' to be 'read off', painted, or photographed, but is lived through and involves a dialectical process, making us and being made by us.

The photographs can be read partly in terms of individual and collective identity – who the individual participants were and/or who they were capable of becoming, both within the immediate foreground of the project and in the (background) beyond. We can identify shifting representations of Leskernick as lived in and through, altered and worked upon, replete with symbolic meaning. We come to see the Leskernick landscape as something dynamic, contested, and polysemic.

Around three-quarters of the photographs depict people-less scenes. The modern aesthetic gaze often involves the exclusion of contemporary subjects, and at Leskernick the individual photographers 'grappled' with the camera, framing, including and excluding to omit and obscure others and importantly, other people's views and perceptions.

Participants were also asked why they had chosen to take a photograph of a particular view or place. In what follows, I attempt to move between the photographic image and textual responses and so begin to excavate the unconscious, or at least unspoken, explanations for identifying with particular places.

Rough Tor – Chris, survey director

The photograph depicts a ridge of land framed by the horizon in the background, with a foreground of unsettled turf and stone. In the midground is

Leskernick Hill. At first, the photo appears similar to a landscape painting. The arrangement is pleasing and harmonious. The components combine to create a specific character pattern that lends distinctiveness to the location. Understood in isolation from the overall context of the project, the photo seems little more than a reflection of a modern aesthetic sensibility. In reality, something very different is going on; it requires an understanding of the significance of this particular location from the point of view of the subject taking it.

The view is of Rough Tor and Brown Willy. As will have become apparent to readers of this book, the image of Rough Tor was very important to Chris (Color Plate 9a). Before the excavations had even been thought of, at a time when he was working on his own, Chris had discovered that, at a particular point along the prehistoric stone row at the foot of Leskernick Hill, at the moment of crossing a large depression that was probably filled with water during the Bronze Age, Rough Tor suddenly came into view from behind the ridge. For Chris, the effect was startling; it reverberated with ethnographic associations having to do with transition and the ritual purification of the body passing through a watery threshold.

By the 1997 fieldwork season, a 'tradition' had been invented involving the induction of new project members. Led by one or two survey directors, the participants were taken on a tour of the site and were initiated into the Leskernick 'story'. The site tour became a sort of rite of passage that, following van Gennep, involved stages – separation, marginalisation, and reaggregation (van Gennep 1960). Separated from the rest of the group, the initiates were led along the stone row and across the once water-filled leat where the Rough Tor 'effect' was theatrically revealed to them by a knowledgeable guide. A further period of liminality followed as initiates were steered across the hill to view other sites and to meet other participants. The last feature of the tour to be visited was the Propped Stone at the top of the hill. Since early on in the project, this stone had assumed the characteristics of a shrine or sacred place for many of the participants. Finally, the initiates were appointed to their supervisors and were reincorporated into the team to begin work.

The whole process of site touring becomes an exercise in instilling communitas and reinforcing the symbolic transition into a mythological landscape. When interviewed some time after the site tour, many initiates (now participants) claimed that Rough Tor possessed a certain resonance for them: a 'cathedral' according to one, 'sometimes threatening and sometimes mystical', according to another. Although some project members, mainly excavators contested or rejected the claims made by Chris and others, all agreed this topographic feature was spectacular, perhaps possessing some significance in the Bronze Age.

Chris wrote:

> My picture shows the Rough Tor effect from the Stone Row terminal. It was the first time I visited Leskernick on my own and I discovered this perspectival effect after crossing the leat. I remember thinking how weird Rough Tor looks from here with

its crenellated effect, and being confused whether it was actually a part of Brown Willy. This area is a part of the fascination
and power of the place. It is a place away from civilisation and
approaches the past. The photo represents the genesis or origin
of the project.

Through the medium of the photograph, Chris constructs a particular
representation of Leskernick. The absence of people in the photo, especially
other archaeologists, disguises a subtle power that Chris exerts by focusing
on his own interpretations. Indeed, by the 1997 project season, the Rough Tor
effect came to assume the importance and status of an origin myth.

'The Detective' – Gary, student excavator

Less than one-quarter of the project members chose to depict the archaeological trench. Of those who did, an effort was made to present the traditional
site of excavation in an unusual way. Asked to name a significant place on the
hill, Gary chose the cairn that provided the setting for 'working and being
with friends' (Color Plate 9b). The photograph depicts Helen, the excavation
supervisor with whom Gary shared a caravan (along with the project sociologists). Helen lies in the bottom of the trench surrounded by archaeological
equipment including photo-scales and a ranging rod. Gary describes why he
chose to photograph this particular setting:

> It's like a murder scene photo. There are several reasons why I
> decided to take it. Firstly, the most significant thing is that we're
> recreating the landscape ourselves. In archaeology the people are
> missing and it was my attempt to reintroduce human beings and
> personality. Second, it was Helen I took because I spent most of the
> time with her in the trench. Third, I used the pole to show that we're
> detectives studying dead people.

Through juxtaposing a human being with the trench and archaeological equipment, Gary offers a discourse on the practice and conventions of
archaeology. Whereas Chris's photo asserts his distance from 'traditional'
methods and techniques of archaeological practice, Gary's photo actively
incorporates archaeological practice, but presents a controversial image filled
with his own assumptions concerning the epistemology of archaeological
practice. Furthermore, by photographing his own trench, Gary authorises
his interpretation.

The next two photographs refer to intimate places of 'private' discovery,
rather than public or communal knowledge and activity. Leskernick's contemporary treeless landscape of knee-high stones provided little opportunity
to 'escape' from the gaze of others. In the face of extremely harsh weather

conditions, a strict work ethic developed and surveillance by colleagues and trench supervisors ensured no individual strayed from the trench for too long. However, participants spending eight or so hours every day on the hill working and socialising with others found opportunities for their own private withdrawal from the group.

The 'nursery' hut – Fay, student excavator

Fay's photograph focuses on a heavily striated stone within House 29 located on the periphery of a circle of houses in the southern settlement (see Figure 5.8d). Fay discovered the circle within the first few days of the project whilst excavating at H39 a small distance to the northeast. Two or three times a day, participants gathered for rest and food breaks at another house circle (H28) located about midway between the southern and western settlements. Fay passed by House 29 and the stone every time she made her way across site to H28. Most excavators working with her ignored the houses, either walking alongside them or directly through them, hardly ever stopping to look. Fay, however, took time to examine them more closely. For Fay, the house came to represent a very personal place of evocative meaning:

> I took the photograph because I'm particularly fond of this little house. I often pass it when I move around on site. I picked this particular stone because of its character, as well as its lichen and moss. It's a storytelling stone that may have had the same significance in the Bronze Age.

Fay's photo is very focused and foregrounded. Whilst taking the photograph, she expressed concern that the textures and colours might not reproduce well. The grasses that frame the stone are purposefully included in the foreground. The framing of the photograph is antithetical to archaeological convention; no attempt is made to include the entire circle, an effect that could easily have been achieved by standing further back. Indeed, the most objective way of recording the house would have been a photograph taken from the top of a ladder – like Gary's. But this would have altered the meaning altogether. The low angle of the photograph expresses the intimacy of experience and engagement that Fay had with the place.

Although Fay mentioned that she was keen to develop her skills as an excavator, she frequently remarked that her artistic background affected her perception of archaeological practice. For her, the hill held a particular mystical resonance, it was a 'beautiful, special place ... where one can find tranquillity, serenity and peace'. Other participants used similar adjectives to describe Leskernick, but Fay used them more frequently in ordinary conversation. The house chosen is unusual because it does not contain within its walls a large earth-fast boulder and, in comparison to most others, contains many moisture-loving plants. As such, its relatively 'undomestic' appearance may have been important to Fay. At first, Fay was reluctant to speak about the house and the stone, as if its resonance would diminish when shared with others:

> Photographs today of our favourite place naturally saw me back in H29 and the stone. I initially felt quite uncomfortable and protective about revealing my thoughts and feelings about the stone; it felt like a secret.

Fay developed her theory about the house, suggesting that because of its dissimilarity to the other houses, its small size, and the unusually shaped stones it incorporated, it might have been used for some alternative purpose, perhaps a nursery.

The embracing stone – Penni – amateur archaeologist

Penni, an experienced amateur archaeologist, takes a similar, closely focused photograph of a large recumbent stone (Figure 12.1b):

> I took a picture of my embracing stone. A stone that says 'come rest you're tired'. I think I'm using it exclusively. I use the stone to cut off the trench and everyone else from my thoughts.

Penni spent most of her time excavating H23, situated at some distance away from the house H28 that many participants used for rest breaks. Some of the excavators decided not to 'waste time' travelling across the hill, preferring to take rest-breaks at the side of their trench. Penni adopted a similar practice but moved a small distance away from her fellow excavators, finding her 'embracing' stone at an appropriate distance 'not too near, or too far' from everyone else at the trench-side. The stone's shape and height, she said, made a comfortable reclining seat, the grass acting as a cushion. Penni's exclusive use of the stone, as mundane as it appears, constitutes a minor act of resistance through her refusal to use either the socially prescribed space of House 28 or the side of the trench. Penni's 'discovery', and use of a stone as a seat, involved an act of bodily incorporation of an unfamiliar reality (Lang 1989). Through the gradual 'inhabiting' of the stone, Penni transforms space into place. By naming it, she domesticates it.

Both Penni and Fay select places on Leskernick Hill that represent the embodiment of their personal attitudes and feelings towards the project. Like Fay's photograph, Penni's is taken at a low and rather intimate angle, concealing the 'world' beyond the stone and everyone else within it.

'Me' – Dan, student excavator

Dan's desire to create a particular effect – his (disembodied) self in the landscape – necessitated someone else taking the photograph (Color Plate 9c). Under Dan's direction, I carefully composed the image until all the various elements he demanded were focussed within the frame. The effect achieved seems to convey an even greater sense of agency than if he had chosen to photograph, or have photographed his entire body. The image of Dan's combat trousers, booted feet, and widely separated stance expresses a certain control, even dominance over Leskernick and the wider landscape towards the horizon. Dan had previously picked up some empty bullet cases found near H39 where he had been excavating, and he placed these next to his feet. He then asked me to frame the view through his legs looking towards the wind machines in the north.

> The idea behind this photo is that we're doing a lot of walking on site. I want to capture *my* feet, my boots to signify *my* activity. I wanted to remember *me* in the landscape rather than what I did. I placed the shells in the picture because they are extremely prominent in the landscape. The area is used by a whole range of people and we tend to forget that we are not the only ones who use and perceive the site (emphasis added).

Dan's photograph confirms his agency as a participant in the project, even though a photograph of him working in the trench might have expressed a more 'authentic', less ambiguous presence. A photograph possesses an artefactual longevity, and it is perhaps unsurprising that no one wanted to be pictorially 'remembered' purely in terms of their labour, although respondents frequently noted their most significant places as those in which they worked.

The photograph also works on a biographical level, given the military metaphors represented through the clothing worn and the spent cartridges carefully laid upon the grass next to Dan's feet. Dan made many references to time spent in the Territorial Army (TA), and artefacts like bullets and other material left over from the military exercises carried out on Bodmin Moor provoked memories and stories. The metaphors of power, control, and discipline are well known in archaeological circles and Dan's agency as a former soldier in the TA memorialised by his clothes and interest in military hardware reconfirmed his status as an excavator.

'Planning' – Justin, professional planner

Justin's photograph is like Dan's, a depiction of a disembodied self actively engaging with the landscape at Leskernick (Figure 12.1c). The body, albeit only a wrist and hand, confers and conveys identity (Palmer 1997: 185).

I had difficulty deciding which picture to take. I would have taken a picture of a trench, but it's quite irrelevant since I've been working in all of them. The picture I decided on was taken close-up to get my hand all blurry. I've been planning this project and my photo remembers that. This one is specific to me. When I draw, my hand is all out of focus and the tape measure and rock thoroughly in focus.

Justin's engagement with the landscape is related to the sensations he experiences when drawing plans of archaeological trenches. Through the medium of the photograph, Justin describes how it *feels* to plan and the focusing required to draw intricate details within a trench. The use of the tape measure and pencil authenticates the image and confirms Justin's identity as a professional planner/excavator. Although project participants were reluctant to depict themselves directly engaged in archaeological activity in the trench, Justin remarks that his photo 'remembers' rather than accurately represents the practice of planning. When Justin was asked to take the photograph, he was drawing a plan of H39. Rather than take the photograph there, he chose to walk some distance away to an unexcavated area. Justin is directly referencing his own practical activity in the project, but he, like Gary, offers an interpretative discourse on the sensory experiences involved with archaeology.

It is interesting to compare Penni's photo with Justin's. Both appear very similar in terms of their composition and arrangement; the thin line of sky above the horizon and the hint of a landscape beyond. Little attempt is made to produce a photograph with depth and perspective. In contrast to, say, Chris's photo of Rough Tor, these images are firmly foregrounded in the present rather than some imagined past. But despite their similarities in appearance, the photos convey very different experiences of place.

The photos and accompanying explanations are very evocative of individual engagement with Leskernick Hill. Although some communicate aspects of shared archaeological practice and process, others convey a different 'sense of place' and past, privacy, and solitude. All of them 'work' on an individual and shared level.

All the participants were given a fixed-lens camera that was capable of taking either panoramic or 'conventional' portrait-sized photographs. Interestingly, only the males chose to use the panoramic option, although some of them took 'conventional' photographs. It may be inferred that choosing to depict a view or scene using panoramic-sized photographs, which appear more encompassing and assertive compared to 'conventional' ones, somehow relates to a gendered 'gaze'. In Western culture, Rodway argues, vision has mainly been defined in terms of a 'masculine hegemony', whereby male eyes define visual styles including the female body as object and spectacle (Rodway 1994: 122–23). Thomas (1993: 23–25) elaborates: 'the male gaze is … the gaze of the voyeur, taking pleasure without engagement. The male gaze is all encompassing and totalising'.

This characterisation of the male as a distanced voyeur is overly unsympathetic to the intimate engagements males have with their surroundings, and, although it is probable that males' and females' feelings and understandings of the world are gendered, this gendering is both complex and often contradictory. Certainly, Dan's photograph of himself rooted firmly in a wide, deep landscape is very different to the close focused intimacy of place depicted by Fay, Penni, and certain other female participants. On the other hand, Justin's photograph exemplifies a profoundly intimate relationship with the landscape. Dittmar's study of people's responses to material possessions suggests that female gender identity is most often culturally constructed and characterised by an emphasis on interpersonal relationships, emotion, understanding, and sensitivity, whereas males are assumed to be individualistic, independent, and pragmatic (Dittmar 1989; 1991). The photographic representations certainly indicate that female participants tended to hold a more emotive view of place.

Gendered differences could also be discerned in relation to the choice of participants most 'significant places'. Asked to list three significant places on Leskernick Hill and provide reasons why they were favoured, male participants more frequently described places they had excavated (worked): House 39 ('supervising the excavation'); House 39 ('working there most'); House 23 ('work'); SE quad House 39 ('planning nightmare'); House 39 ('I did the surface plan, hence it's mine'). In contrast, many females quoted places that had little or nothing to do with the physical activity of excavation or survey: House 28 ('for tranquillity, communality, rest'); House 40 ('because we all eat and relax there'); tool-shed ('that's where everybody gathers and meets in the morning'); Stone Row ('weird feeling, calm area, the unknown'); the 'ritual' landscape ('has a calm, undisturbed, relaxing feel to it').

Imagining Leskernick through sociality

Most archaeological sites share similar spatial arrangements that structure the activities and movements that occur within them – trenches, spoil heaps, and post-excavation areas are often similarly linked and widely used and discussed. However, within any archaeological excavation, a 'backstage' area of activity usually exists that is construed as less important or more 'trivial' because the space appears to be more intimate and unofficial. Often extremely discrete, these places are capable of mobilising profound meaning for people and may only be found by tracking participant's movements across the landscape.

Participants were asked to map their movements and encounters with places and people at Leskernick Hill onto a copy of the RCHME Leskernick settlement map. On the one hand, the maps reveal a network of fairly discrete pathways carved across the hillside linking together the excavation trenches at House 39, House 23, and Cairn 5. On the other, they reveal networks that extend between these 'official' and other 'unofficial' places.

Movement in a landscape is always to some degree socially constrained, and this is particularly obvious within and around the archaeological trench. Following Foucault (1979), we could, indeed, define the space of the trench as 'disciplinary' space within which various social and archaeological technologies, knowledges, and procedures attempt to create the 'docile' body.

> Discipline proceeds by the organisation of individuals in space, and it therefore requires a specific enclosure of space. In the hospital, the school, or the military field, we find a reliance on an orderly grid. Once established, this grid permits the sure distribution of the individuals to be disciplined and supervised. (Dreyfus and Rabinow, quoted in Shields 1991: 40)

Archaeological trenches present another such enclosure. Excavators are required to deposit their belongings some distance outside the periphery of the trench before gaining entry to it after asking permission from the excavation supervisor. Once inside, individual behaviour becomes subject to control and surveillance: smoking, eating, and drinking within the trench are forbidden and certain items of material culture including tape measures, planning boards, photo-scales, and boundary tapes can only be moved by persons authorised to do so.

Stuart, student excavator, June 1997: Mike asked if I had any objections to the tasks he was giving me, which felt strange as I felt almost like I didn't need to bother doing the task but Mike is the supervisor and I carry out whatever task he gives me to do.

Surveillance and discipline may extend to nearby features associated with excavation like spoil heaps and tool stores, and even further afield. One excavation supervisor went so far as to claim that his 'authority extended in all directions over the hill, at least to the point where someone else (another supervisor) was working and commanding'.

Alongside these official spaces, both excavators and surveyors condensed a plethora of meanings around other meeting places. For the excavators, one such was the apparently mundane space chosen for the overnight storage of excavation equipment. Much of the equipment was stored in an old stone sheep pen. This tool store not only provided a safe haven for tools, but participants often commented upon the protection it gave from wind and rain and on its function as a meeting place. The tool store was mentioned as one of the most significant places on the hillside by a quarter of the excavators: 'because that's where everybody gathers and meets in the morning'; 'because it signifies the beginning and the end of the day'.

For the surveyors, two particular, but very different, locales became significant both in binding the group together and in separating them from the excavators. The first place, House 3, which later became named the 'Shaman's Hut' by the surveyors, is located on the furthest fringes of the western settlement. The naming of the Shaman's Hut deserves some attention.

> By the process of naming places and things become captured in social discourses and act as mnemonics for the historical actions of individuals and groups. ... In a fundamental way names create landscapes. (Tilley 1994: 23)

The naming of the Shaman's Hut is referenced on its marginal status beyond the settlements and on its orientation towards Rough Tor. As we have noted, Rough Tor is the distinctive shadowy topographic feature that looms large in Chris's interpretations. For the surveyors, the significance of the Shaman's Hut is unquestioned, and perhaps becomes more entrenched when Chris names it among his three most significant places, and Henry, one of the surveyors, photographs the Shaman's Hut and Rough Tor with the two survey directors in the foreground.

The second place of importance to the surveyors was a tent belonging to one of them. This tent, pitched close to the communal tea-hut (H28), became an exclusive refuge:

Henry, surveyor, June 1996: We go to the tent. Drink coffee and smoke cigarettes. I'm impatient to get on with surveying. ... Just as people started to pack away their coffee filled thermos flasks and finish their cigarettes the rain began and we thus retreated back into the shelter of Wayne's tent.

Although the surveyor who brought the tent intended it to be used as a communal shelter, excavators chose not to use it and for some of them suspicion surrounded the surveyor's activities and conversations within the tent. Both Giddens (1984: 122–26) and Goffman (1959) use the terms *front* and *back regions* to refer to the regionalization of time-space in relation to differing contexts for social action and the sustaining of ontological security. The tent might be seen as a *back region*. For the occupants, its intimacy and closeness permitted social solidarity. For those eying it with suspicion, it was a place of social interaction that was closed to outsiders and allowed the concealment of activities and discursive practices that might discredit the activities taking place in front regions.

So far, certain biographical experiences of Leskernick Hill have been analysed in terms of the locales associated either with excavators or surveyors. Attention now shifts to a place of shared, but tensioned meanings. Located approximately midway between the southern and western settlements, in a somewhat isolated and marginal position near the boundary walls that define the outer limit of the settlement, House 28 – the tea hut – became the focus for social interaction between excavators and surveyors. Its particular location made it an appropriately neutral place. At the beginning of the season, most, if not all, participants gathered at the hut at mutually agreed-upon times to rest and take tea breaks and lunches. Students were delegated the responsibility of tea making by the excavation director.

Lesley, student excavator, June 1997: At lunchtime Stuart and I are volunteered (by Sue) to be tea boy and girl. We are in Hut 28 and the view from here is fantastic. This is Chris Tilley's favourite hut. The whole site has a really nice atmosphere but there does seem to be something special about Hut 28. Is it possible that it was used for some religious purpose? Who knows?

After the first few days of the 1997 season, it became apparent that a particular ordering of space had evolved with the excavators and surveyors clustered together in opposite ends of the house. The spatial separation slowly began to erode when a number of objects collected from the hillside began to appear within the tea hut. A horseshoe, deposited by the female survey director, signalled a largely symbolic termination of the separation (Figures 12.2a and 12.2b). No sooner had the horseshoe been propped up on the back wall of the house, than further items collected from the hillside began to appear:

Fay, student excavator, June 1997: Found part of a bone on the way to tea and decided to add it to the 'material culture' collection accumulating there. It had wonderful shape and form and I wanted to add it to the military shrapnel that the collection appears mostly to comprise in the hope that it might be a more wholesome addition.

Mike, excavation supervisor, Trench diary, June 1997: There is a small collection (of 'military hardware') near Hut 39. 'Excavators' and 'surveyors' alike pick it up. There is a small collection now next to Hut 23 and the least attractive of the artworks around Hut 28, which reminds me of a fetish, incorporates a few more pieces.

The incorporation of material objects in the communal space of the house was democratising in the sense that anyone, regardless of status, expertise or group affiliation, could add to 'the collection'. The objects themselves ranged

fig.12:2 a) the Collectors' Stone in House 28; b) The wrapped stone in House 28 with overt 'peace' messages.

from bones, sheep's wool, and tin cans to used thunder-flash flares, tripwires, and spent cartridges left over from military exercises conducted on Bodmin Moor since the First World War. Finding 'things' became important for some of the excavators, especially as these objects partly compensated for the lack of finds from the archaeological trenches. The act of incorporating material from the hill also seems to relate to a group domestication of unknown or unfamiliar space. As discussed below, many of the objects eventually found their way into participants' caravans.

Imagining Leskernick through material culture

Archaeological practice depends upon the interpretation of a wide range of material culture in order to make statements about the past. Archaeologists recognise that objects are meaningful and that they are important to people's sense of identity and locatedness in the world. In this section, this archaeological acknowledgment is turned around and the material culture associated with, and belonging to the participants at Leskernick, is analysed.

Practising archaeology involves an array of material culture: picks, cameras, photo-scales, mattocks, dentistry tools, ranging rods, drawing boards and, of course, the trowel – the most recognisable archaeological tool of all. Although some participants brought more equipment with them than others, no excavator was without a trowel. Individuals would relate stories about their trowels to others, often referring to previous excavations where they had used them. To distinguish one trowel from the others, many excavators marked the handle in some way.

Some markings made on trowels were very simple – a spot of nail varnish on a female excavation director's trowel – but others were far more elaborate. One handle had been whittled with the owner's name; another had been marked with the message 'To Steve with Love'. Many trowels had originally been given as gifts, thus consolidating the symbolic resonance of an object that operates almost as an extension of the self. Without the possession of the 'correct' or 'appropriate' tools for the 'job', an archaeologist is less able to demonstrate status or prestige. The trowel thus represents a definitive moment in the biography of the owner as well as the tool.

The consumption and display of goods involves the construction of identity and expressions of taste and style. One of the most conspicuous and universally recognised forms of identity display is bodily adornment, including clothing. Apart from clothing's ability to express cultural principles, processes, and even social distance, it is especially useful in signifying cultural categories such as age, gender, and status. Clothing can also indicate the type of work undertaken, and uniforms assist in the articulation of social relations between people participating in similar activities.

Archaeological practice involves shared activity, and at Leskernick a proto-uniform seemed in evidence amongst excavators consisting of cotton fleeces, combat trousers, Gore-Tex jackets, army boots, and waterproof over-trousers, jackets, and coats. Many excavators wore at least one item of military-style clothing that potentially evoked metaphors of power, sacrifice and a sense of collectiveness. Certain participants 'worked' harder than others to express their commitment to the shared meanings and values articulated through archaeological practice via clothing. One student excavator wore a T-shirt designed for the Institute of Archaeology's 'Student Archaeological Society' (the 'SAS'). The shirt displayed the insignia of the British military elite Special Air Services, with the original parachute motif transformed into an archaeological trowel with wings. The SAS motto 'Who Dares Wins' had been altered to read 'Who Digs Wins'. It is unsurprising that in a civilian context, combat-style clothes should undergo alterations whilst retaining many of their original metaphors. For another male student excavator, wearing combat-style clothing seemed to offer both a partial acceptance and rejection of the intended meanings as he had chosen to dye some of it purple:

> I don't have a sole excavation kit but I use certain outdoor clothes for digging. My Berghaus jacket purchased specially for Bodmin (£180), Danner boots that are U.S. Army, Fibrepile trousers, American lightweight Army poncho, rip-stop summer trousers that are lightweight and quick drying, dyed purple combat trousers, a cycling glove to prevent blisters while I'm digging, a 'snoogie' hat, purple neckscarf. That's it.

Dan explained that since he was well aware that many other excavators adopted a military-style 'uniform' whilst excavating, he wanted to position himself apart whilst still retaining a sense of affinity. For Dan, military clothing not only served a practical purpose, it was also biographical since it referred to his TA past. Helen, a female excavation supervisor, who also chose to wear combat-style clothing on-site, expresses similar biographical feelings towards her clothes:

> I've brought my army surplus trousers, army surplus sweater, steel Doc Martins, hooded top, two vests, excavation bra, long wax jacket, and waterproof trousers that Alan gave me. I got most of these clothes from other digs I've been on.

The clothes Helen wore had been either purchased, or borrowed, or given to her by fellow excavators at previous digs. In the 1997 fieldwork season, Helen received a hat from another excavator that she had worked with that, she claimed, would immediately become 'dig gear'. Dan's and Helen's clothing and the life stories they relate to take on a narrative quality.

Whereas a proto-uniform could be detected amongst many of the excavators, the surveyors dressed in similarly structured sets of clothes that were quite distinct: soft shoes or Wellington boots, casual jumpers, and jeans. For many surveyors, including Barbara, a survey director, excavators wore uniforms whilst they (surveyors) wore 'conventional' clothes:

Tony then interviewed me. He took me through my list of what I'd brought with me. What was digger-specific? What had I bought specifically for Leskernick? I denied having any sort of site uniform – I wear the same sort of floppy nondescript clothes at home. What I had done was to renew them – socks, sneakers,

underwear. Signalling a sense of identity; scruffy, somewhat
disorganised, last minutish, not very groupy etc., June 1997.

An acute sense of self-awareness regarding the expressive properties of clothes is displayed in Barbara's comments as she attempts to convey a sense of her own individual identity, whilst at the same time expressing who she is *not* through her denial of the possession of a 'site uniform'. Similarly, Chris, also a survey director, describes the 'everyday' clothes worn for fieldwork in the following way:

> All my clothes that I wear here are everyday. Jeans have become 'project', as they're too scruffy for lecturing in. I don't dress up in the evenings, just what's clean and dry.

Through a gradual transition across a value-laden boundary of acceptability, Chris's jeans are status reassigned from 'appropriate to teaching' to 'project'. Both his and Barbara's fieldwork clothes were more or less identical to those they wear at home or lecturing. By maintaining a familiar image and identity through the adoption of similar if not identical clothing, they seemed engaged in maintaining their social and intellectual identities and statuses within the project.

Although clothing worn by male and female participants on Leskernick Hill tended to suppress 'structured' expressions of gender differentiation, at the holiday park more marked statements, primarily among female participants, were made. At certain social events, at the bar, or in caravans, many females abandoned the masculine or nongendered varieties of clothing worn on site and wore make-up, perfume, and jewellery. Because certain types of clothing are considered appropriate for particular social contexts, it is not surprising that deliberate efforts were made to mark gender off-site. That material culture objects like clothes permit or facilitate as well as constrain certain kinds of social behaviour seems obvious in this case.

I have discussed various ways in which participants engaged with the world at Leskernick through language, image, social movement and action, and material culture. Now the focus shifts towards the activities of the participants at the holiday park. Because social space is formed from 'stretched out' social relations consisting of networks of interaction and interconnection, places and the material culture found within them are rarely bounded or settled (Allen and Hamnett 1995; Massey 1995: 54). Although Leskernick Hill operated as the main 'stage' upon which the archaeological or anthropological gaze was directed, we cannot ignore the other activities occurring in quasi-private 'backstage' areas, for they help shape the performance itself.

Caravan culture and the domestication of space

For four out of the five years that the project ran, the fieldwork participants were accommodated in static caravans at a holiday park near Camelford, north Cornwall. From here, they 'migrated' to Leskernick and its environs in the early morning to undertake excavations and surveys and to here they returned in the late afternoon to wash, eat, socialise, and sleep. The holiday park boasted a grocery store, bar, laundry, fast-food restaurant, swimming pool, and volleyball courts. The owners had clearly tried to plan spaces for interaction and sociality between guests and to engender a community atmosphere through the design and positioning of roads, car parks, static caravan pitches, and washing facilities. The arrangement of caravans was not unlike a modern housing estate: equally dispersed from one another in 'snaking' rows, the caravans were positioned close enough to facilitate communication whilst at the same time retaining an impression of privacy (see Southerton, Shove, and Warde [1998] for an analysis of recreational caravanning).

> Our mobile homes are located in a selected eight-acre part of the park and sited on split-levels in areas surrounded by mature trees. You'll enjoy the totally relaxed and informal freedom of the park's 28 rolling acres, where those who simply want to get away from life's hustles and bustles can always find a quiet spot. (An up-to-date version of Holiday Park's website [accessed December 2006] is available on http:www.juliotswell.com/juliotswell/)

Although the publicity might espouse 'relaxed and informal freedom', guests are nevertheless subjected to certain rules and regulations concerning dogs, noise, speed limits and 'appropriate' uses of the swimming pool.

Patterns of movement around the holiday park reiterate some of those on Leskernick Hill. Just as the hill became domesticated through the socialisation of informal places including, for example, the 'tea-hut' and 'tool store', the holiday park also possessed social spheres, including the bar and project participants' caravans. To move between such points, participants used the shortest routes wherever possible, often cutting across paths and other guests' quasi-private spaces surrounding their caravans. Again, this parallels participants' movements between trenches, tea hut, and spoil heaps up on site.

The caravans as domestic and creative spaces

Caravans operate as domestic structuring spaces for social interaction between relatively exclusive though interdependent groups of project cohabitants. Many new arrivals to the project expressed a keen desire to examine their new 'home':

Stuart, student excavator, June 1997: I was allocated my caravan, number 31. I couldn't believe it; it has a telly, a proper toilet, shower, fridge, and one double bedroom and another with two beds. The caravan is far more equipped than I thought it would be.

The caravans all share a similar internal spatial arrangement, approximating to that of a conventional Western home: three bedrooms, bathroom with toilet, sink and shower, a fully fitted kitchen, and a living room.

Living in close proximity with unfamiliar others demanded skilful negotiation and cooperation. With up to four persons sharing a caravan, space was at a premium, and highly personalised activities such as washing, cooking, and eating required constant compromise and negotiation. In most caravans, a gradual patterning of routine domestic activities emerged, with cooking and cleaning duties being shared more or less equally among occupants. With fieldwork scheduled to commence on site at a similar time each morning, occupants established a preparatory routine that permitted equal access to bathrooms and kitchens.

Just as homes are often worked upon to establish and maintain collective and individual identities, meaningful and symbolically laden alterations to the caravans occurred during the project. Lang (1989) has argued that a home becomes an 'intimate hollow' only after an act of appropriation and familiarisation. Even before home-improving activities like decorating or 'do it yourself' have begun, a range of 'mini-rituals' such as cleaning to symbolically erase the 'presence' of previous occupants, or throwing housewarming parties to consolidate the occupants' sense of ownership occur. The caravan occupants performed similar 'ownership' rituals that helped overcome an immediate sense of displacement. The most noticeable act of domestication involved the gradual takeover of the interior through the positioning of certain objects. On arrival, participants immediately set about ordering and arranging their belongings; a few occupants receiving greetings cards from distant others displayed them in living rooms; others picked wild flowers and placed them on dining tables or on top of the caravan television in a replicative symbolic act of 'house-warming'.

Control over the material world takes many different forms, not least when mass consumer goods are modified and personalised (Appadurai 1986; Miller 1988). The standardised interiors of the caravans were neither unaltered nor radically transformed, although occupants frequently mentioned that the caravan decoration did not reflect their style. Strategies were deployed within limits of acceptability to overcome a sense of alienation, impart control, and differentiate caravan interiors. The most obvious site for such a transformation was the publicly accessible and communal space of the living room. Despite the differences in the quality of materials in each grade of caravan, this room presented a more or less similar coordinated and functional aesthetic: one or two fitted settees placed along the walls of the caravan faced a built-in wall unit housing a TV and a very 'homely' gas fire with fake surround. Whereas the 'deluxe' grade caravans contain dark wood wall-units with glass doors, the 'economy' grade caravans exhibit lighter-coloured wood units with no doors. All the caravans incorporate a dining suite, including a round dark wooden table and soft stools in the 'deluxe' and 'superior' caravans, and a fixed rectangular light chipboard table and benches in the 'economy' grade.

During the project, each caravan used slightly different communicative codes in an attempt to domesticate space through the subtle rearrangement of existing fixtures and fittings and the addition of certain objects.

With little opportunity or motivation to ornament the caravans with more 'conventional' items like family photographs, furnishings, knick-knacks, and so on, occupants performed a creative act of *bricolage*, whereby objects underwent a process of recontextualisation and meaning reinscription. The range of objects was limited to personal possessions brought to the project by participants or more commonly objects purchased from Camelford town or acquired from Leskernick Hill. In a caravan occupied by female participants, a map of Cornwall was placed on the kitchen wall. In another caravan, postcards and empty fudge boxes depicting local Cornish scenes were conspicuously displayed. In one male-occupied caravan, living-room objects included a sheep skull and various other animal bones and stones collected from Leskernick Hill.

In others, spent rifle cartridges collected from the hill were exhibited. Given that participants were deeply involved with the excavation of archaeological material from Leskernick Hill, it is not surprising that souvenirs associated with the past and place were brought into the domestic space of caravans. As Belk (1997: 32) argues, such souvenirs not only have a status-claiming capacity but also represent an attempt to transport some 'sacred' quality of a place across boundaries, in this case from hill to holiday park.

With the exception of books, magazines, and radios, very few personal items were exhibited in living room or kitchen areas. Female participants brought predominantly fictional or archaeological or anthropological books, whereas males tended to bring a far wider range of books on subjects as diverse as birds, exotic cookery, travel, and record production. Books written and edited by two of the site directors were amongst the most common archaeological books belonging to students, suggesting a desire to demonstrate understanding and accord with the 'intellectual capital' of their teachers (Bourdieu 1984). Although participants tended not to bring many personal items from home, in the 1998 fieldwork season one mature male surveyor who travelled to the project alone by car brought a plethora of items from home including a CD player, directors' chair, lamps, tablecloth, seat fabrics, and a potted plant.

In this case, a single occupant was transforming the caravan into a replica of his permanent home. The same individual was responsible for bringing the tent to the project in the previous season. Privacy, even exclusivity, seems to have been judged an important value.

The level to which communal areas became transformed often related to the degree of sociality amongst caravan habitués. Thus, during the 1997 season, it became apparent that two site directors who shared a caravan spent little time together in the caravan preferring to visit, socialise, and eat with others.

Barbara, survey director, June 1997: I spoke to Sue for a while who joked about Chris's awkwardness in their caravan. Apparently Chris has shoved all his stuff in his room and has yet to cook there.

Barbara, survey director, June 1997: Chris is sitting on his caravan steps smoking a fag. Some catch-up conversation. I'm fretting that Sue is feeling left out and feel somehow that Chris is boycotting Sue by refusing to leave a mark on their caravan. I mention this, but meet resistance.

The use and control of space is a potent means for the expression and negotiation of social relations, and an implicit line was drawn between the two directors through a mutual separation of the caravan's communal spaces, including the use of separate exterior doors to enter and exit the caravan. Besides either door, personal items belonging to one or other of the directors were placed. Chris placed his ashtray and wine box near one door; Sue placed her kitchen utensils by the other. Through such material expressions, the social division between the two directors was made visible to all, and the internal spatial arrangement of the directors' caravan became a metaphor for the social divisions up on the hill.

Social relationships between participants were also negotiated through another form of material culture – food. Food is, of course, integral to the maintenance or deterioration of bodily health but, more symbolically, it can communicate affluence, sophistication, social cohesiveness, distance, or even alterations in social status. Not unlike clothing, as well as other forms of material culture, it may also be used to define a sense of individual and collective identity (Lupton 1996; Mennell, Murcott, and van Otterloo 1992; Palmer 1997; Van Gennep 1960). Mary Douglas (1972), in an influential article 'Deciphering a Meal', suggested that food categories encode and structure social events which, in turn structure other events. Social interactions between persons depend upon the sort of meal being shared, and, although the dividing line can often be breached, meals or drinks define intimacy and distance, so that strangers and acquaintances are offered drinks, whereas family, close friends, and honoured guests are given meals (Douglas 1972: 256).

In the context of the project, the sharing of food facilitated the crossing of social boundaries – from distance to intimacy – whilst also marking an alteration in routine. From the first day, food sharing facilitated a sense of group cohesion, no more so than at the 'traditional' first-night party. At the beginning of the 1996 season, the female survey director had orchestrated this event in her own caravan. The following year, with an almost identical menu to that used the year before, the same director chose an alternative setting – the sociologists' caravan. Partly because of perceptions of the divisions that existed between surveyors and excavators, the sociologists' caravan seems to have been selected as a more neutral space for the sharing of food and drink on the first evening. The sociologists' caravan was not only a space where academic and intellectual divisions could be breached, but where social distances relating to unfamiliarity, age, status, and caravan occupancy could be narrowed.

A number of other 'special' meals were shared by all project participants at certain times throughout the period of fieldwork (Sunday lunches, for instance), although food was mostly prepared and consumed by participants within individual caravan domains. Until recently, most research into food consumption was conducted either in 'private' homes or 'public' spheres such as restaurants, although there are notable exceptions. Valentine and Longstaff's (1998) research into the meanings and uses of food as an exchange commodity in the negotiation of power relations took place in the institutional setting of a male prison. Neither exclusively 'private' nor 'public', the preparation and consumption of food in prisons shares many similarities with the fieldwork context. Like the prison, the holiday park assumed a rather ambivalent status through its marginal status on the fringes of the local town. Caravans may be considered as essentially private domains, but shared temporary occupancy often with unfamiliar others alters the meanings associated with domestic freedom and privacy. Although participants occasionally took meals in the camp-site restaurant or bar, or less frequently in a restaurant or café in nearby Camelford, most dinners were prepared and consumed with co-occupants.

Food not only facilitates cohesiveness, collectivity, and a sense of belonging in its own right, it may facilitate further episodic events of sociability. In certain contexts food can also be used to define and maintain boundaries of identity. Although attention is directed more often to cultural groups (e.g., Okely 1983; Palmer 1997), certain practices relating to food preparation and consumption may be seen as affirmations of individuals' sense of identity. Thus, for example, a vegan diet may be viewed as a manifestation of identity formation that implies a certain separation between persons, although negotiable contexts can, again, breach any perceived distance. The relatively mundane drama of food sharing finds its significance not so much in the food eaten, but the event itself. However, when varieties or categories of food, or methods of eating, are considered by others to diverge too widely from consensual norms, a sense of social and cultural cohesiveness may be called into question:

Barbara, survey director, June 1997: Noticed the contents of Sue's sandwich tin – little, broken-up bits of pumpernickel. Bird-like.

Mike, sociologist, June 1997: Sue maintains an absolute separation between her own diet and that of other people on site, even to the extent that her utensils (Chinese bowl and chopsticks) are her own rather than using the ones provided by the camp site as the rest of us do.

It is apparent that food and associated material culture are significant features in the reproduction of social relationships. Food has exchange value, and the gifting of food amongst participants can be explained as a way of influencing and negotiating social relations. In the 1997 fieldwork season, as in previous seasons, parties were often organised by the site directors to mark the departure of a project participant. At these parties, unlike the first-night party, participants were expected to bring food and drink. Most guests also made an effort to 'smarten up', or, in the case of some female participants, to wear make-up and extra jewellery. One particular party for an excavator leaving the next morning involved the sharing of celebratory foods.

Dan, student excavator: It's Penni's party tonight in honour of her leaving, so everyone is cooking food and buying booze. It should be a good night...

Fay, student excavator: Barbara held a party (for Penni) in their caravan this evening. We are all scattered on site, it was a good idea to get together in one place. A lovely atmosphere and a rather impressive 'cairn cake'.

Henry, surveyor: I bought a chicken in Camelford for the dinner party and spent the early evening catching up on my diary as it roasted. Most people had made a real effort in terms of preparing nice food. People had also showered and changed into smart clothes. I felt a bit shoddy arriving in muddy jeans clutching a rather overcooked chicken.

Despite any real or perceived conflicts existing between the excavators and surveyors, the party implied a level of social cohesion as well as an affirmation of project group unity. The party itself acted as confirmation both of the separation of a participant from the group and the resultant change in status her departure would inaugurate.

Conclusion

This chapter focuses on the complex relationships that exist between a group of archaeologists and anthropologists, the landscapes they inhabited over a few short summer seasons, and the wider world beyond. Why should we care about how project participants used and thought about spaces and places, or how they stamped their individual or collective identity through their clothing or food? There are two reasons. The first is that archaeology and anthropology are social practices; the processes and procedures employed are socially constructed; and process, practice, and procedure inevitably colour the form and outcome of their enquiries. The second is that by analysing how we engage with the world around us, we come to a better understanding of the issues raised, questions to be asked, and ambiguities to acknowledge when we try to understand how other people, at other times, thought about and interacted with their world.

In this chapter, the landscapes of campsite and hillside interweave. And just as in chapter 1 the idea of nested prehistoric landscapes is created, so we come to understand that the contemporary landscapes are also nested. In this chapter, I have been content to describe the more intensely occupied spaces and places in which the summer work took place. If this had been a different sort of book, and if there had been more time, I could have opened out towards the other landscapes that the practitioners' inhabited, and tried to understand how they affected, or were affected by, the perceptions and understandings that emerged at Leskernick and at the campsite. Equally, I have chosen to focus on the phenomenological and material world of every-day existence – the 'foreground actuality' mentioned at the beginning of the chapter, rather than the 'background potentiality'. This background potentiality – the constraints and possibilities of historically specific social, political, cultural, and economic relationships – was given more attention in the last chapter. The two chapters – this one primarily about landscape and material culture, the last more concerned with social practice – are intended to work together.

Acknowledgments

A huge debt of thanks goes to the Leskernick Landscape Project team who allowed me the opportunity to intrude on them at inconvenient times. Special thanks to my co-sociologist, Mike Wilmore, for his help in the formulation of this chapter and useful comments on earlier versions. Any errors are entirely my own. Thanks also to David Thackray (National Trust) for his support and financial assistance. Last, thanks to Emma for her unfailing support and encouragement throughout periods of fieldwork and writing-up.

Chapter Thirteen

Art and the Re-Presentation of the Past[1]

Introduction

In this chapter, we consider the relationship between contemporary environmental art and the interpretation of prehistoric lifeworlds in the context of our work at Leskernick. We argue that the production of art in the present can be dialectically linked to an active interpretative understanding of the prehistoric past. We see it as part of the process of interpretation.

We did not start out with the idea of creating installations. Rather, these ideas developed out of our research and a series of practical and methodological problems we faced in the process of recording archaeological evidence and in thinking about how we might present our research to others and represent the past. As the summers went by, we tried our hand at different things; there was much trial and error, but gradually we became more confident, understood better what was possible, and why and what their relevance was to our attempts to interpret the past.

By now, you understand that we were immensely privileged in our work at Leskernick. Not only was it a place of singular beauty, not only was the work absorbing and mind bending, but given its remote situation, we could experiment without distraction and out of range of the public gaze. You will also, we hope, have a feeling for the low grey hill of Leskernick, with the rough moor stretching on all sides, and the encirclement of higher hills, including, on the western side, hills that are rugged and spinal with dramatic granite tors breaching the skyline. Already in our first year we had been struck by the nested nature of the landscape – the lived space of the settlements; then, beyond, the stone row and stone circles, a space of ceremony, memory, and legend; and, still further away, the cairns and tors, reminders of the larger geographies and genealogies of the moor. As time went on, it was the intense relationship between the people of Leskernick and their stone world that often preoccupied us.

The landscape that we were recording, when considered through a contemporary aesthetic lens, was already a cultural 'sculptural' form marked and transformed through thousands of years of human activity. The most striking topographic features of the landscape on Bodmin Moor are the dramatic rocky tors. These have been a constant source of fascination and awe from the past to the present: rock sculptures marking the land, orientation points, sources of myths and stories (Tilley 1995, 1996). Leskernick Hill, though it lacks dramatic tors, is covered with stones many of which have unusual and interesting shapes and deep weathering lines – 'sculpted' monuments with specific densities, masses, forms, and surface textures constantly altering with the qualities of the light and angles of view.

We have discussed the way in which the prehistoric inhabitants of the hill incorporated some of these natural stone sculptures into the walls of their houses, usually upslope and opposite the single entrance downslope. Others were linked or incorporated within the enclosure boundaries and compound walls. Free-standing stones were sometimes emphasised by having stones cleared away from them or, alternatively, heaped around them. There is, for us as contemporary beholders, as we look from a distance or walk more intimately among the stones, an aesthetic pleasure to all this, a pleasure heightened by our particular romantic appreciation of things ruined and patinated by time. No doubt, too, for the prehistoric people, there was also an aesthetic; at the very least, it was not just about surface or form or juxtaposition but more profoundly about the quality and power of the stones. For us, the stones are inanimate; for them, profoundly animate. We respond to the end product of their labour, to the stones *in place*. For them, the creative *process*, the making of the meaningful places, was at least as important. The nested landscape referred to above is an attempt to think ourselves into their world view, their sense of how things relate one to another. This nested landscape works in dialogue with a more intimate relationship to the stone world. And it is both distance and proximity, world view and intimate creative process, and our imaginative response to their way of being, that we are trying to find ways to engage with and to represent.

Equally, we conceive of our work at Leskernick as being as much about process as product. This is why we wrote, and used, our diaries, and why we undertook the sociological investigation of ourselves as a – temporary – community up on the hill. And it is why, as part of the process of documenting the hill, and our work, we experimented with various forms of visual representation from maps to plans and sections, from photos to paintings and drawings, to 'installation art'.

From Archaeology to Art and Back Again

Archaeological remains from Palaeolithic cave paintings to Bronze Age rock art to megaliths, stone circles and stone rows, to earthworks such as Silbury Hill and the Mississippi snake mounds have provided inspiration for a great many environmental artists. In the 1930s in Britain, the sculptural qualities of megaliths were explicitly recognised by Nash, Moore, and others. In the case of Michael Heizer whose work was formative in the development of U.S. 'land art' (see the discussion below), the connection is even clearer. Heizer's father was the famous U.S. archaeologist, Robert Heizer. Some of Heizer's forms are clearly inspired by Aztec architecture, just as some of De Maria's work is inspired by ancient Peruvian Nazca lines in the landscape. In contemporary British environmental art, Long, Fulton, Goldsworthy, and others have expressed interest and inspiration in prehistoric monuments, in particular stone circles (e.g., Goldsworthy 1994; Long 1980, 1996; see also chapter 15 this volume).

As archaeologists, we need to recognise that this inspiration works at a very generalised level. Lippard, an influential art critic, describes the process as 'weaving together ideas and images of very different cultures by making one a metaphor for the other and vice versa' (Lippard 1983: 2). For her, many archaeological statements about the past are 'boring' and 'limited', and the empirically constrained attempts to understand prehistoric monuments by archaeologists are no more or less relevant than statements of mystical belief by 'popular' writers evoking 'earth powers', ley-lines, and other generalised notions such as ideas about 'femaleness' and mother goddesses being embedded in the contours of the British countryside. In other words, ideas about the past are simply 'lifted' to produce work in the present. Noble, in the introduction to the catalogue for an exhibition at the South Bank Centre in London that brought together work inspired by prehistoric art forms, makes this point very clearly:

> There is always a danger when bringing together ten artists under a title *From Art to Archaeology* that they might be seen as a group of 'artist-archaeologists' whose work is directly influenced by ancient source material. Nothing could be further from the truth. Artists are by nature visual magpies collecting bits of information from diverse sources. What is at issue in this exhibition is the transformation of the past through artists' eyes. By crossing disciplines, from art to archaeology and back again with the artist as guide, we are given a door through which we enter the artists' extraordinary vocabulary of experience. (Noble 1991: 4)

We can link this statement to some critical comments by Tiberghien:

> These references to primitive civilizations simply allow the artists to create their art within an atemporal realm, between humanity's most distant past and the sophisticated scientific world. … Their objective is to return to perception and the search for a 'naive realism'. … The aesthetic linked to it, which stresses daily perceptive experience, does not have recourse to any conceptual or theoretical instrument other than ordinary reasoning. (Tiberghien 1995: 226)

Clearly, the concern in Noble's introduction to the Art to Archaeology exhibition is about preserving the disciplinary autonomy of art and the status and role of the artist.

There is no reason why artists should not be 'visual magpies', but we need to be clear that their practice and product is very different from the archaeological artistic practice that we are proposing. In relation to Tiberghien's comments about the lack of any significant theoretically informed position behind land art, we might ask: What if this practice was informed by a more considered understanding of space and place? Furthermore, what if an archaeologically and theoretically informed understanding of place resulted in the production of art in the environment, a practice linking past and present, place and landscape? Might this produce something more profound? Or is the attempt invalidated because the person producing the art has training in archaeology rather than the art academy?

The closest that archaeology has come to art is experimentation with various modes of visual re-presentation: models and three-dimensional depictions of the past as opposed to the flattened spaces of distribution maps and site plans. A standard way to put flesh on archaeological bones has been the museum exhibit or the picture in a book of a Bronze Age chief dressed in ceremonial regalia, or the reconstruction of the interior of a house or tomb, or people wandering around in a 'prehistoric view' of Stonehenge or Avebury. Most of these supposed windows into the past have been produced by graphic designers or artists who inevitably know considerably less about the past they are supposed to be depicting than the archaeologists. It is, perhaps, not surprising that the majority of these 'realist' images have a somewhat bizarre and unreal character, half-way between art and cartoon, seriousness and farce.

In a different manner, Shanks has recently expressed a desire to explore the visual as a means of addressing the 'dismissal of feeling' in a contemporary archaeology in which, too often, scientism has embargoed the subjective (Shanks 1992: 2–3). His book, *Experiencing the Past*, plays with different forms of images: picturesque views of castles and megalithic tombs, photomontages of monuments inspired by Hockney, still-life juxtapositions of broccoli and classical Greek pottery, etc. They illustrate his text and reiterate the important point about the subjective dimension to any experience of the past, but do little more. Deliberately ambiguous and bizarre and virtually undiscussed, their presence evokes a sense of the past in the present. There is a conflation of the personal and the subjective. But the two are not the same. No doubt contrary to Shanks's intentions, the visual images simply reproduce the gulf between past and present, subjectivity and objectivity, rather than attempting to create an informed dialectic.

What we have attempted at Leskernick is the production of art in the landscape as part of the process of interpreting the past. Although the aesthetic qualities of things are sometimes acknowledged in the archaeological literature, they are rarely discussed. Might a consideration of aesthetic qualities also be an important element in the interpretation of the past? For us, the most important point about contemporary environmental art is the way it is created in the landscape and 'artfully' related to space and place (e.g., Beardsley 1989; Fagone 1996; Hall 1982; Kepes 1972; Ross 1993; Sonfist 1982; and see the discussion in Tilley et al. 2000). Despite the important caveats noted above, we have been much influenced by such developments.

Placing Art Works in the Land

From an archaeological point of view, what is most significant about contemporary environmental art is that the work becomes part of the landscape. In the movement away from the confined institutional spaces of museums and galleries, a new and highly specific relationship to place is asserted in which concepts become materialised through the transformation of materials usually found *in place*. In the tradition of landscape painting, landscapes are viewed as if through a window bordered by a frame. The illusion of perspective associated with this tradition creates an even stricter perceptual frame. And the act of framing in Western culture is indelibly associated with the notion of the picturesque.

But to really see the landscape, one must go through the window, feel the land, and bodily experience the place. Environmental art is neither sculpture nor architecture but nonetheless retains aspects of both. The materials used have a mass and volume. On canvas, the artist can choose the point of view or perspective on the landscape, the light, the colours, and textures, and these become fixed. In environmental art, control of all these parameters is lost. The work is constantly changing and so, too, the reaction to it. This encourages self-reflection on our relationship with, and experience of, the work. The intimate knowledge of raw materials and processes that underpin Goldsworthy's work cannot be derived from scientific abstractions but occur through intimate emotional engagement and observation.

Time as well as space becomes embodied within environmental art, in a multiple sense. Time is present not simply in the production of the art but in the act of encountering and experiencing it: traveling to the site, the duration of the visit, the hour of the day, the season of the year, and so on. Experiencing the art thus involves a phenomenological synthesis of anticipation, perception, and memory. Of course, all this is also true of a visit to an art gallery; the difference is that our appreciation of the work becomes anchored in the landscape and the process of walking to the site, the horizon it stands against, the colour of the earth or vegetation, and the position of the sun in the sky and qualities of light, which create meaning. Time also has the effect of decomposing environmental art from the moment of completion: earth erodes, ditches silt, leaves rot, and blooms lose their colour. For some environmental artists, documenting this process is also part of the work rather than leaving it frozen in time through the photograph taken on completion. Just as the piece of environmental art changes, so does the surrounding landscape. Time and change become an intrinsic part of our experience of both.

For many environmental artists, the impermanence of their works is a strategy to combat an emphasis on precious commoditised objects in our culture. The setting of the work in a space without studio walls physically and conceptually limiting creative possibilities provides a new background and a new set of references. The object is no longer self-sufficient and self-referential. Traditional sculpture is something to be looked at, but many earthworks can be walked in, the viewer is inside rather than outside the work, in and of the place that has its own history and character. The primary means of documenting the existence of much environmental art is the photograph, sometimes in combination with plans, drawings, and sketches. This is usually both a way of remembering the art work and an integral part of the project. De Maria's Lightning Field, a one-mile-square grid containing 640 18-foot steel poles, reaches its artistic culmination when lightning strikes one of the rods and the photograph is the only means of testimony to the event. What one chooses to document for posterity in environmental art is what Smithson (1972: 231) calls the non-site. He draws the following distinctions and suggests the site and the non-site exist as a dialectic:

open limits	closed limits
series of points	array of matter
outer coordinates	inner coordinates
subtraction	addition
indeterminate certainty	determinate certainty
scattered information	contained information
reflection	mirror
edge	centres
some place (physical)	no place (abstract)
many	one
SITE	NON-SITE

For Smithson, the site expands experience, the non-site – the re-presentation of site as in a photograph, drawing, map, or plan displaced in a gallery or book – contracts experience. Not everyone would agree with this. Most people – who only view the non-site – may well recognise that the shift from three dimensional to two, the removal of context, movement, variable conditions, and the creation of hard borders transform and diminish their experience.

Environmental art is not primarily an art *of* the landscape, it is a situated art involving a complex of relationships between work and concept, work and text, work and its re-presentation (usually photographic), work and place, and work and the materials manipulated, which are themselves bearers of meaning, work, and space. The form created is thus at the centre of a node of relationships serving to articulate them. What, then, is in the work and what is outside of it becomes consistently blurred. The work spills out beyond itself and is thoroughly mediated.

Environmental Art and the Significance Of Place

> Recently I have been working in the country, where, carving in the open air, I find sculpture more natural than in a London studio, but it needs bigger dimensions. A large piece of stone or wood placed almost anywhere at random in a field, orchard, or garden, immediately looks right and inspiring. (Moore 1937)

Moore's comments about sculpture 'looking right' in an outdoor setting are, according to Biggs, only explicable in terms of a prior 'recognition' on the part of some British artists in the 1930s of the landscape itself as having inherent sculptural qualities (Biggs 1984: 20). A combination of the surroundings and the work could help create a new kind of experience of form. Yet the consideration of place by Moore, perhaps the most innovative sculptor of his generation, hardly seems profound. In the case of Moore's works, the sculptural form is evidently site *dominant* and virtually any setting would, apparently, do. Alternatively, outdoor art works may be dominated by their landscape settings and appear trivial in comparison.

Much contemporary environmental art has a far more sophisticated concern with the landscape setting of the work that is crucial to its creation, perception, and reception. Crawford (1993: 194–45) usefully defines two radically different relational dynamics between environmental art works and their settings. First, there may be an *aesthetic symbiosis* in which an attempt is made to create a harmonious relationship between the piece and its setting. The work draws attention to and enhances its setting and vice versa. Second, there may be a *dialectical relationship*, in which interaction between the work and its setting brings into being a synthetic third object, the product of this interaction. In our view, the most successful and powerful works of contemporary environmental art fall into this last category.

Over and over again, environmental artists stress the importance of place. This is not a process of placing a sculpture in the landscape or depicting a picturesque view but a matter of interaction in which both the art work and the landscape are more than the sum of their parts. Art is no longer mimetic but becomes part of the land. The landscape is not something to be copied but is a primary source for the genesis of the work. The place and the setting mould the work, which is rooted in place. Static, set in place, its meaning and identity is not transferable to another location: the place is the work and the work is the place. The distancing so much emphasised in traditional art and aesthetics (we see the world through a frame) is blown away when one is surrounded by the art object, part of the same place. Smithson notes that for him 'perception is prior to conception when it comes to site selection or definition. One does not *impose*, but rather *exposes* the site' (Smithson cited in Tiberghien 1995: 94). We will consider three specific examples.

Smithson was interested in creating a piece of art in the Great Salt Lake in Utah. The general choice of the location was influenced by colour, areas of the lake in which micro-bacteria give it the colour of tomato soup, but the specific location and the idea of building a spiral jetty were profoundly influenced by the specific local topography:

> I selected my site. Irregular beds of limestone dip gently eastward, massive deposits of black basalt are broken over the peninsula, giving the region a shattered appearance. It is one of the few places on the lake where the water comes right up to the mainland. Under shallow pinkish water is a network of mud cracks supporting the jigsaw puzzle that composes the mud flats. As I looked at the site, it reverberated out to the horizons only to suggest an immobile cyclone while flickering light made the entire landscape appear to quake. ... This site was a rotary that enclosed itself in an immense roundness. From that gyrating space emerged the possibility of the spiral jetty. (Smithson 1972: 223)

John Maine describes the Chiswell earthwork on the Isle of Portland, a place with many quarries and complex exposed geological strata, on the south Dorset coast of England in the following way:

> The proposal takes the form of a landscape work, rising in terraces from the coast path. The curved walls will create wave-like patterns, and support undulating platforms of earth. ... The higher walls will be made of stone found in the upper strata of the quarries (e.g., 'Slate'), and lower walls will be constructed from a sequence of different types, in the descending order of stone layers found naturally. ... Each type of stone will suggest a different method of wall construction. (Maine cited in Morland 1988: 62)

Keir Smith discusses one of his wooden sculptures, Seven Stones before the Old Man, in the Grizedale forest in the north-west of England:

> The sculpture overlooks the Grizedale valley. The highest local Peak, the Old Man of Coniston, is seen in the distance. The work is in two parts, a palisade of larch logs cut to the shape of the mountain, and, in front of this, a row of seven 'rocks', carved from wood. One rock, the largest, contains a deep reservoir filled with metal powder. This *Quarry Stone* refers to the metal workings in Coppermines Valley which leads to the summit of the Old Man. The remaining rocks have implement shapes cut into their top surfaces. ... These shapes are ghosts of potential within the metal ore. They were suggested by Bronze-Age flat moulds from the British Museum. (Smith 1984 in Davies and Knipe 1984)

What is clear from these accounts is the manner in which the artworks relate to the subjective experience of place of the artist. This is a contemporary and personal impression that may come about in various ways. Smithson

318

found his site by driving around areas of the Great Salt Lake with a suitable water colour, his initial point of fascination. Maine had worked as a sculptor for over 20 years in the Portland quarries. The idea for Smith's sculpture in Grizedale came about after a period of residency in which he lived in the place. It has little, or only a tangential relationship to the past. Some of the forms used by environmental artists may be influenced by knowledges of prehistoric monuments, but they clearly do not have the same meanings and a common understanding is not usually being promoted. Long makes this clear in relation to his own work: 'Stonehenge and all the circles in Britain … came about from a completely different culture. …They were about social, religious art. I make my work as an individual' (Long 1986: 7). Goldsworthy, one of the most successful and influential of contemporary British environmental artists, comments:

> My art is a way of learning in which instincts guide best. It is also very physical – I need the shock of touch, the resistance of place, materials and weather, the earth as my source. It is a collaboration, a meeting-point between my own and earth's nature. … Looking, touching, material, place, making, the form and resulting work are integral. … Place is found by walking, direction determined by weather and season. I am a hunter, I take the opportunities each day offers – if it is snowing, I work with snow, at leaf-fall it will be leaves, a blown-over tree becomes a source of twigs and branches. I stop at a place or pick up material by feeling that there is something to discover. (Goldsworthy 1990a: 161–62)

Art at Leskernick

Initially, in attempts to represent our experience of the hill, we experimented with *writing* the stones (Bender, Hamilton, and Tilley 1997). We opened up our text by juxtaposing diary entries with conventional prose, but our illustrations remained traditional 'scientific' abstracted re-presentations. We needed more open-ended drawings and images, ones that were more subjective, full of question marks, and in some way more indicative of our various interpretative leaps, perspectives, and knowledges. We believe that art provides us with another way of telling, another way of expressing the powers of stones on Leskernick Hill. We want to try and capture the powerful sense of place that the rocks evoke through their inherent sculptural properties, and their positioning, whether these be stones incorporated into the houses, or stones in clitter spreads, or stones in the fields or clearings. We cannot aspire to recreate the specific meanings that the stones had to the Bronze Age inhabitants of the site. Our work is our creative response to their creativity or, better, the ruins of their creativity.

The ways in which we have begun to explore this are:

1. Through investigating how our *practical* engagement in archaeological recording and excavation can produce and inform imagery.

2. Through *physically* transforming, and adding to, the surface structures of the hill by wrapping stones and creating installations.

3. By *materialising our surface activities*: placing markers (such as flags) in the landscape signifying the loci where at any one time we are surveying and investigating connections between places.

4. By *constructing visual re-presentations* of our multiple perceptions/understandings of the site and our activities.

At first we wondered whether we ought to get artists to do these things for us. It seemed presumptuous, for instance, to think that we could arrive on site with swathes of textile, or rolls of cling film and pots of paint, and wrap a stone and produce a 'convincing' art work capable of effectively communicating something meaningful to others. We worried that we might be graphically appropriating another discipline's 'language' – a form of plagiarism. But *our* starting point was to try and physically re-present our various reactions, knowledges, and interpretations that had grown out of *being* archaeologists and *being* on Leskernick Hill. Importing an artist from outside, attempting to explain the hill to him or her, and then expecting them to produce some informed response to our work seemed a futile exercise. Anyway, the exclusivity of the category 'artist,' and what object 'art' is supposed to be, has been effectively challenged and debunked in the postmodern discourses of the last 20 years, beginning with radical environmental artists such as Joseph Beuys (Adams 1992; Gandy 1997).

Although an environmental artist is free to respond to a sense of place in the landscape in any way that might seem interesting or appropriate, we are relatively constrained insofar as we only want to respond to what we have found, through our fieldwork, to be archaeologically significant. We cannot, then, wander around Leskernick and create installations on an *ad hoc* basis. Precisely because of this constraint, we regard our art works as being relatively empowered rather than relatively diminished in significance. This is because there is the potential of establishing, through the creation of the art work, a genuine dialectic between past and present. Rather than being regarded as something outside and alien to a discourse of archaeology, the process of producing art becomes an integral part of the process of recording, writing, interpreting, and re-presenting the past in the present. In this respect, we find it significant that although many environmental artists make frequent reference to time in their works, in almost all cases this refers not so much to human time, the landscape as a cultural palimpsest that develops through human agency over time, but to environmental or geological time: weathering, erosion, decay (processes of entropy in the case of Smithson).

It is worth pointing out that a great deal of our knowledge of the hill is of a practical, routinised, nondiscursive character that we cannot yet, if ever, express effectively in words or verbally communicate to others. It stems from spending considerable amounts of time there, being in place, crouched within a trench, feeling the wind and rain seep into our bones, walking through the mists, sheltering behind the stones, making tea in the ruins of a prehistoric house. 'The most rewarding thing ever said to me was by a Dutch woman of a shape I had carved in sand. She said "Thank you for showing me that was there"' (Goldsworthy 1990a: 163). It is this that we are trying to achieve in our artworks at Leskernick: seeing and showing *what is there*.

We conceive of the role of art in the Leskernick project as a means to renegotiate a relationship with the past, a response to our alienation from that past. We work in an unpopulated village that has been abandoned for over two and a half thousand years. We try to create a sense of a particular past and a particular place through our own contemporary experience of the hill and through the process of *making*. The artwork permits us to reveal aspects of reality that would otherwise be both overlooked and impossible to represent in any other way. What we produce is a synthesis of subjectivity and objectivity. For example, by wrapping cling film on a stone, and subsequently painting it, we are creating something new: a synthesis of the stone shape that we have not created and something that we have added to it. We now discuss our work of representation in more detail, addressing each of the four themes mentioned above in turn.

As an excellent exemplar of contemporary environmental art, we cite Goldsworthy's words frequently in what follows. In part, this is simply to acknowledge that, together with the work of Christo, he has been one of our main inspirations. The purpose is also to bring out essential differences between his approach to place and landscape and ours.

Practical Engagement: We Are Participants

When he first began to work in the landscape Goldsworthy stated: 'I felt the sand – in a way I didn't know before ... up until then my art had been expressing ideas, whereas now it became an art which taught me through my hands' (cited in Matless and Revill 1995: 425).

It is paradoxical that archaeological excavation is 'work with hands', a practically engaged discipline, yet in publication the resulting plans and sections emphasise sanitised, detached observation. Conventional archaeological drawings have a highly codified format that requires knowledge of the 'conventions' to translate the image. If you do not know the code, the plan or section looks bizarre. For an outsider, they are elitist, exclusionary, and esoteric. They are part of the interiorised disciplinary power of archaeological discourse. The plans appear so strange because they are produced from an aerial or bird's eye perspective rather from that of an on-the-ground embodied and bodily experience of place. In many ways our scribbled notes and sketches seem to be more accessible. These are the sorts of things *not* usually published. A notepad page has no rules to obey. It arouses no expectations of ordered juxtaposition and, as such, is something closer to human experience and perspective. The need for a measured plan and section for what excavation reveals and destroys is not at issue. But these are not enough, given that they fail to provide so much. There is a need to experiment with multiplex page images, juxtaposing and creating montages of measured plans, sketch plans, paintings, and photo-collages to convey the duality of measured perception and physical experience within the practice of excavation and fieldwork. Thus, a painting or sketch (Color Plate 2a) can give a sense of the textures and presence of the stones far more sensuously than any measured plan and provide the additional advantage that fallen stones can be visually resurrected into their original positions in house and field walls.

Excavation creates its own imagery, reworking the past into the present. The sharp edges of an excavation trench frame have their own modernist and military aesthetic displaying an internal world of textures, patterns, and colours and a potent sense of what potentially lies beneath the turf elsewhere. Visually, time is reversed and ordered in what we extract and sort: turf stacks, earth piles, stone piles, artefacts, environmental samples. At Leskernick, we photographed, and restructured, our 'waste' piles as tangible monuments of our activities (Figures 13.1a and 13.1b). Our spoil heaps, rather than simply being means of getting rid of the detritus of excavation, became part of a creative process of responding to place. We remodelled the spoil heaps so that they mimicked the shapes of the distant tors, reiterating elements in the distant skyline that relationally constitute Leskernick as a distinctive place.[2]

CT (21 June 1996): Late in the afternoon I transform the heap by the stone row terminal into an image of Rough Tor. This appalls the diggers who look at me with complete disbelief. Here is one of the site directors playing at sandcastles. I couldn't care less … of course I do!

Backfilling, too, is often a focus for our ideas about a place and our sense of digging the past in the present. There is a long tradition of placing objects in the backfill, ostensibly to date the excavation for posterity. But there is also a sense of having buried something of ourselves there.

Temporary Physical Transformation of Sight and Place

I have collected stones [to make cairns] that glowed white under a full moon, pebbles at low tide, earth-stained stones at the end of the day, and worked when it was cold enough to freeze one stone to another. … Each pile is much more than its material. They are cairns of light, colour, cold, water … and stone. I have gathered the moonlight, setting sun, incoming tide, hard frost. (Goldsworthy 1995)

fig. 13:1 a) Spoil heap mirroring the profile of Brown Willy, a hill that dominates the skyline at Leskernick; b) stone cairn built during the excavation of 'House' structure 23.

As archaeologists, we find the cairn. How can we inscribe that process of collecting, selecting, choosing, timing, placing? One key response we had to the stones was to wrap them. In doing this, we were acknowledging and making tangible our actions within, reactions to, and interpretations of Leskernick's stoney landscape and the possible significance of these stones to its prehistoric inhabitants. The process of stone wrapping served to *energise* the stones with our ideas and thoughts. In doing this, it clearly mattered *which* stones we wrapped, and where. We wrapped stones of particular shapes – triangular, 'whale backed', and pyramidal stones – that seem to have been significant to the prehistoric inhabitants of the hill. Within the houses, we wrapped some of the backstones opposite the entrance ways that appeared to be, almost without fail, the most prominent stone within the wall's circumference (Figure 13.2a and 13.2b. We wrapped the very large lozenge-shaped

a

b

fig.13.2 a) Henry alongside shawl-covered stone; b) Wayne and Chris adjusting the shawl over the backstone of 'House' 23.

stone that we had identified as a possible 'shrine-stone' or offering place (Figure 13.3a), and some of the circular stone arrangements set among the clitter masses on the hill, which had previously been regarded by archaeologists and geologists as purely natural boulder spreads. We wrapped stones on other sites across the moor.

CT (24 June 1997): After lunch we wrap the [shrine] stone. This takes most of the afternoon as the only way we can get the cling-film round the stone is to unravel part of the roll and pass it through a small hole at ground level. ... The stone looks dramatic in white, especially at a distance, and with the small triangular stone painted red in front of it, but I think that I prefer it in its natural state. This stone somehow seems to evade or resist transformation. Some stones seem to work better being wrapped than others. Perhaps I just need to get used to the stone being wrapped and painted, it will 'work' on me like listening to a piece of unfamiliar music.

Both the materials used for wrapping (fabric during the 1996 field season; cling-film and paint during the 1997 field season) and the colours produced striking effects and impacts on site. Wrapping with fabric curiously confounded the observer's perception of depth and volume (Figures 13.2a and 13.2b). The previously static fabric of the stones had been turned into a mutable one. Fabric, although highlighting, had the effect of obscuring the shape of the stone. Wrapping the stones with cling-film altered and obscured surface texture but still preserved the shape. We regard shape as a key element in the choice and arrangement of stones on the hill, whether it is a stone incorporated into a structure such as a house or compound wall or a stone of especial importance in a field. Wrapping stones within cling-film and highlighting them with paint was found to be particularly effective in visually expressing the significance of these stones (Color Plates 1b, 5a, and 5b).

Using the cling-film, the hard, heavy masses metamorphosed into softer shapes of arresting colour (poppy red, acrylic white, cornfield yellow, navy blue, holly red). Colour, used in this way, no longer has the function of filling an area, as on a canvas, but alters the character of place, according to the qualities of light and weather. Colour, as Goldsworthy puts it, is not simply pretty or decorative, but raw with energy, form, and space. In place, rather than on canvas, it cannot lie flat and passively (Goldsworthy 1994: 6). Our use of colour was a creative response to the ambiguity of Leskernick's landscape, where natural stones and 'cultural' stones (field boulders moved to form part of structures, earthfast stones enshrined into walls, field boulders selectively emphasised by clearings) blend into each other to the point that it is often nearly impossible to distinguish between the two.

Because the hill is covered with stone, photographs are rarely an effective means of visually re-presenting the significance of any *particular* stone. One photograph of stones on the hill looks much like another. Unless we annotate our photographs very carefully, after a short while we have only the haziest idea of which wall, or house, or stone spread on the hill they are supposed to be depicting. Yet, we know from our careful planning and through weeks and months of observation and movement that some stones are more significant than others. Dressing is a way to bring this out. It emphasises the role of stones as signs referring beyond themselves to the houses, clitter spreads, fields, etc. in which they are sited. The stones become concretised, individualised, their specific relationship to place, whether a house interior or the slope of the hill, becomes emphasised. It allows us to *think* about relationships in a manner that would not otherwise be possible. Wrapping stones further served to highlight for us the extreme limitations and basic distortions of linear perspective and mechanical drawings that we have already mentioned. Wrapping the stones is a way of re-presenting the past in the present.

Wrapping the stones takes time. This is important because whilst we are producing a visual display, we are also creating mental notations of shapes, textures, etc., in our minds. Our process of wrapping is additive – we add material, texture, and colour. The photographs we take are a choreographed metaphor for our own interaction with and engagement with the landscape.

fig.13:3 Works in progress a) the Shrine Stone, Leskernick; b) the southern end of Brown Willy; c) stone row at Carneglos; d) solution hollow at Brown Willy.

We are responding to the stones not rearranging or altering them. We do not decide where to place a stone on the hill. It is already in place. Our level of decision-making is at the level of which stones to wrap, which materials and colours to use, how to photograph the result. We emphasise by this process of wrapping that seeing is not a passive receptive act but an active process requiring participation and accumulated stocks of knowledge through repeated visits to a site.

CT (1 June 1998): When we start painting the mini tor the clingfilm covering starts to rip and separate in the wind. The threads of cling-film start to twang and hum in the wind.

CT (7 June 1998): I later learn that this June (1998) was the fourth wettest on record in the century. The previous June (1997) was the wettest since 1879!

CT (30 June 1999): Our techniques have improved considerably in their sophistication. The easiest type of stone to wrap is a single upstanding thin orthostat with good edges. This can be incredibly quick and can be done by one person provided that it is not too large. A low rounded stone is much more difficult because the cling-film keeps on slipping off. One can try and press the film down into the turf or create a 'rope' affect with it to grip on a small protrusion on the stone. Some stones simply have to have a cap of cling-film that will blow off if it is at all windy. Starting the stone is the most difficult before the cling-film starts gripping to itself. Here one can use a foot clamp to keep the cling-film in place or sitting astride it a thigh clamp, a new method that H developed today. A whole glossary of cling-film wrapping techniques could be produced: clamping forms, roping forms, twisting techniques, ring bases of sellotape, loose caps, hard caps, etc. (Figure 13.3).

For us one of the purposes of wrapping the stones was an attempt to evoke a ritualised world of stone that linked the Bronze Age people to the ancestral past in a world replete with myth and memory, nurtured through ritual and ceremony. It was an attempt to evoke the fact that these stones must have been familiar faces, old friends to the people who lived with them in their houses and encountered them daily in their movements around and up and down the hill. The experience of place is always, of course, synaesthetic. The visual is only one sensory cue. The *process* of stone wrapping highlights this experience of place for us, although the photographic re-presentation (the non-site) remains just visual. Much of what we have been doing has a sense of the fleeting in terms of our actual presence on Leskernick. One evening in June 1996, we created, and photographed, our shadows on the stones, as a metaphor for our slight touch on past and present, a brief moment in the lives of the stones photographically frozen in transit (Figure 13.4). The effect of wrapping the stones was also interesting sociologically; we did not rest and sit against *these* stones, as we might with other stones.

fig.13:4 Hand shadows on the enormous grounder that forms the backstone of house 20.

CT (1 July 1999): I will end this year's account with a few statistics. ... We have used 86 rolls of Tesco non-PVC cling-film at 60m/roll – 5,160 m this year. We have used 30 cans of gold spray paint (various kinds), 4 cans of silver spray paint and 26 litres of gloss paint in all, 16 litres of tomato juice and 24 litres of milk.[3] Total costs for all the wrapping and painting and play-dough materials and the milk and tomato juice, bin liners and kitchen towels, turps, paint brushes and paint brush cleaning fluids, staple gun, fluorescent card for the flags etc = £512.49.
... I estimate we have wrapped and painted at least 400 stones, probably more, across the whole of Bodmin Moor.

Materialising Our Surface Activities

During the first field season, we spent much of our time looking out through the doorways of the houses to the distant hills and tors. We were interested in recording the directional orientation of the doorways in relation to the tors and monuments in the landscape beyond. Because the houses are ruins and many have been robbed, to record the landscape we built our own wooden doorway and framed it. This had practical benefits: we had framed what we were to record. It also had surreal effects like Magritte's painting of a landscape seen from a window in which the window is in the landscape (Figures 3.1a and 3.2b). We solemnly carried our flimsy door from house to house to house.

Because Leskernick is an exceptionally stony hill on which the houses and compounds and walls, rock outcrops, and clitter are all stone constructions and rock formations that almost seamlessly merge we had, at first, great difficulty in even finding the houses. No sooner had we moved on from a house, or cairn, across the hill to the next, than it became swallowed up by the great stone spreads. Many of the stones in the ceremonial monuments have either fallen – or been pushed. It was a constant visual strain to attempt to locate them again and again. To facilitate our experience and mapping of intervisibility and movement within and between the houses and enclosures, we flagged the stone row, individual houses, and lengths of field walls. The positions of these flags were predetermined by the prehistoric architecture. In the first year, we used flimsy bamboo canes with white cloth. In subsequent years, we attached fluorescent paper to stout poles:

CT (3 June 1996): I, B, P, and M start to axe the marker flag poles into shape so that they can be hammered into the ground. We have decided to colour code different parts of the site: yellow and orange for the stone row, stone circles and cairn, green for the houses in the southern settlement, and pink and red for the western settlement. We try to affix the fluorescent card we have bought to the poles with U nails. This is quite difficult and not satisfactory. The paper is getting soaked and starts to tear off in the wind. The fluorescent card really stands out in the landscape and can be see from a great distance remarkably easily. But will it be robust enough to withstand three weeks of rain? Will we be? The U nails are useless. We must have a staple gun and tape to keep the paper on the flag poles.

The visual effects of our door frame and the flags were quite dramatic. The former limited, controlled, and defined our field of vision. It standardised and served to objectify. We only recorded the names of the hills, tors, monuments, and landscape features visible through the frame. The latter transformed the landscape that we were looking at (Figure 3.1, and see Chapter 3).

CT (June 1995): Our flags made a presence out of the past: a kind of consolation for the failure of the prehistoric architecture. The fabric moving with the wind created a kind of continuous dynamic. The dynamic of movement of people, of all that was now lost amongst the stones. With their removal what our flags had revealed was gradually slipping back again into the wider landscape. The cairns and the stone circles and huts all disappeared one by one.

The flags fluttering in the breeze seemed to bring life and movement back into the prehistoric settlement. We were also struck by the similarity of their effect to Christo's Umbrellas art project of 1991. Christo had simultaneously erected 1,340 blue umbrellas in Ibaraki, Japan, and 1,760 yellow umbrellas in California. Each umbrella was surrounded by a small platform, an invitation for people to sit beneath them, experience the light rippling through the fabric, and see the landscape in a new way. The work, a temporary installation, was dismantled in a matter of weeks and only materially survives in its lavish documentation.

During the first field season (1995), our 'art' was an unintentional product of the practical methodologies we had developed for recording information about the landscape. Yet, once in position, the flags became installations in their own right, and we subsequently built this perspective into our project design. This led us to reflect on the difference between Christo's transformation of landscape and ours. Where did 'art' begin and where did it end? Christo's work, unlike ours, becomes ritually legitimised through the appendage of an unwritten (but necessary) label 'this is art' and through the power of the institutional structures and critical apparatuses of the art world and art market.

CT (12 June 1996): According to S the flags on the stone row were all toppled over yesterday and the poles snapped off by cattle who have also smashed through the fence wiring around the stone row terminal excavations in an incredibly willful way. They have left the flags marking the houses in the settlement alone. In the rain and fog the Moor seems so bleak, grey and colourless.

CT (May 27 1998): The weather makes such a difference here between feeling happy and quite depressed. Collect the flag poles and start stapling the fluorescent card onto them next to the stone row terminal. ... There is now a stiff breeze and it soon becomes apparent that the paper has to be taped as well as stapled onto the poles or it will just rip off. Even so, the flags have to be orientated in relation to the wind direction. ... In the process [of flagging] I realise the wind has helped us. The fluorescent side of the card faces along the east-west axis of the stone row, the white side in the opposite direction. It is this side which is visible from the settlement. We take photos from various places: along the stone row, from the settlement, and from Black Rock. The flagging dramatises, enhances and strikingly visualises the stone row. ... 7 p.m. and it is wonderfully light. Estimate I have walked 17 miles today and my legs are beginning to give way. Wrap the flags in a bin liner to protect them from the rain and hide them behind the shrine stone by House 28.

fig.13:5 a) Horizon silhouettes (3–26) seen through the doorways of houses in the western settlement; b) horizon silhouettes (28–40) seen through the doorways of houses in the southern settlement. Based on photos by C. Tilley; drawings by Jane Russell.

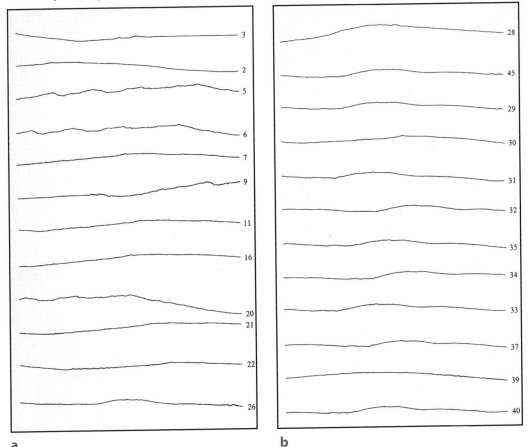

a

b

We were aware that our use of the door frame, despite its somewhat surreal character when seen on the hill, was imposing a linear perspective vision on the landscape in the manner of traditional British 18th- and 19th-century landscape art with changing horizons and fields of vision. We decided to use another method to think about and represent the specificity of place. Figure 13.5 shows horizon silhouettes seen from the doorways of the houses at Leskernick. This is an idea stimulated by Bachelard who remarks that for each object, distance is always present. The horizon exists as much as the centre (Bachelard 1964). The idea becomes graphically expressed in some of Fulton's artwork in a novel fashion. He sometimes draws horizon lines to encapsulate the experience of his walks through the landscape (see the discussion in Reason 1996). In our case, where we chose to record horizon lines is highly specific: we drew them from each of the house entrances. A step forward or backward would alter them. The 'here' of the doorway and the 'there' of the landscape are mutually related through this form of re-presentation in an act of transformation showing neither.

Other installations grew out of our resolution of issues of replication and replacement. Our excavation of the terminal setting of the stone row terminal during 1995 and 1996 had located the positions of the original stone holes for the large recumbent and partially buried stones which marked the spot prior to excavation. Our remit was not to re-erect these stones but to backfill them, post-excavation, in their pre-excavation position. An experience of their original configuration was, however, of great importance because their positioning in relationship to other monuments and landmarks, including the two stone circles and the rocky crenellations of Rough Tor, appeared to be of the utmost significance (Bender, Hamilton, and Tilley 1997). Our solution was to make accurate replicas of these standing stones.

Constructed of wooden fruit crates and covered in grey-painted fabric, these mock stones had the appearance of laughable pastiches as they were transported and erected on site. However, when seen from a distance they worked in the landscape in a convincing way that heightened our perception of the original placement of the stones (Figure 4.9b). In 1997, the backfilling of our excavation of Cairn 5 and House 23 necessitated further considerations on the appropriateness of reconstruction/replication. There was no way in which we could exactly replicate the ruined architecture of the structures that we had dismantled during the excavations. Yet not to leave a sense of what had been there would have destroyed the integrity of the site. Our solution was to construct sympathetic approximations in size, scale, and general configuration of what had been there. These are our 'permanent', present-day installations and versions of the past. Complex issues of appropriate imagery, the role and ethics of archaeological replicas, and pragmatic solutions to site integrity are all bound up in these installations.

Constructing Visual Re-Presentations of Knowledge and Experience

We wanted to experiment with photography to encapsulate and develop our experiences and knowledges of Leskernick and its landscape. The stones at Leskernick, like much contemporary environmental art, occupy a place between sculpture and architecture. They have a mass, form, volume, surface, and colour, and they are organised in space internally and externally in relation to the imposed architecture of the hill. They alter according to diurnal or nocturnal light, the sunrise and sunset (when they glow pink as opposed to being soft shades of grey); according to whether they have a horizontal or vertical character, the topography, their human associations and histories; and whether seen in summer haze or autumn mist, according to the sun and cloud, rain, and damp.

A stone is both singular and many changing, from day to day and season to season. We are attempting to understand the stones in the places of which they are constitutive. This is both an exploration of the stone itself and its relations to others and the spaces surrounding it. This directly connects our work to that of Goldsworthy, who states: 'I am drawn to the stone itself. I want to explore the space within and around the stone through a touch that is a brief moment in its life. A long resting stone is not an object in the landscape but a deeply engrained witness to time and a focus of energy for its surroundings' (Goldsworthy 1994: 6); 'I feel a difference between large deep rooted stones and debris lying at the foot of a cliff. They are loose and unsettled as if on a journey. To take a large resting stone is like extracting a tooth and I would have missed the greater opportunity of knowing the stone in the place it has become part' of (Goldsworthy 1994: 34); and 'When I touch a rock I am touching and working the space around it. It is not independent of its surroundings. ... In an effort to understand why that rock is there and where it is going, I must work with it in the area in which I found it' (Goldsworthy 1990b: Introduction).

Goldsworthy primarily seems to conceive the spaces of his stones and 'where they are going' as part of an order of nature. For us, they have instead a fundamental cultural significance in relation to our own activity on the hill and the actions and events of people in the past. One way we attempt to represent a sense of the present-past of the stones of Leskernick is simply to take close-up photographs of striking and impressive stones on the hill. Some of these are gnarled and weathered grounders, stones that have never been moved by human agency (Figure 2.2); others – in other parts of the moor – are riddled with solution basins, and the resulting images highlighted by use of fluids and other materials are illustrations of their intrinsic aesthetics (see chapter 19) (Figure 13.3d).

We have also experimented with taking photographs of stones that have been used as components of the prehistoric architecture and were originally situated inside the darkened interior spaces of the houses but are now, para-

fig.13:6 Photomontage of cairn 5 during various stages of excavation. Photo: F. Stevens: *'Through the process of excavation, I felt the inner rhythms of the cairn's buried architecture had become unbalanced. To trace the process of reconstruction I decided to take photos of four textural stages. The fragmented montage reflects the disruption of the previous underlying equanimity of the cairn, for although it has been reconstructed, in essence it has been deconstructed.'*

doxically, situated outside in the landscape. By so doing, we are playing conceptually with the theme of inside/outside suggested to us by the very character of the ruins on the hill. We experimented with lenses and filters and constructed photo-montages (Figure 13.6). The latter has obvious parallels with a cubist picture in simultaneously presenting the multiple facets that cannot be seen from one viewpoint, but that you know are there.

In one experiment, we attempted to capture the perpetually shifting sense of place as one walked along the stone row towards the terminal in a series of photo frames. As one walks down the stone row, Rough Tor comes into view, in the far distance, immediately after one crosses a boggy area marking, on the ground, a visually important point of transition. Thereafter, Rough Tor becomes visually more and more prominent as one approaches the stone row terminal. This particular experiment failed to realise our sense of meaningfulness at the point that Rough Tor comes into view. We quickly learnt the obvious: that the 'real' image is not enough. For us to visually represent this shifting change in the landscape, we needed to play 'tricks', to 'distort', to 'emphasise' in precisely the same kind of way as we had achieved by dressing the stones. Contrasting scales and picture angles are all needed to explore the paradoxes of camera vision and the viewing experience of the participant observer. We need to draw out 'reality' and explore various aspects of our experience, inevitably simplifying and reducing its complexity to aid an interpretative understanding.

Images and Words

We have wanted, in this book, to try and create a dialogic relationship between images and words to convey an impression of the power of the stones for the prehistoric peoples. Because our art is ephemeral, we have had, like many environmental artists, to record what we have done in photographs. You, the reader, have to be content with this non-site image. But left to itself, the photograph floats free of context, time, and narrative. Its radical ambiguity means that, without text, they cannot realistically constitute 'another way of telling' (Berger and Mohr 1982) about the past. But, as Burgin notes, although photography is a 'visual medium', it is not a 'purely visual' form. Photographs are typically invaded by language from the very moment we start to look at them. They presuppose words to think about and to be able to understand them (Burgin 1986: 51). This does not imply that photographic images are reducible to words. All it suggests is that without words, they remain so radically underdetermined as to be incapable of constituting a narrative form.

The 'purity' of captionless images undermines the necessary closure of interpretative possibilities that narrative requires. To believe in the purity of an image unsullied by words appears today as somewhat naïve. An image without captions and text may preserve a certain degree of visual purity but the way in which we take such images, they way we look at them, and what we see in them is anything but pure. We take our entire cultural and verbal baggage with us. What images need to work forcefully and effectively is not separation from language but to be put on an equal footing with words (Mitchell 1996). Images have the capacity to 'hit us' bodily and emotionally, all in an instant, by-passing words – this is what Barthes refers to as the 'punctum' of the photographic image – and he opposes it to the denotative and connotative codes ('studium') by means of which we may linguistically appropriate it (Barthes 1980). The capacity of images to effect such work depends very much on our own cultural background. What 'hits' or strikes a nerve is rarely an entirely personal affair. Our cultural background predisposes us in important ways to be effected by some, rather than other, image effects – thus Barthes's reduction of the 'punctum' to a matter of personal subjectivity is a mistake.

Words have always been used to paint pictures and describe landscapes. The technical term for this is ekphrasis: the linguistic re-presentation of visual experience. But however adept the writer or poet, we do not arrive back at these pictures or landscapes. At best, a sense of place may be evoked in words and texts. Images provide us with another means to feel and imagine landscape and place but neither word nor image can be substitutes for being bodily in place. Both are secondary and vicarious in their nature – however, our contention in this book is that combining words with images provides us with the most powerful means we have to represent a phenomenological experience of landscape and place to others.

Reactions

So far, this chapter has been written in terms of creating and re-presenting the Leskernick artwork and how it felt to those involved. Your reaction as reader will always be mediated through photograph and text. But, of course, there were people on the hill – primarily the excavators – who were not involved in creating the artworks but who had to walk past them, sit close to them, see them at a distance. Patrick Laviolette, a postgraduate student at UCL, interviewed many of the team members and asked, amongst other things, 'What do you think of the wrapped stones? Do you like them, dislike them or are you indifferent?' Reactions were rarely indifferent. Of 28 people interviewed, 19 reacted positively, four negatively, and only five with indifference. The negative responses were by males, two of whom were professional field archaeologists and two undergraduate students. Here are some of their responses:

> Intensely dislike. Makes me want to avoid them, not look at them, walk away from them.

> Dislike intensely. Visually offensive, obtrusive. I was offended when I realised that my orientation and behaviour was influenced by the wrapped stones.

> Dislike, largely based on what they want to get out of it. If someone else did it you'd get completely different results.

> The wrapping is overdone, there's just too much of it on the hill. Doesn't work as an art form but it's a lot more valid as an emphasis of relevant stones.

Indifferent responses were exclusively male:

> Don't find them as good as expected. Some are okay. They make good markers.

Roughly equal numbers of male and female participants responded positively for a surprisingly wide variety of reasons.

> Like them but will be happy to see them go. Stones are very powerful in terms of expanding what would otherwise be chaos. Some of the groups of stones work well. I was saddened when the blue stone lost its top.

They help one think about how we make things important and significant. I think 'like' and 'dislike' are the wrong words to use here. I believe it's a useful way of generating thought and meaning.

I like the close engagement with the stones. Entering into a hesitant dialogue about them. I also like putting the sharp colours on them; it's as if we were blending culture and nature.

Helps us translate our stories about the site through feeling the stones.

They're good for navigation on the site. They emphasise hut and clitter features rather well. They're also good because of their temporary nature; if they were permanent they'd be awfully intrusive.

Like them. Don't like the red ones. Interesting way of doing archaeology, instead of uncovering, you're covering.

The participants were also asked: 'Why do you like or dislike the art side of the Leskernick project? And do you consider it to be environmental art?' Of the 27 responses to this question, 15 were positive, seven negative, and five noncommittal. Again, negative responses were strongly worded and came from both from professional archaeologists and students:

Find it trivial, derivative, unoriginal. Visually pollutes the landscape and imposes other people's intentions on my experience of being here for five weeks. Don't think it is environmental art or even objet trouvé art. What's being done could have been done with other means, like photo colouring, computer graphics, etc.

Think they look awful, worse than digging the site up; however, it's untraceable afterwards. Don't consider it to be art, let alone environmental art.

Don't know if it's environmental art. I like it to the extent that it succeeds and dislike it when it fails. More often than not it seems to fail. The flags seem to have been the most successful aspect.

Environmental art?? I don't have much patience with self-indulgent contemporary artworks that I think applies to the art stuff of this project.

Don't like it. Chris's agenda seems to overbear the reactions of other people. Not sure what environmental art is, but I probably think it is because it seems to highlight our awareness of things a la Christo. Doesn't seem to communicate anything human.

The noncommittal ones were all made by undergraduate students, all but one of whom were male:

Don't think of it as art at all. It's more a highlighting of rocks, of group formations of stones that have some significance. That is an endeavour to understand the landscape but not really art.

Don't think it's environmental art because it doesn't repeat what is there. It's almost a form of abuse. I like it though, because this art dislocates perception of the landscape and relocates human beings – something that environmental art shouldn't do, which is why it isn't!

Don't understand the phrase 'environmental art' or perhaps I don't accept it. I very much like it, though. It's attractive and I like the pretentiousness of it. Also, it focuses on the contemporary perception of significant points, most of which probably would not have been in the Bronze Age.

And, finally, the positive responses were made by roughly equivalent numbers of male and female professional archaeologists and students:

Helps you see, think, they jump out. Provides landmarks. Flags especially allow you to imagine/see divisions and barriers. I just feel I'm coming to grips with my orientation on site in large part because of the art work. Think that people's reactions can tell you a lot about them. The excavation is problematic because the questions are often charged. The environmental art allows more new and different questions.

I do like it. Think it's interesting and innovative in trying to express certain ideas in visual form. Like the way it changes the space. Yes, it's definitely art because it takes place within, and responds to, the environment.

Like it at a broad scale. Good visual imagery that displaces your thoughts enough to enhance your thinking. Relationships between things are improved by the art. More different types are needed. I like the process of why the art comes about. It's evocative, whether good or bad it gets a reaction. It's very much art in the present which creates a sociability in the group.

The art side allows a sense of nearness to prehistory by physical engagement. I especially like the idea that it's our creation. Guess it's environmental art; it's definitely installation art because we are speaking to cultural phenomena instead of natural ones.

The painted stones have helped me understand the moor enormously by allowing me to invite local people to the site to show them what we are doing, thus leaving the door open to ask them about their experiences and knowledge of the area. In this sense, the stones in their painted form are ethnographic tools, windows of opportunity, methodological devices. They are not only good to think but also good to understand how other people think. I equally find they are intentionally reactionary, purposefully shocking – instruments of contemporary archaeoanthropological praxis geared towards inviting discussion – encouraging participation, promoting environmental embodiment.

What these responses show very clearly is the gulf that exists between *relating to the art in place* and *seeing it reproduced.* They vividly confirm the point made earlier that 'however adept the writer or poet, we do not arrive back at these pictures or landscapes … neither word nor image can be substitutes for being bodily in place.' For those on site, it was the physicality of the artwork, their direct relationship with it, the way it helped or hindered their understanding of, and movement around the settlement, the enclosures, the hill. Their reactions are *in place*; and, again a point made earlier, the variability of their reaction is by no means simply a personal matter. It is about social and cultural understanding and relationships and about the particularity of context and moment within which they are working and responding to the world around them (Figure 13.7).

fig.13:7 Cartoon by Biff by kind permission of author.

Conclusion

It is clear from the responses that not everyone agree with what we were doing, artwise, on the hill. But then not everyone agreed with what we were doing archaeology- and survey-wise! That is as it should be. But, in conclusion, we would like to reiterate, and expand upon, the need for archaeologists to try to find ways of making our recording of the past, and our engagement with it, more *three* dimensional.

> Anne de Charmant: Lately it seems you have been more involved with art projects than with cinema. Is your career changing direction?
>
> Peter Greenaway: I've become increasingly disenchanted with cinema and its inability to serve the imagination. I want to find

a way of making three-dimensional films, but in a 'real' set as opposed to an artifical one. (de Charmant 1994)

Working *with* Leskernick Hill and its landscape, we *start* by eschewing the frame of a book, camera, or computer screen. These non-sites come second, as a means of documentation, not first. They are a result of our practice, not a reason for it. We are producing ephemeral exhibitions in a real setting; recreating past creations in the present, for the present. Our work is not about replication but about *in situ* transformation, reworking a sense of place into our present-day consciousness.

In our approach to making artworks at Leskernick, we are attempting to forge a middle way between the personal idiosyncratic approach to landscape characteristic of contemporary environmental artists and the disengaged and disinterested 'objectivity' of visual re-presentation in contemporary archaeology. We are working on a hill in which a symbolic geography of place has been preconstructed for us by its Bronze Age inhabitants. We attempt to create a dialectic that mediates between it and ourselves, past and present. The meanings we create are a product of our encounter, and participation and personal involvement creates perceptual intensity. Our wrapped stones mark a place; they also mark a situation, an orientation, a relationship.

Wrapping stones, attempting to emphasise their form and character, their particular properties, has involved being *object*-ively guided. There is an important distinction to be drawn between the appreciation of objectivity in this sense and the disinterested appreciation of things, stemming from a tradition of Kantian aesthetics in which we become isolated from the object and the flow of experience. The object remains mute and passive; something to be incorporated in the measured plan. The other sort of *object*-ivity involves awareness, knowledge, alertness, animation, rather than the contemplative stare (Carlson 1993: 203).

Our artwork has helped us in interpreting the past in the present. It can also be appreciated – or dismissed – as a contemporary cultural work. This ambiguity, this being *of* the past and *of* the present, again forces the recognition of the multiplicity of meanings in a particular place and a particular landscape.

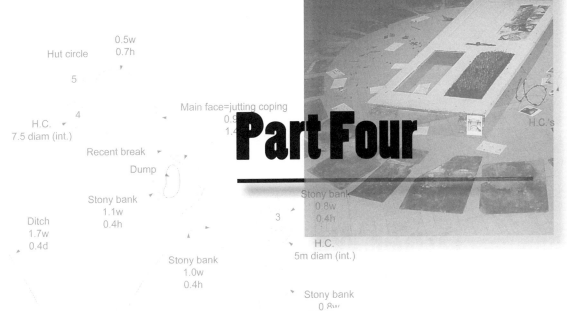

Hut circle
0.5w
0.7h

5

H.C.
7.5 diam (int.)

4

Main face=jutting coping
0.9
1.4

Part Four

Recent break

Dump

Stony bank
1.1w
0.4h

H.C.'s

3

Stony bank
0.8w
0.4h

Ditch
1.7w
0.4d

Stony bank
1.0w
0.4h

H.C.
5m diam (int.)

Stony bank
0.8w

Beyond the Hill

There was never a time when there weren't relationships beyond the hill. The prehistoric people of Leskernick came from somewhere, left for somewhere, moved around, and had contacts that extended far beyond the moor. The archaeologists and anthropologists who worked on the hill came from, and left for, somewhere else. The next chapters are about moving out beyond the hill. First, in the present, chapter 14 is about the creation of an exhibition, and chapter 15 is about allowing the exhibition to be 'hi-jacked' by other people. Our website (http://www.ucl.ac.uk/leskernick), designed by Paul Basu, creates another beyond-the-hill forum. Then, in the past, chapter 16 looks at Bronze Age settlements and contacts across the moor, chapter 17 looks at Bronze Age settlements and contacts across the moor, and chapter 18 moves to the world beyond the moor.

Chapter Fourteen

Other Ways of Telling
The 'Stoneworld' Exhibition

Landscapes, Place, and Past

We always intended to have an exhibition. We wanted to find ways to communicate what we were doing to both local people who knew the moor and to a wide range of other people, academic and nonacademic. We wanted to solicit responses. But we held off during the first three years of the project. It is difficult to be involved on-site, battered by the daily grind, *and* to stand back sufficiently to mount a work-in-progress, and we probably also felt diffident about expressing our half-formed ideas. We had the same difficulties with getting the website up and running. It was only in the summer of 1998, when we had a certain degree of confidence in what we were doing and had already begun to express our ideas by more conventional means, that we moved into these interactive media.

With hindsight, it would have been much better to have started earlier and to have had an on-going local exhibition in which we explained who we were, where we came from, what we wanted to do and why, and how we intended doing it. It would have given people the opportunity to voice their opinions. We might have been able to work with their suggestions, and we could have discussed how our ideas were changing. We would have forged stronger links with the local communities.[1]

Robin Paris, local artist (Leskernick website, 19 August 1999): I do think it would have been more appropriate [for the exhibition] to be shown in maybe your second or third year on Leskernick, which in the subsequent years (or in the fifth year) could have been developed into something more substantial and focused on Leskernick – and 'giving interpretations'.

Several of the people on the project had had some experience of creating exhibitions. BB had been involved in creating a travelling exhibition about Stonehenge that tried to create spaces for people with very varied attitudes to the stones and the landscape to voice their thoughts and for people visiting the exhibition to respond (Bender 1998). It had been a fraught but intensely interesting experience, and she was keen to create something for Leskernick that would be both accessible and intellectually stimulating to a wide range of people. SH had been involved in an arts/archaeology exhibition focussed on her work at Caburn hillfort, East Sussex. WB, one of the surveying team, was the director of an adult education centre and had had considerable experience in creating exhibitions. TW was working for the National Trust and had, in 1998, put on an unusual exhibition about the servants rather than the owners of the 'big house' where he worked. There were also postgraduate students for whom the exhibition held a particular interest. HB was writing his PhD thesis on how Cornish people used the past as part of the construction of a contemporary sense of identity/ies, and PL was working on different contemporary encounters with the Cornish landscape.[2]

Then there were those who were interested in exploring the images that would carry the story (CT, J S-D, FS, LS); there was one person with technical expertise in computerising text and image (AR), and another with the ability (and desire) to creative a CD-ROM to accompany the exhibition (PB).[3]

We mention this variety of starting points to emphasise the way in which the creation of the exhibition cut across the 'normal' archaeology/anthropology divide within the Leskernick Project. It is true that, in the first instance, it was the anthropologists, taking a lunch break amongst the Bronze Age houses at Brockabarrow or on a wet day back in the caravans, who mulled over ideas about the exhibition. But this was because, on-site, the archaeologists were under more pressure to complete the current season's excavations and had little time or energy to reflect on other issues. Off-site, back at University College, as the discussions intensified, several archaeologists became involved. Precisely because the creation of the exhibition occurred away from the intense preoccupations of working on the hill, it drew upon a new group that cut across somewhat entrenched positions.

This chapter is in the form of a narrative. It is about how the exhibition was created and consumed. The exhibition is an artefact, and, like any artefact, it is not stable. Its initial shape and form is already responsive to an earlier history and biography, then it accretes history during its life and, in the process, changes. In the first instance, 'we' create the exhibition and invest it with meaning. Or, more accurately, meanings, because even this initial 'we' is not homogeneous. Then, as it moves on, from birth to biography, it accumulates new meanings, and not just other people's, but also ours. We begin to see it differently. The exhibition was intended to be open-ended so that we and other people could add to it and change it. Like any artefact, like any person, the exhibition's identity and physical presence will be in process.

Again like any artefact, any person, the identity of the exhibition works within a larger context. It is affected by people's interactions, by questions of place and time. And these circumstances and interactions are both cause and effect of larger configurations – social, cultural, economic, and political. Although, in the next pages, the exhibition takes centre stage, the political and social shufflings in the wings and backstage will frequently be audible.

An Exhibition in the Making

Ever immodest, we had in mind not just a one-off exhibition but a blue-print for small travelling shows.

> BB (11 June 1998): [Making the exhibition would allow us] to really think through the whole idea of communicating with local people, creating dialogues, getting people involved, and providing mobile, flexible exhibitions that could move between small museums and libraries – places that are strapped for cash and find it hard to inject change into their exhibits. Exhibitions that could also go to schools, and other places we haven't even thought of ...
>
> I'd like to create something that would work at a local level, but also at TAG[4] or in a university context ...

What sort of exhibition?

We wanted, first of all, to get people to think about their own sense of involvement in the landscape: to suggest that landscapes were not just about 'seeing' but about experiencing; that people's experiences were all different, dependent on happenstance, context, and history, and that they drew on different sorts of knowledge; and that a person's sense of place was full of movement and change.

Then we had to introduce ourselves and our way of experiencing and engaging with Leskernick and Bodmin Moor and the different sorts of knowledge we drew on.

And then we would move to the Bronze Age landscapes – to prehistoric people's experiences of place and landscape – but admitting all the while that what *they* felt and saw was always filtered through *our* understanding of how things are and were.

In the early discussions amongst the anthropologists, further ideas were suggested.

> *BB (13 June 1998): Chris was worried that there wasn't enough on the sociological aspects of the enterprise – the reflexive movement between what we experienced and our interpretations of the past. So we thought maybe there should be a final board on 'The Present Past'.*
>
> *Talking about it again this morning with Henry, Wayne, and Patrick, it also seemed a good idea to use this last board to get across the idea that people need to know more about the past and the creation of landscapes to be able to take responsibility.*

It seemed important that the exhibition should work at a number of levels: people should have a choice about the depth and range of information they wanted. The main boards should carry a manageable amount of text and images that held peoples' attention, but there should also be plastic pockets or something similar containing more detailed information. Someone might want to know more about the art and archaeology aspect: no problem – a couple of pages would be provided. 'Excavation Techniques'? 'Small-Scale Societies'? 'Clitter Structures'? Whatever was needed. And we could add to them. We also needed to find different ways for people to offer their responses and their own ideas. We would have flip-boards and questionnaires. We would have liked to have an interactive CD-ROM, but this, we quickly realised, could not be done in time for 1999.

Who was it for?

In the first instance, the exhibition was for local people. We owed it to them: the commoners, people in the local villages, the Cornish Archaeological Unit (Pete Herring had been an amazing ally and inspiration), Dave Hooley from English Heritage – a tower of strength, Tony Blackman and the Young Archaeologists. We owed it to them to explain what we had been doing and to make it clear that what we did and thought were only some amongst many ways of engaging with the moor. We had to find a place to acknowledge their feelings and their knowledge.

We were aware that this local agenda wasn't entirely unproblematic. We knew that although the 'locals' might be interested in our work, they had no desire to have Leskernick 'put on the map'. It was *their* moor; they did not want to be invaded.

BB wanted to involve the local Young Archaeologists, or other local school children, very directly. She liked the idea of using children's drawings: a child's eye-view. She thought it might be possible to work with a local school and produce a three-dimensional *papier maché* model. CT was against this: he thought it would be patronising to use children's work.[5]

Well, if not the children directly, then indirectly. Tony Blackman and the Young Archaeologists had created a Bronze Age house at Trewortha (see p. 79) that took as its starting point the dimensions of a nearby Bronze Age house circle. It would be good to ask him to contribute some information on the work they had done. Photos of the reconstructed houses would allow people to make the connection between the low circular foundations that remained at Leskernick and real houses, just as discussing present day small-scale societies in different parts of the world and showing photographs of shrine-stones, offerings, and house interiors that are still used today might fire people's imaginings.

So, we would start with local people and local venues. Later, we could go a bit further afield within Cornwall, to the museums at Bodmin and Truro and so on. CT suggested that if we were really trying to open up and be democratic, we should take it to the local supermarkets. HB was, initially, horrified at the idea.

HB (13 June 1998): They are not Cornish spaces. Supermarkets may make shallow gestures to locality by placing Cornish flags and mead on their shelves. But isn't that just marketing? ... Supermarkets are the cathedrals of consumerism. People who may just want to see the exhibition will have to enter into a space where everything is designed to get you buying things ...

And beyond Cornwall? Well, we would see. Obviously, we would want to bring it to University College London (UCL), and to TAG. But, with luck, it would develop a life of its own.

We approached our first venue: the small Lawrence House Museum in Launceston.

BB (26 June 1998): Between the car-park and the museum the skies opened and the rain swept down. I arrived dripping. The museum is in a fine old house and seems wonderfully eclectic. A bit of this and a bit of that. A motherly woman came down the stairs, offered me tea, and took me into the temporary exhibition room which housed a very user-friendly exhibition on hats. She started rather cautiously [to think about our exhibition] but then became very keen.

She took me down and showed me a smaller room that we could use next summer [the larger one was already bespoke]. It

---

housed a small rather dog-eared permanent exhibition on the convict colony in Tasmania – founded by King, a Launceston man. ... There were some sickening accounts of, and by, convicts sent out from Cornwall.

The room is small but will do well. We then retired to her room and Mrs Brown came up with an amplitude of ideas ... about grants and so on.

Raising the money

We estimated that we needed about £1,500 to £2000. We tried all Jean Brown's ideas for local Cornish funding, but to no avail. Local funding was for local people.[6] Over the winter and spring, we managed to raise £1,900 from various UCL sources.[7] Retrospectively, it was too little but that was mainly because we had not expected to employ graphic designers. A more realistic figure would have been £2,500. How many small museums and local venues or organisations can afford that amount?

Working on the text and images

During February and March 1999, a small group congregated at UCL.[8] It would be early evening, some wine and food, time to catch up on gossip, then attention would turn to the flipchart on which BB had written up drafts of texts for the different boards that were to be questioned, annotated, and changed.

There was, as always, a hierarchy of decision-making. Although there was a lot of discussion, the directors retained a great deal of control over the larger structures within which questions, procedures, and interpretations were generated.[9] In the creation of the exhibition, as in other aspects of the project, aspirations to greater democracy rubbed up against an agenda that was less open to negotiation.

HB talking to BB, 20 June 1999:

HB: You had too many people in the meeting and there was ... [a] kind of looseness to it which was nice in terms of them being social occasions but they kind of broke down and you got ... people talking amongst themselves, and things weren't properly discussed. ... You had all these different people with different ideas ... of what the exhibition was about. I think also you got very possessive about the text and it became very much your thing ... would you agree?

BB: It's true that I had already envisaged the … structure. … The more I think about it, the more each part of this [the Leskernick] project has had someone who … structured the inquiry. And then what has happened is that [people have] worked on it and the working on it has in a sense refigured it …

I don't see a way round it, if you go for a co-operative endeavour … you lose the sense of a strong narrative. So, in the end, we create the frameworks, but they are the outcome of a million conversations.

Although the text remained relatively intact, the discussions were fruitful and changes were made.

BB (24 June 1999): The exhibition text started by asking people what they felt about the moor: did they see it as a wilderness? a place of natural beauty? of history? Henry said crossly, that this was far too romantic. It was, he said, for many people, a working landscape. He was quite right and I liked this insistence on a more workaday place. …

Much later, and rather abruptly, HB said he was worried that the exhibition was going to be too untheoretical, too bland. This time I was irritated. I suspected that this was something that Chris had been worrying about and that he'd said something to Henry who was now passing it on. Nonetheless, I suspect that [this] comment rather galvanised me into action. Up to this point I'd sort of been waiting for reaction and interjection. Now, with Easter approaching, I decided I'd stop trying to be so democratic and just get on and write it, and Henry (or Chris) needn't worry – of course it'd be theoretical, though not in any overt way, and (bloody hell!) it certainly wouldn't be bland!

The group also worked on the images. We brought in heaps of photographs and began to sort them so that they matched the story-line. Agreement on which ones to use was easily achieved, based on a combination of image and quality of print.

Over Easter, BB rewrote the text, showed it around, made minor emendations,[10] and took it down to Cornwall to test for a Cornish response. It was important to be sure we had not done anything that might be hurtful to people's sensibilities. She tried it out on Pete and Cathy Herring: some small changes and much enthusiasm.

Looking at the photographs had made us realise how (over)focused our camera work had been. It was not that we had not seen or commented on the palimpsest of past activities on the moor or on contemporary working practices, but they had not been part of our recording brief. At most, we took a picture on a sunlit evening when the old field systems suddenly materialised, or photographed an abandoned millstone that caught our attention; but the great majority of images were of the prehistoric landscape or our contemporary interactions. When, in the exhibition, we wanted to open up to other ways of seeing, the images were missing. We had to go to the Cornish archaeologists for the pictures of Bodmin Moor as palimpsest or working landscape. Equally, there were gaps in our knowledge about these aspects of the moor. We asked Pete Herring to write the leaflets on 'Landscape as Wilderness', 'Abandoned Landscapes', and 'Working Landscapes', and Tony Blackman to do the ones on 'Peat Cutting' and 'Reconstructing a Bronze Age House'.

We were glad to ask for help. It fitted in with our understanding that there were many different ways of negotiating the landscape. We had come to the moor with our own rather odd agenda, one that involved a stop-start sort of history, focussing at one moment on the deep past, and at another on our own contemporary engagement with the landscape. The local archaeologists (and, as we came to find, many other local people) created no such divisions; for them it was the continuous reworking of the moors that held the fascination. Pete Herring was as interested in the reuse of the Leskernick Bronze Age houses by medieval transhumant pastoralists as with the original settlements; Tony Blackman was as authoritative about Bronze Age building methods or prehistoric propped stones as medieval millstones or 20th-century peat extraction.

Our need for their help and advice also reflected our status as visitors. We may have been on the moors each summer for five years; we may have sometimes felt, as we arrived at the beginning of the season, that we were 'coming home'. But we always arrived from 'somewhere'; it was not our place or our community. We could not be sure how people would react to our 'viewpoints'. We were aware, for example, that in a climate of increasing Cornish nationalism, some questioned our right to be on the hill. Talking to Tony Blackman, asking him if he would take part, was important not just because he knew many things about which we were hazy, but because he was one of the people who felt strongly about English 'invasions'. We needed to feel that he approved of how we were going about things.

It was decided that Pete Herring's and Tony Blackman's leaflets should have their names on them to acknowledge their contribution, but the rest (written by CT, SH, HB, BB, and TW) should be nameless – underlining that we were part of a co-operative.[11]

Returning to the question of outsiders and insiders: it was around this time that, having created a Leskernick website, we put out something about the forthcoming exhibition and, quite soon, the question of Cornish identity and our role as 'outsiders' came up.

> *Adrian Watts (Leskernick website, 13 March 1999): If such artworks [or exhibitions] are to succeed 'as a powerful and empowering means of interpreting the past in the present' are they intended to benefit the host land, landscape and people of the country into which they are projected or merely another case of the outsider exploiting the host community? Whose past is to be interpreted, and who is to be empowered today, at whose expense? Who are the winners or the losers in the unequal contemporary power contest between Englishness and Cornishness?*

Pressure accelerating – bringing in the designers

Easter was over, time was getting short, people – students and lecturers – were busy with exams. The working group began to evaporate. The idea was mooted that we should bring in a graphic designer. Vic, HB's former partner, was approached. Vic had only just completed a graphic and design course and was keen to enlarge her portfolio. She and her friend Abi were prepared to take on the job for a very low fee.

The timing was very tight. There were meetings, more meetings, and technical problems. Decisions were made on the hoof, and there was no time to vet all of the proofs.

The relationship between exhibition curators and designers is a curious one. Not unfriendly but rather nerve racking because, by definition, the designers bring, not just their skills, but their ideas. Some of their input is obvious, some almost subliminal. Vic and Abi were determined to create something that was, both technically and visually, all of a piece. They were insistent that the format must not chop and change, that there had to be an overarching integrity to the whole exhibition. So, for example, they created wonderful headers that held the boards on any given screen together. They created an overall tonality to the exhibition. And because of their expertise and vision, the whole thing looked both beautiful and professional. The text was very clear; the images (often blown up from nothing at all) were magnetic.

But what also happened – which we didn't really appreciate until the exhibition was in place – was that they subtly wove their sense of place and landscape into the presentation. Their 'viewpoint' was romantic and holistic. So, from beginning to end the boards blurred into each other, and the overall colouring was green and grey, very 'natural', and 'organic'. Hard-edged plans and sections did not fit this vision, so most of them got eliminated. And what also got lost along the way was some of the intentional grit that formed part of *our* vision.

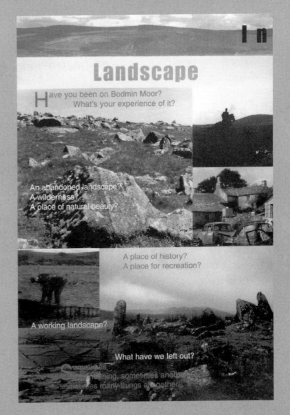

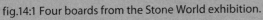

fig.14:1 Four boards from the Stone World exhibition.

For example, when we cling-filmed and painted the stones, CT had chosen bold colours that marked our intercession in the landscape. In the photograph that he had chosen for the exhibition, the stones were vivid red (Color Plate 5a). But these got toned down. Or again, the photographs that illustrated contemporary ethnographic round houses or spirit figures, or the experimental reconstructions at Trewortha, could have been marked up with brighter colours, emphasising the break between past and present. Or, as another example, we had wanted to have moments of informality. In opening up towards other people's ideas about the moors, we had in mind an almost pin-board effect for one of the boards: a kaleidoscope of people's impressions of, or feelings about, the moor. But this interruption, which was supposed to snag against the more formal text, got ironed out and the little sound-bites were given the same weight as the more formal bits of text. If we had been more expert, and had had more time, we might have been more alert to these things. But to be honest, some of the effects were ones that we had envisaged rather than verbalised. It was not until we had lived with the exhibition for a while that we came to recognise the interplay between our way of seeing and the designers'.[12]

HB talking with BB, 20 June 1999:

HB: It'd be much better it we just got a scanner and learnt how to do it and we were in control. ... There's a subtle knowledge of place that we've developed over working here, and that needs to come out in the design, and I don't think it has as well as it could have done (Figure 14.1; Color Plate 10).

Arrival

HB had got permission for us to use the church hall at Altarnun, the closest village to Leskernick. The Women's Institute had coffee mornings there on Thursdays to raise funds for the church, but otherwise it did not seem to be greatly used. The fact that it was less used than the village hall was perhaps a disadvantage, but the fact that it was only a couple of hundred metres from the very fine and much-visited church meant that we would draw in both local people and tourists.

One problem we should have foreseen in our quest for local venues was that we would have to provide exhibition minders throughout the times of opening – a considerable drain on our (meagre) labour resources. Another was that we were bound to be invading some one's territory.

BB (10 June 1999): Although we had tried our hardest to get the tables in the right places, they're not the 'right' tables!
'We were not pleased,' said the chief lady, arms akimbo. They

352

have also removed our sign which had been covering theirs (a dreadful oversight on our part) and flung it onto the grass. ... I hasten round tacking up the boards, making rather a lot of noise in the disapproving silence. ...

By two o'clock, the WI lady had become quite friendly and promised to keep an eye on things ...

BB (17 June 1999): Henry and I had set out the right tables in the right order the night before. But no, there she was, arms more-or-less akimbo: 'We weren't pleased with you'. The self-same words of the week before. Oh dear – this time we hadn't put our [clean] cups away, and I had left two bags on the kitchen surface. 'We don't do that!' No! I tried to mollify, and helped move furniture ...

The church hall was once the village schoolroom. There was one big room that was large, somewhat gaunt, and painted a rather sharp apple green. One half was taken up with tables and chairs set out for coffee mornings. The other half – our half – was filled with elderly tables, chair stacks, and boxes of much-remaindered jumble-sale items.

BB (3 May 1999): Start to haul the tables around a bit ... trying to make it look less institutional. ... We start to put up the stands and screens. Or rather Henry and Patrick do [the work]. We decide on a horse-shoe shape – two screens on one side, two on the end wall, and one round the corner. ... Henry starts attaching the boards. ... Patrick folds leaflets ...

BB (2 June 1999): We deliver posters in Camelford ... Jamaica Inn ... Endless Xeroxing ... food buying ... wine ... plastic glasses ... flowers ...

Final go round. The pouches go up. The blue table clothes go on. The cheese gets cut, and the bread. The flowers look great. We look at each other: it looks good (Figure 14.1).

There is FS's 360-degree photo of the hill mounted and placed on a central table; there's a flip-chart for comments, a table with a pin-board complete with Post-Its for people to write down their feelings about the moor and the past, and a children's corner.

People Reacting

Over the next three weeks, the visitors came. Not in droves, but in quite satis-factory numbers. Perhaps 300 in all: with about two-thirds from Cornwall (of which 50% were local – Altarnun and Five Lanes) and one-third 'from away'.

There was someone at the desk all the time, and we showed people round, talked with them, gave them coffee and tea, and watched them. Mainly BB, HB, and PL were in charge, but the archaeology students took over on a few occasions. We would have liked the students to have spent more time look-ing after the exhibition – but the pull of the hill and the constraints of time and weather made it difficult. Being around, spending time with the text and images and with the visitors, would have allowed them to think about how we had presented things and how they might do it differently and about exhi-bitions as a form of communication and how to find ways to talk to – with – a wider audience. They could have thought about their own responses to some of the questions posed in the text, and, talking to the visitors, gained insights into how they responded – to the exhibition, to the moors, to the past.

Below, we discuss some of the variety of visitors and their responses. These findings are only sketches – a *sense* of what was happening rather than an interrogation. But it was not only the visitors that reacted and interacted, it was us, the producers. We start with the visitors, and then turn to our own reactions.

'Local' visitors

'Local community' is something of a Blairite buzz-word. Like many buzz-words, it is fairly meaningless. Local communities are increasingly heteroge-neous. Quite apart from more obvious class, age, and gender divisions, a major divide is between those born in a place and 'incomers'. An incomer may have lived in the village for 30 years, or have married in, but they are never quite the same as someone born there. There need not be hostility, just difference.

> BB (17 June 1999): There was a lady from Trewint. I asked if she'd lived here all her life and she stressed that it was only the last 50 years – she'd married in from ... Polyphant. [Polyphant is about three miles away!]

On the other hand, some incomers may only just have arrived – to be greeted with as much suspicion by the established incomers as by those who have lived in the village all their lives.

BB (15 June 1999): Three men come in. Londoners. The two younger men were – I'd guess – a couple. They are doing up their house in the village and they hadn't really had time to get to know people. They came once every three weeks. I'm not sure what they expected: they weren't interested in the exhibition, but they were interested in how to get to Leskernick. They glanced around, signed the book and left.

On the whole, the locals who came were 'incomers'. And on the whole, they were 'educated', usually middle class, and knew how to cope with an exhibition. Often, as they arrived, they established their credentials.

BB (3 June 1999): One [was] a Friend of the Lawrence House Museum at Launceston. She'd heard Pete Herring lecture; thought he was wonderful.

BB (5 June 1999): A large lady arrives. She's brought some pottery. … She was at the Institute of Archaeology at the time of Shepherd Frere. She remembered Mortimer Wheeler. She married an Egyptologist. … She's come with another grey-haired, rather quiet woman. This one had dug at Dorchester. As usual these bits of information are greeted with surprise – people haven't known that their friends or acquaintances were interested in the past or had these connections.

More local women than men came. We suspect that, as in many other small villages, a disproportionate number of incomers are widows or single women. It is probably also true that women are more often interested in the past than men. The men, when they came, tended to come with their wives. The women came alone or with a female friend. The women often talk to people, both those they know, and those they don't, and to us. It seems that the exhibition provides a safe, communal space.

And what of people who had lived in the area all their lives? Admittedly on a very small sample, it seemed that a distinction could be made between older and younger inhabitants. Some of the old ones came into the hall for lunch on the Women's Institute days. It seems likely that they had often left school when they were quite young. For them, the exhibition was very foreign, and they were correspondingly diffident.

BB (3 June 1999): They cast fugitive glances in the direction of the exhibition, and when we're not too close, some of them make a brief sortie.[13]

Some of the older people were braver. They might stand by the boards and use them as a backdrop to – or rather as reason for – a conversation or monologue about events or places.

BB (3 June 1999): One man, on a stick ... hovers close to the last board and when I approach starts telling me about being a home guard and going up on Bray Down. He talks about other interesting things – farm labouring, low wages.

BB (June 17 1999): There was a lady from Trewint. ... She didn't want to look around too much. She just wanted to be.

One couple, who seemed not to want to talk, stayed and stayed. And in the end they wrote something lovely in the book. ... Turned out she'd lived close by in an orphanage, and they were both quietly passionate but not vocal about the moor. She said she wanted to come again – to Jamaica Inn, to Launceston ... she would follow the exhibition round!

An older inhabitant might also get courage by being accompanied by someone younger.

BB (3 June 1999): There's a group of three: an older couple and their middle-aged daughter. The wife was from Altarnun; she'd married a Scotsman and moved north. Their daughter had studied archaeology at Southampton and then moved to Canada. She worked in an open-air museum. She did most of the talking.

A grand-mother and her [young] grand-daughter [went round]. The old lady has often walked to Leskernick. The grand-daughter hadn't, but she had seen the reconstructed house at Trewartha.

The grandmother and granddaughter offer interestingly different *generational* ways of accessing the moors and the past: the old woman walks across the moors to Leskernick; the granddaughter is taken to see the reconstruction by her school.

Younger people who have lived in the area all their lives were perhaps less inhibited; they had probably had more schooling.

BB (5 June 1999): When DN meets one of the older incomers [at the exhibition], the incomer is quite surprised to see her. Part of the perceived divisions within the village. ...

DN is a local woman, born into one moor-farming family, married into another. There was not enough work (or land?) for her husband, so he drives a JCB. On the second day of the exhibition, she comes in by herself:

BB (5 June 1999): A youngish woman with dark hair. ... She has a strong local accent. She stops at the picture of the peat cutters. She knows it [and them]: they're related to her. Her husband will know their names, she'll ask him, they'll come back tomorrow. She says she has found some flints, she'd like to bring them in.

Via the photo, DN lays claim to an intimate knowledge of place, one that has a time depth. On the other hand, she also *dis*claims the knowledge – her husband knows more. He – the man – must come and name the names.

BB (5 June 1999): DN left saying I wasn't to let on that she'd been, because she should have waited for her husband. ... But she went off clutching a handful of leaflets!

The next day, she returns with her husband. They (he) have written out a list of the names of the peat-cutters. Alongside each name, he has written how they relate to each other. We stick the list to the comments board. He is pleased. He is older than she is, and somewhat ill at ease. He has come because she wants him to be there.

Visitors 'from away'

The locals who came, with the exception of those that drifted across on the WI days, came because they wanted to know more about a place and a landscape that held a lot of meaning for them. The visitors 'from away' were more mixed. Often they had visited the church and then, having seen the poster, popped in. They were more likely to be couples than solitary. Often they did not stay long.[14] Again, there was the divide between those who had more, or less education, and again, often the older people made it clear that they felt their children would understand the exhibition better.

> BB (15 June 1999): Two very shy people crept in: an elderly couple who live in a small hamlet near Truro. They had come to see the village. ... I would show them something on the board, and they'd look with interest but without comment. ... A couple of times she'd mention how much her daughter would like it – she was a schoolteacher in Penzance.

It was not until we looked closely at the visitors' book that we realised that many of the visitors 'from away' came from other parts of Cornwall. If we had recognised this earlier, we might have noticed differences between them as a group and those who had come from outside Cornwall.

We found, again, that the woman was often regarded as the 'guardian' of the past.

> BB talking to TW and MW, 20 June 1999: One couple came in from Camelford yesterday and he said: 'Oh, it's the wife who finds it really interesting.' ... I went away and I came back two hours later, and they were still there. ...They just wanted to know everything, they were going to read it from top to toe and back again. ... I said, 'Are you archaeologists?' 'No, no, no, but we've seen those circles on the moors and she's always wanted to know. ...'

Already, in talking about the different sorts of visitors, we have begun to talk about their different responses. But we can take this further.

Local people, by birth or arrival, undoubtedly linked the exhibition texts and images to their own understanding and memories of the moor. They would not necessarily take in the whole exhibition, but rather dot around, picking up on certain images or bits of text. They named places, and we became aware that we should have named all the places shown in the photographs.

> *BB (3 June 1999): One woman liked recognising places in the photographs. She asked me where some of the places were – she'd like to visit them. … I realised (too late) that it's important – particularly for local people – to have places named so that they can cross-check with their own memories and intimate knowledge.*

Often they would turn their backs on the screens and start talking to each other.

> *BB (5 June 1999): [Three of them] were standing by the board with the bog and turf and sky and discussing how the bird life on the moor had declined. The lapwings … had gone. The older woman was very knowledgeable. It was clear that the images/text had triggered the conversation.*
>
> *Then all five started talking to each other. There was some talk about the horses that had died on the moor and how the RSPCA had come. I asked whether [the horses belonged to] the people who lived in **** on the way to ****? I rather think they confirmed it, but they also glossed it – 'It could have been'.*

This group comprised four incomers and one local. They could gossip amongst themselves, but part of the gossip was coded so as to exclude snoopers – in this context, us.

> *BB (5 June 1999): They talked about the destruction of the hedges. They assumed that people had been given subsidies to grub them out and noted wryly that they'd soon have subsidies to put them back!*

Sometimes the images elicited more direct responses:

BB (5 June 1999): The woman from next door, encouraged by the picture of the bog, and egged on by her husband, recounted how she'd once gone off the path and had sunk [into the bog] up to her arm-pits. A good graphic yarn.

It became clear that many people, both locals and those 'from away', liked being shown round by one of us and that our presence and conversation encouraged a more direct interaction with the exhibition and allowed them to communicate their knowledge and to talk about their memories.

BB (6 June 1999): I show A the aerial photo … He's gobsmacked. 'By golly, is that right!' He admits that he's not been able to 'see' the houses in amongst the stones when he's been up at Leskernick …

We walk around the exhibition slowly. A tells me that in the old days chunky lime was brought up onto the moors. Sometimes it contained flints. We talk about the difficulty of knowing how things had got to be where they are now.

In this case, talking with a local person, he displays an intimate knowledge of the moors:

BB (3 June 1999): [The man-from-next-door] said he wasn't so interested in earlier history, he liked industrial archaeology. He often walked on Bray Down and there were lots of abandoned millstones there. He'd found a quarried stone that still had a bunch of feathers in the hole.

He is commenting on the things that he sees when he walks the moor. He is also noting – without comment – the gaps in our coverage. He makes it clear, and we suspect many other people felt the same, that he was more comfortable with the more recent past – probably because he could relate the remains to things that are still extant.

HB talking to BB, 20 June 1999: Notions of the Bronze Age are so distant, ... so other, that it doesn't form part of their life. Except the hard-line nationalists who project a sense of their notions of Cornishness onto the Bronze Age and stuff.

Sometimes local people brought things for us to look at:

BB (22 June 1999): A very well built lady arrived, hair like the prow of a ship, denim skirt well belted. A tough face. She had brought a poem.[15]

BB (June 5 1999): The couple from next door come in. He's brought a lump of 'soapstone' carved with a cross. He'd found it in his garden and thought that it was old, but then discovered it'd been made by a lad in the schoolhouse (which is now the church hall) as part of his craft education.

Occasionally, they brought in artefacts that they had found on the moors. It was a sort of exchange: they brought in something that they knew would interest us, and we, the 'experts', 'named' it, and in so doing increased its value.

BB (talking to HB, 20 June 1999): The flints are the things that they have found, which they ... feel tie them [to the land] – which is their knowledge, but which they know they don't understand very well. And I guess one of the things we have perhaps achieved is ... just being available to create some of the links between things they have found and a past that is so far back – and that they haven't really been told about ... at school.

One person brought in some pottery. DN and her husband brought in both flints and pottery.

BB (6 June 1999): DN gets out her flints. Boxes and jars: some from Dozmary pool, some from [where they had built] their bungalow. … The ones from Dozmary are mainly pebble tools, the ones from the bungalow are fine little bladelets. … I explain [about how the blades have been struck, and about the sort of tools that had been made and how they might be used]. She's delighted, and he's impressed at her cleverness [at finding them]!

They then get out an old treacle tin. He'd been working with a friend 20 years earlier, and they had sliced through a pot. He reckoned there was ash in the bottom. His friends had kept the bits for 20 years! He was right: it was half of a [fine] collared cremation urn …

Visitors 'from away' also liked being taken round, liked having things explained. They, too, proffered information but, of course, it was more generalised and often involved comparisons.

BB (14 June 1999): The noisesome lady … mentioned some place she'd been to in Africa a long time ago. She seemed to remember that they had very similar houses to ours and that they included shrine stones. She'd try and find out more and let me know. … Then some [of the rest of the family] gathered round me … and talked about prehistoric stones they'd seen in Ireland.

Compare the following conversation with people from Truro, in which the moor is not named, and the question of access is generalised, with one in which a somewhat discontented incomer, also talking about access, offers very precise locations.

BB (15 June 1999): An elderly couple who live in a small hamlet near Truro [came in]. … They stood and talked about changes in their hamlet: the incomers; the forestry people who had both opened up the forest and planted conifers; the vandals. … Some interesting stuff about the ongoing fight between ramblers and commoners over access. I would show them something on the board and they'd look with interest but without comment. Then talk some more about something else. … And so we progressed for about an hour.

And

BB (22 June 1999): People [she said], were ignorant. They parked across the farm gate at Westmoorgate. Mind you, the Commoners arrogated power to themselves that they did not have. ... One day she had [let] one of her dogs ...out on Davidstow common. It ate some poison and died. ... The commoners admitted putting down the poison against the buzzards. But in fact they had known that some White Goddess people were going to camp [there] the next day – they had been putting down the poison to kill the dogs.

Visitors, on the whole, did not enter into philosophical or intellectual discussions. On the two occasions when they did, the couples were 'from away'.

BB (16 June 1999): He was English, she was German. They'd lived in Delabole for ten years ... They looked around the exhibition carefully. And then he said, rather hesitantly, that he couldn't see the point in going so far back, and more, he felt uneasy that we were disturbing the dead. I said I sort of agreed. We had a long conversation about that.

BB (17 June 1999): Another young couple came because they'd stumbled on the house circles on Brown Willy and wanted to know more. They genuinely wanted to talk about the past – what was it like to live at that time? That sort of desire to imagine the past hasn't been particularly noticeable up till now.

The two-tier system of information seemed to work well. We charged a small amount for the leaflets (mainly because otherwise people would just take one of everything as freebies), and they were steadily removed, with people often picking and choosing amongst them, although, in the end, no great preferences emerged.[16]

People seemed to feel comfortable with the exhibition. They felt drawn in.

BB (3 June 1999): [A woman born in Altarnun, who'd married out] said: 'I like it. I don't know much about archaeology, but I feel that the person who put it together is talking to me'.

[A woman working at the Indian King Centre in Camelford] said she'd read every word of it, and it made her understand much more about things.

Many of their responses – direct or indirect – to the questions we were asking on the exhibition boards were elicited in conversation either amongst themselves or with us. The comments board was more or less ignored. The sparse comments ranged through:

> Wonderful images – well chosen words!

> Very imaginative presentation of information – well done!

> What tools were made from beach pebbles?

> Compare Zulu huts at museum in Kwazulu, and the Tukuls of Ethiopia

> Symborska – poet – Conversation with a Stone

And (nice intercession from a local):

> Where is everybody? Please tell others about the exhibition and get them to come along.

The relative paucity was interesting when compared to BB's Stonehenge exhibition. There, the comments board had been fiercely scribbled on. But that, it seems, was because Stonehenge, or rather access to Stonehenge, was a contentious issue and people used the comments board to argue with each other. Here, at Altarnun, the content of the exhibition was not immediately contentious, and people, we felt, were probably inhibited by the public nature of the board.

At first glance, the visitors' book seemed rather bland, but closer investigation proved interesting. People do not necessarily want to sign, and the 92 entries probably represent about a third of the number of people who came. Fifty-four of the 94 entries were from people who lived in Cornwall, and of these, 35 were from Altarnun or Five Lanes. Twenty-two people from other parts of Britain signed, and 16 came from abroad. Not everyone made a comment, and many took the form of a descriptive adjective. Not unexpectedly, the words interesting/very interesting/most interesting figure most often (19); followed by fascinating (seven), enjoyable (three), wonderful/wonderful work (two), excellent (two), informative (two), evocative (two), and then one each of the following: exciting, inspiring, refreshing, good, great, beautifully done, enjoyable, provocative, intriguing, lovely, really enthralling.

Sometimes, several were used in conjunction; once a small in-joke was made. The photographs were singled out for praise five times, the pamphlets only once. Several times we were thanked personally for being present, and four times people paused to praise the accessibility of the exhibition (Figure 14.2a). Ten people stressed that they felt they had learned something from the exhibition (Figure 14.2b), and five recognised that there was something 'special' being put across (Figure 14.2c). Only one person offered a criticism (Figure 14.2d). And finally, the one thing that distinguished the comments of people from Cornwall from the rest was that, on seven occasions they said how pleased they were to have a local exhibition for local people (Figure 14.2e). Two out of the seven were from Altarnun/Five Lanes.

fig.14:2 Entries in the Exhibition visitors' book.

We also had a Post-It board. Across the top it asked 'What do you feel about the moor?' and we provided small Post-It labels and drawing pins. These were more like little secret messages, and they were nameless. They were accordingly more personal. There were 17 of these messages, a couple were by children, and a couple by archaeologists (Figure 14.3). They were visual, sensual, often romantic. They mentioned time passing and past, the elements, spiritual feelings, fear. Only one or two referred to things that are specifically contemporary – wheel ruts, dead animals. We suspect that those who wrote were reasonably confident of their literary skills, that they were not the older inhabitants, nor those who work the moor, but rather those, locals or visitors, who walk the moor.

Even with the Post-It board, people were quite shy. Often they would say something in conversation and we would encourage them to post-it.

BB (3 June 1999): [She] wrote on the Post-It board that she thought that the moor was friendly. She didn't agree with the person who had said the moor evoked death! But she wouldn't have written the message if I hadn't encouraged her to ...

Perhaps we shouldn't be surprised at the central importance of conversation at the exhibition. We *wanted* to enter into dialogue; we *wanted* to hear what people had to say. So we needed to be there to listen and encourage. But this begs the question of how well such an exhibition works when there is no one there to elicit responses.

Perhaps, too, we had to be there because the exhibition was quite ambitious and also ambiguous. We shall return to some of the communicative failures a little later, but there is no doubt that by being there we could help people to navigate between different boards.

One of the failings was a lack of maps. There were plans of the settlement and a map of Leskernick and the surrounding hills, but no map of how to get on-site or of its relationship to the larger region. People wanted to move between the exhibition and the site. Where was it? How did they get there? And it was not just the 'from away' people who asked. Some of the incomers, though they might walk their dogs or ride the moors, did not necessarily know the names of places. They might have been to Leskernick without even knowing it.

BB (6 June 1999): Rounding the hill ... I found DN and A moseying along. I felt really pleased to see them. With hindsight I wish I had asked them more about what it felt like to move from the exhibition to the site.

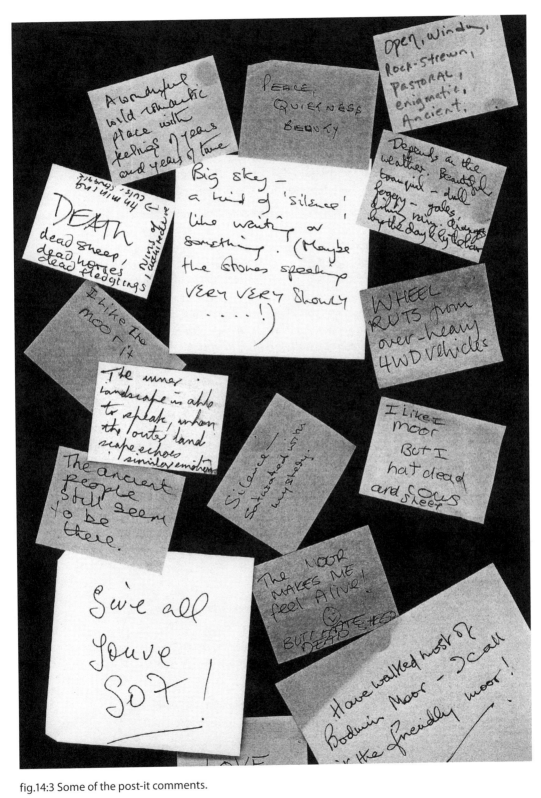

fig.14:3 Some of the post-it comments.

We had left out the detailed maps because we feared that local people would not like us publicising the moor. There are no public footpaths to Leskernick, and they feel protective of the moors. But in retrospect, we should have been less cautious. If we wanted people to make the connection between the exhibition space and a real place in the landscape then we had to provide the means. Quite soon, we Xeroxed and handed out when asked, a section of the ordnance survey map marked with the route from the church hall to Leskernick.

We had a website and this was another place where people could communicate about the exhibition. And they could do it in the privacy of their homes. Here was a site where people could express their views more vehemently.

Robin Paris, local artist (Leskernick website, 10 June 1999):
What sort of after-effect will [the book and CD-ROM] leave on the communities that live around Leskernick today? And how will they affect the future of Leskernick itself? It's your last year here (officially) – you can walk away from any changes you may bring to the area, we will have to live with them.

I'm not wholly against anything you are doing – I just think we need to know about it openly ... and have an input into what you do or don't do. The exhibition is very good, not only for the information and presentation sides of it, but also because you are suddenly communicating openly with us.

The exhibition workshop

Whilst the exhibition was on at Altarnun we thought we might try another way of talking to people. We would organise a workshop on the last night. It would be a good way to bring things to a close.

BB, HB, and PL came up with three themes:

1. People's reaction to the exhibition and to the excavation, and the connections people made between the two.

2. People's sense of the moor: what did it mean to them? How had it changed, and what do people feel about the changes? Are there things that concern people about how the moor is being used today?

3. Responsibility for the moor? Questions of management and tourism? Of access? The responsibilities of archaeologists and anthropologists?

We decided not to call it a workshop – it would be an alien word to most people and perhaps intimidating. We called it a Wine/Cheese Talking Evening.

HB felt that we should break up into small discussion groups. BB thought that this might be somewhat intimidating. In retrospect, she was probably right, but, on the other hand, the awkwardness of the small discussion groups created some interesting dynamics.

As with the opening night, we had no idea who, or how many, would come. As it was, the room filled to capacity – 50, 60 people. The vicar, unsolicited, opened the proceedings. The Cornish archaeologists came. Jack the peat cutter, who figured in one of the photos, came. The students, a lot of locals, some 'ramblers', and others from further afield came.

CT (22 July 1999): Much to my amazement there are about 40 cars parked [outside the church hall] and people have come from as far afield as St Austell.

Whilst the exhibition had been running, PL had created a small installation – a large stone, a fine piece of peat and grass. Something to break up the formality of the exhibition. As the workshop got under way, people added some sweat and labour – Henry's boots and the contents of Fay's rucksack – and some mementoes – the two Andys' collection of bullet cases and the man-next-door's carved stone.

We will not narrate the whole evening, just three episodes.

The first episode

The local people had become more confident. Whilst the wine was going round, they asked what was going to happen, and several made it clear that they did not just want a discussion. They wanted us to tell them what we had been finding. They wanted a mini lecture. CT and SH, both exhausted, rose to the occasion. SH talked about the excavation, and, in a roundabout fashion, addressed the potential sensitivities of Cornish people. She stressed how prehistorians had tended to think about prehistoric development in terms of southern England, and had failed to recognise how different the southwest was. She stressed the importance of regional identity – even Bodmin Moor and Dartmoor differed from each other. CT made connections between past and present, took the audience on an imaginative tour from wrapped stones to prehistoric stones. Stones that were powerful and empowering. He 'walked' them over the moors to the other settlements. The audience's attention was absolute.

When it came to questions – which were mainly directed at SH – they were, as one might expect, the usual gritty questions that bother people: What were the dates? What did they live on? Did they stay at Leskernick all year round? We had addressed these questions in the exhibition, but had stressed that it is not possible to divorce what people do from what they think, and that, equally, we cannot divorce the past from the present because we can only 'see' the past through the present. But these ideas were not picked up on. In wanting us to talk to them rather than have a discussion, and in the questions they posed, people returned to more traditional formulations. Does that mean that they only took from us and from the exhibition those things that conformed, and confirmed, their prior understandings? We do not know; it could also be that new ideas take time to shake down, and that, particularly in public, people (unless they are academics!) are unlikely to want to explore unfamiliar intellectual territory or to try out new vocabularies.

The second episode

After the talks, we broke up into discussion groups. Quite a lot of people left at this time. Some went outside and chatted; others hung around the edge of the circles, half listening but not contributing. One woman left rather dramatically. She was a young woman, and she had brought her father – Jack the peat cutter – and her mother. Now she abruptly ushered them out. She was angry, and before she went she talked to one of the site supervisors. He wrote down some of the things she said:

> *22 June 1999: They come from [a] poultry farm near Brown Gelly.*
> *She thinks that discussion groups are more than alien. It's an alien culture to the local people. Archaeologists go off and study and [learn to] talk. Can you remember what it was like the first time you had to stand up and make a presentation? It's just not what local people do. ... She'd been to art school and was somewhat used to it, but for her parents it was completely different.*
> *There's not a lot of local people here – 'not what I think of as local'.[17] Locals are different – they're classed as peasants by the EU! Local people do not sit around and talk in groups. The way they do it would be to go up to someone in a field ...*
> *She had to go and shut up the poultry ...*

She was angry because we had taken people out of their own space and set them down in alien space and had asked them to communicate in alien ways. She was saying that the only way to level the playing field was for the discussion to be on the other person's territory, where *they* could set the form and tone of communication.

Her comments had more generally applicability: we had brought the exhibition to a local place, but in the process had alienated the space and made it ours rather than theirs. But perhaps if an exhibition remains in place long enough it becomes familiar, and if it is open ended and people's comments and ideas are included, this alienation can be reversed and local people can begin to lay claim to the space and its contents.[18] We shall return to this point at the end of the chapter.

The third episode

The discussion groups got under way and, as good discussions should, they generated dissent and allowed ambivalence to surface.

In BB's group, the question of access came under discussion. We had put this on the agenda as a general issue but also because, following something that had been said on the website, we were aware that people might feel that the exhibition, and the book that would eventually materialise, would bring unwanted publicity to Altarnun and Leskernick.

Almost immediately, someone expressed worry about the moor being spoilt by development. What sort of development? Tourism: 'People were ignorant'; 'They take rare mosses from Golitha woods to make Christmas decorations'; 'They let their dogs roam …'

What should be done? 'Education, education, education!' says a woman, vehemently. But when it is suggested that to educate people you would have to make information available – that maybe there should be pamphlets, or maps, even a sign-posted path, the response was instantaneous. 'They've got maps. People who are interested will find their way,' said one; 'There should be access to knowledge, not sites', said another. 'What about access for dis- abled people?' said a brave woman. 'No!' they chorused.

They also said that even if you told people how to get to Leskernick, they would not go: 'People don't walk that far'; 'And if they did, they would only be disappointed when they got there!' One person admitted that there might be a touch of Nimbyism[19] in all this, but he didn't care!

Quite apart from the Nimbyism, what is striking is the ambiguity about knowledge and education. People should be educated into behaving in a responsible way. But – at the same time – knowledge should be limited to those who know how to use it (i.e., those with education). This fault-line has been noticeable ever since museums started to be open to the general public in the 19th century. On the one hand, they were designed to be places of edi- fication for the masses so that they understood (and stuck to) their place in the scheme of things. On the other, they were intelligible only to those with the education to appreciate them, those able to crack the codes involved in the presentations.

At one level, questions of access were understood in terms of locals v. tourists. But occasionally another 'them'/'us' divide emerged: Cornish versus Other. In the course of discussion in HB's group, it was mentioned that some (unspecified) people had not wanted us to dig this year. 'Who were they?' Silence. 'Oh,' someone said, 'Nationalists.' Our silence was taken as affirma- tive and people were dismissive and quite angry. And yet, within that group and hovering around the edge, were people who we knew felt ambiguous about our presence. They would not, perhaps out of politeness, voice their discontent in this context and on this (celebratory) occasion, but it would surface in private, or on the website.

These various tensions should alert us (and anyone else hoping to engage with local communities) that there is never going to be a unified response to one's presence and one's work. People's reactions will be manifold, contradictory, and dependant upon the context of the encounter.

Rethinking the Exhibition

It was not just the visitors that consumed the exhibition, but us, the producers. Whilst it was at Altarnun, we had time to reconsider what we had done, think about what worked and what did not, and take on board people's responses. Sometimes our concern was directed at the message – the effectiveness of the content – and sometimes the messenger – the effectiveness of the display. Often the two merged.

Thus, HB focussed mainly on the message. Here he is talking to Brian on the website:

> *HB (Leskernick website, 2 August 1999): We wanted to contextualise our work within the present and more recent history of the moor. While I still think that this was a good intention I am beginning to wonder whether or not we were being too ambitious given the restrictions on size that come with producing a travelling exhibition. I think that [the first] section is good but would be better as part of a different exhibition concentrating on peoples' engagement with Bodmin Moor in terms of Past-Present and thoughts about the future. My reasoning ... is that the focus ... should have been about presenting the Leskernick Project rather than trying to encompass broader stuff about Bodmin Moor. I am currently ... beginning research on Bodmin Moor and I have become acutely aware of our [the Project's] collective naivety concerning current and recent engagements with the moor. Locals who have visited the exhibition have generally been more interested in what we've done rather than our rather impressionistic feelings about Bodmin Moor. ... Asking them about their 'feelings' about the moor does not illicit very much response.*
>
> *If we could start again I think that I would leave the core of what we have done but devote more space to:*
>
> 1. *The different modes of thought/ways of investigating the past that have been employed during the last five summers. Rather than having only one board about small scale societies, we could have had a whole screen explaining some of the ways in which we can use anthropology (both ethnographic data*

and social theory) to think about and interpret the past. This could have been juxtaposed with a screen on excavation. Given that most people's ideas of excavation are either some form of treasure hunt (aka Indiana Jones) or a mad/fun long weekend (Channel 4's Time Team) a little more space given over to the long and painstaking process of excavation would have been educational.

2. *A screen about the sociology that Tony and Mike have been doing with photos of caravans, landscapes etc. This would again bring across to the public more about what goes on amongst archaeologists.*

3. *More space devoted to our interpretations. If we had given more space to 1) ... our interpretations would make more sense. Very many people have said to me "What do you mean ... shrine stone?" and I think that this does show that in some ways we haven't fully succeeded.*

But it's easy to say all these things in retrospect. It is only by doing things like this that we learn what to do/not do next time. ...

CT thought that the exhibition was too tentative.

CT (2 June 1999): I don't think our interpretations of the hill have been made strongly enough. Too much of: 'it could be this or it could be the other'.

BB remained convinced that explanations and interpretations should be tentative and wanted to retain the balance between our engagement with the moor and other peoples'. People should be allowed to locate themselves and their views before we embarked on our stories. Although HB was probably right that people often do not verbalise their everyday sense of being in a place, nonetheless, as we have seen, people do respond indirectly or in rather private ways. Perhaps we could find better ways to enter into dialogue.

Apart from the style, and creating a sense of questioning, there were also, as we recognised with hindsight, many ways in which we could have made things clearer. We should have located the moor, the place, and the time more firmly. We should have had a time line and a three-dimensional model of the hill.[20]

There were image juxtapositions that were meaningful to us but not explained to the visitor.

The pictures should have been annotated more fully. This would have offered another level of information and interpretation to be seized on or ignored. The example that comes to mind is a photo of someone holding a flint arrowhead (Figure 14.4). We could have written something very simple on the photo: 'This brown flint comes all the way from Beer in Devon – or from even further afield.' No more than that, but it might have set people thinking about the contacts and exchanges that occurred. How did people move around? What were their relationships with people 'from away'? What other ways might there be to obtain foreign materials or objects?

The beauty of a cheap, flexible exhibition is that it can be changed. Indeed, as the exhibition moved on its way, we started the process of accretion and change. A new board incorporate some of the visitors' comments and perceptions; another offered Leskernick poetry. We began to add work by other people reacting to the exhibition and reacting to the hill (see chapter 15).

The open-endedness of the exhibition allows us to end where we began: with a commitment to the notion of landscapes that are multivocal; an acknowledgment of the fluid and changing nature of people's sense of place.

a   b

fig.14:4 It's a pity we didn't annotate the photographs: a) the flint, for example, comes from Devon, 150 miles away. How did it get to Bodmin Moor? b) people wanted to know the names of places.

Chapter Fifteen

Letting Go
A Dialogue

BARBARA BENDER WITH MARTIN HUBBARD,
SIMON PERSIGETTI, HEATHER KEIR CROSS,
AND MIKE VENNING

We added things to the exhibition, then we allowed other people to create their own work around the exhibition and their particular perceptions of Leskernick. In the first instance, Martin Hubbard and Mike Venning from Falmouth College added an Analogue Metaphor Machine, then, as part of a conference called 'Between Nature' held at Lancaster in 2001, Martin and Mike worked with Simon Persigetti and Heather Keir Cross from Dartington College. This combined exhibition and installation worked very well, and the following conversation took place in the afterglow.

Martin Hubbard: I first saw the exhibition in the church hall at Alternum and then, the same afternoon, Barbara and I went up to Leskernick. The transition between exhibition and site was quite rapid, and my overwhelming astonishment was at the difference between the order of the exhibition and the jumble of the site – I hadn't been prepared for how unreadable it was without expert or local knowledge. I found this fascinating and quite amusing and a few days afterwards I woke up early in the morning with the wish to make something more complicated – something in terms of three dimensions, in terms of surfaces that weren't so flat. It was the disjunction between my experience of the site and the seeming order of the exhibition, even though the words of the exhibition talked about disorder. ... I wanted to move it away from a solely visual reading to something more experiential ...

Mike Venning: Martin talked to me about it, and amongst the things that came up was that it would be good to have photographs that were local – of people who lived near the site. By sheer chance – serendipity – my great grandfather farmed Hendra just over the hill,

fig.15:1 Andy Jones
investigates the
analogue machine.

and, even more surprisingly, I had only just got hold of some old photographs of that side of the family from a recently deceased aunt. So we discussed and worked on the analogue metaphor machine (Figure 15.1).

BB: Could you describe the analogue machine?

MH: It was made from a navy surplus ship's radar screen. A mirror replaced the body of the machine, and you could look through a series of holes in the mirror. These showed a further series of mirrors, reflecting a panorama of the site, Mike's photographs, and a collection of objects from Leskernick that could be touched by inserting your hand into a rubber glove and groping into the machine. The peculiarity of the reflected perspective meant that you could see your hand between the photographs of the people and the landscape impossibly far away.

BB: You say you think it didn't work very well?

MH: I was hoping people would get down on their knees, but, as someone pointed out, what we were asking people to do was to stick their bums in the air which is not a thing to do among strangers. ... It was a failure to understand the sort of nervous concern that people have about moving out of the upright in the company of strangers. ... I had expected something a bit more elastic from archaeologists since they spend most of their time on their knees.

BB: It's also a question of context. The analogue metaphor machine went to two academic conferences, one in Bournemouth, the other in Cardiff, where people weren't expecting art installations. The Dartington installation, which came later, was created for a conference that was specifically about the interface between environment and performance and so people were much more open to what was on offer.

Simon Persigetti: Yes, I saw the Leskernick exhibition and the analogue metaphor machine when it was shown at Dartington. I work there in the Theatre Department, and I'm particularly interested in site specific work. I work with a company called Wrights and Sites, which is based in Exeter and via that kind of practice I've slowly been drawn towards issues of place, particularly those about the way people move in place and what memories of place are.

What excited me about the exhibition and made me think I wanted to do something was that I had always thought of archaeology as a science that was extremely wary of assumptions, so it was exciting to see an exhibition in which Martin and Mike were responding as artists to a site using their tools of excavation – which are to do with perception, colour, light – and to see this in combination with the effort of physical digging and analysis.

BB: The Dartington initiative involved Martin, Mike, and Simon – and then Heather.

HKC: I had been working on a mine site last summer in Cornwall. I found lots of quartz there and it worked wonderfully because I like to use ice, and ice reads very like quartz – its veining when it's frozen and the way it reflects. Martin talked a bit about the exhibition and we talked about doorways and entrances …

BB: Would you say that you were more inspired by the actual site of Leskernick, and less by the exhibition?

SP: No! What the exhibition suggests is an active response to site. … Here was a place that is normally hedged about with so many rules and regulations, even though it appears to be a wilderness, and here's an archaeological dig that says something about the potential fragility of the site, and here's a place that is being interpreted in a very interesting way.

BB: When I was asked to talk at the Lancaster conference, I didn't have a problem with talking or showing the exhibition, but I couldn't see how to take things further. There's this split between the academic and the performative. Then Martin said he would do something – that I should let go of it and let myself be surprised. So it was all new to me when I got here. Tell me about the process involved in creating the exhibition.

SP: OK. What interested me was the chaos of the site and yet how, via a particular lens, particular groups of people had been able to interpret it via archaeology and anthropology. It was like a kind of paradigm of the creative process. … So my response was to look at what would happen if you created a pseudo-landscape – and so the idea of creating a mini landscape made of hunks of stone came about. There was also some collaboration with the others – the idea of the mirror kept coming up ... and so I used the circular mirror as the base for this landscape, which allows the person looking to be part of the landscape, evolved. It was a provocation – I wanted people to look at this landscape and create their own mapping of the site and to name the place, and to name what they thought were significant aspects of the site – to engage in the process of interpretation. The inference is that maybe this way of seeing might transfer to all kinds of other places.

MV: My part went in two strands, and I've not resolved them yet. One was this personal narrative thing that started when I realised I had the photographs. When we did the presentation at Dartington I talked about how photographs are incomplete as evidence and how there was one photograph in the collection that might have had nothing to do with me or my family. And so the other strand was thinking about how we record all this stuff – the idea of the record and the incomplete record. I had a nice idea for a photograph with a mirror in the doorway of an Iron Age hut near Penzance – the idea being that to look at the past you have to get past your own reflection. Then I accumulated information and decided to do it as a kind of memory of artworks of the past that I and others had done – hence the book on Robert Smithson. Then I did a journey to another site near Lands End that was a travellers' site and there were two round hut bases where they had made benders, and these were just as mysterious in the landscape as Leskernick. What was even stranger was that I had decided that I would do a spiral walk to Leskernick and spiral round the hill, and someone else had made a spiral at Lands End, for the millennium or something. My project worked out, but I feel that having so many strands means that the secrets are still closed. Perhaps it's a bit like aspects of archaeology!!

MH: I followed what was actually one of the themes of the exhibition – it seemed that the archaeologists had found that the house-doors were orientated to points in the landscape. I was interested in why this was such an evocative idea to me – what kind of contemporary myths were functioning in me that made it so evocative? And having thought a lot about framing and about cosmology I decided to look at the inside-outness that seemed to be implied in the description of a house circle facing from its inside out towards the landscape. There was also in the exhibition a 360 degree panorama that was laid out in a straight line. This seemed very easy to read but a very strange object, and I thought perhaps we could make the object stranger and see if it was still possible to read it. So I took a 360 degree panorama from the centre of a house circle and then joined the ends of the panorama together so the landscape was turned inside out and now looked like a hut, so that there was a play between inside and outside. What I hoped it showed was that our ideas of inside and outside are not simply oppositional, they're much more complex; they can be inverted and converted and transported …

HKC: Being on site, there were two things that occurred to me as being very important for the people who inhabited the site. One was their water supply, the other their source of light. The water had a lot of other connections – it's just so precious, it has magical qualities, and yet we can't live without it. Those people would have had need for water, and where they got their water from would be very important. So rather than freezing some water from somewhere else, I thought it would be really nice to take the water from Leskernick and use that. It was a bit problematic because it was very heavy and I'm very bad at working out quantities, and we collected far more than was necessary. We carted vast amounts of water across the moor in the worst weather imaginable!

The moon shape has a magic quality, and although not knowing the religious beliefs of the people who lived there, it would have had something to do with this sort of magic in the sky and the way things react to it. So I made the moon from the water from the site, and it was frozen on an industrial site here called the Lune Industrial Site.

BB: How much did you talk to each other in the process of making the separate parts of the installation?

HKC: Oh, we had long meetings. When we'd mapped out what we were going to do, we went to Martin's and physically tried the things – the slates and the door and moved them around until we came to an agreement that something looked right and had some meaning for the whole thing.

BB: So the door and slates that form the centre part that holds it together was a combined effort, but you let each other just get on with the installations around the edge (Figures 15.2a and 15.2b)?

SP: We had an agreement that we would have four separate responses, but the hut circles suggested the idea of a central circle, and the issue of entrances and exits and which way do we face was quite a strong line through the collaborative discussions …

BB: What do you mean by 'Which way do you face'?

SP: We called the installation 'Face This Way', which had to do with the position of the doorways in the hut circles, but also to do with our position as perceivers of place. So doorways of perception.

MV: We wanted a door, and the one position for a door that is not going anywhere is flat on the floor.

SP: Martin's provocation was to ask people to make a map of where they would like to be buried – in a funny way the horizontal door is maybe the last door.

fig. 15:2 a) The slate circle and door, the ice moon to the right, the inside-out panorama at the back; b) the slate circle, the door – earth/air/fire/water.

BB: And the peat in the door frame? What's that?

MH: The four panels of the door frame are earth, air, fire, and water (Figure 15.2b). The earth has watercress growing in it, the air has an empty panel, the water has a shallow filling of water, and the fire has been scorched – and there are some scorched photographs. In a way I'm relieved that it wasn't easy to read, otherwise it would have been too obvious – but then again, it's a bit worrying if an anthropologist can't read it!

BB: I got the fire and scorch – I thought it was about fire and growth! You put some objects in the circle – did you know ahead of time that you wanted people to add to them?

MH: A very early idea was that the installation should accumulate – that it should layer itself. So if you came in one day it would be different from the next.

HKC: On our first visit to the moor, we collected 'kick off' objects from the actual site. All those things – the sunglasses, the beret, the can, the wool, they all came from the site.

BB: I find it interesting – being such a literal and academic person – that you don't feel the need to explain. You had the four elements on the door, but you didn't tell people; you had the objects from Leskernick but you didn't talk about layering.

SP: It's an important question – this is another sort of engagement.

BB: It's been a lovely three days. People have come in and they've stayed, they've busied themselves and committed themselves – they've come up with a dream, filled in cards, taken photographs. Although you didn't mediate with the written word, you mediated with the spoken one.

MV: It's true – I felt like a seaside photographer: 'Excuse me, sir, would you like to …?'

SP: I feel the room has an invitation, whether anyone is here or not, and I feel that, whether consciously or unconsciously, we have created a social space where people are free to stay and talk in a different way to the way they would if they went to an art gallery where there's a hushed silence and reverie and bodily positioning. I looked across the room at the height of the activity yesterday and thought that this is more than an exhibition, more than installation, in a funny way we've created a community. It's a pseudo community, but the configuration of exhibition, of objects and of us being present with our work was a kind of celebration that I feel is the great achievement of any communication. It goes beyond our expectations.

BB: It is a puzzle. Both here and when I sat with the exhibition at Alternum I had the strong feeling that we have to be part of the exhibition. That the engagement happens at least in part because of our presence.

HKC: There are two interesting points. I think it has to be strong enough visually so that if none of us are there people still want to look at it – that it's feeding their senses and so they get drawn in. The second is that I like to get as far away as possible from the written bits, because the spoken word is very important. It's more immediate, they get more from it, and they can look around at the same time.

MV: If you make something visual, it's visual; it's not words in a different form. That's why there's an aesthetic to that circle of slates.

BB: Maybe I'm a creature of words. Your ice moon is incredibly beautiful, but I'm infinitely touched when you tell me that the water came from Leskernick, and that the water and the moon reflect off each other. I'm moved by the personal. The aesthetic is one thing, but there's also this other.

MV: It's a balance.

BB: The interactive bits of the exhibition. Did you think them through in advance?

MH: We were going to do something, but didn't formulate what it should be until the last moment. We had the postcards and we had a lot of Polaroid film and we wanted to use the idea of the message on the postcard and something on the film that would allow for nonverbal interactivity. With the Polaroid, they could seize a little image without having to verbalise it – the idea was for them to look for entrances, whatever they might be.

BB: And the burial?

MH: The postcards. You and I once talked about how the difference between the living and the dead was less sharply defined in prehistoric times than it is now. I wanted to bring that in, and I also wanted to find a way for people to name their own affectionate landscape. The idea came to me, at six o'clock in the morning after the conference had started, that if I asked people where they would like to be buried, if it was near their home they would find salient features that would explain that choice, and these would be things they love.

BB: Do you think that your installation interacted with the Leskernick exhibition, or was really very separate from it?

SP: There was quite a lot of discussion about the relationship between the exhibition and the installation, and we originally had a plan that the spectator would pass through the exhibition to get to the installation, like a doorway opening up. But, of course, we had visualised a much larger room. Having to reconfigure the exhibition changed the dynamic of the space, and we were sensitive that we were maybe running counter to the exhibition in some ways.

MH: My own feeling is that many of our understandings are echoes of ideas on the boards.

BB: Did you hear any comments?

MH: I caught quite a lot, some easy interest and some fiercer curiosity, and some people extremely shocked by how intensely they felt. I had someone fill in a postcard on where they would like to be buried who said 'I don't have a home, I don't live anywhere, I'm not going to have anywhere to be buried, I'd never thought about it – I'd better start thinking about it'.

SP: This is one of the interesting things. This is about a specific site, Leskernick, but it opens up towards an engagement with objects, space, entries.

MH: And then it allowed them to return to the boards. They went from one to the other, and some of the questions had been illuminated by the exchange of seeing the ice melt from the river, and the bookshelf, and playing with the landscape and the Polaroids and postcards. They were in motion in their understanding.

Chapter Sixteen

Movement across the Moor

Introduction

We have talked of a nested landscape (chapter 1), with Leskernick at the centre of the nested circles, but we have talked very little about how the people on the hill engaged with other places, or other people, and of how the hill was part of a network of settlements and relationships that encompassed all of Bodmin Moor and extended well beyond.

To pose questions and attempt answers about how people might have interacted, we need to look at settlements across the length and breadth of the moor. This chapter is based on work undertaken in the last two seasons of the project – the summers of 1998 and 1999 – by some of the anthropologists. In chapter 19, we discuss relationships beyond the moor.

The Bodmin Moor survey based on air and ground survey between 1978 and 1985 (Johnson and Rose 1994: Map 1) identified at least 92 discrete settlement areas. Some of the larger settlements can be broken down into smaller sub-units, giving an overall total of well over 100 moorland settlements. More than half of these settlements are small, with less than 10 houses and structures. A further 20% have between 11 and 20 houses/structures, and the remaining 20 settlements have more than 20 houses/structures. In our survey of Bodmin Moor, we sampled 23 settlements from across the entire moor (Figure 16.1). We included some of the very largest sites such as Black Tor (90 houses) and Garrow Tor (174 houses in four areas); some of the smallest such as the Beacon (two houses), Alex Tor (seven houses), and Codda Tor (eight houses); and some medium-sized ones, in a wide variety of different landscape locations.

The results of this survey work are neither comprehensive nor 'authoritative'. Our main aim was to look for general trends in the data so that we

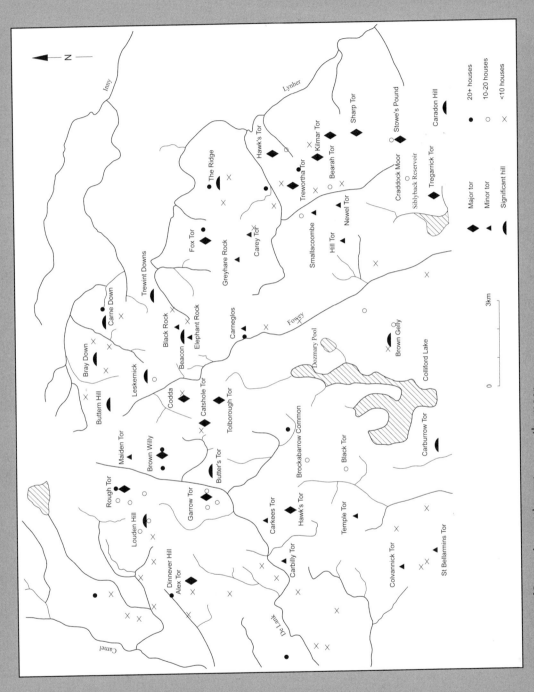

fig.16:1 Map of Bronze Age settlements across the moor.

could compare Leskernick with other settlements, think about the variety of settlement forms and locations, and consider possible relationships between people across the moor. At some of the very large sites, such as at Garrow Tor, we looked at a sample of houses on different sides of the hill. At other sites, such as at Carburrow (39 houses) and Louden Hill (46 houses), we surveyed all known structures. The information that we gathered could easily constitute another book.

Methodology

Although, in this chapter, we only include excerpts from the analysis of the different settlements, we felt that we should explain the strategies behind our surveying so that the reader could get an idea of how the data were assembled.

The aims of the survey were twofold:

(1) documentation of the variability in architectural form across Bodmin Moor. For this, we employed special house recording forms based, in part, on the experiences we had gained from surveying the houses at Leskernick.

(2) investigation of the relationship between the pattern of settlements and the wider landscape setting. To do this, we looked at the way settlements related to tors and rock outcrops, hill morphology, clitter masses, and ceremonial monuments such as cairns, stone circles, etc.

A further interpretative aim was to understand how the people who lived in the settlements within the moor landscape related to each other.

There were three stages involved in the survey. The first involved visiting a settlement area, identifying the locations of the houses and structures, and looking at the relationship between them and the clitter masses, rock outcrops, and so on in a general way. Depending upon the overall size of the settlement and its landscape location, this took between one and two days. During this period, nothing was recorded. The idea was to orientate ourselves and to acquire a general feeling for the place.

The second stage, taking anything up to two weeks per settlement, was to find and identify each individual house and structure on the ground and record the individual architectural details on the recording forms. Because vegetation and stone cover were frequently very heavy, we used numbered flags to identify the location of each structure. These flags made it possible for us to investigate spatial relationships that would not otherwise be readily apparent.

The last stage involved investigating the relationship between the houses and structures and the clitter masses and rock outcrops on the particular hill or tor. We produced sketches, took photographs, and wrote up a general description on site. Writing up the description in place was an essential part of the process of understanding and was quite different from the sort of description created at a desk using maps or plans. The interpretative conclusions are in part drawn from the general on-site description and in part from later, desk-based analyses of individual house and structure descriptions.

Settlements across the moor

All the settlements on Bodmin Moor have their own individual characteristics, their particular relationships to landscape, and their own sense of place in terms of the internal structuring of houses, boundaries and enclosures, the hills on which they are situated, and the cairns, tors, clitter masses, and grounders. No two are exactly alike; indeed the variation in house form is often as great within as between settlements. In the accounts of each settlement, we attempted to describe these particular characteristics. In the next section, we draw out some of the general principles that seem to structure the relationship of settlement form to landscape. Then, in the following section, we turn towards settlement structure and morphology; and in the last section, we offer a general discussion about social relationships between people on the moor.

Settlements within a landscape

Tors, hills, and settlements

An initial analysis of the map produced by the earlier Bodmin Moor survey shows us that the western and southern sides of hills were particularly favoured for settlement. Virtually no settlements are located on the north and fewer on the eastern side. In addition, there are substantial numbers of small settlements sited in almost flat lowland locations or on the top of low ridges. Settlements on high ridge tops such as at Rough Tor, Craddock Moor, and Berry Down (just to the south of the moor today) are exceptions. This pattern occurs irrespective of settlement size: the larger sites are found in similar situations to the smaller ones and, in this respect, are not in particularly favoured or unusual landscape locations. The location of the settlements on the western and southern sides of Leskernick Hill is typical for the moor as a whole.

   The preference for settlements to be sited on the western as opposed to the eastern sides of hills is interesting in terms of weather conditions. The prevailing wind and rain direction is now, and we presume was also in prehistoric times, from the north-west. Therefore, it would seem that shelter was not the *only* concern, and this is borne out by other evidence. Some settlements, such as the western settlement at Leskernick, Catshole Tor, or part of the western and southern settlement areas at Garrow Tor, are high up the slope in quite exposed locations. In all these cases, the houses could have been sited further downslope. In contrast, other settlements, such as Brown Gelly, Brown Willy East, Hawk's Tor East, Alex Tor, Rough Tor South, and Carburrow, are sited very low down the hillslope in much more sheltered locations.

There is a strong connection between settlement and the topography of high tors and significant hills. The greatest concentration of surviving settlement is in the north-west part of Bodmin Moor. There are at least 182 houses and structures on the southern and western sides of Rough Tor, 174 around Garrow Tor, 46 on the south and east sides of Louden hill, and 28 at Stannon to the north-west of Louden Hill.

In the south-east, Stowe's Hill, which has the most significant tor in this part of the moor, has over 80 structures on its northern end, and there are substantial settlements at Craddock Moor (44 houses) and around Tregarrick Tor.

In contrast, in the south-west of Bodmin Moor where the rock outcrops on St Bellarmins and Colvannick Tor are low and only locally significant, there is virtually no settlement.

Although almost all the high tors and high hills on the moor have larger or smaller settlements associated with them, the relationship is complex. Brown Willy, one of the most important moorland landmarks has almost no settlement (see below). Caradon Hill, Kilmar Tor, Hawk's Tor West, Hill Tor, Trewint Tor, and Carbilly Tor have no associated settlements, whereas Sharp Tor, Bearah Tor, Trewortha Tor and Hawk's Tor East, all dramatic landmarks of major significance, have only small settlements associated with them. Clearly, there are wrong and right sorts of tors and hills in relation to settlement concentration. Most of the tors in the south-east of Bodmin Moor – Kilmar, Bearah, Trewortha, and Hawk's Tor East – are long, narrow, and jagged ridges running east-west topped by a series of often dramatic rock stacks, and there is comparatively little settlement on or around them. Compared with circular or oval hills such as Leskernick, Carburrow, or Black Tor, or broader and flatter topped north-south ridges such as Stowe's Hill, Rough Tor, Garrow Tor or Brockabarrow Common, their lower slopes are not favoured for dense settlement.

The heavy concentration of settlement around Rough Tor and Garrow Tor in the north-west of Bodmin Moor must surely relate to the special spiritual powers of those hills and the dramatic rock formations that occur on them.

However, other clearly important hills and rock formations seem to form set-aside areas. Hawk's Tor West was probably not chosen for settlement because it was a reserved special hill in the centre of the moor with a Neolithic henge on its southern slopes. Brown Willy, a spectacular and commanding ridge in the north-west part of the moor, has no house circles or platforms on the summit area, and only 17 houses and platforms have been recorded low down on its eastern slopes with a further 23 on the western slopes.[1] Most of these are little more than rough platforms and were probably used only on a seasonal basis. We suggest that Brown Willy was a communal place where people from different settlements came together, and that the ridge formed a ceremonial processional way. In the photo essay on p. 231 we walked from south to north along the length of it. Stowe's Hill may have worked in much the same way as Brown Willy, for although there are many platforms on the ridge top, there are no houses or substantial settlements around its slopes. Caradon Hill (see below) was another reserved ceremonial space covered with cairns.

Settlements and clitter

The relationship between houses and the spatial distribution of clitter on the hills is very marked at virtually every settlement. As at Leskernick there is a clear preference for locating settlements on the sides of the hills where the densest clitter spreads occur. At Brown Gelly, the settlement is located on the eastern side of the hill where the heaviest clitter occurs, and the same is true for the Beacon, Garrow Tor, Carburrow Tor, Rough Tor, Black Tor, Brockabarrow Common, Catshole, Codda, and Hawk's Tor East. Hillsides lacking clitter are usually avoided.

At some settlements, including Leskernick, Catshole, and Carburrow South, the houses are built within the clitter masses. At others, such as Rough Tor South and Brown Gelly, Carburrow West and the Beacon, Garrow East and West, the houses occur in a band below the densest clitter masses but in areas still containing substantial numbers of stones and grounders. At Rough Tor South, the compounds on the eastern side of Garrow Tor, and at Hawk's Tor East there is a marked spatial zonation of high rocky tors, areas of denser and lighter clitter and lower settlement areas. At Brockabarrow, the area of very dense clitter occurs below the main settlement area and to its north, whilst the settlement at Codda is located between two distinct higher and lower areas of clitter. Settlement areas that do not occur in areas heavily littered with clitter blocks such as Alex Tor, Louden Hill, and Craddock Moor South appear to be the exception rather than the norm, but even at Louden Hill, some houses are built into the sides and base of a short clitter stream.

Clitter structures

In the survey, we documented the various forms of clitter structures at all the settlements. These structures included circular arrangements of stones, encircled grounders, propped stones, arcs of stones in front of, or surrounding large grounders, circular features resembling cairns, spiral-like forms, lines of stones of orthostatic form running through the clitter, chamber-like spaces and 'megalithic' formations, low stone walls running through the clitter as at Brown Gelly and Brockabarrow, and massive stone banks as at Carburrow.

Here are a few examples:

Brown Gelly

On the eastern side of the hill, above a shelving area with many stone platforms and the lower settlement area, is an area with extremely dense clitter running all the way up and around the hill to the tor at the southern end of Brown Gelly. Towards the northern end of this clitter spread, there are very clear *stone wall-like features* running north-south across the slope and west-east downslope (see plan). Associated with these are three *roughly circular clitter structures* focussing on and emphasising prominent exposed grounders that have walls running

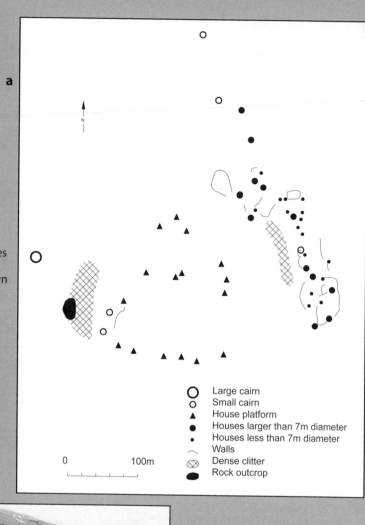

fig.16:2 a) Sketch plan of houses and clitter structures at Brown Gelly; b) view across dense clitter at Brown Gelly; c) sketch plan of houses and clitter features at Carburrow Tor.

a

N

○ Large cairn
○ Small cairn
▲ House platform
● Houses larger than 7m diameter
• Houses less than 7m diameter
⌒ Walls
▨ Dense clitter
⬤ Rock outcrop

0   100m

b

c

N

Wall running through dense clitter

Canon stone

Large cairns on hilltop

Rock edge
×
Chamberlike feature

South settlement

West settlement

Carburrow Tor

0   100m

above them and *arcs or circles of stones* creating spaces below them (Figures 16.2a and 16.2b). These structures and walls are located in the middle of the clitter mass so that one must slowly and arduously move through it to reach them. To move safely, one has to be attentive to every step and every stone. The contrast between moving through the clitter to reach these structures and walking between and around the stone-free area with the cairns on the top of the hill could not be more marked physically and visually.

Brockabarrow Common

One distinctive house with an adjoining pound entered from the south is built right on the southern margins of the main clitter mass (Figure 16.3). This is one of the lowest houses in the settlement area. Quite remarkably, running through the clitter mass there are traces of *a single boulder wall* running east away from the house and then dividing. Such a wall has no conceivable functional significance. It would not keep anything in or out, it does not divide the clitter mass, but its presence is felt …

Carburrow Tor

The two great cairns on the top of the hill are highly visible across the moor, but are invisible from all but the southern edge of the settlement areas situated on the lower southern and western slopes of the hill (Figure 16.2c).

A *stony bank* runs up the north-west slope of the hill and joins the northern cairn. This is not a normal enclosure bank and appears to have no functional purpose. It varies in width between 4 m and 8 m and is 130 m long. It is built of large blocks. There is no orthostatic facing. The bank both incorporates and bifurcates to include large grounders as it meanders up the slope. *Some of these grounders are encircled by smaller stones* within the bank structure. Towards the top of the slope, a short distance below the Propped Stone, there is a large rectangular slab covering *a cist-like chamber* in the bank. In places, the stone bank is virtually indistinguishable from the clitter blocks that surround it; in others it is clearly defined (Figure 16.2c).

At the break of slope with the flattish hill top on which the cairns are sited there is an *enormous propped stone*, known locally as the Cannon Stone (Figure 16.4b). From the bottom of the stone bank this stone is sky lined and the cairns are out of sight. Between capstone and propping stones there is a 'chamber' space with a hole and two step-like features at the top end through which one can squeeze. It is only when passing through this space that the largest cairn at the top of the hill becomes visible for the first time.

The stone bank continues across the hill top for a further 54 m until it reaches the massive cairn. In some respects, the bank resembles

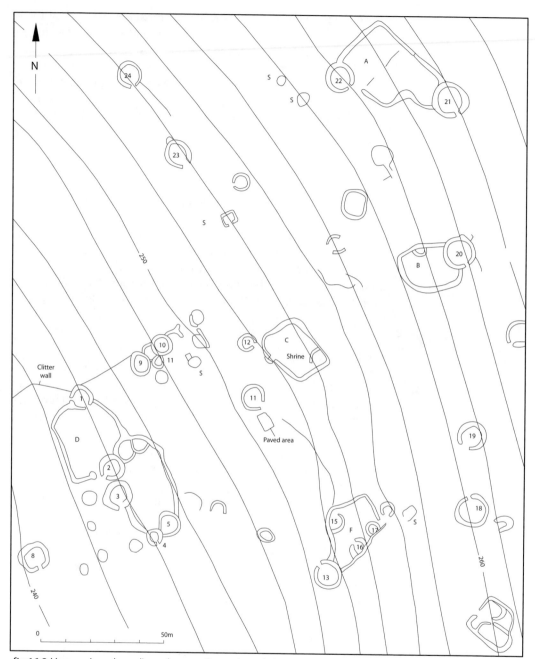

fig.16:3 Houses (numbered), enclosures (letters), and clitter at Brockabarrow Common. S = subrectangular structures. After Johnson and Rose (1984: fig. 11).

a clitter stream; in others, it appears very artificial in character. It links the cairn at the top of the hill to the base of the hill slope and, as it flows through the clitter, it connects the megalith-like chamber underneath the Cannon Stone with the cairn. It seems very likely that this bank served as a processional way to the cairn at the top of the hill.

fig.16:4 a) Carburrow Tor – looking up the clitter wall from the Cannon Stone to the Great Cairn; b) the Cannon Stone. The Propped Stone is 4 m long, 1.6 m wide, and 1.4 m thick; the prop at the front is 0.9 m high, the one at the back 0.3 m.

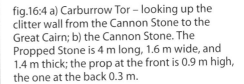

Codda Tor

The settlement at Codda Tor is on gently sloping land about 200 m to the east beneath the tor. It consists of eight house structures, five of which are associated with a compound, together with numerous small cairns. These are all situated between a clitter mass immediately below the tor and another lower down the slope to the east about 120

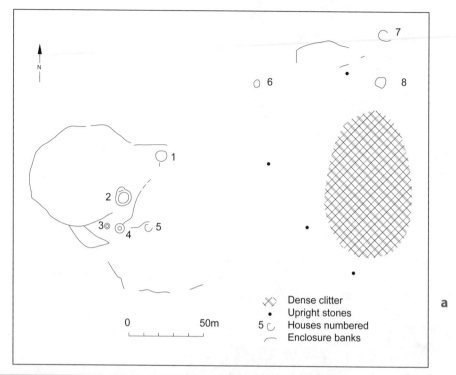

fig.16:5 a) Sketch plan of the houses and clitter at Codda. Based on field survey by Peter Herring; b) Field shrine on the Beacon wrapped with cling film.

m to the south and east of the compound (Figure 16.5a). The latter is a roughly rectangular clitter mass, measuring about 100 m north-south and 50m west-east. This is bounded on the west, north, and south sides by a series of *four standing stones* positioned between 50 and 80 m apart. These are sited 10–20 m away from the edge of the clitter mass and appear to deliberately bound it off. A large pit to the east of the clitter might indicate that another stone was originally placed on this side too. The stones in the clitter mass are incredibly dense, both confusing and exciting the eye, some appearing as a *series of spirals* depending upon where one stands and how one looks, lost or changing as one moves. We wrapped and painted two of these spiral forms (Color Plate 7d). These are entirely 'natural' and fugitive forms.

At half the surveyed sites in our sample, we found large grounders with cleared spaces below them. As at Leskernick, we have tentatively identified these as field shrines or offering places.

The Beacon

On the southern upper slopes of the Beacon, immediately below the summit cairns but not intervisible with them or Elephant Rock, there is a particularly impressive *field shrine* (Figure 16.5b). This consists of a large grounder on top of which there are two leaning stones orientated north-south encircled by a 4.6 m diameter arc or setting of smaller stones.

We have talked about these clitter structures at some length in chapter 9. It is clear that some of them are human creations. It is equally clear that others are natural. As at Leskernick, most are thoroughly ambiguous and it is really not very important whether a particular 'arrangement' is the product of geology or of humanity. Just as we recognise these patterns, so did the people that lived in these settlements. Occupying a world of stone, the patterning would have been invested with meaning and, when it was felt necessary, or served some purpose – creating an activity that was both socially encompassing and, perhaps, socially exclusive – a natural pattern could be enhanced, clarified, or conjoined to other stone markings.

Cairns

Small cairns within settlement areas are found at a number of settlements besides Leskernick. There are some at Black Tor, Hawk's Tor East, Garrow Tor, Catshole Tor, Codda Tor, and Louden Hill, and below the Craddock Moor South settlement area, close to an embanked avenue, there is a substantial cairn-field.

Large cairns sited on top of the hills below which the settlements are located occur at all the surveyed sites except at Codda, Hawk's Tor, Garrow Tor, and Louden Hill; 60% of the 92 settlements documented from the moor have associated large hilltop cairns. There is no particularly favoured cardinal direction between cairn and settlement area. Except for a few of the houses in the southern settlement at Carburrow, these cairns are not visible from the settlement areas. However, it is normal, as at Leskernick, for the skyline to be punctuated by the hilltop cairns and tors associated with other settlements. Those on the top of Brown Gelly and Carburrow Tor are particularly prominent in this respect.

From within the settlement areas situated at various points on the hill slopes, the view of the surrounding landscape is always restricted, always blocked in one or more directions by the hill on which the settlement itself is sited and by surrounding hills and ridges. Often the settlement can be strikingly insular and restricted as at Brockabarrow Common, the eastern side of Garrow Tor, or at Brown Gelly. By contrast, moving up to the tops of the tors and hills where the large cairns are situated and the jagged rocks and solution hollows are to be found is a process of revelation. A world dominated in the settlement areas by the intimate topography of nearby linear ridges, boggy areas, and hills becomes transformed into a distant and panoramic view across Bodmin Moor in which the horizon is no longer a series of lines but appears circular in form, with tors and hills marking the edge of the world. For sites on the edges of Bodmin Moor, the sea marks the edge. The circularity of the world, as mirrored in the circular architecture of house and cairn and stone circle, is only apparent from the tops of the high tors. The spiritual power of the tors is thus intimately associated with this unfolding panorama. Next, we will consider the intriguing case of Caradon Hill, the largest ridge-top cairn cemetery on Bodmin Moor.

Caradon Hill

Caradon Hill is an impressive north-east/south-west ridge on the far south-east edge of Bodmin Moor (Figure 16.6). It rises to a height of 371 m and is the sixth-highest hill on the moor. It dominates the skyline for miles around, yet has no tors or extensive rock outcrops except at the south-west lower end. There is no evidence of any prehistoric settlement on or around the hill. Instead, it has the greatest number of massive cairns on the moor, twenty in all, in sizes that range from 10–15 m in diameter to over 30 m. The one exception is a small cairn that forms an appendage to one of the large ones.

It seems clear that Caradon Hill was a reserved cemetery for the ancestral dead. Today, because the cairns have been plundered for treasure and much mutilated in the process, they are not very visible, but in prehistoric times many of them would have been as prominent and visible in the landscape as those that still crennelate the top of Brown Gelly. Most particularly, for people casting their eye towards Caradon from the Hurlers Stone Circles and Stowe's Pound a short distance away to the north-west, the highest summit cairns would have formed a spectacular skyline.

The cairns are strung out along the gently sloping summit of the hill in two distinct groups. The lower group at the south-west end consists of 10 dispersed and scattered cairns Two of these (Cairns 1 and 3) are tor cairns. The lower one (Cairn 1) is built on top of a small rock outcrop 10–15 m across with a 5 m drop on the north-west edge. It would have been particularly prominent when seen from the south, from off the moor in the direction of Trethevy Quoit. The

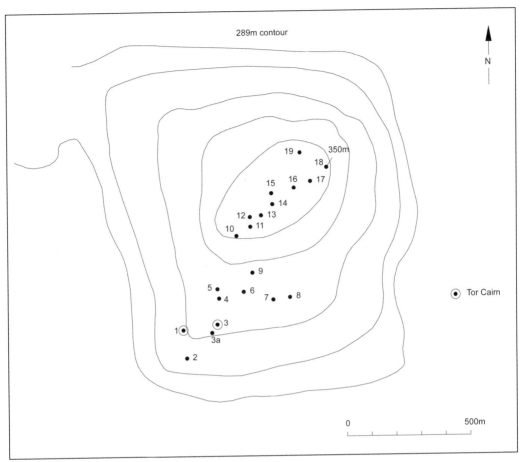

289m contour

N

19 •
18 •
350m
15 • 16 • 17
•
14 •
12 • 13
10 • 11
•

9 •

5 •
6 •
4 • 7 • 8 •

⊙ 3
1 ⊙
3a

2 •

⊙ Tor Cairn

0   500m

fig.16:6 Plan of Caradon
Hill cairn cemetery.

second tor cairn (Cairn 3), slightly higher up the slope, is the largest in the group and has a much smaller cairn appended on its southern side (Figure 16.6). In the centre of the Great Cairn is an elongated and extremely weathered rock stack up to 1 m high and 22 m long that may originally have been covered and concealed by the cairn material that still rides over it in places. The other seven cairns in the group, ranging in diameter from 11 to 24 m, appear to have had a variety of forms. There seem to be round cairns, ring cairns, and platform cairns, but the extreme mutilation of the majority precludes further description.

There is a high degree of intervisibility between most of these cairns, and between this lower group and the ridge top group. Only two of the lower group are not intervisible with the higher ones – Cairn 2 situated low down the slope to the west and Cairn 8 to the east of the ridge top.

The cairns have been built not only for intervisibility between upper and lower groupings, but to be highly visible from across the moor. Seven of the 10 cairns in the lower group have extensive views to the north and west over Bodmin Moor, with up to seven major tors in sight. The Hurlers Stone Circles, Stowe's Pound, and The Cheesewring are prominent to the north-west. From six of the cairns it is also possible to see Dartmoor to the east and the sea to the south.

The higher group of 10 cairns form a staggered north-east to south-west line along the top of the ridge, which slopes gently up to the north-west and is virtually free of clitter blocks or large grounders. This roughly linear distribution contrasts with the lower south-west group. The very largest cairns are found high up on the hill top. These range in size from 15 to 30 m in diameter and include a variety of different forms including cairns with rims and platforms. An off-centre pit in the northernmost of the cairns has exposed a large grounder originally covered by the cairn material. Grounders are also exposed in the outer edge of Cairn 17, and a number of the other cairns in this group may also be built around and conceal grounders. The largest of these, Cairns 15 and 19, are at least 30 m in diameter. The latter, with the partial remains of a central cist, is situated on the highest point of the ridge.

All the cairns in the group apart from Cairn 18 situated slightly downslope from the summit, have a high degree of intervisibility with between six and 15 of the other cairns being visible. Cairn 18, like Cairn 1, must have been sited to be seen off the moor, in this case to the north.

Only the northernmost cairns (16–19) are not intervisible with any of the cairns in the lower and southern group on the ridge, and from all but Cairn 17 situated on the eastern edge of the ridge top there are extensive views across Bodmin Moor to Brown Willy in the north-west, with between seven and nine major tors in sight. From the highest and largest cairn (Cairn 19) situated in the middle of the flat summit top, the panoramic view includes Bearah Tor, Kilmar Tor, Trewortha Tor, Sharp Tor, Stowe's Hill, and the Hurlers Stone Circles below it, Brown Willy, Brown Gelly, Tregarrick Tor, and Carburrow Tor, and extends to Dartmoor to the west and the sea to the south. There is thus a visual explosion and expansion of perspective as one moves up to the ridge top and the massive summit cairns.

Settlement patterns

We now turn to look more closely at the internal form and patterning of settlements and enclosures across the moors.

Settlement form

At Leskernick, there is a clear spatial separation between the western and southern settlement areas. This pattern is repeated at Carburrow, Craddock

Moor, Rough Tor Garrow Tor, Louden Hill, and other sites where different settlement areas are not intervisible and are dispersed on different sides of their respective hills. At other large settlements such as Black Tor and Brock-abarrow Common, settlements are much denser and more nucleated and only occur on one side of the hill. Black Tor, for example, looks quite different from Leskernick:

> The settlement consists of about 90 houses and ancillary structures packed densely together in a honeycomb-like manner in an area of only 3 ha. In many cases, the houses are strung out along their linking walls like beads along a string giving the strong impression of successive construction down a wall line. … The enclosures seem almost secondary or incidental features of the settlement and it is doubtful if they were used either for cultivation or stock keeping. There is a general lack of differentiation between the houses in terms of size and their construction seems highly individual in character. Black Tor might be a specialist tin procurement site – hence its proximity to the Warleggan River.

In other cases, as at Brown Gelly, the settlement is again limited to one side of the hill but is much more spread out and linear in form.

These three different types of settlement structure: segmentary, nucleated, or linear are not confined to one part of the moor or another, they are found scattered across the moor. The greater majority (81%) of the smaller settlements are either clustered as at Catshole, Hawk's Tor East, and Trewortha Tor or linear spreads as at Smallacoombe and on East Moor.

Associated fields or enclosures

At Leskernick there is a plenitude of accretional enclosures.

Roughly speaking, about 18 (20%) of all the larger and smaller settlements have substantial systems of accreted enclosures. Take Craddock Moor:

> The settlement at Craddock Moor spreads around the southern and western slopes of a rather topographically indistinct north-south ridge.
>
> The southern area of the settlement has 26 houses and structures. These form three distinct clusters in a virtually clitter-free area on very gently sloping land towards the base of the slope. These houses are all incorporated into the walls of a well-defined accretional enclosure system that was built from the west to the east across the slope. To the north of one of the houses (House 5) there is a clearly defined drove-way that leads up the slope and out of the field system. A further three houses are associated with another small accretional system to the west.
>
> The houses in the western settlement are located approximately

midway up the slope in a rather exposed position. The houses in the northern part of this settlement area are associated with a well-defined large enclosure with linear subdivisions.

In contrast, at least five settlements are associated with coaxial or linear field boundaries. Smallacoombe, East Moor, and Dinnever Hill are the best examples.

Still others, particularly some of the very large settlements, for example, Garrow Tor, Brown Gelly, Rough Tor South, Brockabarrow Common, Black Tor, and Carburrow, have walls and enclosed areas associated with the houses but no clear system of either accretional or linear field enclosures. Alternatively, in some cases, for example at Sharp Tor and around Tregarrick Tor, although the enclosure walls are primarily accretional they also include elements of a linear or more planned structuring of space.

Finally, about 12 (13%) of the moorland settlements have house clusters but *no* associated enclosures. Catshole and Brown Willy East are two such settlements.

Part of this variability is surely temporal, and part, no doubt, reflects different economic practices, we return to these questions later in the chapter.

House morphology

The houses at Leskernick are mainly circular in form and have a single entrance that usually faces downslope. The same is true for the rest of the moor. The most obvious dwelling places, and the most commonplace at virtually all the settlements, are circular, built of stone, and have wall facings. Although we assume that most were indeed dwelling places, it is quite possible that some were built as non-domestic ancillary buildings, and, of course, even where they did start life as domestic dwellings they will have had individual biographies; some, as they deteriorated, or as familial demography changed, were turned over to storage or used to house animals, and some, eventually, were 'closed' and used as houses for the dead.

Sometimes, these houses were built of coursed walling, but much more often walls were built of placed slabs or orthostats with a rubble and boulder infill. Some houses only have facing on the internal walls, some on both internal and external walls. In all cases where the houses are double faced, far more care and attention is taken over the choice of the slabs for the internal wall face. Sometimes the external facing is only partial; in others it completely surrounds the exterior.

These houses have a single doorway that generally faces downslope. Where there is another entrance, it seems to be the result of a later breach or of stone robbing. Occasionally, the orientation may vary. Thus, for example, at Garrow Tor and Carburrow Tor, some doorways face across-slope rather than down to maintain a consistent doorway orientation.

Although circular in form, many houses are rather roughly so. In most cases, this can be accounted for in terms of the exigencies of building amongst the clitter and incorporating grounders in the base of the wall circuit. At some settlements, including Leskernick, Garrow Tor, Carburrow Tor, Craddock Moor, and Brown Gelly, there are occasional oval or subcircular houses that have been built by tacking a structure onto an enclosure or compound wall. These are often rather rough and ready structures and they may have off-centre entrances. In contrast, there are occasional settlements, for example, Louden Hill and Black Tor, where oval and subcircular-shaped houses are the norm rather than the exception.

In addition to these easily distinguished round stone houses, there are other structures that are much more ambiguous. They are often labelled as 'house structures', but their useage is often far from clear. At least three different forms can be distinguished.

The first are stone-cleared platforms. Here, roughly circular spaces have been cleared within the clitter and the cleared stone piled around the perimeter. It seems probable that wooden structures were erected in the cleared area. They may have been dwelling places, and, if so, they may have been more temporary or seasonal in nature than the stone houses. Or they may have been used for storage or as animal byres. Such cleared circular areas have been found at the Rough Tor enclosure and at Stowe's Hill, where over 80 have been documented (Johnson and Rose 1994: 53). They also occur immediately to the south and east of Tregarrick Tor, and others may be identified elsewhere on the moor in the future. The association of these cleared areas with the Rough Tor and Stowe's Pound enclosures, which date back to the Neolithic, may mean that some at least of the cleared areas are fairly early in date.

The second type are stone banks built to create circular spaces or platforms. They have no internal- or external-facing stones and often seem to have no entrance way. They often appear to be levelled into the slope. Sometimes the circular banks are open on the downslope side and, in such cases, more often than not, no attempt is made to level the land surface within the structure.

At some settlements, such as Leskernick and Black Tor, there are no such circular platforms; at many other settlements across the moor they are commonplace. Sometimes, as at Carneglos, all the structures are of this nature; sometimes, as along the eastern slopes of Brown Willy and at Codda Tor, most of them are. Sometimes, a settlement may have both circular platforms and the more substantial house structures with faced walling but the two are spatially separated. Thus, at both Brown Gelly and Garrow Tor West the platforms occur on shelves of land above the more substantial houses. At Louden Hill, they are found low down the slope or high up above the other houses with stone facing. By contrast, at Brockabarrow Common they are scattered in among the more substantial houses. Again, these circular platforms *may* have been associated with wooden constructions, and they may, like the cleared house stances at Rough Tor and Stowe's Pound, be fairly early in date, possibly Late Neolithic. Some, though, may be much later in date and may have been built in the Late Bronze Age or Iron Age as transhumant huts.

House circles at Brown Willy East

On the lower eastern slopes of Brown Willy there are 17 dispersed house circles in an area of almost flat land with relatively few clitter blocks (Figure 16.7). The majority of them are small slight circular platforms of single boulder or rubble construction lacking clearly defined entrance ways and orthostats. The most northerly one is associated with small enclosures and boundaries, perhaps for stock. Only one of them, House 4, is convincing as a substantial domestic structure that might be more than temporarily or seasonally occupied.

... and those at Brown Gelly

There are two distinct settlements areas on the eastern side of the hill below and between dense clitter spreads and streams and clearly located with reference to them. The upper settlement area consists of 16 structures situated on a broad shelf of land, about 250 m wide, before the hill slope starts to rise up steeply. These consist of little more than small stone platforms or rings between 3.5 and 5 m internal diameter. Most are levelled into the slope but lack internal or external orthostatic facing or clearly defined entrance ways, being built of small blocks and stones. Five appear to have double walls. These structures are widely dispersed and lack connecting walls or associated fields or enclosures.

The third type of structure is a single boulder platform. These structures lack orthostats and are little more than circular rings of larger stones. Such structures are found on virtually all settlements on the moor. They are frequently small in size, are almost certainly of a non-domestic nature, and frequently form ancillary spaces along compound or enclosure walls or abut onto, or are associated with, more substantial houses.

House size

The houses at Leskernick are very variable in size – they may be as small as 4 m or as large as 10 m.

Right across Bodmin Moor, house sizes are highly variable both within and between settlements. Of the 346 surveyed houses for which accurate measurements could be taken, 19% are small with an internal diameter of less than 4 m; 51% are between 4 and 6 m; and 30% are large structures over 6 m in size. Bockabarrow Common is exceptional in having a large number of houses over 7 m in diameter. The southern settlements at Leskernick, Brown Gelly, and Craddock Moor also have substantial numbers of very large houses

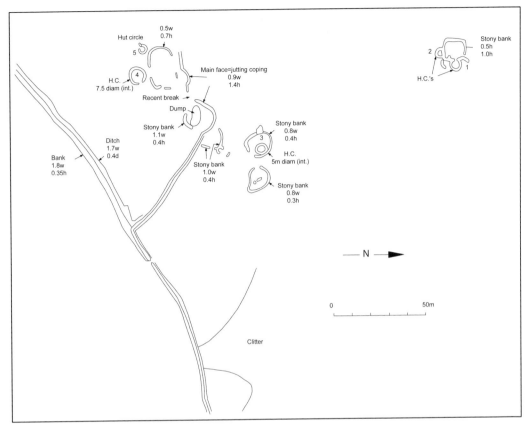

fig.16:7 Brown Willy, East – the northern house cluster. Surveyed by Pete Herring.

(30–40%), whereas those at Garrow Tor and Louden Hill are markedly smaller and much more standardised in size. The norm is to find a small number of large structures with the majority ranging between 4 and 6 m. The western settlement at Leskernick is typical of this pattern, which seems to reflect a spatial organisation in which there are a few principal dwelling houses, and a larger number of smaller houses and associated ancillary structures that are usually organised within, or strung out along, compound or enclosure walls.

Architectural form

It seems that at Leskernick, most of the houses incorporate grounders as part of the foundation courses. There are also many instances where large upstanding grounders are deployed in the construction of the house. In a number of the Leskernick houses, carefully chosen orthostats are used, most particularly as backstones or to mark cardinal points.

Although hard to detect from surface surveys, it seems likely that grounders were used as part of the foundation course in many, if not most, of the houses across the length and breadth of the moor. However, the use of large *upstanding* grounders as a major component of the architectural morphology of the walls seems to have been confined to the north-west part of the moor and, even then, to only some of the settlements. Thus, they are found in a substantial number of houses at, not just Leskernick, but also Rough Tor South, Garrow Tor, Catshole, Codda Tor, and the Beacon. They are used as backstones, incorporated in the external or internal wall faces, and employed around entrance ways. But such upstanding grounders are completely absent from other settlements within this north-west part of the moor, for example, at Brown Willy East and, with one exception, Louden Hill. Over the rest of Bodmin Moor, they are either completely absent or appear architecturally insignificant.

The use of fine orthostats is also rather regionally specific. They are used much more frequently in the northern than in the southern parts of the moor. In the south, the larger domestic structures on settlements such as Craddock Moor, Brown Gelly, Carburrow Tor, and Black Tor are all rather similar in appearance and have very solid walls built of large stone chunks and slabs that are often terraced into the slope. Where orthostats are found within these houses, the large and impressive ones are almost always placed at the entrances to the houses. This emphasis on entrance areas, either through marking them with particularly large orthostats, incorporating large grounders, creating long corridors into the houses as at Carburrow West and Garrow Tor, and/or a thickening of the walls of the house at this point in the house circuit is a consistent feature found across the entirety of Bodmin Moor.

In the northern part of the moor, where orthostats are much more frequently deployed, the largest, highest, and most finely shaped are always used for the internal walls. However, the use, at Leskernick, of particularly large and fine well-shaped slabs to serve as backstones in the internal wall face, is a rather particular development. Rough Tor South is the only other settlement where they appear regularly. Otherwise, there are only eight settlements or settlement areas where they found and even then they occur in only one or two houses. It is true that some may have been robbed out or destroyed, but it seems likely that this particular feature is very locally specific.

The use at Leskernick of large orthostats in the internal or external wall face to mark the cardinal directions occurs in a few houses in a number of the settlements: Rough Tor South, Garrow Tor, the Beacon, Craddock Moor, and Louden Hill. Given the ruinous state of the wall circuits in most cases, it is possible that this marking of the cardinal points may have been more widespread – the consistent entrance orientation of the houses in settlements such as Garrow Tor South, Rough Tor South, and at Craddock Moor South suggests that this is likely.

The use of quartz in the wall facing is rare. We recorded only a few examples at Leskernick, Brockabarrow Common, Garrow Tor, and Craddock Moor. Similarly, deeply weathered stones are very rarely employed as an architectural component of the houses. One clear example occurs at Leskernick and another at Garrow Tor.

The provision of porches or annexes to the houses is fairly widespread across the entirety of Bodmin Moor. Their form and size is extremely variable and has no regional or local significance. Internal subdivisions within houses also occur across the moor. They were almost certainly quite common but are often difficult to detect by surface survey alone. The north-east compound at Garrow Tor is architecturally unique in having large triangular-shaped orthostats set off from the back upslope wall of some houses with cist like spaces in-between. The settlement at Garrow South is unusual in having roughly concentric enclosed spaces defined by single rows of orthostats and blocks surrounding some of the houses. We have not documented this elsewhere.

The possible conversion of houses into cairns or the building of cairns in part of their interior is widespread. We noted examples at Codda Tor, Black Tor, Rough Tor South, Brockabarrow Common, and Garrow Tor, but in every case only a few of the houses in each settlement can be interpreted in this way.

What emerges from this brief survey of house morphology is that there are certain design and construction principles that are widespread across the moor; there are others that are more regionally or even locally specific. We shall return to the meaning of this variability in the last section.

Doorway orientation

The dominant doorway orientation at Leskernick is to the south and south-west, nearly always in the direction of prominent tors or hills (Figure 16.8).

Clearly, no one builds their doorway facing into the prevailing wind, thus none on the moor are orientated to the north or north-west. At the same time, within the remaining spectrum some very strong preferences emerge. The main orientation is to the south or south-west. Out of 23 settlements, only three have doorways that predominantly face to the east or north-east, whilst another three have *some* that face in these directions. Of the 23 settlements or settlement areas sampled doorway orientation to the south, south-east, and south-west are the dominant directions in 15 cases. In three cases, Louden Hill, Brown Willy East, and Codda, the dominant direction is to the east, with other houses facing to the south at Louden Hill. Houses in the north-east compound at Garrow Tor face north-east as well as to the south, and in the northern part of Brown Gelly the dominant entrance orientations are to the north-east and east. One house on the Beacon is orientated to the south, the other to the east. In the western part of the Craddock Moor, settlement houses face south-west or west. Entrance orientation at Carneglos is uncertain but was again probably to the west or south-west.

Within the general south/south-west trend, there is a small subset of settlements or settlement areas where the house doors face due west. Thus, at Leskernick, although the main orientation is south and south-west, four houses in the western settlement (thus 26% of known doorway orientations on this side of the hill) face to the west. The only other settlements with houses facing to the west are Catshole Tor, Craddock Moor, and Garrow West.

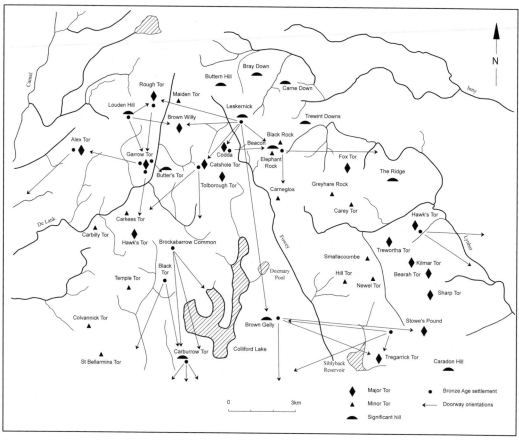

fig.16:8 Map showing house door orientations across the moor.

Because in each of these cases the houses are located on the western side of the hill, it might be postulated that the doorway orientation was simply dependent upon hillside orientation, but although this may have some relevance it is not a sufficient explanation as there are many other settlements on west-facing slopes where the doorways do not face west. Thus, at Garrow West all but one of the houses have entrances that face south across the hillslope; at Craddock Moor, the majority of the houses face to the south or south-west; and at Carburrow all the houses on the western side of the hill have entrances orientated in a southerly direction.

At nearly all settlements, the doorways face towards important hills and tors. There are five exceptions to this rule (26%), and they raise some interesting questions:

Brockabarrow Common

Only one house, which is both exceptionally large and associated with the most substantial pound, looks out to Carburrow Tor and its cairns in the distance. All the others face to the south or south-east but are not orientated to a specific tor. This might be interpreted as an attempt to restrict and control entrance orientation in the propitious and most cosmologically powerful direction so that it became the preserve of only one household.

The Beacon, Alex Tor, Hawk's Tors, and Carburrow Tor

The two houses at the Beacon respectively face east off the moor and south but again not to a specific tor. At Alex Tor, Hawk's Tor, and Carburrow Tor, all situated on the edges of the moor, doorways are orientated off the moor in a southerly direction. The general emphasis on a south doorway orientation at these moor edge settlements might be interpreted in genealogical terms as the ancestral direction, the place where the ancestors came from and populated Bodmin Moor.

The possibility that ancestral affiliations are fossilised in the doorway orientations may hold true for many other moorland settlements. If we take Leskernick: in the southern settlement some of the houses are orientated towards the Beacon and its summit cairns and to Catshole, Tolborough, and Brown Gelly, but the majority of the houses face Brown Gelly, the most important ancestral hill and the furthest away. In the western settlement, the dominant orientation is to Brown Willy and Catshole Tor. In one instance, the orientation is to Brown Gelly and in another, the doorway of the high and isolated House 3 faces Rough Tor. Perhaps what is happening at Leskernick is that for the majority of the houses, tors with ancestral/genealogical significance are being sign-posted, whereas a few of the larger, more significant houses are connected with tors that have huge symbolic and ritual significance.

The possibility that many of the house doors are pointing to tors of ancestral and/or genealogical significance seems to hold good for many other settlements on Bodmin Moor. Four of them have houses that are all orientated to a single tor: the houses at Codda look out to Black Rock; those at Black Tor to Carburrow Tor; those at Rough Tor South to Carburrow; and at Craddock Moor West, to Brown Gelly and off the moor. It is interesting to note that orientation to a single tor is not related to the number of houses. There are very few houses at Codda; Black Tor has the greatest concentration anywhere on the moor. Five settlements have houses orientated to two tors, two settlements have houses orientated to three tors, whereas, like the southern and western settlement areas at Leskernick, doorway orientations in the northeast compound at Garrow and in the southern settlement area at Brown Gelly are towards four different tors. With two exceptions, all these tors have settlements associated with them. The exceptions are Hill Tor, towards which some of the houses at Brown Gelly face, and Hawk's Tor West, towards which many of the houses at Garrow are orientated. The latter was undoubtedly a very significant ancestral hill because it has the Stripple Stones circle henge on its southern side.

So far, we have offered 'thick description' with interpretative interleavings; now we turn more directly to questions of social relationships across the moors.

Discussion

Social relations across the moor

Given the evidence that we have assembled on settlements and landscapes across the moor, and the interpretations that we have begun to proffer, there are a great many questions about social, political, and economic relationships that immediately come to mind.

> Who, we might ask, walked the processional ways?
>
> Who watched?
>
> Who built?
>
> How were the people related that lived within a house? Within a settlement? In different settlements?
>
> How were the people who lived on the moor related to those who lived beyond? (This question may be improperly posed. Why are we assuming that people lived either on or off the moor? Might they not, as we discussed in chapter 2, have lived close to the high places on a seasonal basis?)
>
> What of gender relations?
>
> What of social hierarchy?

The dearth of material culture makes it hard to answer these questions. We have the stone skeletons of the settlements and hilltop structures, but not the human bones or pots or tools or animal or crop remains. Or, at most, we have minimal amounts of these things. In the earlier chapters on Leskernick, we touched on economic strategies, on household composition, and hierarchy or lack of hierarchy within the community or communities. Based upon survey alone, how far can we open out these discussions to take in connections across and beyond the moor? Rather than directly answering the questions we have just asked, we try to come at them through another set of questions – about time and variability.

What time depth is involved?

Before we start, we have to return to the question of time depth. There are over 100 prehistoric settlements, small, medium, and large, on the moor; there are the stone-free stances, stone-ringed platforms, and circular stone banks; and there are many and varied circular stone houses. There are also pounds, accreted enclosures, and some coaxial ones. We need to know whether this variability is contemporaneous, or whether these patterns have developed over time.

At Leskernick, we suggested a history that involved many generations and several centuries. Leaving aside whether the well-worn Neolithic/Bronze Age nomenclature is appropriate (see chapter 1), we place the stone row and circles below the hill in the later Neolithic, third millennium BC; we have the settlements on both sides of the hill expanding and then contracting over several centuries during the second millennium in the Early to Late Bronze Age; and we set the final withdrawal at the beginning of the first millennium BC.

Having considered the other sites across the moor, we suggest that many of the stone-cleared stances or the stone platforms, and the wooden houses that were erected within them, also date to the Later Neolithic and are therefore probably not coterminus with the more substantial stone round houses often found on the same sites. It could well be that the stances and platforms, the stone rows and circles, are associated with a more seasonally mobile people who may have lived off the moor for part of the year. Thus, for example, at Brown Gelly, where the platforms and stone houses occupy different parts of the site, and where the stone houses, representing a much more substantial labour investment, are built downslope in a more sheltered position and closer to water sources, it seems likely that the building and occupation of the stone houses coincide with a later and more permanent settlement of the moor.

What is of interest is that there are very few sites where there are only platforms. In other words, when people settle in, they create a continuity, they build on memories and understandings. However, there are relatively few such mixed sites. It seems clear that the number of people on Bodmin Moor, and the number of settlements, greatly increased during the earlier Bronze Age.

Equally, at the latter end of the settlement story, there are relatively few coaxial field-systems and, when they do occur, they are found either in conjunction with the earlier accretional systems, for example, at Sharp Tor and Teregarrick Tor, or on their own, as at Smallacoombe, East Moor, and Dinnever. Based on the evidence from Dartmoor (Fleming 1988), the coaxial field-systems date to the Middle Bronze Age, probably post 1600 BC. It would seem, therefore, that where accretional and coaxial field-systems are found together the associated settlements must have been occupied for a considerable time. In the rare cases where the coaxial field-systems are found on their own, they represent later and more short-lived occupations. However, we cannot assume that just because a settlement only has accretional field-systems, as at Leskernick, they are of shorter duration. The coaxial field-system may indicate a shift in land tenure and a greater degree of control over land that occurred at some, but not all, settlements.[2]

This chronological sequence is coarse grained. We have, as yet, no way of making temporal distinctions between the smaller, medium, and large settlements of stone houses. We are assuming that, for much of the Bronze Age, they coexisted, and that there was, therefore, both a relatively dense Bronze Age occupation of the moor, and a considerable variety in settlement size and form.

How do we explain the settlement variability?

So, how are we to explain the variability within and between settlements? We discussed the internal variability between houses at Leskernick and we won't rehearse the arguments in any detail. Generally, we believe that the Leskernick houses were occupied by extended families; that in both the southern and western settlements there were large founder households and then smaller ones ringing them about. We also suggested that there were two 'set-aside' houses (Houses 28 and 3) that, because of their position and orientation, were probably associated with initiation ceremonies and were perhaps the dwelling places of ritual leaders. We do not know, but it is possible, whether there was a degree of social differentiation within the settlement – there may have been a sort of truncated pyramid in which a number of people had authority based on expertise in different activities: household heads, elders, people with acknowledged expertise in, for example, hunting or metal-working activities. We do not know how, or in what way, these different statuses might have been gendered. Although there may have been different statuses, we find nothing in the record to suggest a more entrenched social hierarchy.

Leskernick is a relatively large settlement. But there are larger ones, such as Garrow Tor, Brown Gelly, Rough Tor, Brockabarrow Common, Craddock, Black Tor, and Carburrow. We have tended to assume that the social relationships at these sites were rather similar to Leskernick, but it is, of course, possible that at these larger settlements there was a stronger sense of social heirarchy. It may be that the people who were carried on their death across the moor to the great Caradon cairn field were important and greatly revered leaders within these settlements.

Connections across the moor

Communality and social hierarchy are not necessarily oppositional, but clearly, in trying to understand relationship within and between settlements, it matters where the stress is placed. For example, some of the connections between settlements may have to do with subsistence practices. Some of the smaller sites may have been only seasonally occupied. Thus, the small settlements on Codda or the Beacon, both close to Leskernick, may have been associated with seasonal herding activities. Individuals or families may have moved out from Leskernick for part of the year. Such subsistence strategies would be part of the more encompassing social relationships. The particular way in which such activities were carried out, and the process by which people chose, or were chosen, to go would be dependent upon how the people of Leskernick organised themselves.

However, the small settlements may have been daughter settlements. A family or two have moved away from the main settlement and set up in a new place. And again who went, and under what conditions, and what the relationships were with those in 'the old place' would depend upon the social ordering of things. It may even be, as we have discussed before, that a big settlement like Leskernick was itself only seasonally occupied, and that, for part of the year, the Leskernick people lived at one of the very big settlements, or even off the moor. We have tended to downplay this possibility because it seems to us that the complexity of building, enclosures, ritual places, and processual ways is more suggestive of year-round occupation.

But if there had been seasonal movement between Leskernick and somewhere else, then, once again, the conditions under which it took place would be inscribed and negotiated within the larger social order. In our rather communitarian scenario, the occupants of the different settlements would have had considerable decision-making autonomy. If, on the other hand, we opt for a greater degree of entrenched social hierarchy, then the decision-making process would have been circumscribed; production, circulation, and exchange would have been funnelled up the hierarchy, and more wide-ranging exchanges would have been negotiated between elites on and off the moor.

A range of economic activities may also account for some of the variability between settlements. During the Bronze Age, tin was being extracted from the streams on the moor. It may well be that at a settlement like Leskernick, tin exploitation was a seasonal activity. It might also be that there were specialist settlements, either seasonally or permanently occupied. Black Tor, for example, with its honeycomb of oval houses, its lack of enclosures, and its proximity to the Warleggan River might be one such. And some of the dozen or so small settlements with no enclosures may also have been specialist camps. Again, the question immediately arises: what would the relationship have been between such specialist settlements and the other communities on the moor? How and where did the tin get processed? It is possible that the people at Leskernick and many of the other communities smelted the precious particles of tin that they dug from the stream beds into ingots – although we have found absolutely no evidence for such activity. If they did smelt them, did they also work them up into objects? Or did they exchange their ingots for other commodities? Or were the ingots – or perhaps the particles of tin – brought as gifts or tribute to the big settlements and were they worked up there and then fed into the exchange system? We discuss these questions at greater length in chapter 18.

'No man is an island' – nor settlement either. One way or another, there was a criss-crossing of pathways and of movement over the moor. Movement between seasonal and permanent places, between specialist and farming communities. People making their way across the moor on feast days and high days, up to the high places – to the 'cathedral' of Rough Tor, the great processual ways of Brown Willy or Stowe's Hill, the sacred cairn enclosures on Caradon. There were times and places to forge ties, find marriage partners, and to exchange – both things and news.

As we suggested earlier, it may be that we can distinguish something akin to tribal areas within the moor. There is a broad regional distinction in house morphology between the north part of the moor and the south. The houses of Craddock Moor, Brown Gelly, Carburrow Tor, and Black Tor are rather different from those further north: they tend to be very solid and to be built of large chunks or slabs often terraced into the hillslope.

It may also be that house door orientations tell us something about the

social ties between the different settlements. If, in a settlement, the majority of the doorways are orientated towards a particular tor, might this not
indicate the presence of strong ties to the people in the settlement associated
with the tor? Thus, the map shown on p. 406 could be interpreted as showing
dominant kin links, perhaps in terms of a hierarchy of husband and wife giv-
ers and takers in which indebtedness was displayed, materialised, and concretised through the symbolism of doorway orientation. So, for example, in
terms of this interpretation, the people at Rough Tor South received spouses
from Garrow Tor, who received spouses from Carburrow, Brown Willy West
(Fernacre), and Butter's Tor; whereas the people at Carburrow had kin links
with people living off the moor. It is fascinating to note that there are two
houses in the southern settlement at Leskernick with doorways orientated to
the small settlement on the southern slope of the Beacon. Most of the other
houses face Brown Gelly with a much larger settlement on its eastern side,
comparable in size to the southern and western settlements at Leskernick.
Two other houses look out to Catshole and Codda Tors with their small settlements. It is interesting that there are no houses in other settlements with
doorways orientated towards Leskernick. Even those at Codda are related to
Black Rock on the lower northern slopes of the Beacon.

We are left with more questions than we started out with. All we can do
for the moment is to sketch in potential scenarios. And, having focussed in
this chapter on relationships across Bodmin Moor, we need to turn to relationships, people, and places beyond the moor.

Chapter Seventeen

Between Moor and Plain
Trethevy Quoit

We have talked about the way in which the people on the moor invested the stones with meaning; how they saw and sometimes drew out a patterning from the stones; and how, sometimes, they copied the ancestral creations, and thereby learnt the art of transforming ideas and understandings into material forms that could then be located in new places. Eventually, the copyings and transformations from nature could serve as blueprints for monuments built hundreds of miles from Bodmin Moor, but at Trethevy Quoit, a mere half mile from the moor, we see – or think we see – a small example of one such off-moor creation (Figure 17.1). It is worth pausing and circling round the Quoit to try and understand what was happening.

Trethevy Quiot is one of the most impressive and best-preserved dolmens in Britain. It lies to the south-east of Bodmin Moor and is separated from it by a broad upland valley. It is separated from it, but it is constructed out of stones that originated on and around the high tors.

Trevethy Quoit is an isolated dolmen. There are none like it on Bodmin Moor or in the immediate vicinity. The nearest comparable ones are 80 km to the west in West Penwith.

According to the dry typologies into which megalithic structures in all their infinite subtle variability have to be squeezed, Trethevy Quoit is a classic portal dolmen. The wedge-shaped chamber is formed by six large granite side slabs creating an internal space of about 3 x 2 m. The supposed antechamber is at the wider eastern end, over which the capstone, measuring 5 x 4 m, juts out. There are slight traces of a cairn around the base of the chamber.

The chamber has changed little in size and appearance since it was first illustrated in 1858. Then as now, only one of the portal stones forming the supposed antechamber survives to the left or south of the entrance and there

is no documentary evidence to suggest that another ever existed. Then as now, the capstone leans at a distinct angle – it is 3.2 m high at the eastern end and only 2.7 m at the western end. The collapse of the backstone inwards has resulted in the capstone resting askew on the side slabs, but whilst this exaggerates the difference in height, the distinct east-west slope of the capstone was undoubtedly an original feature as the supporting upright at the eastern end is higher than the rest. This upright, which divides the chamber from the 'antechamber', has a gap at its base on the right-hand side just large enough for a person to crawl through. No other portal dolmen in Cornwall has such a feature, and this has led to suggestions that it may have been cut at a later date to force an entry into the chamber. This seems unlikely because there is no trace of any such stone cutting and, moreover, it has long been possible to enter the chamber over the collapsed backstone or by squeezing over the top of the uprights on the southern side.

The leaning angle of the Trethevy capstone is directly reminiscent of natural fallen slabs resting against others to form chamber-like spaces directly below the high tors of Bodmin Moor. Equally, the gap in the base of the upright forming the chamber entrance has all the characteristics found in naturally weathered rocks that occur on the high tors. Weathering patterns caused by frost heave and other processes frequently produce rock formations that look strikingly artificial in form. One of the most impressive examples of this is the enormous tunnel like gap in the granite on the peak of Rough Tor.

All things considered, it seems likely that the upright and the capstone were very carefully chosen and transported from one of the high tors of Bodmin Moor, most probably from Stowe's Pound, which lies 3.5 km due north of Trethevy Quoit, or perhaps from the south-west end of Caradon Hill, visible 2 km to the north-east.

There is another exceptional feature to the capstone. There is a subrectangular hole, 23 x 18 cm, in the capstone directly above the entrance to the chamber. It has never been satisfactorily explained – suggestions range from its being used to hold a flagpole to its being a chimney! The most satisfactory explanation of this curious hole, which, significantly, is directly above the chamber entrance so that people pass below it before entering the monument, is that it is a natural solution hollow that has been eroded through, thus creating a hole. If this interpretation is right, it signals another transference – material and ideational – from moor to quoit. In the last chapter of this book, we talk about these solution hollows and note that they are usually found only on the very highest of the Bodmin Moor tors or on collapsed slabs close by (see chapter 19). On occasion, these hollows weather right through to form a hole in the rock and, indeed, excellent examples are to be found in the south-east of Bodmin Moor at Bearah Tor, Trewortha Tor, and Hawk's Tor.

On the left or southern side of the entrance stands the supposed 'portal' stone. It is very different in character from the other stones used to construct the Quoit. Instead of being a relatively flat and thin slab, it is a rounded pillar. The shiny quartz face that is visible on entering the chamber is heavily weathered. Again, such heavily weathered stones with quartz vein faces generally occur around the high tors on Bodmin Moor. The weathering, suggesting age, and the shiny character of the quartz face again suggest careful choice and attention to detail in the construction of the monument. Rather than being a remnant portal stone, this may originally have been a menhir against which the dolmen was later constructed with the entrance positioned so that the weathered and shiny face be visible on entering the monument.

The small cairn of stones around the chamber is directly analogous to the later tor cairns of Bodmin Moor, for example, Catshole Tor, where a small cairn was built around the base of natural rock stacks whose formation resembles that of a dolmen.

Thus, we suggest that Trethevy Quoit may have been constructed in three different phases, with perhaps a fairly long duration between them. First, the menhir was erected; second, the chamber was constructed to its west; and third, the low cairn was built around it.

If these arguments are accepted, they would explain many of the remarkable differences between Trevethy Quoit and the dolmens of West Penwith. Trevethy Quiot was a local monument in the sense that its significance was directly related to place, and, in particular, to the high tors of Bodmin Moor. It was a cultural monument that in its major constructional features imitated the natural megaliths found all over the moor around and beneath the high tors. It drew its inspiration and perhaps its power from nature and the work of the ancestral beings and at the same time improved and enhanced them.

Chapter Eighteen

Beyond the Moor

Introduction

Early in the book, we used the term 'nested landscapes' as a way of describing the interactions and relationships that criss-crossed the moor. In the last chapter, we extended the story a little way beyond. But, of course, there were other actions and interactions that played out much further afield. We, in the present, draw boundaries, but they are arbitrary and in our work at Leskernick we did not have time to develop this theme of the many different sorts of movement and contact that the Leskernick people would have had, including some that involved only the movement of the mind and imagination.

At a more local level, we should have taken time to walk out one day from the moor. We should have followed the Bowithick pathway north from the Hill, walked across the Davidstow Common and continued down to the coast, for there's no doubt that people would have gone that way, down to the beach to hunt for suitable pebbles, particularly flint ones, to scavenge the foreshore, and perhaps to do some fishing from the sea's edge or in small dugouts. We should also have spent time in the lowlands around the edge of the moor pondering how people *might* have moved seasonally, or, even if they were permanently settled on the moor, what sorts of expeditions there might have been to exchange goods, livestock, people, and stories.

But beyond these webs of activity were other contacts, at first-, second-, and third-hand with more distant places, and it is to these that we now turn.

Bodmin Moor in the larger scheme of things

When we came to Bodmin Moor, we came from 'outside' and, mainly, from the east. Still today, for us, Cornwall was a long way away. For us, partly because we hold the map of England in our minds, it seemed like a western outpost, tethered, like Wales, to the bulk of England. And, as an outpost, we imbued it with a romantic sense of the other, of a place less caught up in the hustle and hassle of the great Wen, less 'busy' than the Home Counties, less manicured than Hampshire, Dorset, or even Devon. We felt even more privileged because Bodmin Moor seemed more remote, more off the tourist trail, its prehistory less well known, than Dartmoor.[1]

This 'peripheralisation' or marginalisation of the west, irritating enough to local Cornish people in the present, also makes its way into the general histories and prehistories of the area, to the exasperation of archaeologists who live and work there.[2] For most of the 20th century, the assumption made by non-Cornish archaeologists has been that Wessex is the hub of the prehistoric universe of southern England and that places like Cornwall or Wales are the periphery.

The way the story is often told is that in the Early Bronze Age there was an uptake of new land and a corresponding spread of ritual monuments into both lowland – the New Forest, and Wealden Sands – and upland areas – Bodmin Moor, Dartmoor, the Derbyshire gritstone, and the North York Moors (Bradley 1984: 89). Much of this up-taken land was adjacent to areas where complex burials and ritual sites pre-existed, and the spread is thus seen as part of a core/periphery phenomenon. So Bodmin Moor and Dartmoor are envisaged as operating on the distant fringes of a hub of action that focuses on Wessex (Hampshire, Dorset, and Wiltshire). The Early Bronze Age Wessex elites, characterised by wealthy burials (furnished with daggers, cups, necklaces, and maceheads often made from 'exotic' materials including jet, shale, amber, and gold) and with major ritual centres, are envisaged as interfacing (via exchange) with, and affecting the social structures of, other areas of southern Britain, including the moors. These 'peripheral' areas, within which there is no evidence of earlier marked social hierarchies, are supposedly characterised by the emergence of Wessex-dependant elites, distinguished by occasional 'rich' burials with Wessex-style grave goods.

We tell the story this way, and yet, at the same time, we talk about the diversity and richness of ritual monuments and settlement and enclosure patterns in the south-west. The local story and the core/periphery story don't really gel. Is there another way of telling?

Let us consider the story of the Rillaton burial.

The Rillaton burial: the stories we tell

As mentioned in chapter 16, the Rillaton barrow, situated south of the Cheesewring and north-east of the Hurlers Circle, is the second-largest barrow on the moor. It was 'excavated' in 1837, and a large north-south-orientated cist was discovered holding the remains of an extended skeleton – the only inhumation burial so far found on the moor. A pot covered by a stone slab lay close to the chest of the person, and inside the pot was a small biconical cup of beaten gold. Within the cist, there was also a Wessex-style 'Camerton-Snowshill' type bronze dagger, a metal rivet, pieces of ivory or bone, and faience beads. The cist was built into the outer edge of the east side of the cairn, relatively close to the surface (1 m down in a cairn 2.7 m high), which might suggest that it was a secondary burial. Or it may be that the central part of the cairn was taken up by a large grounder (Barnatt 1982: 213; Borlase 1872; Hencken 1932: 69–70).

In a core/periphery scenario, the man (it's taken for granted that it is a man) buried in the cist was an important member of a local Bodmin elite who owed much of his status to his ability to control the supply of local tin and perhaps gold that was exchanged down the line with the Wessex 'chiefs'. In other words, his group provided 'raw materials' in exchange for finished goods – a very 'colonial' situation.

Teasing apart this story a little further, we might note that although tin was available on the moor and may well have been extracted by, amongst others, people on Leskernick Hill, or by people in more specialist settlements like the one at Black Tor, it seems very unlikely that gold was procured locally. The major sources of gold are the Wicklow Mountains in Ireland and north Wales (Harbison 1971).[3] Alternatively, the gold found in the Wessex burials may have come from Iberia or, in the later Bronze Age, central Europe (summarised by O'Kelly 1989: 173–75).

Another way of telling would be that the Rillaton personage, rather than being a partner in a rather unequal relationship, was a member of a local highly regarded elite who, in important measure, gained authority through living close to the high places that were both created by and creative of the ancestral beings. They were the holders of the ritual knowledge. The personage probably lived in the settlement at Stowes Pond below the imposing hill top tors, in an area of the moor with many ritual sites – the stone row, the Craddock Moor stone circle, the three Hurlers Stone Circles, and a plethora of other barrows. It could well be that access to local precious metals and stones was an *adjunct* to ritual authority, and that the control and manipulation of material resources (both local and obtained through exchange) was a way of signalling and enhancing the social position of the person buried. In turn, the prominently placed barrow and the offerings of rich grave-goods served to enhance the standing of the local group involved (Brück 2000: 297).

The particular form of the Rillaton gold cup, with its corrugated body and the riveted strap handle linking rim to upper body,[4] is very similar in form and technique to cups being produced on the continent around 1900–1700 BC. These continental cups may be made of gold, as, for example, the Unĕtician cup from Fritzdorf in western Germany, or of silver, as in the two Breton cups, for example, the one from St Adrien (Needham 2000: 178). Both the gold cup and the pointillé-decorated Wessex-style dagger are part of a set of widely exchanged elite objects that recur in the Wessex, Breton, and central European Bronze Ages.

We should probably think of these transactions in terms of long-distance down-the-line exchanges, rather than directed exchange with distant, or particular, places. It may be that, within these exchanges, it was Cornish bronze scrap and objects that were being traded and recycled rather than tin ingots, and that tin as a raw material never travelled far from the moor. These exchange trajectories finger out in many directions – to the continent, to the Atlantic seaboard, the Cross Channel zone, and *sometimes* to Wessex. Thus, two other gold items found in Cornwall, the gold collars (lunulae) from Harlyn Bay, probably come from Ireland where more than 80 examples have been found (Taylor 1980). One of the Cornish collars is a 'classic design', generally believed to be an Irish form. The other, belonging to what has been labelled the 'unaccomplished group', may well be an example of local emulation (Taylor 1980).

If we understand the procurement, use, and placement of fine objects, like the Rillaton cup, to be part of a widespread exchange in, and emulation of, elite objects from very dispersed areas, we can dispense with the Wessex-dependant socioeconomic frameworks that have dominated British Bronze Age studies for so long and instead begin to build up a sense of subtle regional variability, widespread exchange networks, and changes through time (Sherratt 1994). We can note the way in which, in the Early Bronze Age, Trevisker-style pottery was found primarily in Cornwall, whereas by the Middle Bronze Age it is found throughout the south-west, shows greater homogeneity of style, and is exchanged as far afield as Wessex (Parker Pearson 1995),[5] Kent (Macpherson-Grant 1994: 64–65), and France (Pas de Calais: Apsimon and Greenfield 1972: 356).[6]

The observant reader might suggest that, once again, this reformulation of social dynamics, with its emphasis on regional and local variability, mirrors contemporary preoccupations and the current political and cultural resurgence of interest in the 'local' or 'regional'. But there is a difference: where contemporary geopolitics are concerned, although we may wish to emphasise the local or regional, we cannot in good faith do so without also discussing 'the global' and the significance of 'core' institutions and societies. In contrast, in discussing the regional and the local in Bronze Age southern Britain, we are suggesting that the nub of the matter is the subtle and variable *regional* connectivity between different societies, a connectivity quite unlike any contemporary Western configuration.

Regional dynamics

The traditional core-periphery framework, in terms of the Bronze Age of south-west Britain, assumes that the upland communities are largely reliant on a pulse of life generated elsewhere. It assumes that people are driven, because of population pressure, to colonise less favourable areas. But in the cases of Bodmin Moor and Dartmoor, we have to recognise that, one, there is no evidence of signs of pressure on the land in the adjacent lowland areas (see, for example, Fitzpatrick, Butterworth, and Grove's [1999] analysis of east Devon, and Nowakowski's [1991] discussion of lowland north Cornwall). And, two, the uplands were much more favourable locales in the Middle Bronze Age than they are now. The peat that blankets the Bodmin Moor today only developed towards the end of the Bronze Age. Before that time, as evidenced in the thousands of stone houses, miles of stone wall, and numerous ritual stone places, these landscapes supported many thriving communities. Given the presence of important mineral resources, the topographic particularity of Bodmin Moor and Dartmoor, and the significance of the high places, it seems likely that, far from the moors being 'last-stand' places, they were highly charged places, and it seems likely that the people who created and used the old ceremonial complexes, and who later built their settlements there, were held in some awe by those living beyond the moors.

Indeed, rather than envisaging the settlement of the uplands as a colonisation of previously unsettled areas, we need to recognise that, although people may not have *lived permanently* on the moor until the Middle Bronze Age, they had a long familiarity with it. This landscape was known and structured by the presence of preexisting Neolithic and Early Bronze Age ritual monuments and the associated cosmology relating to the natural features. In all probability, the Middle Bronze Age communities who built the houses and enclosures on the moor had lineage rights of passage to, and ownership of, the locales of their settlements via their ancestors who used the stone circles and rows and were buried there.

The Middle Bronze Age use of these upland landscapes thus links with an *in situ* past and suggests highly stable and conservative societies, rather than pioneer communities taking up virgin ground. The proximity of Leskernick's Middle Bronze Age settlement to a stone row and circle complex, and to the Propped Stone and large Early Bronze Age cairn on the top of the hill, is part of an on-going story. Again, on Dartmoor, several settlements are located close to stone rows (for example, at Merrivale), and terminal and contour reave boundaries incorporate, or are orientated on, earlier stone rows and cairns (Fleming 1988). Just as the cairns, stone rows, and circles of the later Neolithic and Early Bronze Age were built with reference to landscape features, so, too, were the later settlements. Some of the Dartmoor reaves are orientated on tors (Fleming 1988: Fig. 23); the house entrances on Bodmin Moor are orientated towards specific tors; and the enclosures at Leskernick are focused on and predetermined by clitter runs. This continuity is interestingly *unlike* the Wessex pattern where Middle Bronze Age settlements are mostly in different locations to the dominant monuments of the preceding ritual landscape.

But even if the moorlands were familiar places with long associations, two questions remain. First, why, if there was no land pressure, did people feel the need to move up onto the moors and to create settled communities? And second (the same question that we have asked several times), were the communities permanent or seasonal? The (rather vague) answer to the first might be in terms of a desire to create stronger and closer links with the ancestral places, to lay claim to these places through proximity and everyday practice, and, at the same time, to lay claim to, and exploit, highly desirable raw materials – stone, tin, and other minerals.

In answer to the second, we may perhaps come closer to some resolution by comparing the evidence from the upland settlements of the south-west with the Middle Bronze Age settlements of lowland southern Britain. We suggest that such a comparison makes it more, rather than less, likely that most of the communities on the moor lived there the whole year round.

Middle Bronze Age settlements on Bodmin Moor compared with those from other parts of southern Britain

What do we know about the Middle Bronze Age communities (c. 1500–1100 BC) of southern Britain as a whole? Our traditional referents for southern Britain are the 'Deverel-Rimbury' traditions of the chalk downlands of Dorset Hampshire, Wiltshire, and Sussex (Barrett, Bradley, and Green 1991; Brück 1999; Ellison 1981), and to a lesser extent the Thames Valley (Brück 1999, 2000). In these areas, the distinguishing characteristics are the appearance of enclosed settlements, the prominence of the round house, a relatively wide range of domestic pottery (also used to contain cremation burials), the appearance of cremation cemeteries, and overt land division (Barrett 1994: 92; Barrett, Bradley, and Green 1991: 224; Ellison 1981). Brück (2000: 281ff) characterises this new focus on settlements as the outcome of a fragmentation of the preceding Early Bronze Age alliance structure that had been based on larger-scale groupings and residential mobility. She suggests that in the Middle Bronze Age, the household unit rose to prominence and was central to identity, inheritance, and land tenure.

Many of these characteristics are mirrored in the uplands of south-west Britain. Here also, the Middle Bronze Age is characterised by new features – round houses, a new range of domestic pottery (Trevisker ware), new funerary rites, and major enclosure systems. However, the settlements are often larger than the individual farmstead of the chalklands, and the placement of houses and the enclosure of land is more complex and perhaps more communal.

Let us look more closely at some of the differences and similarities, starting with the 'domestic unit', moving on to life cycles, rituals of the everyday, and, finally, economic patterns and land divisions.

The domestic unit

The prevalent idea of the Middle Bronze Age domestic unit on the chalk downlands of southern Britain derives from Ellison's (1981) identification of a 'modular unit' comprising a major dwelling plus one or two supplementary buildings. On most Deverel-Rimbury sites, both on the downlands and in the Thames Valley, the major dwelling is very uniform in size. Traditionally, these dwellings have been interpreted as being c. 5–8 m in diameter, which, using Naroll's formula, translates into a living space for four to five adults (Bradley et al. 1980). These relatively modest dimensions have been contrasted with the more massive houses found in the Iron Age (Rhatz and Apsimon 1962). However, more recently, it has been recognised that this house dimension was determined by taking the posthole circle as the outer wall of the house; it now appears that this circle forms the roof support *inside* the house, with the outer wall being a much lower structure either in a wall trench, or, where houses have been terraced into the hillside, on the outer lip of the house platform. This would increase the size to 7–8 m for the largest post-built houses, for example at Black Patch, East Sussex (Drewett 1982: 327). This, in turn, increases the potential household size.

The assumption has been that the main dwelling housed a nuclear family and that perhaps the occasional smaller additional buildings were used by dependant relatives (as suggested for Black Patch, and Itford Hill, East Sussex; Drewett 1982). On the basis of detailed recording of all artefacts and ecofacts within the buildings at Black Patch, East Sussex, Drewett has suggested a rather interesting gendering of space, with the major dwellings being primarily associated with male-gendered artefacts, food storage, and craft activities, whereas the adjunct buildings are associated with food preparation and female-gendered artefacts (Drewett 1982). However, the interpretation of the latter is problematic, because it is unclear whether the artefacts recorded were deliberate foundation deposits, closing-down acts, processes of abandonment, *in situ* 'rubbish', or the result of secondary colluvial deposition (Seager Thomas 1999).

How do these findings compare with those from the Middle Bronze Age settlements of the south-west? The evidence for lowland Cornwall is limited but varied. The houses are wooden and quite 'Wessex-like' in their construction, some with a double internal post-ring (two concentric post-rings that supported the wooden superstructures). Some houses/buildings are quite small, like the one at Gwithian (Megaw 1976), others are in the 7–8 m internal diameter range as at Trevisker (Apsimon and Greenfield 1972) and the smaller buildings at Trethellan Farm (Nowakowski 1991). Yet others, like the three main residential buildings at Trethellan Farm, are substantial, with internal diameters between 8 and 9.5 m, providing areas of 60–70 m^2 (Nowakowski 1991: Table 15).

On the Bodmin Moor and Dartmoor uplands, the main houses are generally comparable in scale to the Wessex Deverel-Rimbury ones, but there is a greater range in size and much more variable settlement patterning. Generally speaking, the Bodmin Moor houses have a 5–8 m diameter, with inner post-rings of c. 4 m diameter (e.g., Mercer 1970: Stannon Down), giving a range of internal space of 20–39 m^2. There are, however, some larger ones, with an interior size range of c. 40–120m^2. On Dartmoor, the most common house form falls within the range of 2–7 m internal diameter, with 35% measuring between 4.5 and 5.5 m (Balaam, Smith, and Wainwright 1982: 241, Fig. 19). However, on both Bodmin Moor and Dartmoor, there is a high ratio of buildings of *less* than 4.5 m diameter compared to houses of greater size, suggesting that many small ancillary non-domestic structures were required. These smaller structures are hardly capable of housing a family and may have been variously, or consecutively, used as dwellings for lone individuals, stores and animal shelters, unroofed rickstands, and shrines.

If we now focus on Leskernick, the larger houses are c. 9–12 m across (outer face) with internal diameters of 6–9 m (inner face of wall), with the potential to house up to eight adults. House 1, the largest of Leskernick's excavated houses, had an internal post ring that measures c. 6 m across and had an internal diameter of 8.5 m. Leskernick's excavated houses suggest that a diverse range of domestic/food processing and industrial activities took place within these buildings. They also have distinct internal zoning indicated by the presence of paved and unpaved areas and artefact-rich versus artefact-bare locations. The range of finds and features suggest that a substantial range of activities took place under one roof. The very limited evidence from Dartmoor suggests something similar – the Dean Moor houses are associated with grain processing, weaving, and perhaps pottery manufacture (Fox 1957). These findings suggest a less extreme spatial separation of activities on a work and gender basis than has been suggested – based on limited evidence – for the Middle Bronze Age south-central British settlements (Burstow and Holleyman 1957; Drewett 1982; Ellison 1978, 1987).

Not only the house sizes, but the settlement forms, too, are more variable. As we have seen at Leskernick, there are both closely associated groups of houses and, within the same settlement, individual large houses set within their own fields; and, as the excavations have shown, there is little to distinguish the use of space in House 39, which forms part of a group of three houses probably not all contemporary, and House 1, which is effectively an isolated structure. Both 'neighbourhood' houses and individual houses are large enough to permit occupation by a permanent household, and the range of activities is in line with the notion of year-round habitation.

Thus far, the comparative evidence suggests that the upland settlements were occupied on a year-round basis. We might even want to see them as more intensively occupied, with larger numbers of people, than the lowland sites. However, as always, any hard and fast differentiation between single scattered farmsteads on the lowlands of south-west and south-central Britain and larger and more nucleated settlements on the south-west uplands needs to treated with caution. Although most of the (relatively limited number of) lowland settlements that have been excavated may conform to the single farmstead pattern, the settlement of Trethallan Farm near Newquay forms a planned settlement of seven round buildings, with residential houses on one side of the site, and ancillary structures on the other (Nowakowski 1991: 188).

House life cycles

Brück (1999) has suggested that the majority of Deverel-Rimbury buildings are short lived and relate to the life cycle of a single household, and she makes a metaphoric connection between personal life cycles, house life cycles, and the pots and tools buried/deposited in the houses at the beginning and end of the life of the house. House biographies are, however, not so uniformly simple across southern Britain. The spread of house dates from several of the Sussex Deverel-Rimbury settlements (Hamilton 2003), such as Black Patch (Needham 1996), Varley Halls (Greig 1977), Mile Oak (Russell 2002), and Downs View (Hamilton 2003; Rudling 2002), suggest that settlements on the South Downs were comparatively long lived. Recent work in lowland east Devon (Haynes Lane) provides another example of a multiphased 'household unit' (Fitzpatrick, Butterworth, and Grove 1999).

Work done on the southwest settlements, both upland and lowland, provides interesting insights into both the commencement and closure of structures. At both Leskernick and on several Dartmoor sites, including Shaugh Moor, there is a repetitive act in the placement of 'everyday objects', particularly quernstones and pounders, in house walls. At other Bronze Age settlements in Cornwall, notably Trethellan Farm (Nowakowski 1991: Ritual Structure 2192) and the recently excavated structure at Callestick, 7 km south-west of Truro (Jones 1998–9), there is a ritual deposition of pottery, sometimes curated pottery sherds, in specific key places. At the other end of the house history, the in-filling or burial of Bronze Age settlements and houses appears to be part of a symbolic act of closure (Nowakowski 1991).

The excavations at Leskernick require that we inject a note of caution into some of these stories of terminal closure. All the excavated structures indicate decay (movement of stones in their sockets, wall-bulging), repair (shoring and buttressing), dereliction (wall tumble), reconfiguration and reoccupation (House 1), and terminal decay (wall collapse, stone robbing, and in-fill via colluvium). Some of the houses from the surface survey appear to have been deliberately shut down through 'slighting'. There is one example of crossed door portals, and there are houses that appear to be filled with cairn-shaped rubble. The excavation of House 1, however, shows that some of these seemingly deliberate acts can be explained in terms of an on-going process of decay, rebuilding, and reuse. Nonetheless, it may well be the case that, once abandoned, the houses become cairn-like – and become, through their transformed profiles, 'houses of the dead'.

The ritual of the everyday and life cycles

A Wessex-orientated view of Bronze Age settlement isolates only three types of buildings on domestic sites: major residential structures, ancillary structures, and animal shelters. Increasingly, excavations of Bronze Age sites in south-west Britain have produced buildings that do not conform to any of these categories. Most particularly they have uncovered buildings *within* settlements that are primarily ritual in nature. Such buildings have been identified at Trethallan Farm (Middle Bronze Age, with, in addition, 'ritual hollows'; Nowakowski 1991), Callestick (Late Bronze Age; Jones 1998–9), and 'House' 23 at Leskernick. Although these buildings and structures vary in their construction, artefact evidence, and patterns of abandonment, they all appear to have been places of ritual, and, as such, and, in contrast to the Deverel-Rimbury traditions further east, they provide loci for everyday rituals within the settlements.

We might link this difference with, on the one hand the creation of *new* settlements on the chalk downlands of central southern Britain, and, on the other, the *continuity* between the locales of upland Middle Bronze Age settlements and earlier ancestral monuments. The downland settlements go hand-in-hand with new patterns of land tenure (Barrett 1994), whereas the upland sites mark places and landscapes of ancestral veneration, communal gatherings, and burials. What is new in these south-westerly contexts is the layering of a ritual cosmology at different scales to bind daily practice into the wider ancestral patterns preset by the form and positioning of the Neolithic and earlier Bronze Age cairns, stone circles, and stone rows.

Upland south-west Britain: cultivators versus pastoralists

The examination of settlements across Bodmin Moor in chapter 17 brought out the variability in house size and form and in settlement patterning. In some areas, there are general scatters of less than 10 houses; in others there are settlements of 40–90 buildings. There are houses with no enclosures (e.g., Catshole Tor), houses with small enclosures (e.g. Brockabarrow Common), house groups on the edge of enclosures or surrounded by them, and individual houses set within fields (e.g., Leskernick). This variability suggests a complex socioeconomic and ritual use of Bodmin Moor that stands in contrast to the more uniform settlement configurations suggested for lowland south-central Britain (though, of course, it would only take one or two new excavations for the picture to change again).

The patterning also seems to be more complex than the one generally suggested for Dartmoor. On Dartmoor, a dichotomy between sites with pounds and sites with enclosures has been emphasised, and, although it is accepted that there were variable combinations, the pounds have been assumed to denote a pastoral economy, the enclosures an agrarian one. These differences have, in turn, been coaxed into a narrative of land degeneration in which cultivators with coaxial field systems are replaced by herders with pounds (Butler 1997a). Once again, the small number of existing excavated sites suggests that this is too simple a story. Shaugh Moor, a classic pound-type site, is traditionally considered to be summer pasture, but has evidence for a number of activities. Each house contained a saddle quern, and there seem to have been two building phases spanning 1600–600 BC. It is only in the second phase that the settlement is reconfigured and visited more sporadically. At the Dean Moor settlement, there is evidence for spinning, corn grinding, and cheese making, and it seems likely that these represent something more substantial than a summer sheepfold.

Land division

The creation of land divisions during the Middle Bronze Age has long been recognised (Curwen 1927; Fox 1954a) and has been associated with an intensification of land-use (Barrett 1994, 1995). Many of the field systems of south-central Britain are coaxial (a system that is laid out systematically on one major axis). For south-western Britain, coaxial systems are predominantly associated with parts of Dartmoor, where reave systems regularly encompass many hundreds of hectares (Silvester 1979: 43). By contrast, in lowland East Devon, the A30 Bronze Age settlements suggest a piecemeal development of field systems (e.g., Patterson's Cross and Castle Hill; Fitzpatrick, Butterworth, and Grove 1999: 216).

There are likewise comparatively few examples of coaxial field systems on Bodmin Moor, although the systems on East Moor (300 ha) and Sharptor are similar to the Dartmoor systems (Johnson and Rose 1994: 63, Fig. 43). Most field systems on the moor are typically curvilinear and accreted, having developed organically out of one or more foci, separated by areas of moorland. The completed systems at Leskernick covered 21 ha and approximates to one or two houses per hectare (Johnson and Rose 1994: 59). Leskernick's systems seem to represent a series of identifiable small holdings that have coalesced to form a block of enclosed land, probably with community grazing on the surrounding open land.

There has been considerable discussion of the relationship between Bronze Age social organisation, land tenure, and land division (Barrett 1995; Johnston 2001). Fleming's social model for Dartmoor's land divisions is based on the different scales at which land division takes place. It recognises social groups at the household and neighbourhood levels. In this model, an upland grazing zone above the contour reave is communally shared by several neighbourhood groups, whereas between the contour and terminal reaves there is more tightly regulated grazing that is divided amongst the occupants of the nearest fields. Below this, there is an area enclosed by the parallel reaves, which he suggests was privately owned by individual households within the neighbourhood groups (Fleming 1978, 1983, 1984, 1988, 1994). In terms of social structure, Fleming suggests that the linchpin is the individual household and that it was at this level of social relations that land tenure was invested.

One issue here is how, if at all, this system relates to preceding traditions of landscape ownership. The planned, coaxial field systems could suggest that land divisions were imposed upon the landscape, implying collaboration between households. However, the ring cairns and large cairns within the Dartmoor systems and the utilisation of skyline cairns by the main reaves (Balaam, Smith and Wainwright 1982: 250) might mean that, at least in part, the system articulated preceding landscape divisions. It might further be suggested that the tradition of boundary building could have rested in occupancy and that the layout of Dartmoor coaxial systems was planned around pre-existing houses and households. But recent investigations indicate that the number of Dartmoor buildings that intersect with axial elements of the coaxial land divisions is quite small (Wickstead in prep). Brück's (2000) examination of the coaxial systems of the Marlborough Downs notes that each time a new settlement was established, it was associated with a new block of fields. This might indicate that, rather than rights to land being invested in individual households, they were held communally by lineage clan or community groups.

Conclusion

Putting together these different parts of the jigsaw puzzle, it seems reasonable to suggest that, first, there was no abrupt colonisation of Bodmin Moor, but rather continuity with what had gone before. There was an attachment to place that long preceded the creation of settlements and enclosures. Second, the settlements were so variable, and so relatively complex that they were most probably occupied all year round. And, third, the moor was in no sense marginal. Within a regional setting, it was, if anything, a focus of activity – mundane and ritual seamlessly intertwined, with the high days and high tors punctuating the social landscape and drawing in people from further afield. In a wider setting, the people of the moor were part of an exchange network that tentacled out across the channel and around the Atlantic seaboard. There was an opening out from the moor towards distant places – people travelled, objects that were never just objects but came with stories and biographies were exchanged, and those who stayed at home were regaled with tales and myths and legends about other places, other people. A child at Leskernick had an intimate topography of place but also a part real, part imagined understanding of a much, much wider landscape.

Chapter Nineteen

Solution Basins
Libations to the Ancestors

When we walk the moors, our eyes lift to the high tors and, at some point or another, it seems important to clamber up the slopes, to stop and to look up at the astonishing rock formations and out across the landscape. Most times, the feeling is of awe and wonderment, of 'uplift'. And it is easy to imagine that other people, over the millennia, have done the same. At Rough Tor and the other high places, people have not just stopped and paused, they have stayed and built monuments. It may be the Bronze Age cairns or walls that encircle the tors, or the enclosures that link tor to tor, or it may be a small medieval chapel, or a Second World War memorial plaque. They left their mark.

It is not hard to imagine our Leskernick people, at special times of year, making their way across the landscape, skirting Brown Willy, to Rough Tor. Driving some of the herd in front of them, bringing food and gifts. Meeting up with other people at the straggling settlement at the south foot of the tor. Talking, laughing, paying their respects, exchanging gossip and gifts, bartering, and the young ones eying each other and wondering …

Then it would be time to prepare for the ceremonies. Perhaps it became very quiet, or perhaps there was music. People would begin to move up the pathway leading to the hill top. Moving away from the sounds and smells and preoccupations of everyday life, moving nearer to the ancestors and the ancestral beings. Moving up the hillside was important: children, wide eyed, walking to the special places for the first time; young initiates watching, listening, learning 'how to'; the older ones remembering other occasions, remembering and giving voice to the stories and memories that made this place *their* place.

Towards the top of the hill, some of the leaders – the people 'with the knowledge' – would suddenly disappear from view, moving behind rocks or into crevices. And, as suddenly, they would reemerge and using the acoustics of overhang or rock funnel send their voices echoing out across the land-scape. Voices, songs, smoke, libation, spiralling – upwards spirals.

Throughout our time on the moor, the tors acted as markers and were integral to the stories that we were telling. Towards the end of the project, as we fanned out across the moor, we stumbled upon another, small dimension to the high places, an additional source of wonderment and magic – the solu-tion basins.

The Solution Basins

We were not, of course, the first to have noted them (Figure 19.1). For example, the antiquarian William Borlase commented on them in 1754. But we were the first to systematically search for and record them. We did not particularly intend to do this. We found one, two, three – and then it seemed important to start looking more intensively and widely.

CT (9 June 1999): From the weather forecast it appears that at long last we will have a nice day so we decide to finish Brown Willy. … On the way, we stop to show Jeremy the solution hollows in the tabular blocks on the lower part of the Brown Willy ridge. They are full of water. I scoop some out in my thermos mug and drink and then offer a libation to Henry. The symbolic power of solution hollows as hidden containers for water, blood, offerings hidden on the top of the stones suddenly strikes me. And how would they have explained them in the Bronze Age? Wonder whether all the really important tors on the moor have them. Rough Tor yes. Stowe's Pound: don't know. Tregarrick Tor yes. Wayne says there are three hidden on the top of Showery Tor. How marvellous. None at Leskernick apart from a propped stone in the corridor that must have been taken from elsewhere. When Wayne and I had started the survey of Brown Willy I had noticed a broken edge on one of the stones with a solution hollow in it. I had later dreamt that it was this stone that must have been taken to Leskernick. It would be wonderful to measure the edges and find that it fitted! Must check at Catshole for them and indeed all over the moor. I'm surprised that I have not thought about solution hollows much before or fully appreciated the power and mystery they must have held. I suppose it is because there are none in the stones at Leskernick.

fig.19:1 Solution hollows at a) Rough Tor, b) Stowe's Pond; c) Rough Tor – photo J. Balfour Paul.

a

b

c

The formation of solution basins

The solution basins are a product of normal weathering processes on the granite in Cornwall. They form on the highest rock stacks of Bodmin Moor. They are the result of the chemical solution of the rock surface when water collects in small irregularities, and they always occur in the hardest granite blocks where there is an absence of jointing or cracks. Gradually, through many thousands of years, a small hollow becomes progressively enlarged and deepened and as the matrix of the granite dissolves, crystals of quartz are deposited and form a glistening layer at the bottom of the basin.

Solution basins come in a variety of different forms. Some are almost perfectly circular; others are oval. They can be up to 1 m in diameter and 50 cm deep. Some may even have the size and dimensions of a shallow bath. Often they erode into each other, forming an irregular chain of basins, or, occasionally, on a thin slab, the basin may erode through completely forming a holed stone. Some hollows are permanently filled with water; other, shallower examples dry up during the hot summer weather. Sometimes, where there are solution hollows on both the highest and second highest stone of a rock stack, the water runs down from one to another. Today, buzzards, the wheeling birds of the high moor, frequently perch on the edge of the hollows and drink from them during dry spells.

The fantastic scalloped profiles of some of the high tors are, in part, created by eroded solution basins. Their interconnected shapes can appear quite monstrous and fantastic. The most famous example, known as King Arthur's Bed, is found on a series of rock stacks to the west of Trewortha Tor. Here, a series of interconnected rock basins takes the shape and size of a human figure.

For these basins to form, there has to be a flat-topped, or almost flat-topped block. Because – with rare exceptions – these only occur on the tops of the very highest tors, the basins are invisible from below. They come as a revelation. One moment you are clambering up the tor, the next you come upon this perfect circle of water – sometimes very calm with the shadows of clouds chasing across the surface, other times wind lashed and turbulent.

On Bodmin Moor

We have found solution hollows on 20 of the 38 principal hills. They are absent on hills lacking major rock outcrops, but they are also sometimes absent from ones where there are outcropping rocks, for example Sharp Tor, Louden Hill, Alex Tor, Colvannick Tor, and Newel Tor. The greatest number occur on the rock stacks of the Rough Tor summit area where there are over 30. There are also numerous solution basins (from 15 to over 20 examples) on the rock stacks comprising Garrow Tor, Bearah Tor, Kilmar Tor, Trewortha Tor, and Stowe's Hill.

Prehistoric associations

In 1754, the Rev. William Borlase, founder of Cornish archaeology, discussed the meaning of peculiarly weathered rock stacks, logan or rocking stones, and solutions basins to prehistoric people (Borlase 1973 [1754]). His work has subsequently been ignored or ridiculed by later generations of more empirically minded archaeologists. Borlase remarked on the fantastic forms of particular tors such as the Cheesewring and argued that they must have been sites of worship and places where Druidic orators made pronouncements. He noted that, often, on the great weathered tors and the rocking stones there were basins, and because they were so regular in size and shape he assumed that they had been carved by prehistoric people (Borlase 1973 [1754]: 241–42). Dismissing fanciful arguments that they might be used for collecting salt from sea water, or grinding ore for tin, or that they might have deities erected in them, or be places of sacrifice or where sacrificial fires were lit, he interpreted them as being connected with the purifying qualities of water: 'The purest of all water is that which comes from the Heavens, in Snow, rain or Dew; and of this the Ancients were not ignorant' (Borlase 1973 [1754]: 248).

The solution hollows, he said, were designed to collect this purest of water undefiled by contact with the ground. The interconnecting channels between the solution basins found on some rocks were designed to funnel this special water from the sky into collecting vessels placed below their lips (Borlase 1973 [1754]: 255). The more basins that were carved, the more sacred water could be collected:

> For catching the Rain and Snow, the little Walls, or Partitions betwixt the Basons, are as necessary as the Mountains on the surface of the earth ... for these [the rain and the snow] fall not perpendicularly, but are driven in an inclined direction, and are therefore very artfully intercepted by these screens which at once stop the rain as it drives, and shelter it from being blown out of the Basons when the Wind is tempestuous. (Borlase 1973 [1754]: 256)

Borlase noted the hidden character of the rock basins on the very highest rock stacks and invisible from below:

> From these basons perhaps, on solemn occasions, the officiating Druid, standing on an eminence, sanctified the congregation with a more than ordinarily precios [*sic*] lustration, before he expounded to them, or prayed for them, or gave forth his decisions. ... To these more private basons, during the time of libation, the priest might have recourse, and be at liberty to judge by the quantity, colour, motion and other appearances in the water, of future events, of dubious cases, without danger of contradiction from the people below. (Borlase 1973 [1754]: 257)

He also suggested that the water in the basins might have been mixed with mistletoe, oak leaves, or other substances and that the rocking motion of logan stones could be used to agitate the contents of the basins. Shorn of the references to Druids and the idea that these basins were carved by people, Borlase's interpretations of the potential symbolic significance and use of the solution basins seem very plausible. Indeed, the prehistoric populations may have shared Borlase's view that they were carved, but by ancestral rather than human beings. The use in libations and ceremonies of the purest water of all, that which falls from the sky, seems entirely credible.

During the Neolithic, when the first permanent stone monuments were constructed on Bodmin Moor, two of the three long cairns that were built were closely associated with rocks with solution hollows. The long axis of the Bearah Tor long cairn in the south-east of the moor is orientated directly up to a series of rock stacks with the most fantastic shapes and with more solution basins than anywhere else along the tor. The Louden long cairn, positioned between and beneath Louden Hill and Rough Tor, is situated directly below the western rock stacks of the Rough Tor summit area and honeycombed with solution basins. A short distance to the north east of the long cairn there is a large isolated grounder resting on an area of exposed granite bedrock. On the surface of the grounder are well-developed solution basins. This is one of only two examples known to us of solution basins occurring on low ground. The proximity of the long cairn to this stone seems likely to have been significant.

Trevethy Quoit is one of the best-preserved Neolithic dolmens in Britain. Located just a few kilometres to the south-east of the moor, it has a peculiar hole in the capstone just above the entrance to the burial chamber. As we suggested earlier (p. 415), this slab may well have been brought to Trevethy from one of the high tors, and the hole is probably a solution basin that has eroded through. It is worth noting that all known examples of solution basins that have eroded into rounded holes are found in the south-east part of the moor.

The hilltop enclosure on the southern end of Stowe's Hill, of probable Neolithic date, both links up and surrounds a series of dramatic rock stacks with well-developed solution basins.[1]

During the Bronze Age, the evidence for the symbolic and ritual significance of solution hollows is even more unequivocal.

On East Moor, a particularly prominent Bronze Age cairn, known as Clitters Cairn, is sited right next to an exposed stone, 4 m long and 1.5 m wide, with three well-developed solution basins on its surface. This is the only other known example of such basins occurring anywhere other than on the high tors. The possibility remains that this stone was actually brought here and placed beside the cairn. The nearest source would be Fox Tor, 1.5 km to the west, on which today only one solution basin occurs on a fallen slab near to the highest point.

On Bearah Tor, there is a tor cairn at the eastern end of the long linear series of rock outcrops and there are well-developed solution basins on rocks immediately to the west of the cairn.

The summit cairns on Rough Tor are right next to rock stacks riddled with solution hollows. Showery Tor, surrounded by the largest and most massive ring cairn on Bodmin Moor, has three solution basins on the uppermost stone.

In all these cases, the solution hollows are not visible from below, and the cairn material would restrict access both to them and the rock stack. At Tregarrick Tor, an isolated rock stack to the south of the main tor, with no solution basins on it, is surrounded by a series of six orthostats on its southern side. These orthostats define a space for ceremonies below the main rock stack, the top of which is riddled with solution hollows.

Conclusion

Although Leskernick is a very stony hill, there are no solution basins. With one exception: there is a stone with a solution basin propped up in the corridor leading to the top of the hill between the southern and western settlement areas (see p. 188). Again, this stone may well have been brought here from elsewhere. There are no solution basins on Codda Tor and only an isolated example at Elephant Rock on the Beacon; it would, therefore, most probably have come from Brown Willy or Rough Tor.

The people who lived on Bodmin Moor during the Neolithic and Bronze Ages must have wondered and marvelled at the strange form of these basins and must have read meaning and significance into them. As amongst the Australian Aborigines, such stones may have been understood to be the frozen representations of ancestral forms, or places where they rested or slept. It seems likely that they were used for libations and ceremonies. Their hidden and secretive nature on top of the very highest rock stacks would make them ideal contexts for initiation rites. Their association with the high tors and with the high-flying birds of the heavens, hawks, and eagles, would have given them an added symbolic power and significance, as would the quartz crystals found within them. We know that this gleaming, shiny substance was charged with ritual powers, for crystals were regularly deposited in cairns along with other grave-goods for the dead.

> For us, the solution hollows were particularly moving: within the hardness of the granite they cradled water, they were intimate, full of gentle movement and hidden depth and invited an action of scooping or touching. Sometimes we filled them with white and red liquids, offering our own libations, our thanks, to the ancestors.

Table 19.1 The Solution Basins of Bodmin Moor

These are the hills and tors of Bodmin Moor. These are the heights, types of rock outcrops (of major, lesser or only local significance), and the numbers of solution basins that occur on the main rock stacks.

Tor or Hill	Height (in meters)	Rock Outcrops	Solution Basins
Buttern Hill	436	None	—
Bray Down	346	None	—
Carne Down	297	None	—
Rough Tor	400	Major	20+
Brown Willy	420	Major	6
Leskernick	329	Local	1
Trwint	304	Local	—
the Beacon	369	Local	8: all on Elephant Rock
Codda	318	Major	—
Catshole	346	Lesser	6
Tolborough	348	Local	—
Butters	316	None	—
Garrow	330	Major	15+
Carkees	281	Lesser	2
Hawk's Tor (West)	307	Major	2
Hawk's Tor (East)	329	Major	6
Colvannick	260	Lesser	—
St Bellarmin's	268	Lesser	1

Tor or Hill	Height (in meters)	Rock Outcrops	Solution Basins
Carburrow	270	Local	—
Brown Gelly	342	Local	1
Carneglos	320	Local	3
Fox	323	Major	1
Hill	324	Lesser	2
Newel	346	Lesser	—
Caradon	371	Local	—
Stowe's Hill	363	Major	15
Sharp Tor	378	Major	5: all on stack to west of summit
Bearah	367	Major	20+
Kilmar	390	Major	15+
Trewortha	318	Major	15+
Tregarrick	310	Major	6+
Smallacoombe	330	Local	—
Louden Hill	315	Local	—
Alex	291	Major	—
Carey	290	Lesser	10+
Carbilly	260	Lesser	— (Quarrying may have destroyed some)

Notes

Chapter 1

1.1.   In the early nineties, the discussion of ritual tended to circle around 'ritual sites' – cemeteries, mega-lithic monuments, enclosures, henges, and ceremonial ways (Barrett 1994; Bender 1992, 1993; Hodder 1990; Thomas 1991; Tilley 1993, 1994). Domestic sites tended to be neglected, though Ian Hodder's work on the significance of house spaces in prehistoric Europe, and Colin Richard's work on Orkney were notable exceptions (Hodder 1984, 1990; Richards 1993). A paper on the importance of domestic ritual was presented by B Bender and M Edmonds at the Prehistoric Society Conference held in Dublin in 1995. The similarity between some of the points made in the Introduction to the present volume and those in the Introduction to Mark Edmond's *Ancestral Geographies* (1999) is entirely intentional!

1.2.   Before we started work, we also needed to get permission from the Commoners of Bodmin Moor. Again, with great good fortune, we met no opposition.

1.3.   In this chapter, the diary quotes are mainly limited to those of the three directors. In later chapters, as students began to keep diaries, the voices proliferate.

1.4.   Full details of the excavations, field surveying, and environmental work will be presented in a forth-coming volume (Hamilton and Seager Thomas in prep).

1.5.   In truth, we found two horseshoes – one by the excavated boundary entrance upslope of House 39 and one outside 'House' 23. Both were quite chunky and under several centimetres of peat and could be medieval or later. It is interesting that this metal survives as it makes the possibility of prehistoric metalworking surviving more likely.

1.6.   Mike has since earned his doctorate and taken up a lectureship in Adelaide, Australia.

1.7.   At the time, Paul Basu was a PhD student in the Department of Anthropology at UCL. He is now a lecturer at the University of Sussex.

1.8.   Radiocarbon dates from nine round cairns on Bodmin Moor range between 2450 and 1550 cal. BC (Christie 1988 – recalibrated using Pearson and Stuiver 1986). We presume the Leskernick cairns fall within the same time period.

1.9.   Butler (1994: 1, Fig. 44) has suggested a similar change from houses of the living to the dead at some of the Bronze Age settlements on Dartmoor.

1.10.   This 'cairn' is probably not a prehistoric structure (but see also note 4.4 below).

1.11.   Only two stone circles and no stone rows on Bodmin Moor have been excavated. When we start-ed work at Leskernick there were still no radiocarbon dates or other datable finds. Based on dates obtained in other parts of Britain, the Bodmin stone circles and rows were dated to the end of the Neolithic or the beginning of the Bronze Age (Barnatt 1980, 1982, 1989; Burl 1976, 1993; Miles 1975: 10–12). Our radiocarbon dates for the North Stone Circle suggest an Early Bronze Age dating for the Leskernick complex of stone row and two stone circles (see Table 1.1, chapter 1).

Chapter 2

2.1.   Bodmin Moor was once much more extensive. 'From a coherent block c. 230 square km in the early 19th century, the moor has been reduced to 95 km, broken up into many discrete blocks' (Johnson and Rose 1994: xi); 'Bodmin Moor is now a mere 41% of the 1800 total' (Johnson 1983: 9, Fig. 4; Johnson and Rose 1994: 4).

2.2.   Bodmin Moor was never actually covered by the Pleistocene ice sheets, but lay to the south of them and was affected by them. The Pleistocene (Ice Age) begins up to 2 million years ago, but humans were sporadically present in Britain only from c. 500,000 years ago. In Britain, the effects of the Pleistocene end c. 12,000 years ago.

2.3.   The fact that the medieval 'squatters' recognised the ruined Bronze Age houses of Leskernick is suggested by Leskernick's medieval Cornish name: *lys* ('court') *carn ek* (*ek* is the adjective for 'rock') (Padel 1985). Thus, a rocky court.

2.4.   These straddle stones supported the wooden house frames or posts to stop them from rotting and to raise grain supplies off the ground, making it harder for rats, mice, and the like to get in.

2.5.   Almost all the stone quarries have fallen silent, except the historic De Lank Dimension stone pit and the smaller concerns at Bearah and Notter Tors. Only one china-clay pit, at Stannon, remains operational.

2.6.   Pollen work at Rough Tor suggests that in this area of the moor the hazel had almost entirely disappeared from the higher hillsides by the Bronze Age, and that the flora associated with a pastoral landscape had established itself (Gearey et al. 2000: 503–4).

2.7.   However, two small tracts of peat unrestricted to valley bottoms dating to prehistoric times were found to the east of Dozmary Pool (Brown 1977).

2.8.   Excavations at Garrow in St Breward show that Iron Age people used some Bronze Age houses as shelters.

Chapter 3

3.1.   See our first publication – Bender, Hamilton, and Tilley 1997 – for a more detailed account of our confusion.

3.2.   See Gell 1985.

3.3.   Norman Quinnell very kindly gave us a copy of this hand-drawn overlay.

3.4.   Dave Hooley works for English Heritage covering south-west England. He has been an invaluable source of help and information. During the 1997 season, he very kindly offered his services for a few days.

3.5.   Lynchets result from the downslope movement of ploughed soil. A positive lynchet comprises the bank formed by soil collecting against the boundary (hedge, fence, or wall) at the bottom of the field. The loss of soil from the top end of the field produces a 'step' called a negative lynchet.

3.6.   From the Cornish Archaeological Unit.

3.7.   Pete Herring has written an excellent introduction to the methods used, chronologies enabled, and nomenclature standardised through the examination of stone-built field systems – abutments, entrances, stone piles, and so on (Herring 1986).

Chapter 4

4.1.   Much later, this pool is associated with many Arthurian and earlier legends. Supposedly, a giant chieftain who bade his daughters slay their husbands on their marriage night had his hunting grounds nearby. And this is also supposedly the pool into which Arthur's sword Excalibur was thrown – and a hand came out of the water and drew it down to the bottomless depths.

4.2.   Pete Herring suggests that, for the people involved in creating the Propped Stone, the tabular outcrop on which it rests might have been perceived as a small crested tor (pers. comm., February 2004).

4.3.   The RCHME is the Royal Commission on the Historical Monuments (of England). Their record is the National Monuments Record (NMR).

4.4.   Indeed, Pete Herring has queried our 'closure'. He notes that, contrary to the findings of the RCHME survey, the centre and south-west side of the mound have *not* been removed to ground level but, rather, to about 0.5 m above ground level, and that the mound is made of stones as well as peat. Having made a careful study of tinners' pits across Bodmin Moor, he believes that, although the mound may have been robbed or disturbed by tinners' activities, it was not *created* by them. He also points out that there are other occasional examples of low-lying great cairns – for example, at Louden and Rough Tor – and that, significantly, when approached from the north-north-east along the valley between Bray and Carne Downs the mound below Leskernick is indeed sky-lined (Pete Herring pers. com., February 2004). Another element in his argument is that the north circle, the mound, and the Propped Stone are all in line (Herring 1997).

4.5.   See Hamilton and Seager Thomas (in prep).

4.6.   The significance of the two highest points on Bodmin Moor, Brown Willy and Rough Tor, is underlined by the fact that both are visible from 10 of the circles (63%). The importance of sightings to the tor in the location of stone circles was already noted in 1895 when Lewis remarked: '*I see no escape from the conclusion that each of these circles was placed in the exact spot that it occupies, because that spot was in a certain direction from the hills I have mentioned*'. He noted, too, that given the salience of Rough Tor in the siting of the circles, it '*may be considered to be the sacred hill of East Cornwall*' (Lewis 1895–98: 111, 112).

4.7.   As so often, Pete Herring offers a cautionary note. He points out that the excavations did not extend to include both ends of the stone. The possibility still remains that a hole had been dug at one or other end and that the stone did at one time stand upright (pers. com., February 2004).

SH: Fair observation! Of course, we will never be sure of the absence of a stone-hole for Pete's possible monolith without a complete excavation of the circle. However, what we can say is that if there was a stone-hole for the setting up of the whalestone, and if the stone is indeed in a 'fallen' position, then the hole would have to be far enough from one of either end of the stone so as not to be undermined by the whalestone quarry hole. This means it would have had to be within at least 9 m of the circumference of the circle (and, indeed, perhaps even closer to the circumference), thus making it distinctly off-centre within the c. 23 m diameter circle.

Chapter 5

5.1.   As the careful reader will note, this version of events runs somewhat counter to that suggested by the archaeologists in this chapter – that puts House 40 as the founder house, with Houses 39 and 38 coming later and being roughly contemporary.

5.2.   The radiocarbon dates put House 40 on the border of Early/Middle Bronze Age and House 39 in the Middle Bronze Age. These are fairly meaningless distinctions.

5.3.   For anthropologists, the words 'enclave' or, in the context of the western settlement, 'compound', evoke ethnographic pictures of spaces of more intensive domestic activity. But for nonanthropologists, both words may be uncomfortable:

Pete Herring (pers. comm., 12 April 1999): Compound, to me at least, imposes feelings of negativity. Why, I don't know. I imagine high wire fences keeping

> *people in against their will, like prison yards, or high wire fences keeping people out, like factories. Don't you feel the same? It's odd that since you and Chris have been using compound for the main enclosure in the western settlement I've felt less affection for it. Enclave for the eastern three houses is also disturbing. I think of Berlin before the wall came down. … Feelings of domination and oppression seep out of the word. The change, c. 15 years ago, from hut circle to round houses adopted from Andrew Fleming has significantly altered perceptions of prehistoric settlements. Compound and enclave seem so modern and depressing that, for me at least, it projects worries and sadnesses back onto the people we are studying.*

5.4. It is possible that a rough incomplete 'circle' of larger stones marks the outer perimeter of the cairn, in which case the upright is within the cairn. The larger circle is 4.90 m in diameter.

5.5. There is an additional 'house' – 'House' 36 – that is off centre and is probably not a domestic dwelling.

5.6. We vacillated between using the word 'field' and the word 'enclosure'. Most of the time we used the word 'enclosure' because, as Pete Herring put it, it is 'a remarkably neutral/descriptive word with a lot of meaning driven out of it' (pers. comm., 12 April 1999).

5.7. This sense of using 'natural' markers of space was perpetuated in the medieval grazing of the moor: 'The boundaries of the common land could be marked by well-known points in the landscape such as prehistoric monuments or natural stones rather than actual fences or ditches' (Altenberg 1999: 27).

5.8. Pete Herring protests:

> *(Herring, pers. comm., 12 April 1999): Work on other highland British transhumance [as well as the Irish evidence] indicates that most essentials, at most periods were similar, including the employment of young women in the summer grazings. It's not just romantic, it's probably true, and gives women a strong role in Cornish prehistory. It also provides a good starting point for modelling prehistoric transhumance, and again placing young women at its heart.*

5.9. However, the old land surfaces were implied by the position and orientation of the structural stones lying on top of them. So it was possible to determine where the surface had originally been, which was important because it showed that the walls were built on a preexisting land-surface rather than being dug into the ground (Hamilton and Seager Thomas in prep).

5.10. We have thrown out a third possibility, which is that the houses were built and occupied by some small part of a community – by herdspeople bringing their animals to pasture on and around the hill. We think it unlikely that herdspeople moving on a seasonal basis away from the main community would invest in such large and solid houses and would create such a proliferation of ritual settings. Seasonal pasturage of animals is well attested back to the 14th century AD on Dartmoor (Fogwill 1954), and Herring (1996) has made a case for the use of the moor for transhumance in Romano-British and early medieval times on the basis of place-name evidence and the morphology of several groups of small subrectangular huts, including, he would now add, many at Leskernick. But all these later dwellings associated with high pasture transhumance are fairly mean and make-do places – the sort of shelter that individual shepherds might build.

5.11. We have not said much about tin working. Given that British tin is only found in Devon and Cornwall, its possible exploitation at Leskernick would have provided its inhabitants with a valuable resource. It is generally assumed, in the absence of other evidence, that it was alluvial tin extracted from the streams that was being exploited. We discuss further the possible range of available tin in chapter 7.

Chapter 6

6.1. In many other houses, the floor 'seems' to be levelled, but, again, excavation casts doubt on this. All the excavated houses had sloping floors, but what had happened was that the collapse of the walls created barriers against which sediments accumulated and thereafter development of peat on these surfaces created the *impression* of a terrace.

6.2. One of these circular platform areas, Structure 22, is filled with larger and smaller slabs except for a small clear area just inside the doorway. This may have been a house platform that was later transformed into a cairn.

6.3. House 13 is almost certainly a much later structure created through the destruction and robbing of orthostats from House 12.

6.4. Internal diameters 5.7 x 4.5 m; c. 4 m; 3.6 m x 4.2 m; 4.5 m; c. 5 m respectively.

6.5. Structure 8 is a small oval structure (c. 3.5 m diameter) of single-wall construction. Structure 19 is a small triangular structure, c. 3 m in diameter, made up of small stones. Pete Herring would interpret these and several other houses as later transhumant dwellings. Thus, for example, the structures to the east and west of House 8, House 10 and possibly 16, and Houses 9 and 17 may have been reused by transhumant herders.

6.6. A cairn built around a grounder and with a rough kerb was built into this wall, and there is another cairn in the southern wall. A small, rough circular structure up against wall 5 may well be a later transhumant dwelling.

6.7. Or – Pete Herring's transhumance hypothesis once more – it might be a much later structure.

Chapter 7

7.1. The other small structure, 19, up against the east side of the compound, is triangular in shape, seems to lack a doorway and may also be a robbed-out cairn.

7.2. Recent rescue excavations at Stannon Down (Jones 1998–99, 2001) provide additional insight into the morphology of house/cairn structures. There were four structures that bore a superficial similarity to ones interpreted elsewhere on the moor as roundhouses. On excavation, three, at least, appeared to the excavator to be ring cairns. This is further discussed in Hamilton and Seager Thomas (in prep).

7.3. In all, 15 struck flints, c. 1,000 pieces of struck quartz, 31 pieces of slate, three pounders and two fragments from pounders, and nine body sherds and two base sherds were found.

7.4. A flint edge has a more sinuous edge than a metal blade and would therefore cut a broader groove.

7.5. Quartz occurs naturally on Bodmin Moor in crystal form as part of the granite, or, quite frequently, as veins intruded into the granite. These veins may include cassiterite. When the granite breaks down, the resulting detritus – including any cassiterite present – may either remain *in situ* or be transported downhill. *In situ* 'detrital' cassiterite is known as 'eluvial cassiterite'; redeposited detrital cassiterate is known as alluvial. Historically, cassiterite from all three sources has been exploited. Cassiterite in the granite is mined; eluvial and alluvial cassiterite are streamed (Craddock 1995; Penhallurick 1987).

7.6. The third enclosure would be to the east of enclosure EN7. The remains of a possible wall run from the cairn at the corner of C2 in a south-west direction.

7.7. Later we abandoned this interpretation and assumed that the pile was the result of house or cairn robbing and tumble.

7.8. Pete Herring tells this bit of the story somewhat differently:

Herring (pers. comm., 4 December 1999): I see the equivocal ground evidence differently and have a different story as a result. It means losing the droveway, which is a great shame to a 'functionalist' like me as I would love to see herds being driven down it to the open pastures beyond …
I see SJ and SO as one enclosure, attached to SP and thus quite late,

*but with an east side which curves past House 44 (contemporary) and ends
on House 32. I then have the south wall of SF attached to this, and then SK
attached to SF, leaving the 'drove-way', with its clitter an obstacle to animals,
blocked at its north end. The south wall of SJ includes the southern blocking
of the drove-way whose west wall will have been robbed to leave the flimsy line
we see today. The south wall of SJ seems to me to ride over the abandoned
House 44, and SJ is then the product of a retraction, and one of the very last
enclosures in the system.*

7.9.   North slab of cist 45 x 60 x 12 cm, south slab 60 x 75 x 25 cm, and west slab 45 x 149 x 25 cm. The cap-stone lies close by – 180 x 120 x 15 cm.

Chapter 9

9.1.   A version of this chapter appeared in the *Journal of Material Culture* (Tilley et al. 2000).

9.2.   Stephan Harrison: School of Geography and the Environment, Oxford University; Ed Anderson: Bede College, Stockton.

9.3.   In the context of this paper, 'clast' means 'stone'.

9.4.   Sue (January 2003):

*'Leskernick Hill appears to be circular' – these are somewhat 'weasel words'
– Leskernick Hill is oval. Of course, this is what we know today from the
plan, but the Bronze Age people must have known it took longer to walk over
it one way than the other! ... I personally always see Leskernick as a giant
whalestone, especially when viewing it sitting at Codda or on Brown Willy'.*

Chapter 10

10.1.   It also needs to be stressed that there are many different sociologies in terms of both the theories and methods that can and have been applied to the investigation of archaeology. These approaches include – in no particular order – those derived from the application of theories of political-economy (Carman 1993; Shanks and McGuire 1996), cultural studies (Shanks 1992), postmodernism (Hodder 1997), feminism (Evans 1990; Gero 1985, 1994, 1996), ethnomethodology (Gero 1996), management studies (Cooper et al. 1995), semiotics (Edgeworth 1990), aesthetic theory (Meredith 1990), relativism (Lampeter Archaeology Workshop 1997, 1998), the sociology of science (Jones 1991; Thomas 1991), critical theory (Graves 1991), identity and ethnicity (Rowlands 1994), social anthropology (Shankland 1996), and heritage management (Carman 1991). This is not an exhaustive bibliography, but it illustrates the potential range of approaches that might be drawn upon to examine the social contexts within which archaeology is situated and in which archaeologists work.

10.2.   Anthony Grafton comments that 'Footnotes – since they come from this belief in verifiability – work very well in post-modernity, as a way of producing a text which is constantly cycling around and subverting itself' (quoted in Jackson 1999: 157–59). The use of diary excerpts in footnotes, text that is simultaneously the supplement and foundation of the 'main' text, seems a good way to create a sort of 'dialogical text' (Clifford and Marcus 1986: 1–26). Clifford suggests that such a dialogical approach obliges writers to find diverse ways of rendering negotiated realities as multi-subjective, power-laden, and incongruent. In this view, 'culture' is always relational, an inscription of communicative processes that exist, historically, *between* subjects in relations of power. Such an approach is essential to our concern with understanding how authority is manifested in the Leskernick Project and has had a practical influence upon our own writing as we have tried to decide which diary excerpts to include and exclude when faced with the often candid remarks of the project participants.

Chapter 11

11.1. Brief details describing who each person is are included when they are mentioned for the first time. I have used only a brief selection of extracts to illustrate my argument for reasons of length; many more quotations of relevance could have been included.

11.2. Several recent texts have used the metaphor of reading to describe the process of archaeological interpretation (e.g., Hodder 1986; Tilley 1990), but less attention has been paid to the role of texts in the actual practice of archaeological fieldwork.

11.3. It needs to be stressed that this discussion of archaeological practice is primarily about practice within an academic context. For archaeologists working in the commercial sector, although texts are important, other abilities, such as management skills, carry considerable weight.

11.4. Interviewed, 16 October 1997. Unless otherwise indicated, Chris refers to Chris Tilley.

11.5. A point noted by Tony Williams (10 June 1997).

11.6. Unless otherwise stated, 'Mike' refers to one of the excavation supervisors (Mike ST) rather than the chapter author.

11.7. Some fieldwork projects continue to display formal organisational characteristics derived from earlier historically situated practices – reflecting, for example, the military background of many pioneers of British field archaeology (Locock 1995; MacAdam 1995).

11.8. Some archaeologists had worked in the commercial sector and commented on the differences:

> (Fieldnotes, 24 May 1997): Both [archaeologists] believe that there is an academic and excavator split. Based around the fact that the academic can work, they reckon, without the pressures of the 'real world' impinging whereas the diggers are battling with life amongst the developers and bureaucracy. Especially the latter.

11.9. This point was questioned by Barbara who believed that this was true for some but not all of the archaeological supervisors. The fact that some of their undergraduate and graduate dissertation work was very phenomenological and in line with the theoretical position of the survey directors' own work could, she suggested, be seen as an exception to this distinction. I would argue, however, that this proves rather than disproves the argument presented here. The horizontal distinction discussed here pertains specifically to the liminal moment of fieldwork. Beyond this moment, back in the academy, hierarchy once again becomes the dominant factor structuring relations between students and lecturers. Text-based, intellectual capital becomes the key factor mediating these relationships and it is therefore not surprising that some students who were excavation supervisors might seek to ally themselves with the ideological position of lecturers with whom they have some familiarity.

11.10. Note the conjunction of space (*field*) and time (*season*) in this term.

11.11. The similarity of this diagram to that used by Evans-Pritchard (1940) to illustrate Nuer representations of space is intended.

11.12. An ironic situation, given that in the eyes of some of the Cornish and local residents it was the project participants 'from London' who were the outsiders (see discussion on the Leskernick website). This point was recognised by one of the survey supervisors:

> *Henry (12 June 1997): [Peter, a professional archaeologist and specialist advisor to the project] spoke about the pride locals have in their past. He mentioned how 'Cornish knowledge' is often listened to more than 'outsider' knowledge. Peter was pleased that we wanted to make an effort in making the project open to visitors and in taking on board some of the local knowledge of Leskernick. But I couldn't help thinking that he was also subtly reminding me that we are very much outsiders and, perhaps, [viewed] with a certain degree of scepticism by the local archaeological community. One wonders what sort of discourse goes on about our project between all the local 'keepers' of archaeological knowledge. ...*

11.13. Sue excused Mike's actions by pointing out that 'he pisses in each of his trenches when they are completed as a formal act of farewell'. 'He tends to mark his territory in the same way when out walking', she added (interview 14 October 1998).

11.14. Prior to the incident, Barbara had made the following diary entry:

> *(Barbara, 10 June 1997): Tony says that Mike won't take part in any of the questionnaires. It seems to me that he's terrified of being sucked into something in which he might give away things unintentionally. He needs to defend himself, to control what we know (or don't know) about him.*

11.15. A second analysis of the fieldwork context here described is provided by Wilmore (2006).

Chapter 13

13.1. A longer version of this chapter, including a section on Environmental Art, was published in (Tilley, Hamilton, and Bender (2000).

13.2. This mimicking of land-form does not seem to be found at Leskernick. However, it does occur elsewhere. As far as we know, it has not previously been remarked that the shaped top of the standing stone at Long Meg and Her Daughters in Cumbria directly mimics the two breast-like hills of Knock Pike and Dufton Pike that lie beyond it below the ridge skyline. Equally, at Casterigg, also in Cumbria, a stone on the north side of the circle seems to directly mirror the hill behind. Because this is a natural boulder, we thought it might simply have been chosen for its shape. Closer inspection showed that, in fact, the top of the stone had been roughly flaked to create the required contour.

13.3. Tomato juice and milk were poured into solution hollows.

Chapter 14

14.1. We won't, at this point, discuss the meaning of 'community', but will return to this question.

14.2. BB: Barbara Bender; SH: Sue Hamilton: WB: Wayne Bennett; TW: Tony Williams; HB: Henry Broughton; PL: Patrick Laviolette.

14.3. CT: Chris Tilley; J S-D: Jeremy Stafford-Deitsch; FS: Fay Stevens; LS: Lesley Smith; AR: Ash Rennie; PB: Paul Basu.

14.4. TAG = Theoretical Archaeology Group.

14.5. Later, it came out that HB had had reservations, but for different reasons. 'It was always important for me that it looked professional. … That's why I had this problem with lots of kids' drawings and the model and things, because although it's nice … I wanted it to look slick and professional' (HB talking to BB, 20 June 1999).

14.6. The only exception was the Friends of Lawrence House Museum, which kindly donated £70.

14.7. We are very grateful to the following contributors: the Anthropology Departmental Fund, the Dean's Travel Grant, and the UCL Friends Programme.

14.8. Most of the time, the group consisted of BB, SH, CT, HB, GA (Gary Armstrong), FS, LS, J S-D, and AR. PB came to some of the earlier meetings.

14.9. This was less true for the sociological chapters, although even with these many of the parameters were set in advance by the directors.

14.10. TW made longer comments but they, alas, arrived too late to be included.

14.11. For at least one visitor, this lack of authorship was confusing. She recognised that some texts were written by one of the three directors, but who were the others written by?

14.12. These comments echo ones made in chapter 13, about whether we should do the artwork ourselves or work with artists.

14.13. There may also have been a small technical problem – one or two murmured that they'd have to go home for their 'specs – but they didn't come back.

14.14. Thus, T(anya), one of the archaeological students, noted that whilst two local visitors stayed an hour and a half, one visitor from away stayed 10 minutes, and a couple with two children stayed five.

14.15. This particular incomer didn't go round the exhibition at all. She brought the poem (her passport), and then sat down and launched into a diatribe against the … the village … the ramblers … the Commoners …

14.16. Over one particular week when we checked the leaflet containers quite carefully, 215 leaflets were taken. The Wilderness and Art leaflets scored marginally the highest (20, 19); this was followed by Surveying (17), Turf Cutting (16), House 39 (16); The Corridor (16); Abandoned Landscapes (15), Being on the Hill (15), Enclosures (15), Reconstructing Bronze Age Houses (14), The Public (14), Excavation (13), Working Landscapes (13), and Small Scale Societies (12).

14.17. The local versus incomer issue surfaced over and over again. Later in the evening, a teacher from Boscastle recounted that, during a recent argument over the building of a community centre, someone had eye-balled her: 'And how long have you been here?' 'Sixty years – all my life. How long have you been here'? 'Twenty-seven'!

14.18. Another way might have been to *start* the exhibition at the local level or, at least, collaborate much more tightly with local people right from the start. Amy Hale (Leskernick website, 23 February 1999): 'I think it would be a wonderful idea to design this [exhibition] in collaboration with people who have very different experiences of the Bodmin Moor landscape'.

14.19. Nimby = Not In My Back Yard.

14.20. One way forward was in part suggested by discovering, quite accidentally, that FS's 360 degree photo created a wonderful counterpoint to the aerial photograph. The aerial photograph, the close-up of a hut interior, and FS's diorama all worked off each other. But the connections needed to be explained.

Chapter 16

16.1. Some on the west side, however, may have been destroyed by the later very large medieval field system.

16.2. For a detailed discussion of the possible social distinctions that attended accretional and coaxial field-systems, see Herring (in press).

Chapter 18

18.1.   Generally speaking, the record of excavation on both moors has been relatively modest. This is mainly because they are not under threat from development. The 19th- and early 20th-century excavations
on Dartmoor and Bodmin Moor have been summarised in Radford (1952), Fleming (1988), and Johnson and Rose (1994: Appendix 1). Later in the 20th century, Aileen Fox worked on Dartmoor (1954a,
1954b, 1957), and, on Bodmin Moor, Radford (1935) worked at the Hurlers' Stone Circle, Dudley at
Garrow (unpub) but noted in Johnson and Rose (1994), Mercer (1978) at Stannon Moor, and Christie
(1988) wrote up Croft Andrew's 1941–42 excavations on Davidstow Moor. In the seventies, work on
Dartmoor intensified. The Central Excavation Unit worked at Shaugh Moor (Balaam, Smith, Wainwright 1982; Smith et al. 1981; Wainwright, Fleming, and Smith 1979; Wainwright and Smith 1980);
and Fleming's (1988, 1994) excavated at Holne Moor. Much of the recent discussion of the Bronze Age
of the granite uplands of the south-west has been dominated by Fleming's work on the Dartmoor
reaves. Less attention has been paid to the incredible survey work on Bodmin Moor (Johnson and
Rose 1994) and to the results of excavations on Bodmin Moor, for example, at Stannon (Jones 2001),
and Colliford (Griffith 1984), and immediately adjacent landscapes Callestick (Jones 1998–99).

18.2.   P. Herring, pers. comm., January 2004: 'We *never* see it like this! You're making assumptions, or just
confining yourselves to academic archaeology and its simplifications'.

18.3.   However, this surmise is based on a very limited number of analyses of possible source materials –
only one in Ireland, and none in Wales!

18.4.   There is only one other comparable example in Britain. It comes from Ringlemere, Sandwich, Kent
(*Current Archaeology* 2002, 179).

18.5.   On the other hand, Wessex-style Bronze Age pottery rarely appears in the south-west. Shaugh Moor
on Dartmoor, where Wessex biconical urns appear to the exclusion of other styles, is an extraordinary exception. Parker Pearson (1995: 98) has suggested that perhaps Shaugh Moor was occupied by
an intrusive group from the east – in which case it has little, or nothing, to do with elite exchange.

18.6.   This expanding territorial identity and the more extensive exchanges are also reflected in the distribution of metalwork types (Crediton palstaves, Pearce 1983: 18, Fig. 5; MBA Tumulus pins in Cornwall, Ellison 1980: Fig. 2; Parker Pearson 1995).

Chapter 19

19.1.   A similar association is found at both Carn Brea and Helman's Tor, excavated examples of hill top
enclosures of proven Neolithic date elsewhere in Cornwall (Mercer 1981, 1986a; and see the discussion in Tilley and Bennett 2002).

Bibliography

Adams, D (1992) 'Joseph Beuys: pioneer of a radical ecology', *Art Journal* 51(2), 26–34

Allen, J and Hamnett, C (1995) *A Shrinking World?*, Oxford: Open University

Altenberg, K. (1999) 'Space and community on medieval Dartmoor and Bodmin Moor' in Medieval Settlement Research Group Annual Report 14, 16–28

Appadurai, A (1986) *The Social Life of Things: Commodities in Cultural Perspective*, Cambridge: Cambridge University Press

Appadurai, A (1996) 'The production of locality', in Appadurai, A (ed), *Modernity at Large*, Minneapolis: University of Minnesota Press

Apsimon, A M and Greenfield, E (1972) 'The excavation of the Bronze Age and Iron Age settlement at Trevisker Round, St Eval', *Cornwall Proceedings of the Prehistoric Society* 38, 302–81

Axford, E (1975) *The Bodmin Moors*, London: David and Charles

Bachelard, G (1964) *The Poetics of Space*, Boston: Beacon Press

Ball, D and Goodier, R (1968) 'Large sorted stone stripes in the Rhinog Mountains, North Wales', *Geografisker Annaler* 50A, 54–59

Ball, D and Goodier, R (1970) 'Morphology and distribution of features resulting from frost action in Snowdonia', *Field Studies* 3, 193–217

Balaam, N D, Smith, K, and Wainwright, G J (1982) 'The Shaugh Moor project: fourth report – environment, context and conclusion', *Proceedings of the Prehistoric Society* 48, 203–78

Ballantyne, C (1986) 'Nonsorted patterned ground on mountains in the Northern Highlands of Scotland', *Biuletyn Peryglacjalny* 30, 15–34

Ballantyne, C and Harris, C (1994) *The Periglaciation of Britain*, Cambridge: Cambridge University Press

Bapty, I and Yates, T (eds) (1990) *Archaeology after Structuralism*, London: Routledge

Barker, P (1982) *Techniques of Archaeological Excavation*. London: Batsford

Barnatt, J (1980) 'Lesser known stone circles in Cornwall', *Cornish Archaeology* 19, 17–29

Barnatt, J (1982) *Prehistoric Cornwall: The Ceremonial Monuments*, Wellingborough, UK: Turnstone Press

Barnatt, J (1989) *Stone Circles of Britain*, Oxford: British Archaeological Report 215

Barrett, J (1994) *Fragments from Antiquity*, Oxford: Blackwell

Barrett, J (1995) 'Defining domestic space in the Bronze Age of southern Britain', in Parker Pearson, M and Richards, C (eds), *Architecture and Order*, London and New York: Routledge

Barrett, J, Bradley, R, and Green, M (1991) *Landscape, Monuments and Society: The Prehistory of Cranborne Chase*, Cambridge: Cambridge University Press

Barthes, R (1980) *Camera Lucida*. London: Fontana

Beardsley, J (1989) *Earthworks and Beyond: Contemporary Art in the Landscape*, New York: Abbeville Press

Belk, R (1997) 'Been there, done that, bought the souvenirs: of boundaries and journey crossings', in S. Brown S and Turley D (eds), *Consumer Research: Postcards from the Edge*, London: Routledge

Bender, B (1992) 'Theorising landscapes, and the prehistoric landscapes of Stonehenge', *Man* 27, 735–55

Bender, B (ed) (1993) *Landscape: Politics and Perspectives*, Oxford: Berg

Bender, B (1998) *Stonhenge: Making Space*, Oxford: Berg

Bender, B, Hamilton, S, and Tilley, C (1997) 'Leskernick: stone worlds; alternative narratives; nested landscapes', *Proceedings of the Prehistoric Society* 63, 147–78

Benedict, J (1970) 'Downslope soil movement in a Colorado Alpine region: rates, processes and climatic significance', *Arctic and Alpine Research* 2, 165–226

Benedict, J (1976) 'Frost creep and gelifluction features: a review', *Quaternary Research* 6, 55–76

Berger, J and Mohr, J (1982) *Another Way of Telling*, London: Writers & Readers

Berggren, Å and Burström, M (eds) (2002) *Reflexiv Fältarkeologi*, Malmö, Sweden: Riksantikvarieämbetet and Malmö Kulturmiljö

Berridge, P and Roberts, A (1986) 'The Mesolithic period in Cornwall', *Cornish Archaeology* 25, 7–34

Biggs, L (1984) 'Open air sculpture in Britain: twentieth century developments', in Davies, P and Knipe, T (eds), *A Sense of Place: Sculpture in the Landscape*, London: Ceolfrith Press

Borlase, W C I (1754, revised 1973) *Observations on the Antiquities, Historical and Monumental of the County of Cornwall South-West England 3500BC–AD 600*. Newton Abbot, Devon: David and Charles

Bourdieu, P (1984) *Distinction: A Social Critique of the Judgment of Taste*, London: Routledge and Kegan Paul

Bourdieu, P (1988) *Homo Academicus*, Cambridge: Polity Press

Bourdieu, P and Wacquant, L J (1992) *An Invitation to Reflexive Sociology*, Cambridge: Polity Press

Bradley, R (1984) *Social Foundations of Prehistoric Britain*, London: Longman

Bradley, R (1995) 'Ancient landscapes and the modern public', in Morgan Evans, D, Salway, P, and Thackray, D (eds), *The Remains of Distant Times: Archaeology and the National Trust*, London: The National Trust

Bradley, R (2000) *An Archaeology of Natural Places*, London: Routledge

Brown, A (1977) 'Late Devensian and Flandrian vegetational history of Bodmin Moor, Cornwall', *Philosophical Transactions of the Royal Society of London* B276, 251–320

Brück, J (1999) 'Houses, lifecycles and deposition on Middle Bronze Age settlements in Southern England', *Proceedings of the Prehistoric Society* 65, 145–66

Brück, J (2000) 'Settlement, landscape and social identity: the Early-Middle Bronze Age transition in Wessex, Sussex and the Thames Valley', *Oxford Journal of Archaeology* 23, 167–212

Burgin, V (1886) *The End of Art Theory*, London: Macmillan

Burl, A (1976) *Stone Circles of the British Isles*, New Haven: Yale University Press

Burl, A (1993) *From Carnac to Callanish*, New Haven: Yale University Press

Burstow, G P and Holleyman, G A (1957) 'Late Bronze Age settlement of Itford Hill, Sussex', *Proceedings of the Prehistoric Society* 48, 321–400

449

Butler, J (1994) *Dartmoor Atlas of Antiquities Volume Three – The South-West*, Exeter, UK: Devon Books

Butler, J (1997a) *Dartmoor Atlas of Antiquities Volume Five – The Second Millennium BC*, Exeter, UK: Devon Books

Butler, J (1997b) The Prehistoric Settlement of Dartmoor, UCL PhD thesis, unpublished

Carlson, A (1993) 'Appreciating art and appreciating nature', in Kemal, S and Gaskell, I (eds), *Landscape, Natural Beauty and the Arts*, Cambridge: Cambridge University Press

Carman, J (1991) 'Beating the bounds: archaeological heritage management as archaeology, archaeology as social science', *Archaeological Review from Cambridge* 10(2), 175–84

Carman, J (1993) 'The P is silent as in archaeology', *Archaeological Review from Cambridge* 12(1), 39–53

Carmichael, D, Hubert, J, Reeves, B, and Schanche, A (eds) (1994), *Sacred Sites, Sacred Places*, London: Routledge

Chadwick, A (2003) 'Post-processualism, professionalization and archaeological methodologies, Towards reflective and radical practice', *Archaeological Dialogues* 10, 97–117

Chalmers, J and Bird, S (1998) *Bodmin Moor*, Fowey, UK: Alexander Associates

Christie, P, (1988) 'A barrow cemetery on Davidstow Moor, Cornwall, wartime excavations of G, K, Croft Andrew', *Cornish Archaeology* 27, 27–169

Clifford, J and Marcus, G E (1986) *Writing Culture: The Poetics and Politics of Ethnography*, Berkeley: University of California Press

Collingwood, R (1945) *The Idea of Nature*, Oxford: Clarendon Press

Cooper, M A, Firth, A, Carman, J, and Wheatley, D (eds) (1995) *Managing Archaeology*, London: Routledge

Cosgrove, D (1984) *Social Formation and Symbolic Landscape*, London: Croom Helm

Craddock, P (1995) *Early Mining and Production*, Washington, DC: Smithsonian

Crawford, D (1993) 'Comparing artistic and natural beauty', in Kemal, S and Gaskell, I (eds), *Landscape, Natural Beauty and the Arts*, Cambridge: Cambridge University Press

Curwen, E C (1927) 'Prehistoric agriculture in Britain', *Antiquity* 1, 261–88

Das, V (1990) *Structure and Cognition*, Delhi: Oxford University Press

Davies, P and Knipe, T (eds) (1984), *A Sense of Place: Sculpture in the Landscape*, London: Ceolfrith Press

De Certeau, M (1988) *The Practice of Everyday Life*, Berkeley: University of California Press

de Charmant, A (1994) 'Peter Greenaway: upstairs, downstairs', *Tate* 2, 52–53

Descola, P and Palsson, G (eds) (1996) *Nature and Society: Anthropological Perspectives*, London: Routledge

Dittmar, H (1989) 'Gender identity-related meanings of personal possessions', *British Journal of Social Psychology* 28, 159–71

Dittmar, H (1991) 'Meanings of material possessions as reflections of identity: gender and social material position in society', in Rudmin, F W (ed), *To Have Possessions: A Handbook on Ownership and Property* (Special Issue), *Journal of Social Behaviour and Personality* 6(6), 165–86

Douglas, M (1970) *Purity and Danger*, London: Penguin Books

Drewett, P (1982) 'Later Bronze Age downland economy and excavations at Black Patch, East Sussex', *Proceedings of the Prehistoric Society* 48, 321–400

Edgeworth, M (1990) 'Analogy as practical reason: the perception of objects in excavation practice', *Archaeological Review from Cambridge* 9(2), 243–51

Edmonds, M (1999) *Ancestral Geographies of the Neolithic*, London: Routledge

Eliade, M (1959) *The Sacred and the Profane*, New York: Harvest

Ellen, R (1996) 'Introduction', in Ellen, R and Fukui, K (eds), *Redefining Nature*, Oxford: Berg

Ellison, A (1978) 'The Bronze Age in Sussex', in Drewett, P L (ed), *The Archaeology of Sussex to AD 1500*, Council of British Archaeology Report 39, 30–37

Ellison, A (1981) 'Towards a socio-economic model for the Middle Bronze Age in southern England', in Hodder, I, Isaac, G, and Hammond, N (eds), *Pattern of the Past: Studies in Honour of David Clarke*, Cambridge: Cambridge University Press

Ellison, A (1987) 'The Bronze Age settlement at Thorny Down: pots, postholes and patterning', *Proceedings of the Prehistoric Society* 53, 385–92

Evans, K (1990) 'Sexist language in archaeological discourse', *Archaeological Review from Cambridge* 9(2), 252–61

Evans-Pritchard, E E (1940) *The Nuer*, Oxford: Oxford University Press

Fagone, V (ed) (1996) *Art in Nature*, Milan: Mazzotta

Feld, S and Basso, K (eds) (1996) *Senses of Place*, Santa Fe, NM: School of American Research Press

Fitzpatrick, A P, Butterworth, C A, and Grove, J (1999) '*Prehistoric and Roman Sites in East Devon: The A30 Honiton to Exeter Improvement DBFO Scheme, 1996–9*, Salisbury, UK: Wessex Archaeological Trust Archaeology Report 16

Fleming A (1978) 'The prehistoric landscape of Dartmoor part 1: south Dartmoor', *Proceedings of the Prehistoric Society* 44, 97–123

Fleming, A (1983) 'The prehistoric landscape of Dartmoor part 2: north and east Dartmoor', *Proceedings of the Prehistoric Society* 49, 195–241

Fleming, A (1984) 'The prehistoric landscape of Dartmoor wider implications', *Landscape History* 6, 5–20

Fleming, A (1988) *The Dartmoor Reaves: Investigating Prehistoric Land Divisions*, London: Batsford

Fleming, A (1994) 'The reaves reviewed', *Proceedings of the Devon Archaeological Society* 52, 63–74

Fogwill, E G (1954) 'Pastoralism on Dartmoor'. *Transactions of the Devonshire Association* 86, 89–114

Folliot-Stokes, A (1928) *The Cornish Coast and Moors*, London: Stanley Paul

Foucault, M (1979) *Discipline and Punish: The Birth of the Prison*, Harmondsworth, UK: Penguin

Fox, A (1954a) 'Celtic fields and farms on Dartmoor in the light of recent excavations at Kestor', *Proceedings of the Prehistoric Society* 20, 87–102

Fox, A (1954b) 'Excavations at Kes Tor an early Iron Age site near Chagford', *Transactions of the Devonshire Association* 86, 21–62

Fox, A (1957) 'Excavations on Dean Moor in the Avon Valley 1954–1956', *Transactions of the Devonshire Association* 89, 18–77

Fox, A (1964) *South West England*, London: Thames and Hudson

French, M (1979) *Cornish Gold*, Liskeard, UK: Chantry Press

Gandy, M (1997) 'Contradictory modernities: conceptions of nature in the art of Joseph Beuys and Gerhard Richter', *Annals of the Association of American Geographers* 87(4), 636–59

Gearey, B and Charman, D (1996) 'Rough Tor, Bodmin Moor: Testing some archaeological hypotheses with landscape scale palynology', in Gearey, D J, Charman, D J, Newnham, R M and Croot D G (eds), *Devon and East Cornwall Field Guide*, London: Quaternary Research Association

Gearey, B, Charman, D, and Kent, M (2000) 'Palaeoecological evidence for the prehistoric settlement of Bodmin Moor, Cornwall, southwest England. Part II: Land use changes from the Neolithic to the present', *Journal of Archaeological Science* 27, 493–504

Geertz, C (1973) *The Interpretation of Cultures*, New York: Basic Books

Gell, A (1985) 'How to read a map: remarks on the practical logic of navigation', *Man* 20, 271–86

Gell, A (1992) *The Anthropology of Time*, Oxford: Berg

Gero, J M (1985) 'Socio-politics and the woman-at-home ideology', *American Antiquity* 50(2), 342–50

Gero, J M (1994) 'Gender division of labour in the construction of archaeological knowledge in the United States', in Bond, G C and Gilliam, A (eds), *Social Construction of the Past: Representation as Power*, London: Routledge (One World Archaeology 24)

Gero, J (1996) 'Archaeological practice and gendered encounters with field data', in Wright, R R (ed) *Gender and Archaeology*, Philadelphia: University of Pennsylvania Press

Giddens, A (1981) *A Contemporary Critique of Historical Materialism*, London: Macmillan

Giddens, A (1984) *The Constitution of Society: Outline of the Theory of Structuration*, Berkeley: University of California Press

Giddens, A (1985) 'Time, space and regionalisation', in Gregory, D and Urry, J (eds), *Social Relations and Spatial Structures*, London: MacMillan

Gledhill, J (1994) *Power and Its Disguises*, London: Pluto Press

Goffman, E (1990) *The Presentation of Self in Everyday Life*, London: Penguin Books

Goldsworthy, A (1990a) *Hand to Earth*, London: Henry Moore Centre for the Study of Sculpture

Goldsworthy, A (1990b) *Andy Goldsworthy*, London: Viking

Goldsworthy, A (1994) *Stone*, London: Viking

Goldsworthy, A (1995) Conference paper, Manchester: National Trust Centenerary Conference

Goudie, A and Piggott, N (1981) 'Quartzite tors, stone stripes and slopes at Stiperstones, Shropshire, England', *Biuletyn Peryglacjalny* 28, 47–56

Graves, P (1991) 'Relative values? Criticisms of critical theory', *Archaeological Review from Cambridge* 10(1), 86–93

Greig, I (1977) 'Excavation of a Bronze Age settlement at Varley Halls, Coldean Lane, Brighton, East Sussex', *Sussex Archaeological Collections* 135, 7–58

Griffith, F (1984) 'Archaeological investigations at Colliford Reservoir, Bodmin Moor, 1977–78', *Cornish Archaeology* 23, 49–139

Guidoni, E (1975) *Primitive Architecture*, London: Faber & Faber

Hall, C (1982) 'Environmental artists: sources and directions', in Sonfist, A (ed), *Art in the Land*, New York: Dutton

Hamilton, S (2003) 'Sussex not Wessex, a regional perspective on southern Britain c. 200–200 BC', in Rudling, D (ed), *The Archaeology of Sussex to AD 2000*, King's Lynn, UK: Heritage Marketing and Publications for the Centre for Continuing Education, University of Sussex

Hamilton, S and Seager Thomas, M (in prep), *Excavating Stone Worlds: Critical Approaches to Fieldwork on the British Bronze Age*, Walnut Creek, CA: Left Coast Press

Harbison, P (1971) 'Hartmann's gold analyses: a comment', *Journal of the Royal Society of Antiquaries of Ireland* 101, 159–60

Harris, C (1981) *Periglacial Mass Wasting: A Review of Research*, Norwich, UK: GeoAbstracts

Harrison, S, Anderson, A, and Winchester, V (1996) 'Large boulder accumulations and evidence for permafrost creep. Great Mis Tor, Dartmoor', in Chatman, D J, Newham, R M, and Croot, D G (eds), *Devon and East Cornwall Field Guide*, London: Quaternary Research Association

Harvey, D (1989) *The Condition of Postmodernity: An Enquiry into the Origins of Cultural Change*, Oxford: Basil Blackwell

Hencken, H (1932) *The Archaeology of Cornwall and Scilly*, London: Methuen

Herring, P (1986) An exercise in landscape history, ore-Norman and medieval Brown Willy and Bodmin Moor, unpublished M.Phil thesis, University of Sheffield

Herring, P (1996) 'Transhumance in medieval Cornwall', in Fox H S A (ed), *Seasonal Settlement*, papers presented to a meeting of the Medieval Settlement Research Group, Vaughan Papers in Adult Education, No 39, Leicester: University of Leicester

Herring, P (1997) 'Early prehistoric sites at Leskernick, Altarnun', *Cornish Archaeology* 36, 176–85

Herring, P (in press) 'Commons, fields and communities in prehistoric Cornwall', in Chadwick, A (ed), *Recent Approaches to the Archaeology of Land Allotment*, BAR International Series, Oxford: Archaeopress

Hirsch, E (1995) 'Landscape: between place and space', in Hirsch, E and O'Hanlon, M (eds), *The Anthropology of Landscape: Perspectives on Place and Space*, Oxford: Oxford University Press

Hirsch, E and O'Hanlon, M (eds) (1995) *The Anthropology of Landscape: Perspectives on Place and Space*, Oxford: Oxford University Press

Hodder, I (1984) 'Burial, houses, women and men in the European Neolithic', in Miller, D and Tilley, C (eds), *Ideology, Power and Prehistory*, Cambridge: Cambridge University Press

Hodder, I (1986) *Reading the Past*, Cambridge: University Press

Hodder, I (1989) 'This is not an article about material culture as text', *Journal of Anthropological Archaeology* 8, 250–69

Hodder, I (1990) *The Domestication of Europe*, Oxford: Blackwell

Hodder, I (1997) '"Always momentary, fluid and flexible": towards a reflexive excavation methodology', *Antiquity* 71, 691–700

Hodder, I (1999) *The Archaeological Process*, Oxford: Blackwell

Hodder, I, Shanks, M, Alessandri, A, Buchli, V, Carmen, J, Last, J, and Lucas, G (eds) (1995) *Interpreting Archaeology*, London: Routledge

Hooke, R (1998) *Principles of Glacier Mechanics*, Upper Saddle River, NJ: Prentice Hall

Hooson, D (ed) (1994) *Geography and National Identity*, Oxford: Blackwell

Horigan, S (1988) *Nature and Culture in Western Discourses*, London: Routledge

Ingold, T (1993) 'The temporality of landscape', *World Archaeology* 25(2), 152–74

Ingold, T (2000) *The Perception of the Environment*, Milton Park, Abingdon: Routledge

Jackson, K (1999) *Invisible Forms*, London: Picador

Jacobi, R (1979) 'Early Flandrian hunters in the south-west', *Proceedings of the Devon Archaeological Society* 37, 48–93

Johnson, N (1983) 'The results of air and ground survey of Bodmin Moor, Cornwall', in Maxwell, G S (ed), *The Impact of Aerial Reconnaissance on Archaeology*, CBA Research Report 49, 5–13

Johnson, N and Rose, P (1994) *Bodmin Moor, An Archaeological Survey, Volume 1: The Human Landscape to c, 1800*, London: English Heritage Archaeological Report Number 24

Johnston, R (2001) 'Breaking new ground: land tenure and fieldstone clearance during the Bronze Age', in Brück, J (ed), *Bronze Age Landscapes: Traditional and Transformation*, Oxford: Oxbow

Jones, A. (1998–99) *The excavation of a Later Bronze Age structure at Callestick*, Truro: Cornwall Archaeological Unit, *Cornish Archaeology* 37–38, 5–55

Jones, A. (2001) *Stannon Down, Cornwall 1999: Stage 2 Archaeological Excavations*, Truro: Cornwall Archaeological Unit: A report for English China Clays International (now Imerys)

Jones, M (1991) 'Analysis and synthesis: compatible activities or separate roles in archaeological science?' *Archaeological Review from Cambridge* 10(1), 6–11

Kepes, G (ed) (1972) *Arts of the Environment*, London: Aidan Ellis

Kermode, F (1981) 'Secrets and narrative sequence', in Mitchell, W J T (ed), *On Narrative*, Chicago: University of Chicago Press

Kohl, P L (1993) 'Limits to a post-processual archaeology (or, the dangers of a new scholasticism)', in Yoffee, N and Sherratt, A (eds), *Archaeological Theory: Who Sets the Agenda?* Cambridge: Cambridge University Press

Lampeter Archaeology Workshop (1997) 'Relativism, objectivity and the politics of the past [part 1]', *Archaeological Dialogues* 4(2), 164–98

Lampeter Archaeology Workshop (1998) 'Relativism, objectivity and the politics of the past [part 2]', *Archaeological Dialogues* 5(1), 30–53

Lang, R (1989) 'The dwelling door: towards a phenomenology of transition', in Seamon, D and Mugerauer, R (eds), *Dwelling, Place and Environment*, New York: Colombia University Press

Leskernick website – www.ucl.ac.uk/leskernick/home.htm

Lewis, A (1895–98) 'Rude stone monuments of Bodmin Moor', *Journal of the Royal Institution of Cornwall* 13, 107–13

Linton, D (1955) 'The problem of tors', *Geographical Journal* 121, 470–87

Linton, D (1964) 'The origin of the Pennine tors: an essay in analysis', *Zeitschrift für Geomorphologie* 8, 5–23

Lippard, L (1983) *Overlay, Contemporary Art and the Art of Prehistory*, New York: Pantheon Books

Locock, M (1995) 'Project management in a changing world: redesigning the pyramid', in Cooper, M A, Firth, A, Carman, J, and Wheatley, D (eds), *Managing Archaeology*, London: Routledge

Long, R (1980) *Five, Six, Pick Up Sticks, Seven, Eight, Lay Them Straight*, London: Anthony d'Offay Gallery

Long, R (1986) *Richard Long in Conversation*, Noordwijk, Holland: MW Press

Long, R (1996) *Circles, Cycles, Mud, Stones*, Houston, TX: Contemporary Arts Museum

Lucas, G (2001) *Critical Approaches to Fieldwork, Contemporary and Historical Practice*, London: Routledge

Lupton, D (1996) *Food, the Body and the Self*, London: Sage

MacAdam, E, (1995) 'Trying to make it happen', in Cooper, M A, Firth, A, Carman, J, and Wheatley, D (eds), *Managing Archaeology*, London: Routledge

Macpherson-Grant, N (1994) 'Earlier prehistoric ceramics from the Monkton A253 project', *Canterbury's Archaeology* (1994), 62–66

Malim, J (1936) *The Bodmin Moors*, London: Methuen

Massey, D and Jess, P (eds) (1995) *A Place in the World?* Oxford: Open University

Matless, D and Revill, G (1995) 'A solo ecology: the erratic art of Andy Goldsworthy', *Ecumene* 2(4), 423–48

Megaw, J V S (1976) 'Gwithian, Cornwall: some notes on the evidence for Neolithic and Bronze Age settlement', in Burgess, C B and Miket, R (eds), *Settlement and Economy in the Third and Second Millennia BC*, Oxford: British Archaeological Reports

Mennell, S, Murcott, A, and van Otterloo, A (1992) *The Sociology of Food: Eating, Diet and Culture*, London: Sage

Mercer, R (1978) 'The excavation of a Bronze Age hut-circle settlement, Stannon Down, St, Breward, Cornwall, 1968', *Cornish Archaeology* 9, 17–46

Mercer, R (1981) 'Excavations at Carn Brea, Illogan, Cornwall 1970–7', *Cornish Archaeology* 20, 1–204

Mercer, R (1986a) 'The Neolithic in Cornwall', *Cornish Archaeology* 25, 35–80

Mercer, R (1986b) 'Excavation of a Neolithic enclosure at Helman Tor, Lanlivery, Cornwall, 1986, 'Interim report', Department of Archaeology, University of Edinburgh Project Paper 4

Meredith, J (1990) 'The aesthetic artefact: an exploration of emotional response and taste in archaeology', *Archaeological Review from Cambridge* 9(2), 208–17

Merriman, N (1989) 'Museum visiting as a cultural phenomenon', in Vergo, P (ed), *The New Museology*, London: Reaktion Books

Miles, H (1975) 'Barrows on the St Austell granite', *Cornish Archaeology* 14, 5–81

Miller, D (1988) 'Appropriating the state on the council estate', *Man* 23, 353–7

Mitchell, J. (1996) 'What do pictures really want?', *October* 77, 71–82

Moore, H (1937) 'The sculptor speaks', *The Listener* 18, 339 August

Morland, J (1988) *New Milestones, Sculpture, Community and the Land*, London: Common Ground Press

Morris, B (1987) *Anthropological Studies of Religion*, Cambridge: Cambridge University Press

Needham, S (1996) 'Chronology and periodisation in the British Bronze Age', *Acta Archaeologica* 67, 121–40

Needham, S (2000) 'Power pulses across a cultural divide: cosmologically driven acquisition between Armorica and Wessex', *Proceedings of the Prehistoric Society* 66, 151–207

Noble, A (1991) 'Introduction: the placing of prehistory', in Ackling, R (ed), *From Art to Archaeology*, London: South Bank Centre

Nowakowski, J (1991) 'Trethellan Farm, Newquay: excavation of a lowland Bronze Age settlement and Iron Age cemetery', *Cornish Archaeology* 30, 5–242

Okely, J (1983) *Changing Cultures. The Traveller-Gypsies*, New York: Cambridge University Press

O'Kelly, M J (1989) *Early Ireland. An Introduction to Irish Prehistory*, Cambridge: Cambridge University Press

Padel, 0 (1985) 'Cornish place-name elements', *English Place Name Society* 56 and 57, 38–40, 150–51

Palmer, C (1997) 'From theory to practice: experiencing the nation in everyday life', *Journal of Material Culture* 3(2), 175–99

Palmer, J (1967) 'Landforms', in Beresford, M and Jones, G (eds), *Leeds and Its Region*, London: British Association for the Advancement of Science

Palmer, J and Neilsen, R (1962) 'The origin of granite tors on Dartmoor, Devonshire', *Proceedings of the Yorkshire Geological Society* 33, 315–39

Palmer, J and Radley, J (1961) 'Gritstone tors of the English Pennines', *Zeitschrift für Geomorphologie* 5, 37–52

Parker Pearson, M (1990) 'The production and distribution of Bronze Age pottery', *Cornish Archaeology* 29, 5–32

Parker Pearson, M (1995) 'Southwestern Bronze Age pottery', in Kinnes, I and Varndell, G (eds), *'Unbaked Urns of Rudely Shape': Essays of British and Irish Pottery for Ian Longworth*, Oxford: Oxbow Books

Pearce, S (1983) *The Bronze Age Metalwork of South Western Britain*, Oxford: British Archaeological Reports 120

Pearson, G W and Stuiver, M (1986) 'High-precision calibration of the radiocarbon timescale, 500–2500 BC', *Radiocarbon* 28, 839–62

Penhallurick, R D (1987) *Tin in Antiquity*, London: The Institute of Metals

Plummer, K (1983) *Documents of Life*, London: George Allen and Unwin

Preston Blier, S (1987) *The Anatomy of Architecture*, Chicago: University of Chicago Press

Pryor, F, (1995) 'Management objectives: context or chaos?' in Cooper, M A, Firth, A, Carman, J, and Wheatley, D (eds), *Managing Archaeology*, London: Routledge

Radford, C A (1935) 'Notes on the excavation of the Hurlers near Liskeard, Cornwall', *Proceedings of the Prehistoric Society* 1, 1934

Radford, C A (1952) 'Prehistoric settlements on Dartmoor and the Cornish Moors', *Proceedings of the Prehistoric Society* 18, 55–84

Reason, D (1996) 'Disarticulating art and nature, which nature, which art?', in Fagone, V (ed), *Art and Nature*, Milan: Mazzotta

Reid, C, Barrow, G, and Dewey, H (1910) *The Geology of the Country Around Padstow and Camelford*, London: HMSO, Memoirs of the Geological Survey

Reid, C, Barrow, G, Sherlock, R, and Dewey, H (1911) *The Geology of the Country Around Tavistock and Launceston*, London: HMSO, Memoirs of the Geological Survey

Rhatz, P and Apsimon, A M (1962) 'Excavations at Shearplace Hill, Sydling St Nicholas, Dorset, England', *Proceedings of the Prehistoric Society* 28, 289–328

Richards, C (1993) 'Monumental choreography: architecture and spatial representation in late Neolithic Orkney', in Tilley, C (ed), *Interpretative Archaeology*, Oxford: Berg

Rodway, P (1994) *Sensuous Geographies: Body, Sense and Place*, London: Routledge

Rose, G (1995) 'Place and identity: a sense of place', in Massey, D and Jess, P (eds), *A Place in the World?*, Open University: Oxford University Press

Ross, S (1993) 'Gardens, earthworks and environmental art', in Kemal, S and Gaskell, I (eds), *Landscape, Natural Beauty and the Arts*, Cambridge: Cambridge University Press

Rowlands, M (1994) 'The politics of identity in archaeology', in Bond, G C and Gilliam, A (eds), *Social Construction of the Past: Representation as Power*, London: Routledge (One World Archaeology 24)

Rudling, D (2002) 'Excavations adjacent to Coldean Lane', in Rudling, D (ed), *Downland Settlement and Land-Use: The Archaeology of the Brighton Bypass*, London: Archetype Publications Ltd

Russell. M. (2002) 'Excavations at Mile Oak Farm' in Rudling, D (ed), *Downland Settlement and Land-use: the Archaeology of the Brighton Bypass*. London: Archetype Publications Ltd

Said, E (1995) *Orientalism* (revised with new afterword), London: Penguin Books

Seager Thomas, M (1999) 'Stone finds in context: a contribution to the study of later prehistoric artifact assemblages', *Sussex Archaeological Collections* 137, 39–48

Shankland, D (1996) 'Çatalhöyük: the anthropology of an archaeological presence', in Hodder, I (ed), *On the Surface: Çatalhöyük 1993–95*, Cambridge and London: McDonald Institute for Archaeological Research and British Institute of Archaeology at Ankara

Shanks, M (1992) *Experiencing the Past*, London: Routledge

Shanks, M and McGuire, R H (1996) 'The craft of archaeology', *American Antiquity* 61(1), 75–88

Shanks, M and Tilley, C (1987) *Social Theory and Archaeology*, Cambridge: Polity Press

Sherratt, A (1994) 'What would a Bronze Age world system look like? Relations between temperate Europe and the Mediterranean in later prehistory', *Journal of European Archaeology* 1, 1–58

Shields, R (1991) *Places on the Margin: Alternative Geographers of Modernity*, London: Routledge

Silvester, R (1979) 'The relationship of first millennium BC settlement to the upland areas of the South West', *Proceedings of the Devon Archaeological Society* 47, 205–71

Smith, A D (1986) *Ethnic Origin of Nations*, Oxford: Blackwell

Smith, K (1984) 'Kier Smith', in Davies, P and Knipe, T (eds), *A Sense of Place: Sculpture in the Landscape*, London: Ceolfrith Press

Smith, K, Copper, N, Wainwright, G J, and Beckett, S (1981) 'The Shaugh Moor project third report – settlement and environmental investigations', *Proceedings of the Prehistoric Society* 47, 205–73

Smithson, R (1972) 'The spiral jetty', in Kepes, G (ed), *Arts of the Environment*, London: Aidan Ellis

Sonfist, A (ed) (1982) *Art in the Land*, New York: Dutton

Southerton, D, Shove, E, and Warde, A (1998) Home from home?: a research note on recreational caravanning (draft paper), University of Lancaster

Spies, W (1983) 'Christo: surrounded islands', in *Christo: Surrounded Islands*, New York: Harry N, Abrams

Stuiver, M and Reimer, P J (1998) *CALIB User's Guide Rev. 4*, University of Washington, Quaternary Isotope Laboratory

Taylor, J (1980) *Bronze Age Goldwork of the British Isles*, Cambridge: Cambridge University Press

Thomas, J (1991) 'Science versus anti-science?' *Archaeological Review from Cambridge* 10(1), 27–38

Thomas, J (1993) 'The politics of vision and the archaeologies of landscape', in Bender, B (ed), *Landscape: Politics and Perspectives*, Oxford: Berg

Tiberghien, G (1995) *Land Art*, London: Art Data

Tilley, C (1989a) 'Excavation as theatre', *Antiquity* 63, 275–80

Tilley, C (1989b) 'Interpreting material culture', in Hodder, I (ed), *The Meaning of Things: Material Culture and Symbolic Expression*, London: Harper Collins

Tilley, C (ed) (1990) *Reading Material Culture'*, Oxford: Blackwell

Tilley, C (ed) (1993) *Interpretative Archaeology*, Oxford: Berg

Tilley, C (1994) *A Phenomenology of Landscape*, Oxford: Berg

Tilley, C (1995) 'Rocks as resources: landscapes and power', *Cornish Archaeology* 34, 5–57

Tilley, C (1996) 'The power of rocks: topography and monument construction on Bodmin Moor', *World Archaeology* 28(2), 161–76

Tilley, C and Bennett, W (2002) 'An archaeology of supernatural places: the case of west Penwith', *Journal of the Royal Anthropological Institute* 7(2), 335–62

Tilley, C, Hamilton, S, and Bender, B (2000) 'Art and the re-presentation of the past', *The Journal of the Royal Anthropological Institute* 61(1), 35–62

Tilley, C, Hamilton, S, Harrison, S, and Anderson, E (2000) 'Distinguishing between cultural and geomorphological landscapes: the case of hill-top tors in South-West England', *Journal of Material Culture* 5(2): 177–96

Trudgian, P (1977a) 'Mesolithic flint scatters around Crowdy Marsh', *Cornish Archaeology* 16, 21–24

Trudgian, P (1977b) 'Excavation of a cairn at Crowdy Marsh, Advent, near Camelford', *Cornish Archaeology* 16, 17–21

Tufnell, L (1985) Periglacial landforms in the Cross Fell-Knock area of the north Pennines', in Boardman, J (ed), *Field Guide to the Periglacial Landforms of Northern England*, Cambridge: Quaternary Research Association

Turner, V (1967) *The Forest of Symbols*, Ithaca, NY: Cornell University Press

Ucko, P and Layton, R (1999) *The Archaeology and Anthropology of Landscape*, London: Routledge (One World Archaeology)

Val Baker, D (1973) *The Timeless Land: The Creative Spirit of Cornwall*, Bath, UK: Adams & Dart

Valentine, G and Longstaff, B (1998) 'Doing porridge: food and social relations in a male prison', *Journal of Material Culture* 3(2), 131–52

Van Gell, B, Buurman, J, Waterbolk, H T (1996) Archaeological and palaeological indications of an abrupt climate change in The Netherlands, and evidence for climatological teleconnections around 2650 BP, *Journal of Quaternary Science* 11(6), 451–60

Van Gennep, A (1960) *The Rites of Passage*, Chicago: University of Chicago Press

Wace, A J B and Thompson, M J (1972) *The Nomads of the Balkans*, London: Methuen

Wainwright, G J, Fleming, A, and Smith, K (1979) 'The Shaugh Moor project: first report', *Proceedings of the Prehistoric Society* 45, 1–33

Wainwright, G J and Smith, K (1980) 'The Shaugh Moor project second report – the enclosure', *Proceedings of the Prehistoric Society* 46, 65–122

Waterson, R (1990) *The Living House*, Oxford: Oxford University Press

Wickstead, H (in prep) A study of the socio-economic conditions that structure later prehistoric land division in West Devon, UK: developing analytical approaches to ancient boundaries, PhD research in progress

Williams, R (1993) *The Country and the City*, London: The Hogarth Press

Wilmore, M, (2006) 'Landscapes of disciplinary power: an ethnography of excavation and survey at Leskernick', in Edgeworth, M (ed), *Ethnographies of Archaeological Practice: Cultural Encounters: Material Transformations*, Walnut Creek, CA: Altamira Press

Index

About the Authors

BARBARA BENDER, professor in Heritage Anthropology, has a first degree in Geography and a PhD in Archaeology, and has taught in the Material Culture subsection of the Department of Anthropology at University College London for most of her academic life. Amongst her publications are *Stonehenge: Making Space* (1988); *Landscapes: Politics and Perspectives* (1993); *Contested Landscapes: Landscapes of Movement and Exile* (with M. Winer, eds) (2002). She is a founder member and managing editor for the *Journal of Material Culture*, and has served on the Wenner Gren Foundation Advisory Committee.

SUE HAMILTON is reader in later European Prehistory at the Institute of Archaeology, University College London. Her body of published work covers British and European Bronze and Iron Age societies and ceramics. In recent years, her interests and publications have focused on landscape archaeology – particularly from social and sensory perspectives, and issues of archaeological field practice and its published formats. She has conducted field projects in Britain, France, Italy, and Rapa Nui (Easter Island). Her current work incorporates considerations of gendered landscapes and includes the co-edited book *Archaeology and Women* (2007).

CHRIS TILLEY is professor of Material Culture in the Department of Anthropology, University College London. His research interests are in anthropological theory and material culture studies, phenomenological approaches to landscape, and the Neolithic and Bronze Ages of Britain and Europe. He has carried out fieldwork in Scandanavia, Britain, France, Malta, and Vanuatu. Recent books include *An Ethnography of the Neolithic* (1996), *Metaphor and Material Culture* (1999), *The Dolmens and Passage Graves of Sweden* (1999), *The Materiality of Stone* (2004), and *Handbook of Material Culture* (co-edited, 2006).

LIBRARY, UNIVERSITY OF CHESTER